D#307052

10-3904 8

Crisis-Consciousness
and the Novel

Crisis-Consciousness and the Novel

Eugene Hollahan

DELAWARE

Newark: University of Delaware Press
London and Toronto: Associated University Presses

Associated University Presses
440 Forsgate Drive
Cranbury, NJ 08512

Associated University Presses
25 Sicilian Avenue
London WC1A 2QH, England

Associated University Presses
P.O. Box 39, Clarkson Pstl. Stn.
Mississauga, Ontario,
L5J 3X9 Canada

The paper used in this publication meets the requirements of the American National Standard for Permanence of Paper for Printed Library Materials Z39.48-1984.

Library of Congress Cataloging-in-Publication Data

Hollahan, Eugene.
  Crisis-consciousness and the novel / Eugene Hollahan.
    p.   cm.
  Includes bibliographical references and index.
  ISBN 0-87413-445-5 (alk. paper)
  1. English fiction—History and criticism—Theory, etc.
  2. American fiction—20th century—History and criticism—Theory, etc.   3. Consciousness in literature.   4. Narration (Rhetoric)
  I. Title.
  PR826.H64   1992
  823.009—dc20   91-50883
                                                              CIP

PRINTED IN THE UNITED STATES OF AMERICA

For Mark, Carol, and Brian

. . . but the sons can shield the father . . .

and

For Saul Bellow

scribit ut scribam

What a marvelous book one would write by narrating
the life and adventures of a word.

Balzac, *Louis Lambert*

There are . . . men to whom a crisis . . . comes
graceful and beloved as a bride.

Emerson, The Divinity School Address

Contents

Acknowledgments

Some of the ideas in this book were first tested in articles and reviews that appeared in the following journals: *PMLA, Nineteenth-Century Fiction, Studies in Philology, Texas Studies in Literature and Language, Comparative Literature Studies, Studies in the Novel, Modern Fiction Studies,* and *Novel: A Forum of Fiction.* These exploratory essays are cited where appropriate in the course of my argument. I offer sincere thanks to the editors of these journals.

Three colleagues provided assistance at crucial stages of this project. A good Americanist, Janet Gabler-Hover, vetted an early draft of the introduction, detecting errors and offering suggestions for argumentative coherence and unity. A good Victorian, Paul H. Schmidt, read the entire manuscript and pointed out places where the argument went wrong and where it went right. Another Americanist, James D. Wilson, recognized the "powerful stuff" inherent in my subject and encouraged me to complete the project. My sincere gratitude to these three fine scholar-critics.

Finally, I must thank Sonja Gardner, who combines word-processing technology with a truly humane spirit.

Permissions

Crisis-Consciousness
and the Novel

Introduction: A Model for a Critical History

The first working title of this book—*Concussion of That Great Noun*—identified the object of my inquiry. Beginning with the rise of the novel in the eighteenth century, expanding during the triumph of realism, and coming to cultural fruition in the twentieth century, *crisis* as a signifier has enjoyed a career of perhaps unparalleled impact. The compelling phrase "concussion of that great noun" in reference to *crisis* derives from George Eliot. The prophetic Eliot was the first literary intellectual to call explicit attention to the effects, at once psychological and social, of this powerful word. In *Felix Holt, the Radical* (1866), Eliot depicts a polished London lawyer exploiting the "concussion of that great noun" so as to manipulate naive colliers during the first election held under the Great Reform Bill of 1832. Novelists before her (Richardson, Scott, Austen) indeed incorporated the problematical word into their narrative representations, but Eliot calls attention to it in explicitly special ways. *Felix Holt* thus becomes a major text of reference in a critical history of the *crisis*-figuration which I will posit as a crucial element in modern consciousness.[1] Throughout my investigation, I inquire into the presumed lineaments of greatness Eliot may have perceived in this potentially explosive word. Admittedly a beginning of a beginning, my historical survey will inquire into the various ways human beings, including major authors, respond to and manipulate each other via this "great noun." I will show both that and how it indeed eventually achieves rhetorical importance (and notoriety) in the twentieth century.

The audience for any written utterance may always be a hypothesis.[2] Who, then, is the hypothetically proper audience for the present study? The answer lies with the reader who will entertain this word's—or any single word's—potential power. Can we determine if and how a word attains to greatness? Will it help to discover that it serves major authors to compose renowned books? That it serves grand ideas and influential aesthetic theories? Will it help if we see how it enters into systems bearing upon economics, politics, theology, science, and other important arenas of thought and action? How it becomes crucial to the figurative

1

rendering of modern consciousness? In urging that *crisis* is almost always a figurative element in rhetoric, I am influenced by Saussure's famous remark to the effect that "any word can always evoke everything that in one way or another can be associated with it."[3]

The heuristic model I propose to use will seem like a hybrid—and indeed it is—but in fact it proves in the application to be unified, coherent, and functional. Compounded of elements drawn from many critical sources (including hints from Hayden White, James Mellard, Paul de Man, Hans Kellner, and Marshall Brown), and organized as an undergirding historical narrative, the model both positions and enables me to carry out my intention: a critical history balanced equally between historical description and critical commentary. At the level of practical criticism, I have identified from my own reading numerous novels in which an author constitutes himself or herself a *crisis*-rhetorician. Variously employing Brown's account of crisis as dialectical turning point, de Man's view of crisis-rhetoric as error-prone utterance, and White's consciousness-determining tropology, I will attempt to constitute the biography, as it were, of an important modern keyword. Wherever appropriate, I suggest how a given novel informed by a *crisis*-trope variously, and in some cases sequentially, constitutes a metaphoric, metonymic, synecdochic, or ironic reality. I will argue that we can not understand certain novels without first determining if and how a crisis-trope informs them. If I myself operate via a governing trope, as Hayden White would insist that I inevitably must do, it would be my heuristic acceptance, for the sake of argument, of Eliot's assertion in 1866 that *crisis*, however ironically, was becoming a "great noun." Allowing for occasional lapses in strict chronology, the story I will narrate is, I think, a rhetorical tale of a great if specialized tradition.

I want to begin by positing the following heuristic scenario. George Eliot witnessed the concussive and electrifying effects triggered by and centering on *crisis* in political disruptions, social upheavals, individual lives, and in numerous forms of written and spoken discourse. Recognizing an emergent cultural phenomenon, she then incorporated the "great noun" as a signifier, both literal and figurative, in her rendering of moral conflicts enacted by individuals struggling toward modern self-realization in *Felix Holt, the Radical*. In two greater novels, *Middlemarch* and *Daniel Deronda*, she elaborated even more strenuously an informing crisis-consciousness. Eliot's contribution to an evolving *crisis*-rhetoric begins with her acute realization that this word which originally meant "judgment" was historically becoming not only a device for manipulating or inducing unthinking behavior but also an explosive rhetorical strategy for radical critique of individual and social life.[4]

Eliot and other authors will be seen variously to use *crisis* from their own constructional perspectives, in the process exhibiting the word's manipulation by characters within their fictions. I intend to urge that *crisis* evolves from being a cultural and linguistic phenomenon to becoming also a sign of personal maturity and an essential component of the modern self. The literature that enables and embodies the modern self exists in considerable part because of *crisis*-consciousness. Historically, then, Eliot's attribution of some peculiar importance to one single word proves acutely and achingly correct. In the following pages, I will adopt Eliot's adjective "great," but rather than merely assert its putative greatness I will think of *crisis* as both a question and a quest. Of course, I can not hope to "prove" the figuration of any putative figure. I can only urge and attempt to convince my reader by an accumulation of passages that, to some degree, must speak for themselves. I leave a good deal of work to be done by a willing reader.

I think that *crisis*-consciousness should be seen as a radical form of self-consciousness or consciousness in general. In arguing that *crisis*-consciousness is a historically verifiable element in the formation of modern consciousness, I will first heuristically stipulate that *crisis*-consciousness functions as a trope. In doing so, I am influenced by Hayden White's essay "Tropology, Discourse, and the Modes of Human Consciousness." White persuasively argues that consciousness is "tropic" in that it depends not solely upon the data it perceives but primarily and more so upon the perceptual apparatus of the perceiver. Mental patterns of organization resembling the master tropes described by Kenneth Burke (metaphor, metonymy, synecdoche, irony) amount to structures of consciousness that determine the ways we understand existence or reality. *Crisis*-consciousness, I will argue, may profitably be seen as a figuration consisting historically of many dimensions and implications, functioning in various texts and contexts as a figure of speech or trope (a mindset, so to speak), and representing a stage in human consciousness itself. Thus viewed as at bottom a Kantian strategy for constituting reality, the *crisis*-trope as precipitating event or governing power will be examined in many of its occurrences in the main tradition.[5] I will endeavor to place what I call the *crisis*-trope securely within literary history and also within the episteme or framework of contemporary criticism.[6]

I will show the word used variously by characters within a fictional representation or by an author (as actual author, implied author, or narrator). Similarly, within the very complex behavioral category of manipulation, both artistic and nonartistic, I will show the word used in three main senses (as signifier for stressful circumstances, as signifier for dialectical turning points, and as signifier evoking, inducing, or even necessitating decisions or judgments). Behind all of these usages, of course, stands the literary artist, selecting emphases and ordering intensities. I need not point out that much slippage must inevitably occur between these conveniently distinguished categories. Then, too, the three main usages may sometimes cohere (as when an individual mired in an imbroglio makes a decision so as to effect an existential change in direction).

My chief focus throughout will be upon *crisis* as a narrative trope, but if (under White's influence) I am to speak of crisis-consciousness, I should also establish a connection between crisis-consciousness and the novel as a form. Eliot explicitly concerns herself in *Felix Holt* with the nature of crisis-consciousness. She demonstrates that *crisis* enables a trope of consciousness and thus that an emphasis on heightened consciousness may necessitate the trope of crisis-consciousness. In more than thirty contexts, Eliot signifies *consciousness* as a sign of perception and understanding. Thus, in delineating major characters (Mrs. Transome, Esther Lyon, Rufus Lyon, Annette Ledru, John Johnson, Harold Transome, Matthew Jermyn) and lesser personages, Eliot almost insists upon consciousness as, at crucial moments, the salient feature of moral character and social change. Admittedly, when Eliot writes *consciousness* she usually means mere awareness or alertness. Even so, at times she means something more. A tour de force of mood and atmospherics in chapter 1 establishes Mrs. Transome's exile at Transome Court so that her "high-born imperious air" (p. 29) represents a rotten Tory consciousness "absorbed by memories" (p. 13) that will be swept away as her neighborhood is abruptly stirred into a new political awareness. Likewise, in chapter 3, Eliot harps on the idea that in 1832 England was gradually awakening to "that higher consciousness which is known to bring higher pains" (p. 470) and to "the higher pains of a dim political consciousness" (p. 50). Of considerable relevance on this point is the fact that seven major characters associated with *crisis*-images are likewise signified via *consciousness*.

Despite such evidence, though, one might not feel compelled to make much of Eliot's *crisis*-consciousness motif were it not that in one passage she elaborates a definition remarkably similar to White's tropological definition. In chapter 27, Felix Holt attempts to clarify for Esther Lyon his own world view. Aware of being situated in a historical situation fraught with crisis-induced change, he asserts at one moment that "I have to determine for myself"; almost immediately, however, he contradicts himself by speaking of a "determining reason" in the sense of a compulsion or irresistible inner motive. He seems to anticipate White.

"It is just because I'm a very ambitious fellow, with very hungry passions, wanting a great deal to satisfy me, that I have chosen to give up what people call worldly good. At least that has been one determining reason. It all depends on *what a man gets into his consciousness—what life thrusts into his mind*, so that it becomes present to him as remorse is present to the guilty, or a mechanical problem to an inventive genius." (pp. 266-77; emphases added)

Does not this anticipate, albeit clumsily, what White intends by a consciousness-informing trope? Does not Eliot invite us to see human perception—"what life thrusts into his mind"—in association with a trope or reality-shaping mind-set? I will argue that we may profitably see it this way and, more to my purpose, that modern consciousness, at many crucial points in the history of the novel, equates with or at least expresses itself as acute crisis-consciousness, whether authorial or characterological.[7] As any novel is, almost by definition, a form metonymically and synecdochically full of details and categories of details, I assume any completely worked-out novelistic tropology to move from metaphor (initial stability) to irony (self-criticism), dealing as necessary with things and categories typical of the two middle stages. Historically, I believe, the *crisis*-trope enters into numerous literary representations of the praxis of social and material worlds but also that it is a narrative convention which has scarcely been recognized.[8]

In intricate ways, one kind of figuration embeds itself in and then triggers or governs other figures of speech.[9] Kellner describes a kind of governing trope that shapes and regulates interactions among other tropes (p. 214). I intend to urge that *crisis* functions in just such a way. Is it not the case that to designate an event or occurrence as a crisis is to activate the imagination toward any of a wide variety of metaphors and related figures, most particularly self-reflexive irony? Raymond Williams and Paul de Man will be cited as noting how closely *crisis* and *criticism* stand in relation to each other. This intricate relation becomes even more complex when we remember that *crisis* frequently signifies a "turning point." Ought we to be surprised to discover that the word *trope* itself etymologically signifies a "turning"? In rhetorical criticism, "rhetoric" is sometimes used not in its usual sense of "modes of persuasion" but in an alternative sense to mean disciplined figuration in the widest sense. *Trope* should be defined thus: "All the turnings of language away from straightforward referential meaning."[10] Etymologically, of course, this is literally correct. The conjectured Indo-European base or root [*trep-, to turn] yields the Greek verb *trepein* (to turn) and thence the noun *trope* (a turn). From this process we have the Greek noun *tropos* (a turning, as in a figure of speech). In general, *tropos* refers simply to any and all figurative language. It cannot be noted too often that *crisis*, *criticism*, and *trope* inextricably entwine. Hans Kellner puts the problem for both writer and reader most aptly: "Get the story crooked!"[11]

To some degree, as I focus upon narrative discourse I am attempting to represent what Michel Foucault perceives as a history of a mentality.[12] *Crisis*-consciousness testifies to a crisis of consciousness itself. In my own understanding of the dynamics of reading, the appearance of the great noun *crisis* in a discourse occasions, even compels, a complex readerly experience. Poised between literal and figurative, this word regularly generates energy in a chain-reaction and thus tests one's readerly competence. I think it provides a fleeting sense of systemic but self-reflexive structure in the face of the seamless flux of raw experience. A *crisis*-figure necessitates a radical form of self-consciousness capable of satisfying the rigorous requirements of contemporary criticism. Perhaps as much as any metacritical term, it lends itself to the programs of numerous schools of criticism as well as to numerous writers' purposes, from the mundane (Golding) to the daringly experimental (Joyce). Occurring at the intersection of ordinary language and literary language, the *crisis*-trope exhibits the novel's becoming more self-conscious and philosophical as well as more scientific and specialized. As to its putative figurativeness, I can only urge at this point that this "tropic" word also tends almost always to be "allotropic," i.e., it functions in two or more ways at once, never carrying only one single meaning.

Historically, *crisis* must have begun as a word meaning "judgment" but then shifted toward meaning a situation within which judgment is necessary. The novelists I will cite wish to restore the force and relevance of the original meaning. The word itself bears some looking into. In the *Oxford English Dictionary*, this problematical word begins as a Greek noun meaning "discrimination" or "decision"; then, a Greek verb (*krinein*) meaning "to decide." The *OED* entry opens into five categories of experience: medical pathology, astrology, general human affairs such as politics or commerce (via transitivity and figuration), decision-making, and signs. Not all of these stand in a clear relation to the etymological idea of "judging" or "deciding," and by a curious process the usage meaning (decision-making) that comes nearest to the root meaning has become obsolete.

In pathology, *crisis* refers to that point in a disease when an important alteration leads to recovery or death. In 1543, Bartholomew Traheron translated *The Most Excellent Workes of Chirurgerye by J. Vigon,* in the process offering an ambiguous definition of *crisis* that suggests how the word's import hovered between choice and determinism: "*Crisis* signifyeth iudgemente, and in this case, it is used for a sodayne chaunge in a disease." Here, judgment presumably means someone's choice of possible explanations (hence, judgment) that a change has in fact occurred.

In astrology, with respect to the causes of medical disorders, *crisis* refers to a conjunction of planets determining the outcome of a disease. Or, a critical point in a course of nonmedical events. Citations derive from standard works on astrology, but a 1663 example suggests how the word, in one of its technical senses,
enters into imaginative literature.

> They'll feel the pulses of the Stars,
> To find out agues, Coughs, Catarrhs;
> And tell what Crisis does Divine
> The Rot in Sheep, or Mange in Swine.
> (Samuel Butler, *Hudibras,* I, 1, 611-14)

Another meaning shows how *crisis* transfers into the arena of general human life by referring to some decisive stage in any cultural process whatsoever. It refers to an event perceived as a state of affairs in which a decisive change for better or worse seems imminent. Such usage adduces feelings of insecurity, difficulty, and suspense relative to commercial life, politics, government, history, language, religion, statesmanship, or foreign affairs, as well as external nature. Eight examples establish a range of signifieds: interpretable signs, crucial moments, perceptions of danger, dire straits, change-triggering excitement, and relief from tedium. A historical development inchoately emerges, ranging from politics through Gothic sentimentalism, Victorian commercialism, and naturalistic determinism, ending in a modern thirst for excitement.

The obsolete fourth and fifth *OED* meanings keep more closely to the word's etymology. For decision-making, four examples range from 1621 through 1715. In William Cave's *Ecclesiastici; or a History of the most Eminent Fathers of the Church in the Fourth Century* (1682), *crisis* signifies the study and judgment made of an object under scrutiny: "We have not made . . . a Crisis and Censure of every single Tract." The fifth meaning indicates that *crisis* denoted not only judgment but also a sign by which one could judge something. It meant a criterion, token, or sign. Examples range from 1606 to 1657. Two citations derive from political commentary and politico-religious tractates, but a third example derives from an anonymous work of dramatic literature.

> 1606 (*Sir Gyles Goosecappe*, ii, 1) The Crises here are excellent good; the proportion of the chin good . . . the wart above it most exceeding good.

This semiological example points toward a general connection with literary methods and effects. Thus the *OED* lays down basic guidelines but does not tell the entire story. Other dictionaries and handbooks witness to a more complex and even self-contradictory history.[13]

Grounded in this etymological model, and looked at historically or externally, the problem that interests me appears quite crucial for literary history and criticism. In *The Place of Poetry: Two Centuries of an Art in Crisis*,[14] Christopher Clausen describes a prolonged ordeal by which poetry has been displaced by science and prose from a position of cultural preeminence. Every poet since 1750 has faced the problem. Clausen makes no mention of the phenomenon of poets themselves literally internalizing their continual crisis by incorporating the problematical noun itself into their poems. Nevertheless, he could have cited numerous poets who thus faced the problem head-on. Emily Dickinson's devoting entire poems to a strenuous effort at defining *crisis* would be either a starting point or a culmination.[15] But that would constitute another subject altogether.

One implication of Clausen's account would be that not only the sciences but also other forms of literature, particularly those with a scientific bias such as the novel, would benefit from poetry's losses. Such is in fact the case, but to conclude further that the novel has been spared any and all crisis would be a mistake. Clausen's characterization of poetry as existing in continual crisis applies equally to the novel. Admittedly, novelists created and enjoyed large audiences and a cultural role of considerable importance. Even so, they had to compete with science's descriptive veracity and poetry's stylish expression. Historically, the novel came into being as a problematical form and a revolutionary paradigm shift in epistemology and ontology, in literary knowing and literary being. It has remained in tension, and it has steadfastly internalized and coped with such stress in part by means of *crisis*-figurations.

Beginning with Samuel Richardson's *Pamela* (1740), the novel as a literary form has been greatly altered by cultural changes and predicaments—scientific, philosophical, aesthetic—of the kinds regularly designated "crisis." The novel has undergone continual stress, not the least interestingly, I will argue, in the technical decision faced by each novelist whether and how to use the potent word that was steadily becoming a major figural device throughout western culture. Among literary forms, the novel most fully incorporates the wide range of materials and methods that comprise modern life, and the genre offers good examples for a critical history of *crisis*-rhetoric. No critic has examined the novelists' literal confrontation with the great noun, but it provides a peculiarly rewarding way of looking at the tension-ridden history of the novel, a way to examine how novelists inscribe into their texts not only representations of crisis but also the metacritical term itself.

This study teases out numerous implications of Eliot's ironical assertion that one single word was taking on a special rhetorical role. It seeks to discover why—by 1866 (or 1832)—*crisis* had become peculiarly important and would become steadily more so in the unfolding story of modern life. What makes this noun so variable and yet so constant? Does it serve many different purposes? What, if any, specifically rhetorical, figurative, or critical function does the word serve in a novel?

Clausen does not define *crisis*, leaving it to convey its familiar meaning of a "predicament" or "dilemma" or "emergency." He thus follows a practice consistent with more than five hundred critical and scholarly articles and books listed in a computer-conducted survey of the MLA Database from 1966 onward. These essays employ the word almost exclusively in the general sense of an emergency or the only slightly more specialized sense of an emergency-triggered historical change.[16] My own investigation uncovers several more levels and types of meaning.

To a degree, this book derives some of its motivation from a kind of teleological *terminus ad quem*. In a very special and personal sense, and in keeping with the complexity of the topic under discussion, the beginning of this critical story lies literally in its end. It culminates in a description of a career-long meditation on the great noun carried out by an American novelist, the Nobel laureate Saul Bellow. By 1947, when Bellow began to publish the first of his ten novels to date, he was fully cognizant that Eliot's great noun was leaching into every nook and cranny of western culture. Routine communication had become scarcely imaginable without the concussive word. Bellow witnesses in every book to American versions of this modern phenomenon. From *Dangling Man* through *Herzog* and *Humboldt's Gift* up to *More Die of Heartbreak* (1987), he employs *crisis* to achieve fresh authorial crisis-perspectives in his ongoing analysis of American society. Technically, he experiments with the trope in terms of frequency of use, diegetic placement, emphasis, and effect. For his characters themselves, from the sidewalk to the White

House, the strategy of declaring a crisis becomes a tactic in power struggles. Bellow's major theme, enunciated in *Humboldt's Gift*, takes the explicit form of a *crisis*-utterance: "Under pressure of public crisis the private sphere is being surrendered." My critical history of *crisis*-rhetoric from Samuel Richardson onward, including contextualizing excursions into forms of discourse in disciplines such as philosophy and theology, seeks to describe and comprehend the long foreground that leads up to Bellow's strenuous enterprise. To conclude this critical history with a chapter on Bellow may seem somewhat arbitrary, but as the dedication to this book suggests, my motivation here is in part that of a witness to Bellow's literary achievement.[17]

Bellow places *crisis* like a dragon at the gate in the opening sentence of *More Die of Heartbreak*. No sensitive reader can ignore this challenge. But what exactly is the gauntlet (to change my figure) so defiantly dropped? Is *crisis* a technical device? Does it have a name, a beginning, a history? Is it part of a tradition or a genre? Will it prove to undergo historical or other kinds of development? If so, has it been a favorite method of major artists? In what relations does it stand to other techniques? If Bellow uses it in every novel, is it thus necessarily part of any novelist's equipment? In order to deal with such questions, I attempt a chronological survey including description, analysis, and interpretation. The result, I think, is to discover a strange historical phenomenon indeed. Eliot made history by calling attention to *crisis* as a potentially great noun, but her discovery proves to be only one of many crucial moments in a cultural revolution and continuing evolution.

Bellow's sustained crisis-rhetoric confronts his reader with critical issues that will surface at various points in my historical survey. When a novelist insinuates this signifier into a narrative, he achieves several effects. He expresses a belief that the world itself is structured in word and deed according to the complex principles of crisis. He also brings into his discourse the actual history that is thus structured. The novelist may designate his characters themselves as *crisis*-rhetoricians, and by exploiting this metacritical word, a writer introduces critical analysis directly into a work of the imagination. Literature thus becomes radically self-reflexive and self-critical. On the whole, I will urge, the *crisis*-strategist such as Scott, James, Durrell, or Bellow uses Eliot's great noun as a variable trope that enables other figures of speech (metaphor, irony) to work their effects by appealing simultaneously to many levels of the mind.[18]

In actual practice, *crisis*-rhetoric constitutes an element not only in the rhetoric of fiction but also in discourses by theologians, philosophers, autobiographers, and poets. Their discourses establish a firm historical and rhetorical context for a long line of English-language novelists. The term "rhetoric of fiction" has been a commonplace since Wayne Booth's influential study *The Rhetoric of Fiction* (1961). By contrast, the term "rhetoric of *crisis*" enjoys no such familiar currency, and Booth himself is indifferent to *crisis* in the rhetoric of fiction. Indeed, except for occasional asides or random musings, few critics vex themselves over Eliot's putatively great noun. Almost uniquely, Paul de Man explicitly posits *crisis*-rhetoric as a literary phenomenon worthy of concentrated study. In a general way, he contributes to the heuristic model I will use.

In *Blindness and Insight* (1971), de Man examines the troublesome question whether literature is a primary source of knowledge. Not every part of de Man's argument bears directly upon my topic, but I cite him here as a critic who establishes *crisis* as a term demanding critical attention. Positing literary texts as "elusive enigmas" that provoke critics to make self-contradictory statements, de Man then focuses on an ambitious array of topics: New Criticism, psychoanalytical criticism, Lukács's theories on the novel, Blanchot's impersonalism, Poulet's speculations on origins, Derrida's interpretation of Rousseau, literary modernity, and lyricism. His opening essay, "Criticism and Crisis,"[19] undertakes to defend literature as a special form of language and a primary source of knowledge. Alarmed at having discovered a perplexing "rhetoric of crisis" in structuralist criticism, he subjects crisis-rhetoric to a uniquely sustained examination, as follows.

The structuralist controversy of the late 1960s and early 1970s occasioned a most heated conflict as to which discipline (sociology, anthropology, linguistics, psychoanalysis) would most directly influence literary criticism. One controversial question persisted: whether literary language represents a privileged form of consciousness. Insisting upon the discrepancy between sign and meaning, demystifying critics sought to show that literary language was a part of language in general, no more special than everyday language. However, to demystify literature of all claims to a special status would be to face the "nothingness" of human existence. Better, says de Man, to accept literature as a primary source of knowledge but to remember that the invented fiction, rather than filling the void, asserts itself as "pure nothingness, *our* nothingness stated and restated by a subject that is the agent of its own stability" (p. 19).

In the 1890s, Mallarmé composed a prose text, *Crise de vers*, which expressed alarm over the young poets' adoption of free verse. Mallarmé used a crisis-rhetoric to express his alarm, but the "crisis-like intensity" of Mallarmé's utterance seems to de Man to have been misplaced.

Likewise, too, de Man can not be certain (in 1970) if, despite its crisis-rhetoric, the structuralist controversy itself is truly a crisis ("apocalyptic tempest") reshaping critical consciousness. Even so, "people are experiencing it as a crisis" and "they are constantly using the language of crisis in referring to what is taking place" (p. 6).

Mallarmé himself knew that the modern shift to free verse did not amount to a crisis. Something was indeed complicating practices and assumptions, but the actual crisis was Mallarmé's text itself, the *Crise de vers*, because that act of writing dared self-reflexively to question its own origins. Almost as if acknowledging the tropological movement from metaphor to metonymy to synecdoche to irony, de Man stipulates for a deconstructive definition of *crisis*: "We can speak of crisis when a 'separation' takes place, by self-reflection, between what, in literature, is in conformity with the original intent and what has irrevocably fallen away from this source" (pp. 7-8). Having used a *crisis*-rhetorician (Mallarmé) to establish an ontology (self-reflection) for crisis-rhetoric, de Man equates criticism itself with crisis:

> the notion of crisis and that of criticism are very closely linked, so much so that one could state that all *true criticism occurs in the mode of crisis*. To speak of a crisis of criticism is then, to some degree, redundant. In periods that are not periods of crisis, or in individuals bent on avoiding crisis at all cost, there can be all kinds of approaches to literature: historical, philological, psychological, etc., but there can be no criticism. (p. 8; emphasis added)

The etymological connection between *criticism* and *crisis* enforces itself ineluctably.

De Man admits that by asking whether literature and literary criticism are privileged forms of consciousness, structuralism initially appears to be a genuine criticism. Lévi-Strauss, for instance, argues that the observing subject can achieve anthropological "self-demystification" only by examining his own society. However, de Man illustrates how logically confusing his topic always threatens to become when he objects that for us to equate literature with demystification would be "to cause a crisis." The structuralists' insistence that literature equates with demystification may in fact be "the most dangerous myth of all" (p. 14).

De Man thinks that all statements made in the mood and rhetoric of crisis must share one "recurrent epistemological structure," a structure revealed by the interaction between *crisis* and some other word. He cites the example of Husserl.

On May 7 and May 10 of 1935, Edmund Husserl, the founder of phenomenology, delivered in Vienna two lectures entitled "Philosophy and the Crisis of European Humanity"; the title was later changed to "The Crisis of European Humanity and Philosophy," to stress the priority of the concept of crisis as Husserl's main concern. The lectures are the first version of what was to become Husserl's most important later work, the treatise entitled *The Crisis of the European Sciences and Transcendental Phenomenology*, now the sixth volume of the complete works edited by Walter Biemal. In these various titles, two words remain constant: the word "crisis" and the word "European"; it is in the interaction of these two concepts that the epistemological structure of the crisis-statement is fully revealed. (p. 14)

The two-term structure—*crisis* "of" *European*—provides de Man with grounds for a critique of Husserl. In effect, de Man rebukes one large category of manipulative uses of *crisis*.

Husserl, says de Man, illustrates how crisis-rhetorics may fail to utter the truth. That is, Husserl defines philosophy as self-interpretation, with self-critical vigilance as its dominant trait; but philosophy, he insists, is the unique privilege of European man. De Man objects to such arbitrary provincialism, charging that Husserl fails to examine his own narrow claim and thus "escapes from the necessary self-criticism that is prior to all philosophical truth about the self" (p. 16). As de Man critiques the structuralists' pretension to any ironical self-reflexiveness, he proclaims a shocking paradox:

Speaking in what was in fact a state of urgent personal and political crisis about a more general form of crisis, Husserl's text reveals with striking clarity the *structure of all crisis-determined statements*. It establishes an important truth: the fact that philosophical knowledge can only come into being when it is *turned back upon itself*. But it immediately proceeds, in the very same text, *to do the opposite*. The *rhetoric of crisis states its own truth in the mode of error*. It is itself radically blind to the light it emits. (p. 16; emphases added)

Any description of a crisis must always stipulate for a crisis "of" something, and, never to be taken merely at face value, it must always be interpreted. A crisis-rhetoric will always risk self-contradiction.

Assuming that all genuine crisis statements will be both self-reflexive and paradoxically self-mystifying, de Man goes on to insist that demystifying critics themselves, perhaps unknowingly, employ a *crisis*-rhetoric and thereby actually assert rather than deny the "privileged status of literature as an authentic language" (p. 17). But literature, insists de Man, always offers itself as fiction, and hence it is the only form of language "free from the fallacy of unmediated expression." In effect, he proposes the following syllogism. No criticism that is not cast self-reflexively in the mood and rhetoric of crisis can be considered a true criticism; Husserl's rhetoric of crisis is not self-reflexive; therefore, Husserl's structuralist crisis-rhetoric is not a true criticism.

In commonsense terms, de Man pleads merely that no critical enterprise be allowed to lapse into complacency. He exposes to skeptical analysis the culture-wide abuse of the great noun *crisis* whereby a potentially precise word was steadily being reduced almost exclusively to the status of a manipulative verbal strategy. In semantics a buzzword, such as, e.g., my earlier example of Lawyer Johnson's speech in *Felix Holt*.

Almost single-handedly, de Man foregrounds Eliot's great noun and compels us to deal with it. In a very general but forceful sense, he contributes ideas such as the following to my descriptive model. First, it is proper and even necessary to speak of crisis-rhetoric. Second, in literary criticism, the concepts of crisis and criticism should seem virtually synonymous. Third, *crisis* is preeminently a word able both to signify a set of facts (events, emotions) and also to trigger unthinking responses. Fourth, in every occurrence, *crisis* will signal rhetorical forces bearing upon the human personality or self. Fifth, a text itself may constitute a crisis, and specific texts may occupy unique positions in a critical history. Sixth, as a signifier, *crisis* is not a natural fact but a cultural judgment to be determined by a writer or reader. Seventh, authors devote painstaking care to deciding what parts of their discourse they will designate *crisis*. Eighth, *crisis* functions in the discourse of numerous disciplines. Ninth, *crisis* may be preeminently a signifier that can variously express, suppress, or distort meaning. Tenth, there exists a vocabulary of crisis-rhetoric: *crisis-aspect*, *crisis-like*, *language of crisis*, *crisis-statement*, *crisis-laden rhetoric*, and so on. Eleventh, to define *crisis* beyond its etymological and standard meanings will involve difficulties; witness de Man's various efforts, in which *crisis* variously means self-reflexive separation from an original source, "explosive renovation," "apocalyptic tempest," or simply "literary criticism." Finally, *crisis* will always signal a complex meaning that the reader is obliged to interpret. *Crisis* is a writer's special invitation to the critic to criticize.

De Man's skepticism towards literature as both knowledge and consciousness has influenced literary criticism. Christopher Norris notes:

> texts always generate a history of partial or 'aberrant' readings, the blind-spots of which can be deconstructed but never so completely demystified as to bring criticism out on a level of perfect clarity and truth. 'Criticism' and 'crisis' are linked not only by a punning etymology but by the very nature of

interpretative thought. 'The rhetoric of crisis states its own truth in the mode of error'. This is to say that criticism thrives on an ultimate *aporia* which it may not recognize but which everywhere marks its performance.[20]

Happily, though, de Man's gloomy caveat serves not only as a sober warning but also as a stimulant to critical effort.

Hayden White does not associate a consciousness-trope with any single word, as I intend to do. Indeed, I am aware that to study one single word might seem an extravagance. However, *crisis* witnesses to the violence disrupting the modern world, and hence it merits special attention. A general warrant for this book can be derived from important precursors who identify and interpret crucial words which shape our thinking about life and literature. The concept of a keyword which epitomizes a culture and its discourses has been urged by Raymond Williams. In *Keywords: A Vocabulary of Culture and Society* (1976) and *Culture and Society: 1780-1950* (1958),[21] Williams inquired into a vocabulary of shared words and meanings. In *Keywords*, he examines historical and current usages of 136 loaded and multivalenced words such as *aesthetic, capitalism, ecology, hegemony, welfare*, and *work*. In *Culture and Society*, Williams examines forty English authors ranging from Edmund Burke to George Orwell, discovering in them the keywords *industry, democracy, class, art*, and *culture*. Such complex keywords provide a useful but tricky map enabling us to examine disruptions and developments in life and thought. I am likewise motivated by other studies of isolable words.[22]

Broadly speaking, from such studies I derive operative principles for the model I will use in a critical history of *crisis*. Such a model must inevitably encompass a wide range of critical perceptions and issues. I must emphasize here that I will not use "keyword" in Williams's narrowly Marxist sense but in his (and others') more general sense; thus, I will refer to a "keyword" largely to remind my reader that I am representing the history of one single word. I find that keyword study provides viable if problematical means by which to identify crucial stages in cultural history. One pertinent issue, for example, is each new rhetorician's stipulative construction of a rationale or foundation for a peculiar usage. A keyword interpreter must try to separate out the emotive features from the cognitive features of a given utterance. He must be on the lookout for certain writers who possess a keen sense of the concentrated richness of certain words. A procedure as mechanical as word-counting may prove useful, although multiple and contradictory meanings may complicate any mere quantification.[23]

A single word can convey ideas and doctrines in unofficial and subtle ways, but no word can function without some contextualizing concept or image. Meanings ramify ineluctably; context may or may not insulate a word from adjacent contexts; relations between dominant and subordinate meanings may not be immediately, if ever, completely clear. A dialectic may develop between established meanings and a rhetorician's willed or *ad hoc* meaning. In every case, an interpreter must have recourse to dictionaries as well as to historical circumstances, real-life utterances, and written texts. The interpreter must be prepared to encounter impassioned personal responses to a given word. Repeatedly, I discover that a single word may become burdened with conflicting associations upwelling from the deepest recesses of a cultural psyche. Ambiguities and concealed metaphors complicate utterances, and some slippery words leave much hard work to be performed by the reader. Such explanatory work includes tracking a word through life and literature in order to glimpse the moral life revising itself and shaping human destinies. A word may inform our ways of thinking about human experience and thus contribute to our picture of the modern personality or self. Words provide a mysterious source of art.

A specific word may lead us into numerous fields of knowledge, including literature, politics, psychology, philosophy, science, art, and aesthetics. It will be rooted in figural contexts induced in part by the word itself. In my own understanding of the process, a keyword operates in a wide cultural context, from time to time entering figurative usage as an identifiable trope but always carrying some figurative potential. In the case of *crisis*, a flexible modern keyword becomes a trope under pressure of compelling rhetorical intentions and truth-effects.

Literary texts in general prove to be particularly fruitful places for word study, but novels most fully integrate a totalizing picture of human life and thus peculiarly reward such analysis. Individual novels may embody specific stages in the history of a word, and such a word may fructify a developmental pattern in an author's oeuvre. Writers of genius put their own distinctive stamp and coloration upon individual words. The history of a word resembles the story of a human life. Words enable human beings to invent or dramatize their own existences and thus to participate in culture. Finally, regardless of whether one approaches a word as neutral scholar or impassioned polemicist, whether one regards a word as full of meaning or empty of meaning, one should always think of human beings as social creatures who invent their own lives, consciously and unconsciously, in large part by means of special words. Taken cumulatively, this is the assemblage of ideas I find to emerge from the keyword studies cited above.

In literary criticism it would be valuable to have a statistical analysis of words avoided by an author. *Crisis* almost certainly has shaped modern culture, but it has not been universally embraced. Concordances would have informed Clausen whether certain poets embraced or avoided Eliot's great noun. Given the abundant evidence that the word eventually becomes one of the most familiar and potent words in western culture, a list of writers who ignore the word altogether comes as a shock. As absence rather than presence, they help to contextualize and define my examples, namely, certain key writers who explicitly signal crisis-consciousness.[24]

Admittedly, literature derives much of its substance and meaning from its own place and time, but in the interest of concentrating upon literary history, I deal mainly with the history and culture that finds an organic place in novels and related discourses. I attend only in passing to social and historical context or background. While recognizing the merits of, for example, the New Historicism, I invoke only in passing the historian's concern with any Hegelian transcendence of historical continuity, any sociological positivism or rationalism, any nationalized expression of folk values, or any dialectic between the aesthetically unique work of art and its conditioning historical grounds. In my view here, an aesthetic (rhetorical) critique tends to subsume other concerns.

The novel as a literary form has been undergoing a continual crisis partly of its own making for the two hundred and fifty years of its existence. Novelists acknowledged this widespread external crisis in part by internalizing *crisis* into the structure and meaning of their narratives. Lionel Stevenson concludes his one-volume history of the English novel with a generalization concerning the novel's cultural function: "the inherent qualities of the whole genre have preserved it as the sole adequate vehicle for the complex, pragmatic, fluctuating modern world."[25] Abundant evidence illustrates how novelists incorporated the metacritical term itself into their efforts to examine a society or a culture undergoing constant change and traumatic self-examination. *Crisis*-rhetoric historically converts a word of limited technical use into one of the most flexible and conceptually loaded narrative tropes. It thus contributes to the novel's generic power to render the complex, fluid, at times violent actualities of modern life.

Richardson, I will demonstrate, was unable to compose his masterpiece *Clarissa* without distributing *crisis*-signifiers that complicate vital stages in the conflict between Clarissa Harlowe and Robert Lovelace. Likewise, Eliot could not construct her masterpiece *Middlemarch* without insinuating a systematic *crisis*-trope that establishes Dorothea Brooke and Will

Ladislaw as the bearers of her thematic intention. But, even if as few as fifty thousand novels had been published since Richardson, the few dozen examples that I will cite constitute a severely limited body of evidence. Numerous prose-fiction writers from Barnabe Rich in the sixteenth century to John Fowles in the late twentieth century have been entirely omitted.[26] To that extent, gaps occur in my argument. But no critic can hope to establish an exhaustive repertoire of examples upon which to apply theories, interrogations, and speculations. Given the hundreds of thousands of extant novels, one's chief selections must be stringently economical.[27]

The fifty or so examples I will identify as incorporating a *crisis*-trope in fact constitute a remarkable collection of masterpieces. The list includes novels by Richardson, Sterne, Mackenzie, Scott, Austen, Emily Brontë, Eliot, Meredith, Gissing, Moore, James, Lawrence, Forster, Conrad, Joyce, and Durrell, as well as the American novelist Robert Coover. Examples glanced at in passing, e.g., Virginia Woolf, William Golding, and Iris Murdoch, plus major novels in other national traditions, are intended to augment a convincing set of illustrative materials. The forty-year career of Saul Bellow culminates my history of a master figurative device.

To be unaware of the history and potential power of Eliot's great noun means to be alienated from a central dynamic of modern life. The history of *crisis*-rhetoric from Richardson to Bellow witnesses to profound social struggle and social change. History contrives, so to speak, for crisis-rhetoric to accompany and shape modern consciousness. If history itself is a kind of language, *crisis* constitutes one significant element, in the process becoming "that great noun." Some proponents of historicism insist that for ideological reasons no historian can exert any control whatsoever over the contingent historical materials that flood into a written account.[28] This view is rejected here. What counts finally in a historical study of literature is the history that finds its intrinsic place in the literature itself, and which can be confidently interpreted, if only heuristically.

The pertinent history that enters into the literature examined here can be adumbrated as follows. Within a large cultural framework of revolutionary passion ultimately given political expression by Thomas Paine, the first English novelist Samuel Richardson early on depicts a headlong collision between English aristocracy and an emergent middle class. Henry Mackenzie exhibits the tragic encounter between pre-romantic humanitarianism and old-fashioned human greed. Scott marks the end of the eighteenth century's pure sentimentalism by positing a seriousness latent in Gothic emotionalism. Jane Austen smuggles into one of her novels the Romantic philosophy of esemplastic imagination only to judge it harshly. Eliot includes in three novels much carefully researched materials drawn from the reform period of 1832 and an incipient European Zionism. Meredith witnesses to the dead-end failure of an obtuse aristocracy; Gissing and Moore attest to inherent economic contradictions lurking within Victorian prosperity; Henry James builds class-consciousness into his novels in the form of a conflicted aestheticism. Lawrence provides a compelling portrayal of the mechanization that was ruining the English countryside. Forster sadly notes the failure of Anglo-Indian rapprochement. Lawrence Durrell invents a convoluted literary form in order to suggest the maddening intricacies of Middle-Eastern politics. Robert Coover makes literary substance and form out of a tormented reactionary ideology espoused by Richard Nixon. Finally, Bellow repeatedly witnesses to exploitation of crisis-mentality as a form of sociopolitical manipulation and escapism. At every stage of this turbulent history, history floods into the literature.

Under the cloak of ideas, history enters in another way. *Crisis*-tropes elaborated in polemics, autobiography, philosophy, theology, history of science, and social science are cited whenever they illumine the main subject. Not only eighteenth-century rhetoricians such as Thomas Paine or nineteenth-century thinkers such as Carlyle, J. S. Mill, and Newman, but also twentieth-century figures such as Husserl, Karl Barth, T. S. Kuhn, and Jürgen Habermas bring both intellect and passion to bear upon the argument. To adapt a phrase borrowed from W. K. Wimsatt, my main body of evidence illustrates how the *crisis*-trope has both intricately and gorgeously enriched the English-language novel and, in the process, enabled many forms of modern consciousness. It becomes steadily clearer with each of my historical examples that many important novelists have depended upon *crisis* in the construction of their narratives. It likewise becomes manifest that the serious reader must acknowledge the functional presence of this word-as-trope. As Wolfgang Iser might put it, the *crisis*-building novelist inscribes into his texts an Ideal Reader who must be, among other things, a *crisis*-conscious reader.

Etymology is intricately relevant to the model I will use in this critical survey. The root meaning of *crisis* (discrimination, judgment, decision) presumedly derived from an original circumstance (as conjectured by etymologists) in which a cutting leads inevitably to a separating and then a sifting. As shown in *Webster's New World Dictionary of the American Language* (1986), the process would have been developed as follows. The hypothetical Indo-European base [*(s)ker-] meaning "to cut" yields the hypothetical root form [*(s)krei-] meaning "to sift" and/or "separate," hence "to decide" or "to judge." From these conjectured forms developed the Greek *krisis* (judge; decision). Since human beings possess an ability to construct fictions which liberate the human spirit, fiction-making enables human freedom itself. Assuming the existence of an *a priori* mode of existence that one might designate a "flux," we might plausibly entertain the following proposition: "Each organism initially enacts a *cut* in the flux." Furthermore, such a cut is a selection that cuts out something and thereby distinguishes it from something else. By such a shaping process, categories such as objects, acts, and events are brought into being. Such cuts or decisive actions enable human consciousness to produce complex fictional worlds which interpret the conceived or perceived real world.[29] This compelling version of human imagination bears directly upon *crisis*-rhetoric. The conjectured root, a "cutting" or simply a "cut," suggests that any novel consists externally of an undifferentiated chunk carved out of the flux or totality of things. Does it not follow that a novel may consist internally of a segmented series of parts accomplished and signalled by markers such as incisive *crisis*-images that cumulatively add up to a governing *crisis*-trope?

In my historical account, then, a story will be told relating to an overlooked but genuine problem in literary criticism: the rhetorical status and function of a word employed as early as Aristotle's *Poetics*, current in many languages and rhetorical forms, and arguably one of the most characteristic words in the modern world. The word regularly Englished as *crisis*—call it a critical or a metacritical term—has had an extraordinary career in language and literature, particularly in the novel. My historical survey will demonstrate that this figure of speech plays various roles in processes of individual growth, social interaction, social change, and intellectual advancement. It can lend itself to an Aristotelian readerly structure or enter into a modernist writerly text that flaunts its arbitrariness. Almost always an operative metaphor, *crisis* becomes part of the novelist's code that must be decoded. As an integral part of a narrative, the great noun may operate in a textualism; as an intertextual signifier, it may also demand that a text be read in connection with various cultural contexts (political, psychological, theological, sociological, aesthetic) and thus operate in a contextualism. Without necessitating any specific ideological distortion, *crisis* can enable ideological interpretation, whether Marxist, Freudian, sociological, or some other.[30] If we further hypothesize that this metacritical term acts as a radical means of defamiliarization, we will see that it automatically provides, from an Archimedean point of perspective, something like

Gide's celebrated device the *mise en abyme*, which reflexively enriches a narrative by complicating levels of narration.[31]

A novel expresses time-consciousness. One of the fundamental uses of *crisis* has been as a signifier for turning points in a temporal sequence. With origins in Greek drama as described in Aristotle's *Poetics*, the turning point helps to determine narrative structuring and hence narrative meaning. In this familiar sense, *crisis* denotes the episode or incident in which the situation of the main character, by analogy with the progress of a disease, either improves or worsens. Historically, a certain category of writer has resorted to this explicit method of signalling to the reader a crucial moment of truth. Novelists as varied as Henry Mackenzie, Jane Austen, George Moore, and William Golding have not hesitated to use it thus. Given that even a short novel embodies many hard-to-manage materials, an author's decision to assist a reader by such an explicit device would be understandable. However, comprehending major turning points—from health to sickness, wealth to poverty, or failure to success—might appear to be such a simple procedure that one would not expect any intricate rhetorical interpretation to be involved.

Such is not the case. In attempting to make each new book uniquely and interestingly an exploration of crisis-consciousness, Saul Bellow has discovered that turning points in fact represent complicated moral or psychological or ontological problems. His ten novels illustrate the difficulty of structuring narratives via major twists of fate. In *More Die of Heartbreak*, the main character explicitly reflects upon the paradoxical importance of the turning point in human existence. In desperation, he hits upon the formulation that "our existence was worthless if we didn't make a turning point of it" and, moreover, that one ought to endeavor to make one's life a "turning point for humankind." Even so, such high-sounding generalizations occur in perplexing entanglements where neither character nor reader can easily identify a turning point or even a path. Turning points prove philosophically complex. Because they represent the human personality forming itself within a temporal succession of moments, any descriptive evaluation of such constitutive moments necessitates a strenuous effort of imagination.

Both Mellard and Kellner characterize tropological shifts from metaphor to metonymy to synecdoche to irony as dialectical turning points.[32] In general, crisis-consciousness requires one's being sensitive to dialectic. In a ground-breaking essay, "'Errours Endlesse Traine': On Turning Points and the Dialectical Imagination," Marshall Brown subjects *crisis* to sustained scrutiny. He sensitizes us to intricate tropological turnings from one condition of soul or consciousness to another. Like

White, de Man, Mellard, Kellner, and various keyword interpreters, he thus contributes to my critical model.

Endeavoring to reflect on the way a transition appears "from the inside," Brown meditates upon seven metaphorical images which project and reflect emergent occasions: Mill and River, Wheel and Swing, Revolution, Dialectic, Dancing, Turn Against Turn, and Escapable Romance. He intends to discover not what a turning point or crisis was after the dust has settled but what a turning point is in the "turbulence of its occurrence." The turning point or crisis is a "trial" or a "process." But the word *crisis* itself means "judgment," and Brown desires to learn exactly what is on trial and what conclusions result from crisis-judgment itself. He asks: "When does the judgment come?" Drawing upon literary and philosophical texts, Brown describes dialectical forces triggered by crisis as turning point. On the positive side: freedom and the possibility of benign change. Yet more disturbingly, on the negative side: incomprehension, disorientation, perplexity (aporia), revolutionary violence, disorder, interpersonal conflict, and ontological uncertainty.[33]

Brown's description of dialectical crisis-consciousness as revolution constitutes a major element in my theoretical model and will frequently surface in my historical narrative. Influenced by Brown's speculations (together with Hayden White and de Man, as well as recent studies of narrative framing and the *mise en abyme*), I will delineate a picture of *crisis* as a complicated dialectical trope twisting through the main tradition of English fiction. Obviously, Brown's urging that *crisis* functions as a disorienting trope owes much to the explosive destabilization induced by deconstructive skepticism. He compels us to reopen the entire question of turning points in human experience and in narrative discourse. Brown's basic question—"When does the judgment come?"—will be answered at every stage of this book on the subject of a modern keyword signifying "judgment." I want to suggest at the outset that judgment of some sort must come whenever a writer invokes the unsettling effects of the putatively great noun.

What other critical issues are involved here in my history of one single word in context of many novels? Several, it would seem. For example, tracing this history brings us face to face with the ongoing critical effort to settle the literary canon. In that the *crisis*-trope appears explicitly in some but not all important novels from Richardson's *Clarissa* to the present, it can provide one basis for the heuristic establishment of a specialized canon. Literally, *canon* means a measuring line or rule, hence, a standard of judgment, and it refers variously to books of the Bible as being of divine origin, to lists of recognized saints, or to books attributed on the basis of logical evidence to a given author. But in contemporary criticism, *canon* bears upon institutionalized literary studies. What texts will be included on required lists? On what grounds? In terms of which ideologies? Since critical practice itself necessitates inclusions and exclusions of materials and methods, it enforces canonical problems. In my study, excepting a few peripheral examples drawn from continental literary traditions, plus novels by the Americans Robert Coover and Saul Bellow, the texts derive from mainstream English literature. By and large, they narrow down a well-established authorial tradition: Richardson, Scott, Eliot, James, Forster, Joyce, and the like. Of course, merely to note that specific novels incorporate a *crisis*-trope would not thereby bestow value upon them. Even so, given the rich history of this figure that I will represent, together with the discovery that some writers avoid the increasingly popular word altogether, ought not such a body of crisis-centered narratives be urged as at least one sort of canon?

In addition to problems of the canon, the most vexing critical issue of our day likewise yields somewhat—granted not easily—to our recognition of the critical role of crisis-rhetoric. As conjectured by Derrida, deconstruction represents a radical and abiding skepticism. It seems to me that the *crisis*-trope constitutes the simplest method of deconstruction. Derrida's neologistic figuration attempts to combine two opposite processes—construction and destruction—so that both a linguistic utterance and radical criticism of the same utterance occur, as it were, simultaneously. Any written construct must be recognized to have always already deconstructed or destabilized itself by its own self-contradictory substance. Thus, a novel such as Eliot's *Daniel Deronda* is considered to have smuggled into itself radical features that undermine any presumed integrity or logocentric metaphysic of presence.[34] I feel compelled to hypothesize that, in the case of the *crisis*-trope, the root meaning (judgment) directly signals to the reader that the onward movement of a discourse (particularly a narrative) must be interrupted and at least an *ad hoc* critical judgment be made on the spot. Both utterance and criticism of the utterance thus do occur, to the degree possible, simultaneously. The most characteristic figure of speech for deconstructive (chiasmic) analysis is the metaphor of an explosion. Eliot's concussive *crisis* represents, to my understanding at least, the most radically direct means of concussive deconstruction. Joyce's *Finnegans Wake*, to take one example, perfectly illustrates deconstruction in literary practice, demonstrating—I will urge—the tortuous procedures by which one kind of artist plants a *crisis*-trope in a narrative.

My description of the crisis-trope thus interfaces with (while not being engorged by) various critical issues. As in reader-response criticism, it confronts problematical relations between text and reader. Throughout, I have kept in mind certain language effects regarded both as equipment for living and as locus of meaning effects. Literature, so to speak, designates cultural roles for its readers. A text exists to be read and may exist only in being read. Even if a reader must cope with an author's world view, reading nevertheless constitutes the basis for understanding literature. Whether as catharsis, sympathetic response, guiding assumption, or adaptive gestalt, the readerly activity provides a ground for literary experience. Yet the precise relation between text and reader remains a mystery to be explored. A writer inscribes into any written utterance certain distinctive features that shape a reader's responses. A given pattern of such discursive features is said to constitute a reader—hypothetical, ideal, implied, fictitious, contemporary, privileged, or informed—who embodies an informing principle within the writing itself.[35] Compounded of readerly expectations, the implied reader embodies formal elements which an actual reader is obliged to perceive. In a novel informed by a *crisis*-trope, the hypothetical reader (in reality a cleverly formalistic fiction or trope) must be a superreader who can shake off the spell induced by narrative if and when the great noun compels a critical judgment. Such a technique at intervals requires a reader's adopting a critical stance toward a discourse. No text can really control a competent reader, but does not the *crisis*-trope come nearest to uttering such writerly commands?

On the whole, this book thus acknowledges current critical issues but endeavors to remain basically a critical history. It attempts to demonstrate that the crisis-riddled modern world and the crisis-conscious novel are analogous and coeval. Yet nagging questions dog my every step. Why has *crisis* become historically and culturally so important? What about the very word itself? What makes this single noun so variable and yet so constant? What constitutes the presumed rhetorical, figurative, or critical importance of *crisis* in a novel? How and why has it become a twisting trope that serves so many different rhetorical purposes?

Paul de Man and Marshall Brown in a sense harangue each other over this very question. In the face of de Man's solemn assertion that crisis-rhetoric states its own truth in the mode of error, Brown persistently inquires, "when does the judgment come?" Conversely, to Brown's insistent query, de Man as it were replies that whenever the judgment comes it may be radically flawed. In de Man's radical assertion, a profound skepticism dwells, healthy in its intention and effect. The proper response to de Man is simply to maintain skeptical vigilance in the face of any rhetorical strategy whatsoever. The correct response to Brown is no less radically imperative. In a narrative, judgment will come, at the very least but unfailingly, when a rhetorician invokes Eliot's great noun. A narrative without a *crisis*-trope may move relentlessly toward its closure absent any ineluctably self-reflexive interruption. The reader may not feel obliged, even by narrative segmentations such as chapter divisions, to interrupt and interpret. But every appearance of *crisis* signifies that a fictive character has either made a judgment or himself been judged, or, that the author has otherwise necessitated a judgment.

Empson described the splendid effects of certain magnificently rich words. Ironically, perhaps, *crisis* sometimes seems among the poorest and emptiest of words, but historically it has been loaded down with intricate meanings by a brilliant succession of writers. Oddly, if *crisis* occasions hyperbolic excess in some authors (e.g., Karl Barth and Robert Coover), to others it seems nearly invisible. Raymond Williams does not include *crisis* among his keywords, even though he himself concludes *Culture and Society* as follows: "The human crisis is always a crisis of understanding: what we genuinely understand we can do." Similarly, Marian Cusac makes *crisis* a key term in her analysis of Scott's novels but never even notices the trope itself within Scott's books. Even so, despite such indifference, its metaphoric and metamorphic career has been remarkable. It begins as Aristotle's term for logical plot structuring, becomes Longinus's term for emotional exacerbation, and eventually enters into a variety of critical and narrative formulations: Matthew Arnold's cultural centrality, Henry James's existential aestheticism, Lawrence's self-defining sexuality, Brown's revolutionary turning point, de Man's error-ridden criticism, Merrell's cut into the primordial flux, Durrell's reborn self, Bellow's analysis of hysterical escapism, and so on.

De Man argued that Husserl's crisis-rhetoric swerved into error because of an ill-considered analytical phrase (crisis of European sciences). Yet the great noun also thrives alone, as rhetorical bludgeon, in numerous contexts. Novelists themselves in effect labor to distinguish between the word as a manipulative buzzword or as part of a sustained analysis. In many respects, this potent signifier itself remains uncannily an empty symbol or vessel to be filled out by any writer's or reader's desires or *ad hoc* meanings. It thus hovers precariously but productively between the literal and figurative, the objective and subjective, the manipulative and the communicative. As a powerful word, it can be used, as Foucault says of power itself, both to dominate people and to liberate people (by enabling self-realization and self-improvement).[36]

Throughout this book I am moved to ask, how does a *crisis*-trope figure in a novel? No simple answer is forthcoming, and the answers I propose are most likely mere thought-starters, amounting to an introduction to an introduction. Even so, recent critical theories encourage speculative answers. Two recent books, both coincidentally dedicated to Paul de Man, enable speculation. Peter Brooks's *Reading for the Plot* concentrates upon "our desire and need for such orderings" as those provided by plotted narratives. Plot, conceived of as "the organizing dynamics of a specific mode of human understanding," acts out the implications of metaphor. The metonymic moments which readers seize and valorize are thus the active structuring parts of a text, determining its meaning.[37] Brooks's concept of the organizing line and intention of narrative generalizes my own specific belief in a reader's obligation to seize on any moment signalled by a *crisis*-image. Any such image provides one momentary stay against readerly confusion by guiding the creation of meaning that prevents the reader from losing himself or being totally absorbed in the very act of reading. Brooks believes that narrative is itself a form of thinking. If so, a *crisis*-signal may preeminently induce the critical stance prerequisite to narrative's in truth constituting a form of self-reflexive thought. The word makes us stop and think.

In *Beyond Deconstruction*[38] Howard Felperin explains recent ideological positions and methodological issues in a way that reinforces my belief that *crisis*-tropes bring criticism, as it were deconstructively, into a discourse. Felperin leads me to conclude that *crisis* is always a figure of speech or, so to speak, a fluid critical pun. Felperin praises de Man's clairvoyance in thinking, in 1971, that "true criticism occurs in the mode of crisis," and the critical issues Felperin reprises all bear upon or witness to the potential functions of *crisis* within a discourse. The textual self-consciousness that marks avant-garde criticism assuredly crystallizes in every occurrence of this trope that commands the reader to judge or criticize. More broadly, I believe, any *crisis*-trope will enable or even necessitate a unique confluence of writerly and readerly skills.

Any *crisis*-rhetoric will place interpretative responsibility and authority squarely upon the individual reader. The endless train of error that is human life, when it is converted into a narrative adroitly cut and shaped by *crisis*-figures, reconstitutes itself in terms of a strenuous and almost endlessly interpretable (hence long-lived) discourse. If the masters of deconstruction discover in every text some foreknowledge of criticism, is it not the case that *crisis*-tropes almost uniquely occasion and even constitute such foreknowledge? To the degree that the modern self is a function of language, *crisis*-rhetoric participates (as Eliot hints in *Felix*

Holt, the Radical) in the complex process by which alienated modern individuals desperately make up their own moral histories.

Paul Valéry described the novel reader as being totally absorbed in the story to the point of critical self-oblivion.[39] The *crisis*-trope inscribes into the text a novel reader who, having initially given himself over to Valéry's totally engrossed *"crisis of credulity,"* must simultaneously be prepared to become, when the trope appears without warning, an acutely self-conscious critic. The *crisis*-trope, with its curious combination of emptiness and fullness of linguistic materiality, maximizes the reader's implication in the creation of the text.

I am convinced that every new *crisis*-trope triggers other major figurations partly by coming nearest to the root meaning of *trope*, i.e., a turning away from literal meaning. It thus enables and induces an extraordinary range of rhetorical effects, including major metaphors and ironies. It also enters into the radical problematics of authorship and authority. By inducing critical self-reflexivity, it activates salient critical and philosophical issues. It may prove to be the case that *crisis* achieves greatness simply by triggering a rhetorical tension adequate to the tensions of modern life. In general, this problematical word serves the aims of a master plot extremely flexible and potent, serviceable to many ideologies, systems, and aesthetic purposes. Can a word that so easily lends itself to manipulation attain to greatness? God-terms and buzzwords may be justly held in contempt by a rational mind, but within a modern cultural framework *crisis* is undoubtedly, among other things, a great manipulator. At another level, salutary effects result from its ability to place personal responsibility for moral judgment squarely upon beleaguered and increasingly evasive modern individuals. Late in the twentieth century, Saul Bellow will stubbornly confront this aspect of the word's ironical greatness, a greatness that had by his time been hard-won through a prolonged historical ordeal.

My problem throughout is to mediate between literary meaning and the presumed truth of history. Human life appears to be indeed an endless train of human error, and literature expresses such a flawed condition. All attempts definitively to interpret life or literature likewise are doomed to error. This complex fate surely accompanies all interpretations of *crisis*-language, including my own. But the critic's task is to make the critical effort. Once we see how George Eliot brings the great noun forward in 1866 as a subject for critical interrogation and judgment, criticism of novels can never again be quite the same. In the final analysis, this magisterial trope performs one radical function, the illocutionary act of commanding the reader: Judge! lest the story be not judged!

1

Revolutionary Roots of Modern Crisis-Consciousness:
Samuel Richardson, Henry Mackenzie,
and Sir Walter Scott

If *crisis*-consciousness is indeed a trope, it earns this designation by being one of the most effective means which writers use to induce reality-effects and truth-effects. In our own day, *crisis* has become so prevalent in discourse that a reader sensitized to such a word might be expected to find it anywhere and everywhere.[1] Even so, in my investigation of the narrative impact of this device, I focus mainly on a selection of the most active examples drawn from my own reading.

Aristotle describes a turning as a peripeteia, a reversal or sudden change in fortune or circumstance. Literally, this vivid moment suggests the falling of a feather and thus the dizzying turbulence of dialectical crisis. Aristotle's pioneering account has been neatly assimilated to modern criticism by E. M. Forster: "the advantages of the triple process of complication, crisis, and solution so persuasively expounded by Aristotle."[2] By and large, the *Poetics* emphasizes one main turning point within the patterned action of a drama; without precluding heightened emotions, it strongly implies rational judgment. Five hundred years later another treatise would shift the emphasis from judgment to a more intense emotionalism. Longinus's first-century treatise *On the Sublime* perpetuates Aristotle's *crisis*-terminology but offers another meaning. By *sublime*, Longinus meant greatness of spirit. A genetic critic, he identified five chief sources of sublimity: ability to conceptualize great thoughts, intense emotionalism, powerful figures of speech, selection of noble or lofty diction, and harmonious composition of sentences. In at least one sense, Longinus is a romantic theorist. Emphasizing an exaltation triggered by short passages of pure poetry, he appealed to a psychological intensity which would emerge in full flower in the eighteenth century in Europe. For Longinus, figures such as *efficacia*, *enargeia*, and *phantasiai* result

28

in powerfully affective writing, suggesting causative connections between human passions and bold figures of speech.[3]

Longinus confused rhetoric and psychology with other features of the writing and reading experiences, but his influential statement is enlivened by a powerful *crisis*-image. At one key moment in section 38 of *On the Sublime*, he examines a familiar story for the sources of its energies, variously hyperbolic, grand, and intense. In essence, he constructs and vividly signals a metaphoric equation of blood and mud.

> Possibly then the best hyperboles, as we said above in speaking of figures, are those which are not noticed as hyperboles at all. This result is obtained when they are uttered in an outburst of strong feeling, and in harmony with *a certain grandeur in the crisis* described, as where Thucydides is speaking of the men slaughtered in Sicily. 'For the Syracusans', he says, 'also came down and butchered them, but especially those in the water, which was thus immediately spoiled, but which they went on drinking just the same, mud and all, bloody as it was, even fighting to have it.' That blood and mud were drunk together, and yet were things fought over, passes for credible in *the intensity and feeling and in the crisis*.[4] (emphases added)

Rational judgment begins to yield to the hyperbolic emotionalism that by cumulative association would one day transform *crisis* (*krinein*) itself into a powerful word. Longinus concludes with a warning that tyranny can work deleterious effects on literature. Ironically, the emotionalism he champions would itself become a means for rhetorical manipulation of human behavior and thus impose on all men a form of tyranny. In the twentieth century, human beings would learn to use a *crisis*-laden rhetoric to terrorize and tyrannize.

Samuel Johnson's epochal dictionary (1755) takes note of only two meanings of *crisis*, in astrology and medicine, but other writers of the period were extending the range of meanings into new areas of experience. One 1769 citation in the *OED* offers the following Longinian utterance: "To escape a crisis so full of terror and despair." Beginning in the middle of the eighteenth century and culminating in excesses of Gothic terror and horror, this new Longinian element would color the effects of *crisis*-language. From this point onward, English rhetoric will be influenced by this figure which oscillates wildly between reason and hysteria. We will witness here a special moment of historical transition.[5]

Two nonnovelistic texts (one implicitly Aristotelian, the other Longinian) suggesting the great figure's emerging currency in eighteenth-century England appear in both Richard Cumberland's autobiography and Thomas Paine's *The American Crisis*. Cumberland arbitrarily structures his account of a presumedly actual event in Oliver Goldsmith's life by analogy with a dramatic plot marked by a strong turning point. Paine moves men to political action by using *crisis* for its incomprehensible, emotional effects in a revolutionary rallying cry. These documents establish a broad framework—ranging from reason to unreason—within which to place Richardson as the first English novelist and an important *crisis*-theorist.

Narrative literature results from conjunctions of complex cultural forms and verbal conventions. That any *crisis*-trope represents only one possible division of a presumedly seamless factual event or narrative can be seen in the following example. Richard Altick critiques the excesses of one sort of *crisis*-strategist. He finds his example in *Memoirs of Richard Cumberland, Written by Himself* (1807). This Cumberland was a playwright known for manifestly deplorable tricks such as facile emotionalism, a resort to quick and easy effects, and emotional shortcuts. In order to elucidate the scholarly problem of basic and collateral evidence, Altick examines six different accounts of the sale and publication of Oliver Goldsmith's *The Vicar of Wakefield* (1766). The six versions offer widely discrepant interpretations of certain presumed facts. Altick is led to ask if the episode alluded to by the six commentators actually happened at all, and, if so, how much money Goldsmith collected for *The Vicar of Wakefield* and from whom? Altick's conclusion is that every human being views events through a unique set of mental lenses. Variations of any presumed truth are inevitable.

Five of Altick's examples, excerpted from James Boswell, Mrs. Hester Thrale, Sir John Hawkins, William Cooke, and George Steevens, eschew any *crisis*-figure. Altick prints Boswell's version of Johnson's own account of how he himself rescued Goldsmith from an oppressive landlady by selling "a novel ready for press" in Goldsmith's possession.

I received one morning [said Johnson] a message from poor Goldsmith that he was in great distress, and, as it was not in his power to come to me, begging that I would come to him as soon as possible. I sent him a guinea, and promised to come to him directly. I accordingly went as soon as I was drest, and found that his landlady had arrested him for his rent, at which he was in a violent passion. I perceived that he had already changed my guinea, and had got a bottle of Madeira and a glass before him. I put the cork into the bottle, desired he would be calm, and began to talk to him of the means by which he might be extricated. He then told me that he had a novel ready for the press, which he produced to me. I looked into it, and saw its merit; told the landlady I should soon return, and having gone to a bookseller, sold it for sixty pounds. I brought Goldsmith the money, and he discharged his rent, not without rating his landlady in a high tone for having used him so ill.

Altick notes too that Boswell offers his reader a direct quotation from Johnson.

Not so Mrs. Thrale, who offers a paraphrase. Hawkins offers an even greater variation, making no mention of Johnson's part in the episode. Likewise, Cooke's account does not include Johnson. And in Steevens's version, the entire story is converted into a story of Samuel Richardson's rescuing Johnson from debt! Thus Altick shows how five versions offer variable facts so as to produce such a "welter of discrepancies and outright contradictions" that one is left wondering: "where is the truth to be found?" Or, as we might put it: "when does the judgment come?"

Altick's sixth example, from the melodramatist Cumberland, provides other variations on the presumed facts, including the structuring and heightening device of designating poor Goldsmith's predicament a "crisis of his fate." Cumberland insinuates a metaphor (a human life is a drama) in order to control a metonymically cluttered array of details.

> I have heard Dr. Johnson relate with infinite humour the circumstance of his rescuing him [Goldsmith] from a ridiculous dilemma by the purchase money of his Vicar of Wakefield, which he sold on his behalf to Dodsley, and, as I think, for the sum of ten pounds only. He had run up a debt with his landlady for board and lodgings of some few pounds, and was at his wit's-end how to wipe off the score and keep a roof over his head, except by closing with a very staggering proposal on her part, and taking his creditor to wife, whose charms were very far from alluring, whilst her demands were extremely urgent. In this *crisis of his fate* he was found by Johnson in the act of meditating on the melancholy alternative before him. He shewed Johnson his manuscript of The Vicar of Wakefield, but seemed to be without any plan, or even hope, of raising money upon the disposal of it; when Johnson cast his eye upon it, he discovered something that gave him hope, and immediately took it to Dodsley, who paid down the price above-mentioned in ready money, and added an eventual condition upon its future sale. Johnson described the precautions he took in concealing the amount of the sum he had in hand, which he prudently administered to him by a guinea at a time. In the event he paid off the landlady's score, and redeemed the person of his friend from her embraces. (emphasis added)

Altick derides Cumberland's use of *crisis* for the mere sake of putting a rhetorical twist upon the presumed facts. Cumberland arbitrarily states that Goldsmith's landlady was of an amorous and even marital bent. He uses clichés to heat up his language: Johnson's "rescuing" of Goldsmith from a "ridiculous dilemma" in which he is at his "wit's end" because of a "staggering proposal" from his Wife of Bath-like landlady, and so on. Cumberland's decision to signify Goldsmith's predicament as a "crisis of his fate" gives his account a shocking but controllable effect. He uses *crisis* to impose something like a concussive dramatic structure on Goldsmith's plight and then to construct a sort of master *crisis*-plot of a kind popular novelists would also employ. Accordingly, Goldsmith's perplexity is made to occasion Johnson's wise judgment.

Cumberland's resorting to a *crisis*-image is part of what Altick objects to as the memoirist's playing fast and loose with the presumed facts.

> *What about Cumberland's version, which is conspicuously different from the others?* Sheer embroidery and careless variation on the better attested facts. There is no other evidence that Dodsley was a party to the transaction, and the landlady whose charms were less than compelling is so patently a stock character from comic fiction and drama (remember that Cumberland was a playwright) that we may dismiss her with the same alacrity that Goldsmith, according to Cumberland, did.[6] (emphasis Altick's)

Objectively considered, Cumberland's rhetorical centering on *crisis* comes fairly under Altick's rebuke. But viewed purely as a shaping rhetoric, it effectively illustrates the Russian Formalists' distinction between *fabula* (presumed actual events) and *sjuzét* (rhetorical rendering) as the two poles or levels of any rhetoric of fiction. Cumberland exemplifies the temptation offered to any eighteenth-century narrator to structure a narrative by means of a simple Aristotelian *crisis*-figure. Ironically, by signifying a *crisis* Cumberland merely obliges his reader to perform a serious act of judgment. If the reader is Richard Altick, the verdict boomerangs against Cumberland himself.

Few if any serious writers of any period use the great noun carelessly, and many perceive it as a revolutionary signifier. Numerous authors in a wide assortment of disciplines exploit it. Among the most effective would be the most influential propagandist serving the American cause of independence during a major revolutionary period: Thomas Paine.

The great noun becomes great in part because of the lofty intentions it facilitates. Paine illustrates how the violent progressivism of revolution occasions a classic expression of crisis as dialectical turning point. He produced an electrifying series of thirteen essays (1776-1783) now known as *The Crisis* or *The American Crisis*. Responding to an earlier series of political pamphlets voicing the English argument, Paine's *crisis*-rhetoric enflamed a smoldering American militia. As a civilian aide to the Continental Army, Paine analyzed or intuited the dire political situation.

By general agreement, he possessed as powerfully as Rousseau or Marx the gift of using keywords and phrases with magnetic effects. His pamphlets bolstered morale, rationalized temporary defeats as strategic victories, poured contempt upon the British and the American Tories, derided General William Howe's character, urged greater civilian self-sacrifice, and exhorted the British people to realize how unjust and hopeless was their government's cause against the freedom-loving people of America. Coincidentally, the separation of America from England as urged by Paine perfectly illustrates a tropological movement from identity to difference to classificatory arrangement, falling just short of ironic self-reflexion.

Paine is regarded historically as a genuine master at using an insider's perspective to sum up and interpret dangerous circumstances, critical occasions, and changing events. Given America's historical predicament and the future overuse of *crisis*, Paine used the word itself sparingly; even so, his *crisis*-images add up to a trope that permeates his impassioned discourse. Strangely enough, by far the majority of occurrences of *crisis* in *The American Crisis* are used in the most mechanical fashion, externally as titles to each individual pamphlet and internally as cross-references from one essay to another. Even when he signifies *crisis* within the essays themselves, the reference is usually a practical cross-reference from one pamphlet to a preceding essay or to the series as a whole. At least five pamphlets contain no internal mention of *crisis*, not even of the most mechanical sort. In only four pamphlets (numbers 1, 3, 4, and 7) does the master propagandist develop more organically the implications of his keyword.

Paine's chief strategy was to provide large, unmistakable effects by labelling each pamphlet "The Crisis," but he also weaves in subtle effects, variously rational and irrational. A few lines of his famous opening passage can illustrate his overall effectiveness. At the outset, *crisis* means an imbroglio within the context of which men must make crucial choices. He begins with a seasonal metaphor, one that will transpose itself into synecdochic elaboration via numerous names and facts.

These are the times that try men's souls. The summer soldier and the sunshine patriot will, in this crisis, shrink from the service of their country; but he that stands it *now*, deserves the love and thanks of man and woman. Tyranny, like hell, is not easily conquered; yet we have this consolation with us, that the harder the conflict, the more glorious the triumph.[7]

By emphasizing the element of individual choice in determining a course of action, Paine leaps over other available meanings (medical; astrological) so as to stress the etymological meaning (decision; judgment).

In the third pamphlet, Paine recounts the original state of affairs leading to hostilities; he elucidates the Americans' frame of mind "at this crisis." Via *crisis*, Paine occasions condemnation of the British refusal to redress American wrongs as well as the British decision to use "the East Indian article *tea*" in order to transfer British "rapine" from India to the American colonies (p. 211). Paine's additional theme here focuses metonymically upon American resoluteness and British indifference. He harps upon *crisis* as a dangerous situation within which someone decides upon a course of action, and he goes on to conclude that in "the present crisis" of the British attack on Philadelphia, Americans themselves must determine house by house who is for the American cause and who against it. Then, too, by responding in kind to a British crisis-pamphlet bearing the same title, Paine in effect guarantees that success will come to the party which empowers itself to designate which event is a crisis.

The climax of Paine's argument incorporates an analogy between the Americans' predicament and a disease that is nearing its turning point. More importantly, it establishes an ambiguous relation between rational judgment and deterministic physical illness as well as between danger and opportunity. Such conceptual complication will become an essential element in the unfolding history of crisis-rhetoric.

> There is a mystery in the countenance of some causes, which we have not always present judgment enough to explain. It is distressing to see an enemy advancing into a country, but it is the only place in which we can beat them, and in which we have always beaten them, whenever they made the attempt. *The nearer any disease approaches to a crisis, the nearer it is to a cure.* Danger and deliverance make their advances together, and it is only the last push, in which one or the other takes the lead. (p. 231; emphasis added)

Paine's analogy to disease defines the American crisis as in part a naturalistic problem standing outside the realm of rational choice, but his argument goes on to urge conscious decisions by individuals who may thereby advance the American cause.

Each of Paine's thirteen essays bears the title "The Crisis." His *crisis*-rhetoric climaxes in pamphlet number 7. Appealing to the common sense, fairness, and practicality of the English people, he urges the rightness of the American cause. Warning of a potential war between England and America's ally France, Paine admonishes the English that this "matter is come now to a full crisis, and peace is easy if willingly set about." He concludes his argument in this pamphlet by emphasizing, via a pun, his belief or judgment that the English people have reached "a Crisis" in their relations with the Americans. He refers both to his own literary form (the Crisis pamphlet series itself) and to the "Crisis" (moment of decision in a stressful situation) that must be acknowledged by the English people.

> Here I rest my arguments and finish my address. Such as it is, it is a gift, and you are welcome. It was always my design to dedicate a *Crisis* to you, when the time should come that would properly *make it a Crisis*; and when, likewise, I should catch myself in a temper to write it, and suppose you in a condition to read it. *That* time has now arrived, and with it the opportunity for conveyance. (p. 291; emphases Paine's)

Like George Eliot eighty years later, Paine displays an acute awareness of the problem of which event in a series of events the rhetorician should designate as a *crisis*.

Paine's final use of the great noun (pamphlet 9) drives home the fact that he uses the word much like Eliot's Mr. Johnson or Richard Cumberland, manipulatively to signal a crucial juncture and an emotional call to action.

> *At a crisis, big like the present, with expectation and events*, the whole country is called to unanimity and exertion. Not an ability ought now to sleep, that can produce but a mite to the general good, not even a whisper to pass that militates against it. The necessity of the case, and the importance of the consequences, admit no delay from a friend, no apology from an enemy. To spare now, would be the height of extravagance, and to consult present ease, would be to sacrifice it perhaps forever. (p. 304; emphasis added)

Paine's *crisis*-theme depends upon two of the great noun's paradoxical connotations: danger and opportunity. He urges Americans to script their own earthly destiny by judging, deciding, and acting. As a *crisis*-rhetorician, he generally adheres to his announced rhetorical axiom that the rhetorician should avoid any writing device by which "the eye is diverted" and instead should direct the reader's eye to "a clear conclusion that shall hit the point in question."[8] Paine is not a rhetorician to waste a great noun.

In addition to its being figuratively consistent with the tropological transit from metaphor to synecdoche, Paine's revolutionary call to enlightened consciousness forcefully illustrates Brown's description of revolution as dialectical crisis or turning point. During Paine's own lifetime, the astronomical term "revolution" was taking on the implication of violent progressivism. As a philosopher of reason, Paine situates his appeal for revolutionary consciousness and action squarely within the mixture of error and truth that constitutes the matrix not only of dialectical crisis but of human existence phenomenologically (and properly) understood.

On the whole, *The American Crisis* represents an extreme or classic instance of a parsimonious but effective *crisis*-trope. Paine's rhetoric moved and steered political behavior by invoking the mysterious word. Together with Richard Cumberland, he adumbrates a broad but firm eighteenth-century context for an examination of another revolutionary thinker, the first English novelist.

1. "the crisis for which I have long been waiting"

Colley Cibber's self-serving autobiography appeared in 1740, the same year as Richardson's *Pamela*, arguably the first English novel. In his third chapter, the playwright and poet laureate Cibber recounts how he missed out on career opportunities in church, court, and army. At a key moment, Cibber hints at a shift from metaphor to metonymy by signifying *crisis* in its sense of a fateful turning point determined by the stars.

> I am now come to *that Crisis in my Life when Fortune seemed at a Loss what she should do with me*. Had she favour'd my Father's first Designation of me, he might then, perhaps, have had as sanguine hopes of my being a Bishop, as I afterwards conceiv'd of my being a General, when I first took Arms, at the Revolution. Nay, after that, I had a third Chance too, equally as good, of becoming an Under-proper [sic] of the State. How, at last, I came to be none of all these, the Sequel will inform you.[9] (emphasis added)

Cibber's trope is as manipulative as Cumberland's and as revolutionary as Paine's; given his personal involvement in his own life story, he appears even more manipulative and error-prone than Cumberland. Having laid down a red herring suggesting that he was a plaything of the remote stars, he surprises his reader by recounting his career in literature and the theater as depending entirely upon his own bold enterprise. With Cibber's secular or self-centered *crisis*-figure, literary thought moves toward Richardson's modern-tending view of human beings as self-defining agents in a godless world.

Samuel Richardson spins out his sentimental romance *Clarissa; or the History of a Young Lady* (1747-48)[10] to a million or more words. This epistolary masterpiece narrates the frantic trials and tribulations of Clarissa Harlowe, a middle-class heiress, and her ultimate choice of death as more desirable than a forced marriage with her suitor Robert Lovelace, who has raped her. Elaborated at repetitive length and in minute detail for an audience that was first discovering the pleasures of realistic prose fiction, *Clarissa* can be read as a rambling but convincing set of social and sentimental data. In addition to this cumulative effect, it also shapes itself around an irresistibly logical and tropological story line with structural points highlighted and complicated by at least three *crisis*-signals. To understand Richardson's effects (and those of other examples I will cite), I must resort to a variety of critical methods (e.g., tropology, *mise en abyme*, narrative framing), but undergirding all of these is a basic part/whole analysis.[11]

Richardson's story line runs as follows. Robert Lovelace, an aristocratic rake, antagonizes the middle-class Harlowe family even as he is falling deeply in love with the younger daughter Clarissa. When the Harlowes insist that Clarissa marry the rich but repellent Mr. Solmes, Lovelace contrives for Clarissa to run away with him. He sequesters the girl in a brothel. After many emotional harangues, several attempts at escape, and episodes of foiled passion, the frustrated Lovelace drugs and rapes Clarissa. Subsequently, Clarissa escapes but is recaptured; Lovelace wishes to marry Clarissa; Clarissa deteriorates physically even as she enlarges and elevates her spiritual outlook; the Harlowe family, too late, forgives Clarissa; Clarissa dies; Lovelace provokes a duel with Clarissa's cousin, who kills Lovelace; the dying Lovelace repents his misdeeds. Richardson stipulates that both Clarissa and Lovelace enact their inner desires as *crisis*-rhetoricians. He constructs a dialectical turn against turn in which Lovelace wins a fierce struggle with Clarissa over whose rhetoric shall prevail.

The psycholinguistic processes at work in Lovelace's (and perhaps in any writer's) use of an electrifying, manipulative, but self-delusive *crisis*-trope may best be comprehended by a theory of meaning elaborated, via Wittgenstein's language-games, by J. L. Austin and William Alston. In *How to Do Things with Words* (1962), Austin identifies ways by which humans achieve certain effects upon other humans *by* using sentences; also, a second order of effects that are achieved *in* using sentences. Any command from one person to another to perform a given task may accomplish its specific, explicit goal (performance of the task). In addition, any such command implicitly asserts one's very power or authority to command. Austin designated the first as the perlocutionary meaning of an utterance; the second, its illocutionary meaning. In *Philosophy of Language*, Alston built upon Austin's ideas by elaborating certain rules tacitly followed by users of language in choosing among possible forms of expression. A sentence may be said to have an illocutionary potential when it is understood to involve a speaker's implying certain conditions to hold. Austin thinks that the illocutionary act may take the form of reporting, describing, analyzing, explaining, predicting, or *judging* (emphasis Beardsley's).[12] I wish to suggest that in the case of Lovelace, a brilliant if perverse illocutionary act determines that the speaker holds or takes responsibility for and control over a specific set of social dynamics. Lovelace's domineering word *crisis*, with its roots firmly set in the Greek verb *krinein* (to judge), preempts from Clarissa the right to designate what moment in their relationship will be a *crisis*. Lovelace aggressively represents certain dominance and submission relations to hold and thus effectively asserts his authority. His rhetorical intention and the utterance that expresses it perfectly illustrates Austin's illocutionary act.

Philosophers of consciousness agree that consciousness can best be understood at one level in terms of dialectical polarities, e.g., subjective or objective, active or passive, intellectual or spiritual, horizontal or vertical, and the like.[13] Richardson foregrounds just such oppositions, which thenceforth became elements essential to an historically unfolding *crisis*-consciousness. Clarissa herself dominates the sentimental dimension, but Lovelace offers a more striking representation in that he dominates both Clarissa and the book as a whole. More than a century before *Felix Holt, the Radical*, Richardson discovered or induced the linkage between *crisis* and sociopolitical manipulation. He takes Lovelace through numerous mercurial changes of mind and heart, intricate rationalizations, fluctuating moods, the putting on and taking off of masks, roles, and voices. Lovelace's self-expression takes the form of a sustained attempt to oppress and dominate Clarissa. Philip Stevick explains it thus:

> Lovelace creates his own channels through which to press his advantage, and they resemble the finest refinement of the eighteenth-century mind, its wit and poise, its facility with language, its logical and analytical methods, its enormous learning, its ability to move with grace between play and irony and earnest partisanship. All of these are the fascinating traits of a brilliant age, mirrored in the figure of Lovelace—and they all become means for the manipulation of Clarissa.[14]

The main turning point may be Clarissa's decision not to marry Lovelace after he has raped her.[15] Such a viewpoint is consistent with the Clarissa plot and its eschatological heavenward turn. However, Richardson also explicitly structures the narrative via *crisis*-images that shape another plot, the earthbound Lovelace plot that dialectically and violently deconstructs the Clarissa plot. The initial metaphor of family harmony is shattered by a metonymic and synecdochic violence.

Richardson explicitly introduces a major trope into the English novel when he arranges for Lovelace to become a *crisis*-strategist. In the year-long series of letters that constitute the story (January to December), Lovelace initially designates his deadlocked relation with Clarissa as a *crisis* in a letter to Clarissa (late March) that boldly expropriates the initiative from Clarissa. At this anguished crux, Clarissa still holds out hope that Lovelace may reform and become worthy of rescuing her from her oppressive family. Lovelace writes (from a coppice near her father's house) that he considers her promise to grant him a private interview to be binding upon her. Prior to this crucial event, Clarissa has referred to some unspecified moment in her own tribulations as an impending crisis. Lovelace then both skillfully and arrogantly breaks the deadlocked turn against turn, expropriating the center of dramatic gravity to himself by shifting the designation of *crisis* from Clarissa to himself.

> And *are things drawing towards a crisis between your friends and you?*—Is not this a reason to expect, the *rather* to expect, the promised interview?
>
> Can *I write all that is in my mind*, say you?—Impossible!—Not the hundredth part of what is in my mind, and in my apprehension, can I write!
>
> O the wavering, the changeable sex!—But can Miss Clarissa Harlowe—Forgive me, Madam!—I know not what I write!
>
> Yet, I must, I do, insist upon your promise—Or that you will condescend to find better excuses for the failure—Or convince me, that stronger reasons are imposed upon *you*, than those you offer.—A promise *once* given!—the promis-*ed* only can dispense with;—or some very apparent necessity imposed upon the promis-*er*, which leaves no power to perform it. (Letter of 29 March; emphases Lovelace's)

Having accepted Clarissa's own stipulation of her familial entanglement as a crisis, Lovelace concludes this letter by shifting his rhetorical focus to his own frustrations and distractions and, more specifically, by expropriating *crisis* to himself. He concludes: "My *fate* is indeed upon its crisis." For the scholarly Lovelace, *crisis* emphatically signifies a critical juncture in which a decision must be made. Clearly, he implies here, the judgment will be not hers to make but his.

Ironically, the confusion Lovelace feigns will in fact characterize his own eventual fate. Richardson arranges his early episodes so that Clarissa in effect attempts to wrest what might aptly be called crisis-management away from Lovelace. In that Clarissa represents the bourgeois class and

Lovelace represents the aristocracy, their clash over crisis-management symbolizes an historical class struggle and a tropological paradigm shift. Historically, this type of self-centered *crisis*-struggle will continue to characterize interpersonal conflicts over priorities in self-fulfillment. It will receive its clearest elucidation in the social-science theory of Jürgen Habermas, a twentieth-century thinker who willingly relinquishes the individual self ("European Man") that Richardson champions and in a sense invents.

In Clarissa's epistolary discussions with her confidante Anna Howe as to the course of action she must take with respect to her family and Lovelace, she describes three alternatives. She can escape to London, or put herself in the protection of Lovelace's relative Lord M., or secretly meet and marry Lovelace. In her letter of 6 April, as if to wrest away from Lovelace the *crisis*-control he had seized from her during her own perplexity, she notifies Anna: "The crisis is at hand." Richardson establishes a sharp contrast between Lovelace's confident rhetoric and Clarissa's less secure style. Clarissa writes:

> If *I* am to be singled out to be the *punisher* of myself, and family, who so lately was the *pride* of it, pray for me, my dear, that I may not be left wholly to myself; and that I may be enabled to support my character, so as to be *justly* acquitted of wilful and premeditated faults. The will of Providence be resigned to in the rest: As *that* leads, let me patiently, and unrepiningly, follow!—I shall not live always!—May but my *closing* scene be happy!—
>
> But I will not oppress you, my dearest friend, with further reflections of this sort. I will take them all into myself. Surely I have a mind, that has room for them. My afflictions are too sharp to last long. The crisis is at hand. Happier times you bid me hope for. I *will* hope! (Letter of 6 April; emphases Clarissa's)

In betraying her anxiety and thereby foreshadowing her own premature death, Clarissa's is a restricted viewpoint, extending no further than her parental entrapment. She correctly perceives her predicament as a crisis of familial incomprehension, but she lacks the worldliness to prevent Lovelace's eventually defining and controlling her own worldly if not her heavenly crisis.

Richardson then complicates matters by revealing Lovelace as a revolutionary tyrant who thwarts other revolutionaries. At one point, Clarissa's desire to determine or designate crises in her own life is reinforced by Anna Howe. Two days after Clarissa's letter (8 April), Anna responds to Clarissa by warning her not to run away with Lovelace without first being married to him. She grants Clarissa her designation of her entrapment as a crisis—"now you are upon such a crisis"—but hints that more serious contingencies might face Clarissa if she merely exchanges one predicament for another. Richardson implies that Clarissa uses bad judgment in failing to perceive that Lovelace will tyrannize over her by manipulating her one major crisis.

Richardson constructs a two-level, two-stage story. *Clarissa* has a decidedly secular and a decidedly sacred dimension. In the latter part of the novel, the sullied Clarissa declines into bodily weakness but rises in spirit so that her expectation of heaven convinces many readers that at her death she will enter heaven. But in certain earlier, more secular, parts of the novel (roughly January through June), Richardson actually concentrates more intently upon the characterization of Lovelace. He emphasizes Lovelace's finest traits—wit, poise, verbal facility, logic, analysis, learning, grace, playful irony—which dominate Clarissa via tyrannizing procedures of a *crisis*-trope.

With Clarissa in his clutches but realizing he can never seduce her, Lovelace perversely but logically decides that by raping her he can coerce her into a respectable marriage. Richardson shows Lovelace carefully structuring his own behavior. As if to deflect responsibility from himself even while claiming the glory, Lovelace characterizes his cynical orchestration of the rape itself as "the crisis for which I have been long waiting." On Monday, 12 June, Lovelace describes to his confidant John Belford the actual rape. His scheming reaches a peak of frantic rationalization. In explicit language, he reappropriates crisis-management from Clarissa to himself. Using an array of rhetorical devices, not excluding brackets, Lovelace enumerates his grievances against Clarissa and rationalizes his own criminal behavior.

> Be her preference of the single life to *me*, also remembred!—That she despises me!—That she even refuses to be my WIFE!—A proud Lovelace to be denied a *Wife*!—To be more proudly rejected by a daughter of the *Harlowes*!—The ladies of my own family [She thinks them the ladies of my family] supplicating in vain for her returning favour to their despised kinsman, and taking laws from her still prouder punctilio!
>
> Is not *this* the crisis for which I have been long waiting? Shall Tomlinson, shall these women, be engaged; shall so many engines be set at work, at an immense expence, with contrivance; and all to no purpose?
>
> Is not *this* the hour of her trial—And in *her*, of the trial of the virtue of her whole Sex, so long premeditated, so long threatened?—Whether her frost is frost indeed? Whether her virtue is principle? Whether, if *once subdued, she will not be always subdued*? And will she not want the very crown of her

glory, the proof of her till now all-surpassing excellence, if I stop short of the ultimate trial? (Letter of 12 June; emphases Lovelace's)

Lovelace's *crisis*-consciousness mires down in self-delusion. In the hour of Clarissa's trial, which Lovelace himself designates, she will indeed be judged, and on the secular level Lovelace decides when the judgment comes. Himself now a masterful if wicked *crisis*-rhetorician, Lovelace proceeds to justify his assault upon a helpless woman. In the same letter, he obliquely describes the rape itself, accomplished with the aid of the procuress Mrs. Sinclair. Richardson thus completes the trope that initiates, structures, and coordinates his two major storylines by permeating his book with excitability and hysterical rationalization.

Of course, *Clarissa* is a lengthy text, and Richardson has much more story to tell. Some of his most compelling details occur after the crisis-structure has been completed. But the structure itself, in effect Lovelace's exigent trope of crisis-consciousness, is of chief relevance here. Richardson uses *crisis* to link two very different plot lines. The sacred dimension develops as the despoiled Clarissa, feeling rejected by the world, goes into physical decline and turns her thoughts toward heaven. When she dies (7 September), her unforgettable final words of Christian hope ring as convincingly as those of Hopkins's tall nun in another masterpiece of apocalyptic literature, "The Wreck of the Deutschland." Hopkins's drowning nun echoes Revelation 22:20 by crying: "O Christ, Christ, come quickly." Clarissa also cries out: "Come—O come—Blessed Lord—Jesus!" (Letter of 7 September). By contrast, Lovelace the rapist resolves a tormented psychological conflict by provoking his own death under the rapier of Colonel William Morden (Letter of 18 December, N. S.). Lovelace's final words express perplexed guilt and remorse rather than hope: "LET THIS EXPIATE." Richardson remains true to Christian tragedy by balancing his sacred theme dialectically opposite his secular theme. Lovelace has moved from metaphoric egotism to ironical self-punishment; likewise, we can easily imagine Clarissa, like Chaucer's Troilus, turning at heaven's gate to laugh (or weep?) at the little earth where she suffered so horribly.

Other novelists to be examined as explorers of *crisis*-consciousness include such important names as Scott, Conrad, James, and Joyce. None, however, is more important in this putative tradition or canon than Samuel Richardson. His analysis of manipulative behavior in relation to self-definition has provided an adaptive model for subsequent novelists. Richardson's discovery or invention of a structuring *crisis*-trope appears to have enabled the invention of the novel itself as a new literary form. Although by no means as structurally thought out as the techniques at work in subsequent masterpieces by Meredith, Lawrence, or Forster, Richardson's *crisis*-figure surely leads one to speculate whether the developmental greatness of the great noun in effect dictates that any full-fledged rhetoric of fiction will of necessity include a rhetoric of *crisis*.

Clarissa establishes relevant questions and hypotheses for my historical survey. A *crisis*-rhetoric serves the ends of characterization, particularly with regard to self-expression, life-scripting, manipulation, and interpersonal conflict. A novelist may contrive for some of his characters themselves to recognize and cope with social or personal exigencies by enfiguring a *crisis*-image into his own or another person's life. Two characters may be set in conflict over the question as to whose *crisis*-script will predominate. In effect, the fictive *crisis*-strategist will be a literary person or author, and when he or she is a main character the resultant tension will permeate an entire narrative. Broad implications stemming from social or political crisis may be developed at the existential level of individual consciousness and behavior, though a novelist or character may not take pains to stipulate a definition for *crisis*. In general, principles of characterization such as perceptiveness, alertness, foresight, wit, and aggressiveness may be established or signalled by the keyword. To use a *crisis*-trope is to constitute oneself a judge, albeit one's judgment may be deeply flawed.

The great noun also serves other novelistic intentions. *Crisis* stands in a special relation to dramatic plotting and its distinctive techniques (Lovelace refers several times to his scheme as a drama with an Act I, Act II, and so on). Plot structure may be achieved by a novelist's or a character's judicious positioning of *crisis*-signifiers. As part of a master plot, *crisis* can be used to signal a controlling, informing structure for a very large assortment of narrative data pertaining to emergencies, contingencies, traumas, or trials. Intense emotional effects can be thus created or triggered. Historically, given this problematical emotionalism, the electrifying term will be used sparingly until the tormented twentieth century exploits it as a keyword for an entire age.

Crisis may serve either a novelist or a character as a device for manipulation of other people or of narrative materials. The etymological meaning (judgment, decision) will sometimes enforce itself in a given context and sometimes not. Witnessing to the violence of modern culture, the word itself frequently pulls away from its cool etymological meaning toward heated connotations more violent and dangerous. Paul de Man insists that the epistemological structure of every *crisis*-statement depends upon a two-term structure: noun preposition noun; crisis *of* something (in Meredith's *The Egoist*, "the crisis of doubt and dispute"). Even so, a novelist or character may use the great noun by itself, as grammatical subject or object, without specifying any further phrasal elaboration ("I pledge you my word it's a crisis"). Then, too, *crisis* itself may serve the writer in one way but the reader in a different way. Such a dual function can be understood as the packing and unpacking, encoding and decoding, understood to embody the literary process itself, even if what is unpacked may not be identical with what is presumably packed in. *Clarissa* illustrates how *crisis*-consciousness was from the outset of the genre a part of the novelist's equipment and method as a generic shifter that smuggles criticism into a seamless narrative. Richardson establishes the principle that when *crisis* (judge) signals a stressful moment or turning point in a written narrative, the author has thereby issued a special invitation to the critic (judge) to criticize.

2. "crisis in the corruption of a state"

During the last quarter of the eighteenth century, the novel as a form underwent a crisis. After 1771, when Richardson's moralistic and sentimental mode reached its English apogee in Henry Mackenzie's *The Man of Feeling*, energies that produced the early masterpieces of Richardson, Fielding, Smollett, and Sterne had subsided. During a quarter century of decline, five new lines of development emerged: Gothic terror and horror, social manners, social theories, exotic Eastern fantasy, and didacticism. The early metaphoric identification of novelistic content and form with individual genius, having broadened into the early masterpieces by Richardson, Fielding, Sterne, and Smollett, woefully narrowed down to an ironically reduced prospect. By the end of the century, the novel verged on extinction, and recovery of its early prestige would come only later with Sir Walter Scott and Jane Austen.[16]

The influence of Richardson and Laurence Sterne determined that English novels would delineate not only social manners but also sentiments peculiar to fine sensibility. Lucrative "crying volumes" extended the Richardsonian vein, offering emotional characters charged with fine feelings. Not narrative structure but overall impression was the chief aim of these novels of social concern depicting the pathos of delicate-minded individuals, the frustration of love beyond one's social position, the vanity of riches, the misery of the poor, and the glory of benevolence.

Henry Mackenzie produced a cogent example of sentimental romance in *The Man of Feeling* (1771). This brief narrative metonymically depicts emotional and moral standards of the age via the delicate responses of one Mr. Harley to a dozen social types encountered during the last few weeks of his brief life. Grounded in the benevolism of the Earl of Shaftesbury and Francis Hutcheson, thus positing an innate moral sense expressed in acts of public virtue, Harley naïvely urges that sensibility should lead ineluctably to humanitarian action.

In spite of Mackenzie's studied formlessness, his book exhibits a novelistic structure centered by means of a single *crisis*-image. By this oblique means, he radically questions whether dialectical turn necessarily leads to benign change. The three-part story establishes Harley's rural life style, takes him on a round trip to London for adventures in the problematics of philanthropy, and returns him home where he pathetically dies of injured sensibility. Mackenzie establishes a complex of literary ideas at the main turning point—Harley's return trip—which he blatantly signals via a sustained *crisis*-utterance.

Supposedly preserved in a badly mutilated text, the story line follows a simple pattern. Mr. Harley, youngest member of an impoverished family of gentry, attempts to secure the use of royal lands. Hoping thus to increase his ability to perform benevolent acts, he leaves his neighbor Miss Walton and travels to London to seek the king's approval. In London, he encounters various individuals who test his delicate feelings of benevolence, among them a disguised panderer, a mob of Bedlamites, a gang of swindlers, and other unsavory characters. Eventually he learns that the royal lands had been awarded to the panderer. Dejected, he sets off for home. On the road, he converses with an old man, Ben Silton, with whom he discusses social and moral problems attendant upon philanthropy. Once Harley reaches his own neighborhood, he assists an aged soldier to settle upon a small farm on the Harley estates. Reaching home, he learns that Miss Walton is now affianced to a rich man. Harley falls ill, languishes, and, at the moment when Miss Walton reveals to him that she in fact returns his affection, he abruptly dies.

Mackenzie advances the history of *crisis*-tropes by fusing a plot of action with a plot of thought. He signifies the disorienting turning point of Harley's turbulent ordeal, in a textual fragment preceding chapter 33, when Harley leaves London to return home. Like Cumberland's or Cibber's, his turning point aspires to be of the logical, Aristotelian sort, but it also manifests an obscurely violent turn from path to pathlessness.

Mackenzie structures a tropological plot of thought in chapter 33 as Harley travels the high road homeward toward further disappointment and death. He highlights this episode by stipulating "an alarming crisis in the corruption of a state." His intellectual plot deconstructs or seriously questions the plot of action by means of a dialectical conversation between Harley and Ben Silton. Harley's most forceful utterance climaxes a discussion of vice, poetry, philanthropy, wealth, and filial piety. The conversation between Harley and Silton can be summarized thus. Poets tend toward egotism, but happily the "poetical inclination" induces individuals to benevolent feelings that may result in philanthropic deeds. Even so, prudent people think that the poetical inclination results in a certain "unfitness for the world"; therefore, poetry may ironically militate against practical activities that keep the economy viable. Harley's longest speech climaxes the discussion. Even though poetical feelings may enervate moral fiber to some degree, yet they ought to be encouraged ("Perhaps we now-a-days discourage the romantic turn a little too much"). Since private morals and public virtues are based upon feelings, poetical feelings might mitigate the appalling reduction of pleasure itself to the pleasures of wealth.

Mackenzie converts the disappointed Harley himself into a passionate center of *crisis*-consciousness. Harley wrings his hands over a presumed "alarming crisis in the corruption of a state." He echoes the ancient-modern debate when he condemns present-day "Frivolous" and "Interested" philosophers as being sneerers who lack the critical judgment typical of past ages. Mackenzie has arranged Harley's story to show various responses that sensibility can make to the hard facts of life, and Harley now mounts a desperate effort to rationalize his predicament in terms of a general social malaise.

> "They laugh at the pedantry of our fathers, who complained of the times in which they lived; they are at pains to persuade us how much those were deceived; they pride themselves in defending things as they find them, and in exploding the barren sounds which had been reared into motives for action. To this their style is suited; and the manly tone of reason is exchanged for perpetual efforts at sneer and ridicule. *This I hold to be an alarming crisis in the corruption of a state*; when not only is virtue declined, and vice prevailing, but when the praises of virtue are forgotten, and the infamy of vice unfelt." (p. 57; emphasis added)[17]

A *crisis*-collapse occurs precisely here, as Harley fails in his attempt to force the metonymic and synecdochic fragments of his life into a new metaphor (feeling equals character and fate). Historically, too, Harley's shrill speech establishes that *crisis*-contexts will often stand out in strong relief from the embedding language and thus create confusingly different readerly effects and expectations.

Mackenzie's *crisis*-trope realizes itself in several ways. Besides invoking the general concussive or electrifying effects triggered by the great noun, it also signals a dialectical turning point in Harley's experience. Harley confusedly aspires to perfect in himself the habit of critical judgment he finds lacking in the philosophies of his own day. He will attempt, at the turn, to resist the selfishness he perceives in his fellow Englishmen. His linking of *crisis* and *corruption* establishes an image of physical disease, thus foreshadowing his own decline and death. Mackenzie adds a further deconstructive irony by having Harley attempt to project his own sense of failure off upon society at large, so that at his best moment Harley is also at his worst. Ultimately, Harley proves unable to cope with the cruelly scattered metonymic facts of life. His conventional analogy between a human body and the state backfires. Mired in ontological insecurity, he erroneously rationalizes as a crisis of social corruption a condition which proves to be a fatal crisis of his own character, spiritually and physically. When his judgment comes, it is deeply flawed, so that what ought to be a leap from metaphor to metonymy is nothing more than neurotic projection of danger away from a threatened self.

Other interpretations may be equally plausible, but Mackenzie unarguably followed his master Richardson in structuring this tale of spiritual earnestness and humanitarian zeal via the great noun. Richardson's bold-faced Lovelace puts his own stamp upon the great trope by signifying *crisis* as in effect his own signature; feckless Harley in his prolonged aporia struggles ineffectually to project *crisis* away from himself by a fruitless trope of social concern. By thus structuring Harley's misadventure on the road to London, Mackenzie anticipates Nietzsche's dialectical formulation: "Truth is not a place (*topos*) but a way, and the way is not a road (*hodos*) but a turning (*tropos*) off that deadly high road."

Traditionally, novelists in the mainstream attempt to make organized sense out of the jumble of actual experience. A sort of rationalism colors the main tradition of the novel. Even so, books with a rationalistic aura contrast sharply with other important books that undermine narrative logic and logic itself. Published between *Clarissa* and *The Man of Feeling*, Laurence Sterne's *The Life and Opinions of Tristram Shandy, Gentleman* (1760-67)[18] illustrates how a peculiar sort of story—capricious, freakish, incoherent—makes a very different use of a *crisis*-image. Setting out to interest readers by rendering quirky familiar life, Sterne satirized intellectual pretensions, including the rationalistic assumptions of current literary methods. Sterne purposely jumbled his narrative so as to ridicule the biographical structure that was destined after Fielding to typify English novels until the middle of the nineteenth century.

Tristram Shandy provides nothing like a plot with a crisis (turning point). Rather than the universalistic, *a priori* kind of structure that underlies such books, it is organized according to Sterne's whims and pranks. Such story as inheres shifts capriciously from Tristram's father Walter Shandy to his father's brother Toby. In the first half, an account is given of the odd goings-on in the Shandy household. Sterne focuses on Walter's madly twisted theories. His hopes for immortality in the form of a son who would be properly begotten, delivered, christened, and educated come to a comic end. In the second half, the bashful old soldier Toby is courted at great length by the aggressive Widow Wadman. Conflicts of opinion between the two brothers represent an absurd turn against turn in which the brothers thwart their own purposes by unknowingly converting events and conflicts against each other. Sterne dwells upon the unsettling premise that human experience always moves toward an unknown goal. The melancholy spectacle of error never ends.

The pervasive fragmentation in *Tristram Shandy* represents an ultimate metonymic dispersal of metaphoric (in this case familial) unity, as Sterne's rhetoric disclaims all pretensions to coherence and predictability. It undertakes to destabilize judgment itself: "if I thought you was able to form the least judgment or probable conjecture to yourself of what was to come in the next page—I would tear it out of my book" (p. 80). In keeping with this irrationalism, Sterne decenters *crisis* into a digression placed only a few pages into his perplexed tale. When Eugenius attempts to comfort the dying Parson Yorick, Sterne provides a moving scene but one peripheral to larger developments. *Crisis* carries only the simple meaning of a physical malady that has reached a turning point.

> Come,—come, Yorick, quoth Eugenius, wiping his eyes, and summoning up the man within him,—my dear lad, be comforted,—*let not all thy spirits and fortitude forsake thee at this crisis* when thou most wants them;—who knows what resources are in store, and what the power of God may yet do for thee?—Yorick laid his hand upon his heart, and gently shook his head. (p. 31; emphasis added)

Sterne fits the category of a writer overwhelmingly a crisis-rhetorician but not a *crisis*-rhetorician. Yorick dies brokenhearted because his ungovernable sense of humor had provoked his victims to unite against him. In one sense, then, the charming Yorick becomes irrelevant to Tristram's adventures. Sterne has effectively dislodged Aristotle's keyword (and Richardson's and Mackenzie's) from any major structural role in this novel. He thus adds a small but vital increment to my unfolding model.

Admittedly, of course, *Tristram Shandy* may in fact be a greater book than some others I will use to illustrate my argument. Given the many narrative devices by which Sterne parodies established and subsequently long-lived novelistic methods, his minimalizing of the role of *crisis* may seem a minor point. Nevertheless, in my argument *Tristram Shandy* establishes that Sterne's de-centering *crisis*-rhetoric serves as an important negative exemplum and thus foreshadows such ironical, antirational tropes figures as those in *Wuthering Heights*.

3. "Jeanie's presence of mind stood her friend in this dreadful crisis"

Jane Austen represents a culmination of Johnsonian attitudes, but she will be examined later in this study as an innovator opening up formal possibilities that point toward Eliot, Meredith, and Henry James. Sir Walter Scott points toward the Oxford Movement and Victorian historicism and thus seems suited to the nineteenth century, but his backward glancing via the historical novel, plus his reworking of sentimental and Gothic motifs, connect him with the eighteenth century. Scott is possibly unique in having his entire oeuvre scrutinized by a critic who uses the metacritical term *crisis* in a sustained critical effort. Marian Cusac's commentary proves how the chameleonic keyword can be simultaneously visible and invisible to the critical eye. Cusac first divides Scott's twenty-six novels into two groups, eighteen Romances and six Chronicles. In the six chronicles, Scott's basic structure is a series of episodes involving a passive protagonist and a happy ending. No turning-point occurs in these chronicles. In the eighteen romances, Cusac finds events more causally related. Further subdivision into Comic and Tragic produces a distinction between novels with an active protagonist and a happy ending (Comic) and novels with a passive protagonist and an unhappy ending (Tragic). Cusac further divides two types of romances into three types of structures: crucial structures, progressive structures, and climactic structures. The climactic structure centers on one dramatic moment at the conclusion of a novel; the progressive structure centers on a pattern made by a defining event followed by a confirming event and a culminating event; the crucial structure centers on a pattern made by a defining event followed by a crisis (turning-point) and a catastrophe. Cusac's examination of Scott's comic novels follows the same three-part division: climactic, progressive, and crucial structures.

Cusac determines that only ten of Scott's novels (seven comic, three tragic) are marked by a strong turning point. Placing *The Heart of Midlothian* among Scott's comic romances, she characterizes it as a progressive structure with three episodes (definition, confirmation, culmination) in which the plucky Scots lass Jeanie Deans defines her devotion to duty, confirms it, and in a culminating scene effectively redoubles her confirmation. *The Heart of Midlothian* contains no event resembling a dialectical crisis marked by confusion or uncertainty of purpose in the main character. Jeanie Deans's "active and undaunted habits of virtuous exertion" (chap. 52) result in an unquestioned and unquestioning characterization. During Jeanie's barefoot walk from Edinburgh to London, followed by her successful appeal that Queen Caroline pardon a condemned woman, Scott's heroine never wavers.[19]

Few readers would doubt Jeanie Deans's unswerving devotion. Jeanie displays no dialectical turbulence or ontological uncertainty. If Jeanie never wavers, she certainly never turns; hence, no turning-point (crisis) can be said to mark her experiences. But by failing to perceive Scott's *crisis*-trope, Cusac partially misreads this novel. Scott advances the history of the trope by using the word itself more often than any previous novelist. In a book of fifty-two chapters, Scott distributes six passages throughout the second half (Chaps. 19, 25, 30, 34, 37, and 52), which complicate the story via Eliot's ironizing great noun.

Generally regarded as Scott's finest novel, *The Heart of Midlothian*[20] eschews Scott's standard young hero in favor of a heroine from the lower classes. Set in the Scotland of 1737, it narrates the experiences of David Deans, a dairy farmer, whose younger daughter Effie is illegitimately impregnated by a dissipated young Englishman, George Staunton. Deans's other daughter, Jeanie Deans, saves Effie from a death sentence for her presumed infanticide. Because of a complicated Scottish law, Jeanie can save Effie only by falsely testifying that Effie had informed her sister of her pregnancy. Refusing to lie, Jeanie pluckily travels alone to London, secures an audience with Queen Caroline, and wins Effie's pardon. Subsequently, Jeanie, together with her father and new husband Reuben Butler, settles on a Highlands estate under the patronage of the Duke of Argyle. Effie and George Staunton are married, but Staunton is later killed by his own illegitimate son (the infant grown into an outlaw) who then flees to America. Scott's concerns include the problematics of human justice and the Presbyterian ethos. Moreover, a powerful moral theme is generated by the question whether Jeanie ought to save her condemned sister or maintain the integrity of her own conscience. This moral theme induces a high seriousness not found in Scott's other fictions and in part explains the book's special status.

Scott builds his book in four main sections. Chapters 2-7 depict a riot in which an Edinburgh mob lynches the hated officer Captain John Porteous. Chapters 8-24 depict the Deanses' background; Effie's trial, conviction, and sentencing; also, Jeanie's moral quandary. Chapters 25-39 show Jeanie's harrowing but successful journey to London to win Effie's reprieve. Chapters 40-52 show Jeanie's marriage to Reuben Butler, Effie's marriage to her seducer George Staunton, and Staunton's death. The first section convincingly reconstructs the historical situation of the Porteous riot; the realistic second part is the most highly regarded; the third seems weak in only confusedly emphasizing Jeanie's heroism; the fourth section, with its romantic high-jinks involving bandits and smugglers, seems extraneous to the presumed core of the book.[21] In Cusac's view, Jeanie initially defines, then confirms, then culminates her unwavering commitment to virtuous exertion on behalf of a clear moral precept. However, at one level Jeanie's concern seems to be chiefly for her own tender conscience rather than for her sister's life. The narrative effect of this problematical emphasis can be made clear by cross-reference to an episode in Mark Twain's *Huckleberry Finn* when Huck accepts the certainty of eternal damnation in hell rather than turn over his new friend, the runaway slave Jim, to the civil authorities.

Scott's abortive gesture towards deeper artistic seriousness becomes clearer in light of Jeanie's *crisis*-consciousness as elaborated in the second half of *The Heart of Midlothian*, where he significantly advances the historical evolution of this narrative device. If Jeanie Deans remains her unswerving self from start to finish, not subject even in the midst of life to the ordeal of any disorienting turn, what rhetorical effects result from the six *crisis*-images that strongly mark the second half of the novel? An answer to this query demonstrates that in some respects Scott advances *crisis*-rhetoric far beyond Richardson and Mackenzie.

In the first half, numerous exigencies and entanglements might plausibly be designated as crises but are not. Circumstances of grave danger or trouble appear in chapter after chapter: Effie Deans's imprisonment in the gloomy Tolbooth prison, Captain John Porteous's death sentence for firing into a riot mob, a subsequent riot in which Porteous himself is lynched, and Reuben Butler's horrified witnessing of the lynching. Scott initiates his *crisis*-trope only at the end of chapter 19, depicting Jeanie's visit to her imprisoned sister, where his vivid language induces Gothic emotions of terror and horror. He emphasizes the link between crisis-consciousness and the human propensity to error. I have already cited the *Oxford English Dictionary* as providing a quotation from the *Junius Letters* (1769) that conveys a decidedly emotional twist: "To escape from a crisis so full of terror and despair." Scott exploits this emerging Longinian impulse.

> On the evening which preceded the eventful day of trial, Jeanie was permitted to see her sister—*an awful interview, and occurring at a most distressing crisis*. This, however, formed a part of the bitter cup which she was doomed to drink, to atone for crimes and follies to which she had no accession; and at twelve o'clock noon, being the time appointed for admission to the jail, she went to meet, for the first time for several months, her guilty, erring, and most miserable sister, in that *abode of guilt, error, and utter misery*. (p. 215; emphases added)

The great noun activates a series of atmospheric words (*eventful, awful, distressing, bitter, doomed, crimes, follies, guilt, error, misery*) that very nearly approximate a parody of Longinian or Gothic atmospherics. Scott may be the first novelist to recognize how the curious word itself can be exploited for its horrific potential, yet his purpose goes beyond overwrought atmospherics. He knew that *crisis*-consciousness can be a part of the sensibility even of a character who never explicitly uses the word itself.

A considerable part of *The Heart of Midlothian* consists of passages of thick Scots dialect, and Scott could have used Scots dialectal forms such as *crise* (medical) and *cris* (point in time), but in fact he uses the great noun only in passages where he composes his narrative in standard English. The modest Jeanie Deans herself would never use the self-dramatizing figure, but in chapter 25, when she debates inwardly how she might finance her intended expedition to London, Scott makes crisis-consciousness part of her imaginative equipment. As if to emphasize the etymological base, Scott establishes that "in this crisis" she quite self-consciously considers herself to be more of a "good judge" than her own esteemed father. Like Richardson's Lovelace, she determines that she alone will decide when the judgment comes.

> Without departing from filial reverence, Jeanie had an inward conviction that the feelings of her father, however just, and upright, and honourable, were too little in unison with the spirit of the time to admit of his being a *good judge of the measures to be adopted in this crisis*. Herself more flexible in manner, though no less upright in principle, she felt that to ask his consent to her pilgrimage would be to encounter the risk of drawing down his positive prohibition, and under that she believed her journey could not be blessed in its progress and event. (p. 269; emphasis added)

The pious Jeanie is at least somewhat in tune with "the spirit of the time." The judgment, whether sound or erroneous, comes when she decides to act. She keeps her father in the dark and borrows money from the Laird of Dumbiedikes. At this point in literary history, Scott may be unique in thus emphasizing the great noun's literal meaning at the same time centering an extended crisis-narrative so squarely and literally upon one character.

Having first linked *crisis* with Gothic terror and horror, Scott has now changed direction so as to make Jeanie's powers of judgment the motif of a crisis-episode. In chapter 30, Scott combines his two motifs (terror and judgment) when he depicts Jeanie's imprisonment by a band of robbers. Jeanie will eventually escape and continue her mission to London; Scott stipulates that "in this dreadful crisis" her presence of mind makes survival possible.

> The old woman held a candle in one hand, and a knife in the other. Levitt appeared behind her; whether with a view of preventing, or assisting her in any violence she might meditate, could not be well guessed. *Jeanie's presence of mind stood her friend in this dreadful crisis.* She had resolution enough to maintain the attitude and manner of one who sleeps profoundly, and to regulate even her breathing, notwithstanding the agitation of instant terror, so as to correspond with her attitude. (p. 319; emphasis added)

Scott here shifts toward increased complexity and violent perplexity. In that Jeanie at this juncture has been deflected from the high road to London, this episode demonstrates that truth resembles not so much a high road as a turning (*tropos*) away from a high road. A measurable difference between Jeanie and Mackenzie's feckless Harley is that the plucky Scots lass regains the high road and accomplishes her mission.

Scott's innovations include his structuring *crisis*-images into two subplots. In chapter 34, he provides an intertextual rationale for the wild behavior of George (Staunton) Robertson in the form of six lines of verse quoted from "our British Juvenal." Describing a wild young character presumedly similar to Robertson, the verses allude to a moral disease that has "to its crisis come."

> Headstrong, determined in his own career,
> He thought reproof unjust, and truth severe,
> *The soul's disease was to its crisis come,*
> He first abused and then abjured his home;
> And when he chose a vagabond to be,
> He made his shame his glory, "I'll be free!"
> (p. 375; emphasis added)

By means of this analogy between moral corruption and medical crisis, Scott hints that the headstrong young Robertson may be redeemable. Later, the wild boy in fact matures and redeems himself as Sir George Staunton, a proper husband to Effie Deans. A second subplot, in chapter 37, during Jeanie's climactic audience with Queen Caroline, shows Jeanie naïvely blundering so as nearly to turn a discomfited queen against her. Jeanie experiences an acute confusion. Happily, at this "awkward crisis" (p. 402), Lady Suffolk—who skillfully doubles as the king's mistress and the queen's confidante—smoothes the queen's ruffled feathers so that Jeanie's blunder does not disrupt the interview. Jeanie is afforded the opportunity to learn from this synecdochic doubling of persons and roles.

The passage of Juvenalian verse suggests that *crisis* may operate at the lowest level of moral degradation; Lady Suffolk's maneuvering suggests that *crisis* may denote sound moral judgment at the highest social level. These juxtaposed images rhetorically frame Jeanie's own emerging consciousness with values that implicitly judge Jeanie's own character. Having used *crisis* to signal such a framework, Scott makes it clear that Jeanie is neither high nor low but rather a middling, unambiguously practical heroine. His final chapter shows the violent death of Jeanie's brother-in-law at the hands of his unwitting son "The Whistler," plus Jeanie's own taking charge, explaining what needs explaining, concealing the dead man's private papers from prying eyes, and generally making herself serviceable. Scott drives home his characterization via one final *crisis*-image: "It was in such a crisis that Jeanie's active and undaunted habits of virtuous exertion were most conspicuous" (p. 550).

In general, Scott's *crisis*-trope wonderfully complicates a simple tale. Ostensibly, as Cusac mistakenly urges, he depicts Jeanie uncritically. Quite to the contrary, he depicts Jeanie carrying out a morally ambiguous action but one such as his exacerbated crisis-rhetoric might lead his reader to expect. She illegally releases her incarcerated nephew. Surprisingly, this presumed model of rectitude never reveals her own action and thus in effect compounds a serious crime. Scott never pushes Jeanie past the synecdochic multiplicity of common duties to the final tropological stage of self-reflexive irony. His rhetoric in this novel betrays him into a serious question of moral judgment, yet despite achieving some compelling emphases, his *crisis*-trope remains largely in the service of a one-dimensional characterization yoked with certain shocking emotional effects. But shocking emotional effects henceforth become part of the history of the trope, and *crisis*-consciousness as a major type of consciousness will come to be understood as concern, existential tension, dynamism, and passion.[22]

By the end of the eighteenth century, certain features of a revolutionary new consciousness were emerging. By this time, the potentially great noun *crisis* had established itself as a crucial element of the new consciousness. With ontological and epistemological roots firmly grounded in traditional ideas concerning the individual, society, and moral responsibility, during this period *crisis* added a revolutionary coloring to its range of implications. A *crisis*-rhetoric develops as one means of coping with numerous crises in many departments of human life. As we see in Richardson, Mackenzie, and Scott, the keyword in one of its effects serves as a *crisis*-trope, in the process becoming part of the history of the novel. In general, to be alert to reality now comes to mean being conscious not only of crisis as a principle of existence but also the centrality of the *crisis*-trope itself. Reflexive irony, as Kellner thinks, may prove to be the master trope of any tropological sequence of tropes. I would add that in discourses where it appears, the *crisis*-trope will undergird and permeate all such sequences.[23]

2

Ideology and Crisis-Consciousness:
Jane Austen, Emily Brontë, and George Eliot

Tracing the diachronic development of a figure of speech through several centuries offers abundant pleasure as the journey twists through major literary works. Steadily throughout the nineteenth century, the great noun *crisis* and its attendant form of consciousness became both an individual and a corporate means for dealing with reality. It became increasingly a method for making statements, authorizing opinions, describing and characterizing social changes, and engaging in political and ideological struggles. To ignore *crisis* would be to ignore reality and the means of having control over reality. The century was vexed, enlivened, and radically altered by numerous ideologies, visionary theories, and systematic programs urging conflicting assumptions and goals. Ideologies that provided context and motivation for new forms of consciousness included (to name but a few) romanticism, utilitarianism, positivism, and liberalism. They triggered or enabled *crisis*-structured experiences both actual and fictive. Ideologies always demand an assertive Nay or Yea, and ideologies themselves also undergo crisis.[1] Nineteenth-century authors responded to emergent ideologies in crisis by depicting individuals whose existences are shaped or who self-consciously shape their own existences via a *crisis*-trope.

Three major Victorian sages—Thomas Carlyle, John Stuart Mill, and John Henry Newman—composed famous accounts of their own ordeals precipitated by a powerful utilitarianism or liberalism. They contribute to the context for the history of crisis-consciousness in the novel. A plausible approach to these three writers is afforded by a *crisis*-utterance from another sage, Matthew Arnold. In the same year as Eliot's *Felix Holt, the Radical*, Arnold wittily enunciated his major theme: the cultural centrality of sound critical thinking. For Arnold, to possess crisis-consciousness amounts to standing "at the centre" of things.

I have got into much trouble for calling my countrymen Philistines, and all through these remarks I am determined never to use that word; but I wonder if there can be anything offensive in calling one's countryman a young man from the country. I hope not; and if not, I should say, for the benefit of those who have seen Mr. John Parry's amusing entertainment, that England and Englishmen, holding forth on *some great crisis in a foreign country,*—Poland, say, or Italy,—are apt to have on foreigners very much the effect of the young man from the country, who talks to the nursemaid after she has upset the perambulator. There is *a terrible crisis,* and the discourse of the young man from the country, excellent in itself, is *felt not to touch the crisis vitally.* Nevertheless, on he goes; the perambulator lies a wreck, the child screams, the nursemaid wrings her hands, the old gentleman storms, the policeman gesticulates, the crowd thickens; still, that astonishing young man talks on, serenely unconscious that *he is not at the centre* of the situation.[2] (emphases added)

Crisis-imagination has become essential to a truly civilized life. Twentieth-century novelists such as Forster and Robert Coover will self-consciously echo Arnold's linking of *crisis*-experience to some metaphorical center of reality, nationalistic or metaphysical. In the nineteenth century, Arnold's type of crisis-consciousness reflected a general preoccupation that would animate many forms of discourse.[3]

In his wildly energetic spiritual autobiography, *Sartor Resartus: The Life and Opinions of Herr Teufelsdröckh,*[4] Carlyle employs *crisis* one single time to signal his hero's anguished tropological turn from negativism (pessimism) to positivism (optimism). *Sartor Resartus* urges several kinds of doctrines—metaphysical, ethical, social—intended to redress an insincerely costumed England. It depicts Germanic philosophical idealism in conflict with a shadowy but forceful Calvinism, a turn against turn which produces in Carlyle a painful impasse. Carlyle's own personal turmoil, by which he earned the right to speak as a sage, finds expression in three central chapters. In a prolonged moment of truth—"The Everlasting No," "The Centre of Indifference," "The Everlasting Yea"—Carlyle develops the equivalence of a plotted crisis and climax. In "The Everlasting Nay," Teufelsdröckh reasons that a vast utilitarian machine grinds joy out of human life. The "nay" uttered here is two-pronged. He sadly acknowledges the widespread modern disbelief in life's supposed purpose, but he then defiantly says "nay" to this negative scheme of things. In "The Centre of Indifference," he wanders between two worlds, a mechanistic realism and a dynamic idealism. In "The Everlasting Yea," he resolutely makes a three-part judgment or choice: to renounce false hopes of happiness, accept human sorrow as a holy condition, and carry out a practical plan for his life. By surviving this chastening turn of events, Teufelsdröckh has earned the right to offer his nugget of truth to his bewildered fellow-men.

Carlyle's fictive editor presents an account of Teufelsdröckh's agonies as a fever-crisis.

> Under the strange nebulous envelopment, wherein our Professor has now shrouded himself, no doubt but his spiritual nature is nevertheless progressive, and growing: for how can the 'Son of Time,' in any case, stand still? We behold him, through those dim years, *in a state of crisis, of transition*: his mad Pilgrimings, and general solution into aimless Discontinuity, what is all this but a mad Fermentation; wherefrom, the fiercer it is, the clearer product will one day evolve itself? (emphasis added)

Carlyle enriches the tradition by offering his reader the chemical metaphor of *crisis* as a purifying process within human consciousness. Thus he depicts a tropological shift from metonymic mechanism to synecdochic vitalism. More precisely, Carlyle's economical crisis-trope informs the first half of *Sartor Resartus* so as to depict a shift from metaphor, through metonymy and synecdoche (the sartorial anatomy of society), to irony; then, in the second half, a new metaphor (vitalism of work) appears as rationale and motive for new consciousness and new behavior.

J. S. Mill chose to express his own personal crisis and the new consciousness it afforded him not by means of symbolic narrative but by analytical exposition within an autobiography. As important as *Sartor Resartus*, Mill's *Autobiography*[5] was written over a long period of time, partly before 1861, partly after 1871. An economist, logician, and moral philosopher, he labored to defend *laissez-faire* capitalism even while being acutely aware of its potential abuses. He supported liberal political and social innovations. The *Autobiography* consists of seven chapters, the titles of which clearly display Mill's use of the great noun to structure his anguished, inspiring story.

(emphasis added)

Mill's famous fifth chapter depicts experiences important to his own personal development and to the intellectual history of England. It illustrates Brown's dialectical premise (adapted from T. S. Kuhn) that crisis enables progress. A summary of chapter 5 reveals how Mill, in 1826-27, experienced the personal agony that led him to swing away from subjection to his father's strict Benthamite dogma and regimen.

Mill began his adult life intending to become a "reformer of the world," but at age twenty he fell into an inexplicable depression. His account of this anguish somewhat resembles Carlyle's experience of a rejection by the universe, as it were the negative side of Carlyle's Everlasting No. Like George Eliot, Mill establishes a strong link between *crisis* and *consciousness*.

> In this frame of mind it occurred to me to put the question directly to myself: "Suppose that all your objects in life were realized; that all the changes in institutions and opinions which you are looking forward to, could be completely effected at this very instant: would this be a great joy and happiness to you?" And *an irrepressible self-consciousness distinctly answered, "No!"* At this my heart sank within me: the whole foundation on which my life was constructed fell down. All my happiness was to have been found in the continual pursuit of this end. The end had ceased to charm, and how could there ever again be any interest in the means? I seemed to have nothing left to live for. (p. 139; emphasis added)

Mill judged that the habit of logical analysis had worn away his emotional life, so he decided upon suicide if his problem were not solved within one year. Happily, he found a way out of his despair, beginning with the moment when he was "moved to tears" by reading Marmontel's *Memoires*. He began to make the stressful transition from one system to another. Much like Carlyle, he experiences up to the moment of his crisis a shift from metaphor (filial piety) through metonymy and synecdoche (utilitarian principles and classifications) to irony (self-loathing); then, happily, he reconstitutes a new metaphoric basis for life (affectivity). As candidly as possible, Mill describes his own personal crisis as a turning point in terms of happiness properly valued as a desirable end rather than a means to social improvement. He announces: "This theory now became the basis of my philosophy of life." Premises underlying his tropological shift from an analytical to an affective schema represented for Mill himself crucial "turning points, marking a definite progress in my mode of thought."

Newman likewise structured his own spiritual autobiography—*Apologia Pro Vita Sua*[6]—by using Eliot's great noun one single time. Both

Carlyle's crisis-transition from self-conscious individualism to a self-forgetful work ethic and Mill's crisis-transition from his father's closed system to a more open philosophy are matched in narrative excitement and cultural significance by what Newman—perhaps thinking of Thomas Paine—called his "great revolution." While pursuing absolute truth as well as defying a dominant liberalism, Newman changed his allegiance from Protestantism (metaphor) to Roman Catholicism (synecdoche). Given the suave clarity and clear logic of Newman's thought-style, his argument can be easily summarized. Newman, of course, had spearheaded the Tractarian or Oxford Movement, which sought to restore the Anglican Church to its former legitimacy and glory. Chapter 1 recounts how he modified his narrow Protestant dislike of the Roman Catholic Church. Chapter 2 narrates his participation in the Oxford Movement and its aspirations to return England from pathlessness to the right path. Gradually, he realized that he could in fact accede to some few Roman Catholic dogmas. In 1841, Newman published Tract XC, where he in effect asked himself: "Can I be saved in the English Church?" Compelled to answer in the negative, he decided to enter the Roman Catholic Church and be ordained a priest. In Chapter 5, he argues that for an individual to be tested in a conflict between authority and private judgment can be beneficial to that person's moral fiber. Newman's "great revolution of mind" is free of Carlyle's and Mill's romantic egotism. Whereas their books are explicitly structured by a single *crisis*-trope precisely enabling a moment of change in a main plot, Newman himself in fact uses the great noun one single time but judiciously places it so as to achieve an entirely different, non-egotistical emphasis. The general effect is to convey a quality of modesty unlike the egotism of Carlyle and Mill and much more consistent with the sweet temper normally associated with Newman.

The effect of the *Apologia* was not like a recollection of some long-past event but rather "like a conversational explosion" on the subject of a recent event (London *Times*, 16 June, 1864, p. 12). His single explicit designation of an event as a concussive crisis occurs not at the turning point of his own personal adventure but at the beginning of a collective adventure, the Oxford Movement itself. In Chapter 2, in a context of pious admiration for the men who influenced him in his spiritual development, Newman describes how the Anglo-Catholic party had suddenly become a power in the national church. He designates the early stages of the Oxford Movement as "the birth of a crisis."

Its originators would have found it difficult to say what they aimed at of a practical kind: rather, they put forth views and principles for their own sake, because they were true, as if they were obliged to say them; and, as they might be themselves surprised at their earnestness in uttering them, they had as great cause to be surprised at the success which attended their propagation. And, in fact, they could only say that those doctrines were in the air; that to assert was to prove, and that to explain was to persuade; and that the Movement in which they were taking part was the *birth of a crisis* rather than of a place. (pp. 69-70; emphasis added)

As a crisis-conscious apologist, Newman subordinates himself to the activities of the group. Ironically, of course, the *Apologia* may in fact depict a personal transformation not only as compelling as that in Carlyle and Mill but equally egotistical. Newman could actually intend thus to decenter both Aristotelian logical structure and the members of the Oxford Movement away from any privileged place in his narrative. More likely, though, he expresses an authentic humility.

Carlyle, Mill, and Newman—three sages thrown into crisis by the nay-saying power of dominant ideologies—after uttering an anguished Nay conclude by uttering their hard-earned Yea. These three spiritual autobiographies of Victorian Sages bear directly upon my study of narrative *crisis*-tropes. Although themselves not novels, these self-scrutinizing forms of consciousness nevertheless flesh out my history of *crisis* by contextualizing the novelists who structure their representations via the great trope.

My next three examples (Austen, Brontë, Eliot) are women writers, and inevitably this fact raises the question whether *crisis*-consciousness ought to come under the strictures of feminist criticism. On the whole, my examples are not women novelists but men, a selection that could imply that crisis-consciousness manifests only a patriarchal development of male consciousness. For my own part, on this score I have been unable to discover any deep or radical differences (other than genuinely aesthetic principles) between novels by women and men.

1. "a crisis, an event, a something to alter her"

One unfolding discovery in the history of *crisis*-utterances is that, generally speaking, crisis-consciousness signifies maturity in individuals and communities. Jane Austen provides a forceful example of this principle. We are told to look for the meaning of Austen's six novels by examining in each a keyword (*expectations, sensibility, amiability, liveliness, imagination, submission*). In *Pride and Prejudice*, the keyword is *liveliness*; in *Emma*, it is *imagination*.[7] Given Austen's avoidance of the more violent emotionalism or corrosive ironies that characterize much nineteenth-century fiction, we might not expect to find a stressful word like *crisis* serving the aims of such a modest, restrained author. Even so, the tonal differences between the light, bright *Pride and Prejudice* (1813) and the darker, more complex *Emma* (1816) arguably result from Austen's adoption in the latter book of a *crisis*-trope. *Pride and Prejudice* is strictly a comedy. As David Cecil says: "nothing even potentially tragic occurs in it."[8] And, in fact, *crisis* never once appears. However, in constructing *Emma* with a more somber intention ("I am going to take a heroine whom no one but myself will much like"), the maturing Austen signifies four separate parts of her story with the implicative noun that Richardson established as a richly manipulative device. Austen creates a sharpened focus on three characters (Emma Woodhouse, Mrs. Weston, Frank Churchill) by assigning to each a *crisis*-consciousness as a life-structuring, meaning-enabling principle.

In historical terms, Austen depicts in *Emma* a critical interpretation of the conflict between common sense and esemplastic imagination. Austen marks the distance between Emma's manipulative "errors of imagination" and eventual discovery of her own fallibility by two *crisis*-signals. Early on, Emma willfully misinterprets a conundrum composed by Mr. Elton to mean that Elton wishes to court Emma's protégée, Harriet Smith. Emma, the actual object of Elton's misguided attentions, metonymically but inauthentically projects her own personal conflicts and sexual tensions off onto the hapless Harriet. Just as Eliot's Mr. Johnson would manipulate ignorant working men merely by uttering the electrifying noun *crisis*, Emma deliberately distorts Elton's verse-conundrum so as to manipulate Harriet with a *crisis*-centered, plotlike explanation. She declares to Harriet: "Things must come to a crisis soon."[9] She thus easily convinces the credulous Harriet that the conundrum was "written for you and to you." Austen here displays Emma's self-delusion at its most blatant.

The larger plot movement depicts Emma's gradually amending her errors of romantic imagination by becoming aware that she must cease exploiting other people and instead pursue her own happiness with George Knightley. Austen calls attention to this maturing process by subsequently showing Emma becoming less manipulative albeit still somewhat a self-delusive schemer. Emma's moral and imaginative growth occurs between her decision "not to utter a word that should hurt Jane Fairfax's feelings" (p. 203) and her decision to bend her own efforts to "thoroughly understand her own heart" (p. 283). Austen signifies this change by stipulating that Emma views her ambivalent relation with Frank Churchill as requiring Emma's own stipulation of a *crisis* for its resolution. As with

Eliot and a few other novelists, Austen makes an effort to provide a contextualized definition of *crisis*.

> She wished she might be able to keep him from an absolute declaration. That would be so very painful a conclusion of their present acquaintance!—and yet, she could not help rather anticipating something decisive. She felt as if the *spring would not pass without bringing a crisis, an event, a something to alter her* present composed and tranquil state. (p. 214; emphasis added)

Though not yet fully mature, Emma still has modified her sense of *crisis* from its being exclusively a controlled, manipulative device for directing other people's lives to its being a less controllable eventuality that she must at least in part tolerate rather than dominate. In finally distinguishing other people's concerns from her own personal concerns, she moves from naïve metaphor to more sophisticated metonymy. Emma discovers in herself something resembling negative capability. Austen thereby characterizes her problematical young heroine in terms of a maturing sense of *crisis* as an existential principle of self-discovery and self-acceptance.

Austen uses two other episodes centering upon secondary characters in order to enlarge, intensify, and clarify her crisis-theme. In the case of Frank Churchill, the unsavory "secrecy and concealment" of his engagement to Jane Fairfax becomes forgivable only after he writes a long explanatory letter to Mrs. Weston. In composing this letter (which Mrs. Weston wisely will allow Emma to read) the mortified young man explicates his puzzling behavior by noting that eventually "every little dissatisfaction that had occurred" in his secret relation with Jane Fairfax finally "came to a crisis" (p. 303). Austen thus shows how Frank's reconciliation with Jane parallels, and perhaps results from, his ability to construct a coherent life-script and a rational life based in part on a conscious grasp of the part *crisis* may play in cutting and shaping one's own raw experience.

Austen perfectly grasped the dialectical principle whereby crisis-consciousness can lead to mature freedom but in the process may risk miscomprehension and interpersonal conflict. Prior to the episode in which Churchill's letter mollifies Emma's outrage over his dissimulation, Austen shows Emma being urged to patience by the wise Mrs. Weston. Like Churchill and Emma herself, but with more mature poise, Mrs. Weston explains the predicament of Frank and Jane as being a crisis of incomprehension requiring tolerance and forbearance on all sides.

"There were misunderstandings between them, Emma; he said so expressly. . . . *The present crisis*, indeed, seemed to be brought on by them; and those misunderstandings might very possibly arise from the impropriety of his conduct." (p. 273; emphasis added)

Austen arranges her narrative so that the benighted Emma, hearing Churchill's perplexities interpreted as a crisis, is enabled to grow up. In order to establish Emma's new metonymic objectivity, Austen's narrator notes: "Emma began to listen better." Austen's dialectical theme declares, in effect, that the unruly imagination, presumably a *sine qua non* for humane existence, must none the less be firmly ruled.

An author can not choose whether to use informing figures of speech but only which kinds of figures to use.[10] A writer can thus load the dice by means of rhetoric. The novelist chooses moments to dramatize fully and moments to glide over. In its turn, critical interpretation should be *"based only on those elements that we are obliged to perceive."*[11] It seems abundantly clear that in Austen's ordering and emphasizing intensities in *Emma* so as to advance beyond *Pride and Prejudice*, she decided to secure certain heightening effects by the strategic use of a three-part *crisis*-trope. Like Richardson or Scott, she obliges her reader to become crisis-conscious. Austen's own crisis-consciousness almost assuredly contributes to those features of her work that display what Lionel Trilling called her "new consciousness" of the possibilities of personal growth through the admittedly risky process of imaginative role-playing.[12]

2. "at that crisis, a sudden inspiration descended on me"

Any serious novel represents or depicts a crisis, but only by the insinuation of the word itself does the crisis-trope come into being. One historical peculiarity of the rhetoric of crisis-consciousness has been two widely differing conceptual implications. *Crisis* may suggest dire circumstances, stressful situations, emergencies, and even exacerbated emotions; by contrast, it may also suggest its own root-meanings of cool judgment and thoughtful decisions. In the most complex discourses, of course, it simultaneously designates judgments made in and of emergent entanglements. Eliot's compelling utterance "crises of emotion" (*Middlemarch*) expresses an idea at once literally redundant and literally accurate. Any *crisis*-trope may derive some of its aesthetic effectiveness from Longinian emotionalism as well as Aristotelian form-building implications; the trope can trigger emotional responses or signal a structural turning point. *The Heart of Midlothian* and *The Man of Feeling* effectively illustrate the two methods. However, a writer may choose not to depend upon *crisis* in triggering stress and disorientation within a character or in triggering emotional responses in a reader. As an example, Graham Greene's *The Heart of the Matter* (1948) could accurately be described either as one endless crisis (stressful impasse) or as one acute crisis (severe judgment), but Greene entirely eschews the great noun itself.[13]

Comparable to *The Heart of the Matter* in rendering a prolonged emotional turmoil concluding in general desolation would be Emily Brontë's *Wuthering Heights* (1847). This narrative of the emotional agonies attendant upon an overmastering passion incorporates *crisis*, but, as in *Tristram Shandy*, decenters it away from any major structuring role. By means of this decentering intertextual trope, *Wuthering Heights* perversely affirms the romantic value of imaginative disorder and thus as it were refutes Austen's attempt in *Emma* to chasten or subdue the romantic imagination.

Wuthering Heights[14] represents a strangely impersonal symbolic embodiment of elemental forces depicting extreme emotions associated with frustration, hatred, and revenge. Brontë's characters live in isolation from ordinary moral values. In this extraordinary perspectival experiment, fragmentary impressions of unconventional occurrences filtered through the consciousness of two very conventional narrators (Lockwood and Nelly Dean) engage in a disturbing dialectic between Gothic violence and fatalistic impassiveness. Brontë heightens her effects by omitting any explicit authorial moral judgments whatsoever. To achieve stability, a reader must become metonymically and synecdochically more objective than either of Brontë's major narrators.

The example of Scott would warrant an abundant use of *crisis* to induce and intensify Gothic excesses. Heathcliff's abrupt and disruptive introduction into the Earnshaw household, the youthful adventures of Heathcliff and Catherine, the death of Hindley Earnshaw's wife, Hindley's tormenting of Heathcliff, Heathcliff's overhearing Catherine determine to marry Edgar Linton, Catherine's brain-fever, Heathcliff's return as a prosperous man, Isabel Linton's elopement with Heathcliff, Catherine's death in giving birth to young Cathy, Isabel's flight from Heathcliff, Linton Heathcliff's birth in London, Heathcliff's manipulation of the estates of Wuthering Heights and Thrushcross Grange, the death of the besotted Hindley, the deaths of Edgar and young Cathy's husband Linton—these sensational episodes might have occasioned a *crisis*-rhetoric even more exacerbated than Scott's. Nevertheless, *Wuthering Heights* incorporates *crisis* mainly in an early episode involving the unreliable narrator Lockwood. Brontë intends via one of Lockwood's dreams in chapter 3 to satirize not only Lockwood's own conventional imagination, together with rigidly conventional Christian dogmatism, but also any authorial reliance upon conventional devices such as Aristotelian crisis. She concentrates her spare, dismissive crisis-rhetoric in a single episode in chapter 3 depicting Lockwood's two dreams during a night spent at Wuthering Heights. His second dream prepares the ground for a major plot when he dreams of grasping the "little, ice-cold hand" of the deceased Catherine (Earnshaw) Linton through a broken window pane in the room where she had slept when alive. In this dream, which triggers Heathcliff's own first utterance of his obsession with Catherine's memory, Lockwood emphasizes the Gothic emotions of terror and the "intense horror of nightmare." Reference to *crisis* thus might not be unexpected, but in fact Lockwood foregoes the word in this second dream. Only in reconstructing his first dream, along the lines of a conventional short story, does Lockwood use the great noun to signal a dialectical moment of decision in itself all too obvious.

Lockwood's first dream enacts a sermon on the theological topic "Seventy Times, and the First of the Seventy-First" by the Reverend Jabes Branderham. Jabes develops *topoi* and motifs by no means irrelevant to Brontë's overall satirical intentions: "heavy-headed" moral instruction, orthodox worship as public humiliation, theology as catalogue, intrapersonal and internal conflict, and ritualized violence. The dream itself gathers around a clear, simple plot. Guided by Heathcliff's servant Joseph, Lockwood trudges through the snow to attend chapel together with Jabes Branderham's congregation. Each of the 490 parts of his sermon addresses a separate sin, as Jabes denounces sins unfamiliar to the naïve dreamer Lockwood, sins "of the most curious character—odd transgressions that I had never imagined." Wearied by Jabes's shrill catalogue, and unable to cope with such synecdochic multiplicity, Lockwood yet attempts to wait out the preacher and thus fulfill his church-going duty. When Jabes commences a new list of sins, Lockwood can endure no more. He impulsively turns the tables on Jabes by denouncing Jabes himself as being guilty of the unpardonable sin, presumably the sin of being unforgiving toward other Christians (or simply the sin of bad preaching?). Lockwood structures his dream by means of a plot with an obvious crisis or dialectical turning point.

> I was condemned to hear all out; finally, he reached the "*First of the Seventy-First.*" At that crisis, a sudden inspiration descended on me; I was

moved to rise and denounce Jabes Branderham as the sinner of the sin that no Christian need pardon. (p. 29)

As a result of Lockwood's denunciation of Jabes, the congregation takes up staves and begins a general riot, so that "the whole chapel resounded with rappings and counter-rappings," while Jabes went on pouring forth his self-righteous zeal from the pulpit. At this point in the dream, Lockwood awakens.

Hayden White discusses Freud's tropological account of dream-work in four stages: condensation, displacement, representation, and secondary revision.[15] *Wuthering Heights* on the whole yields to such a tropological analysis, but Lockwood can only dream and analyze dreams in simplistic Aristotelian plot terms. Both as the dreamer and as the dreamed, Lockwood remains mired in incomprehension because of his compulsive need to identify his own self metaphorically (in tropological terms, literally) with the external world. His violent revolt against Jabes's theological tyranny provokes a disorderly turn against turn ("rappings and counterrappings"). By means of this dream episode, Brontë decenters *crisis* away from any presumed turning point or center of Lockwood's framing narrative. Lockwood ends up carrying the same burden of ontological insecurity that he initially brought to Wuthering Heights, and his prolonged disorientation induces much of the interest of this strange narrative. Brontë's crisis-trope effectively undermines the very idea of plot structure by decentering *crisis* away from the heart of the narrative to a remote periphery. In itself a powerfully Freudian episode, Lockwood's dream in which "every man's hand was against his neighbor" serves Brontë's aim of depicting Lockwood early on as a man of limited imagination and conventional wit who will not be able to fathom the problematically dreamlike depths of the love affair between Heathcliff and Catherine, which he learns about from an equally conventional personality, Nelly Dean.

3. "great crises of emotion [reveal] the bias of a nature"

Historically, certain novelists occupy special places in the history of crisis-consciousness. Richardson is the progenitor of the novel and of novelists who depend upon a *crisis*-trope. Much later, Saul Bellow will provide the enlightening spectacle of an entire oeuvre incorporating a crisis-rhetoric that enables an important cultural analysis and a major theme. Between Richardson and Bellow, others occupy special places. Mackenzie first signals the main turning point of an Aristotelian plot by placing *crisis* at a single key moment in a narrative. Sterne first takes pains to satirize the very Aristotelian logic of any structuring crisis-rhetoric. Scott first used the great noun to create Gothic and Longinian emotional effects together with serious characterization. Austen prepares the ground for Meredith, James, and other art-novelists by employing *crisis* in a subtly expressive pattern of thematic development. George Moore first explicitly links crisis-consciousness with the very act of writing a novel. Other special niches belong to James, Lawrence, and Durrell, to name only three. Even so, despite these signal achievements, pride of place belongs to George Eliot for having called attention to *crisis* as a "great noun" worthy of special study, thereby providing a kind of charter for my argument.[16]

As distinct from a Paine or Scott who merely use *crisis*, Eliot may have been the first literary intellectual explicitly to signal that the word was becoming a keyword in the modern world. Even in her own personal life, the word carried a special meaning. David Williams recounts how the aging Eliot, while going through the private papers of the recently deceased George Henry Lewes, was moved by some unspecified emotion to enfigure into her diary a single word: *Crisis*. Although John Bayley believes that Eliot responded cryptically thus to her discovery that Lewes had been sexually unfaithful, Williams thinks that the diary entry "Crisis" in this context is more likely "a private signal to herself that some time—not now but in a little while—she would have to get finally and properly married."[17] In either case, the self-dramatizing presence of *crisis* in such an anguished dialectical moment calling for a firm decision assuredly points to a special significance for Eliot herself of this variously concussive, constructive, analytical, electrifying, and manipulative noun. As a preeminent artist, she would not use it casually.

Around 1850, serious novelists began to witness to a new kind of consciousness, a crisis-mentality centering on radical issues and decisions that would thenceforth shape English culture. In contexts of historical imbroglios and exigencies precipitated by the Industrial Revolution, democratic reforms, and widespread population shifts from country to city, serious novelists observed how human life was being transformed. This new consciousness necessitated their discovering or inventing new feelings and human relationships. Urbanization was producing a community of disoriented individuals lacking social identity. The transitional predicament called for new rhetorical strategies to engage with the emerging modern dilemma of dialectical interaction between a fluid community and anomic individuals. Disorientation meant that the lonely individual with a divided consciousness of simultaneously belonging and not belonging felt compelled to invent his own moral existence.[18]

Felix Holt, the Radical occupies a special position in the formation of the new crisis-consciousness. Raymond Williams notes:

> But the emphasis of want is now specialised to Felix Holt: to the exposed, separated, potentially mobile individual. It is part of a crucial history in the development of the novel, in which the knowable community—the extended and emphatic world of an actual rural and then industrial England—comes to be known primarily as a problem of relationship: of how the *separated individual, with a divided consciousness of belonging and not belonging* makes his own moral history.[19] (emphasis added)

One element in this anomic self-consciousness took the literal form of a structuring *crisis*-consciousness, by means of which a disoriented individual literally shapes his own cultural and moral history and a novelist orders the intensities of his representations.[20]

Life itself begins to equate with crisis, and Eliot witnesses to such a peculiar cultural phenomenon mainly by extending crisis-consciousness synecdochically into more realms of social experience than anything attempted by Richardson or other precursors. Three crisis-narratives by Eliot constitute major texts of reference for my study of this turbulent historical shift. Subsequent to *Felix Holt*, Eliot's crisis-rhetoric will gather to a greatness in *Middlemarch* and *Daniel Deronda*. In these ambitious books, Eliot exploits "uncomprehended" effects of crisis while also exploring or exploiting its root meaning of critical judgment. Without sacrificing Richardson's emphasis on conflicted crisis-management or Scott's emphasis on exacerbated emotions, she extends Austen's existential subject of ethical decisions colored by a heightened crisis-consciousness. In *Middlemarch* and *Daniel Deronda*, the great noun will prove to be a dark but fruitful source of art, and interpretation will be more than ever obliged to take it into account.[21]

Eliot clearly uses *crisis* in her exploration of the mysteries of moral possibility. She manipulates her discourse so that the trope becomes internalized into some select few of her characters as an element of their own consciousness. Thereby privileged characters then as it were shape their own lives by analogy with the composition of narrative fiction.

I have already noted in my introduction that Eliot uses *Felix Holt* to hypothesize a close connection between the novel, modern consciousness, crisis-consciousness, and the *crisis*-trope. As a major text of reference in the present critical history, *Felix Holt* merits closer attention. It shows a major writer coping with unwieldy materials via a narrative strategy that she will master only in later books, a strategy she will then bequeath to other masters such as Meredith and James.[22]

I need at this point to reprise my introductory remarks on *Felix Holt*. Eliot implies that *crisis* is the trope of heightened consciousness, so that an emphasis on heightened consciousness nearly always necessitates the word itself. In more than thirty contexts, Eliot signifies *consciousness* as a sign of perception and understanding. In presenting major characters (Mrs. Transome, Esther Lyon, Rufus Lyon, Annette Ledru, John Johnson, Harold Transome, Matthew Jermyn) and certain minor characters, Eliot signifies consciousness as one of the salient features of moral character and social progress or purpose. *Consciousness* may only mean awareness or alertness, but it may mean much more. Chapter 1 represents Mrs. Transome's exile at Transome Court so that her "high-born imperious air" (p. 29) represents a backward-looking Tory consciousness "absorbed by memories" (p. 13) that will be swept away as her neighborhood is violently stirred into a new political consciousness. Subsequently, Eliot urges her belief that in 1832 England was gradually awakening to "higher pains of a dim political consciousness" (p. 50) and a "higher consciousness which is known to bring higher pains" (p. 470). Of considerable relevance, too, is the fact that seven major characters singled out by *crisis*-images are likewise signified via *consciousness*.

Eliot singles out Felix Holt by permitting him to offer a definition of *consciousness* remarkably similar to White's tropological definition. Aware of being situated in a historical moment fraught with stressful change, Felix asserts at one moment that "I have to determine [my destiny] for myself"; almost immediately, however, he contradicts himself by speaking of a "determining reason" in the sense of a compulsion or irresistible motive. He anticipates White's description of a mind-set: "It all depends on what a man gets into his consciousness—what life thrusts into his mind, so that it becomes present to him as remorse is present to the guilty, or a mechanical problem to an inventive genius" (pp. 266-67). Eliot thus invites us to see consciousness—the dialectical control of "what life thrusts into his mind"—as a reality-shaping mental predisposition, something like a trope.

Perhaps more so than any writer before James or Joyce, Eliot wrote narratives motivated by a concern with consciousness.[23] What Eliot demands of her readers is that we perceive how her books concern themselves with crisis-consciousness and, by extension, with modern consciousness itself. Her variegated trope in *Felix Holt* resembles only slightly the neat single-image crisis structures employed by Carlyle, Mill, and Newman. However, it does base itself solidly in an Arnoldian sense of the cultural centrality of the trope. Applying Hayden White's tropology to *Felix Holt*, I arrive at the following hypothesis. Eliot begins with a historical irony, first establishing in her "Introduction" a parable of English life before the age of reform; at this point, an imagined "happy outside passenger" on a coach enjoys a view of imagined peace and prosperity. Thus, ironic retrospect enables a metaphoric identification of self and other. Immediately, though, in keeping with the revolutionary thrust of the Great Reform Bill, she depicts the wretched Mrs. Transome and other isolated individuals as metonymic fragments of a splintering society. How does the next tropological phase (synecdoche) occur? I think that only the implied author's or narrator's organizing viewpoint manages to classify or arrange the splintered fragments into anything resembling an organic whole. According to my understanding of the book (as influenced by Kellner's tropological analyses), the final phase of irony is reached, if at all, only in the concluding sentence, indeed, the final word: *money*.[24]

The ideal reader of *Felix Holt* will resemble the studious Reverend Rufus Lyon, who approaches an apocalyptic text like the Book of Daniel (p. 394) in the spirit of an "impersonal study of narrative" (p. 368). Eliot enunciates a principle crucial to my general argument. The verse epigraph to chapter 36 asserts: "words embalm / The conscience of mankind." Given her virtual equating of *conscience* with *conscious*, I think that she also means that words embalm or preserve consciousness. Throughout the narrative, she insists via chains of signifiers that her story is a story of "new stages" and "new sympathies"; likewise, that life is an affair constituted by numerous dialectical turnings, which she repeatedly expresses in terms of body language (averted eyes, faces, bodies) and in larger social responses (physical changes of direction, turning of corners, and the like). Thus, I think, Eliot establishes a plausible context for the historical drama of crisis-consciousness centering on Felix Holt.

In *Felix Holt*, Eliot achieves a peculiar focus on her revolutionary subject of rural England at the time of the Great Reform Bill of 1832. She depicts a group of colliers at Chubb's public house in Sproxton being easily manipulated by the "grandeur, the knowledge, and the power" of Lawyer Johnson's twisting but concussive crisis-rhetoric. Given that Lawyer Johnson functions as Eliot's synecdochically linking device between several scattered characters and plot lines, and in that his speech provides a kind of charter for my study of *crisis* as a word of great potency, the scene bears repeating. Here, again, is the passage.

". . . We've got Reform, gentlemen, but now the thing is to make Reform work. *It's a crisis—I pledge you my word it's a crisis.*"

> Mr Johnson threw himself back as if from *the concussion of that great noun*. He did not suppose that one of his audience knew *what a crisis meant*; but he had large experience in the *effect of uncomprehended words*; and in this case the colliers were thrown into a state of conviction concerning they did not know what, which was a fine preparation for "hitting out," or any other act carrying a due sequence to such a conviction. (emphases added)

Lawyer Johnson uses *crisis* as an oratorical bomb. The "concussion of that great noun" carries the day, despite Felix Holt's abortive attempt to urge rational common sense and social justice upon Johnson's audience of excitable colliers. During the climactic election-day riot (chap. 33), Felix inadvertently kills a demonstrator. Eliot specifies that "Tucker was dead from spinal concussion" (p. 330). Thus, "that great noun" literally has a concussive effect on the people in and around Treby Magna.

In *Felix Holt*, we see a novelist systematically attempting to extend the range of the figure previously used by Richardson, Scott, and Austen. Like the *mise en abyme* it reflexively resembles, the crisis-trope distributes its effects variously, both in specific contexts and widely throughout a narrative.[25] Eliot's trope achieves greatness in part because of her Arnoldian insistence on its cultural centrality, as well as its empowerment alternately as a manipulative, a constructional, and an analytical tool. Her Mr. Johnson the *rhetor* represents the literary artist in his power to hold and move men's minds; this crudely manipulative image is balanced over against the independent Esther Lyon, whose "life was a book which she seemed herself to be constructing" (p. 389). The tavern scene is only one of nine turning points where Eliot explodes or otherwise insinuates her great noun. In this novel of fifty-one chapters plus an epilogue, *crisis* detonates in chapters 6, 9, 11 (Mr. Johnson's speech), 15, 28, 31, 36, 38, and 45. Excepting Johnson, no character uses the word itself in direct discourse, but Eliot suggests that other characters (e.g., Rufus Lyon, Matthew Jermyn, Harold Transome, Tommy Trounsem) variously confront the disorienting but potentially life-shaping power of *crisis*. By thus directing the reader's attention, she adroitly influences readerly response.

The general impression is of a scattering of effects, but the scatterings eventually center, however loosely, in Felix Holt's trope of consciousness. Eliot makes it clear that both writerly judgment and readerly judgment must come whenever a writer uses the emergent trope that radically means "judgment." Any human life consists of hundreds or thousands of moments, but which moment among thousands will an author, narrator, or fictive character designate as a crisis? When does the judgment come? A narratorial generalization in chapter 45 somewhat clarifies Eliot's intention. When Esther Lyon visits Felix Holt in jail, Eliot declares that every point may be a turning point: "Every minute that passes may be charged with some such crisis in the little inner world of man or woman" (p. 441).

Any writer must decide what parts to emphasize; in many parts of *Felix Holt* the crisis-trope is less a presence than an absence. Chapters 1-5; 16-27; 39-44; 46-51, plus Eliot's "Introduction" and "Epilogue"—these are unmarked by any *crisis*-signal. Yet chapters 1-5 establish vital matters: the setting, in 1832, in and near the cheerful village of Treby Magna; Harold Transome's return from the Orient to take up his presumedly rightful place at Transome Court; and, the budding if conflicted romance between Felix Holt and Esther Lyon. Chapters 16-27 also develop crucial scenes and subplots: electioneering, with its public and private excitements; the conflict between attorney Matthew Jermyn and his unacknowledged son Harold Transome; the elder Mrs. Transome's self-pitying misery at Transome Court; the market dinner at the Marquis Inn; the discovery by Jermyn of an heir to the Transome estate; the abortive debate between Evangelical Rufus Lyon and High Church representative Mr. Sherlock; the revelation to Esther Lyon that she is the unknown heir; and, Esther's hope that she and Felix might one day be married. Not even Felix Holt's decision to forsake his father's profitable patent-medicine trade so as to become a watchmaker and working-class teacher carries any *crisis*-designation.

Chapters 39-44 likewise synecdochically complicate the narrative: Esther's taking her rightful place at Transome Court; Harold Transome's decision to protect his interests by marrying Esther; Jermyn's agonized confrontation with Mrs. Transome; Mrs. Holt's "striking presentation" of herself at Transome Court on behalf of her incarcerated son; and, Esther's decision to visit Felix in jail. Chapters 46-51 also contribute: Felix Holt's conviction for manslaughter and sentence to four years' imprisonment; Jermyn's public revelation to Harold that he himself is Harold's biological father; Esther's renunciation of the Transome Court estate; Felix's pardon from his prison sentence; and, in the "Epilogue," the wedding of Felix and Esther. Much of the story, then, remains relatively uncut by *crisis*-signifiers.

MacKenzie's *Man of Feeling* had exhibited with strict economy how the linkage between modern consciousness and *crisis*-consciousness may center (however problematically) in the consciousness of one individual. Nothing quite so neat as Lovelace's or Harley's experiences informs *Felix Holt*. Eliot is attempting to represent a much larger, more varied scene, and hence she scatters her crisis-signals so that they suggest how disorientation, marked variously by the presence or absence of crisis-consciousness, characterizes a new set of social conditions. In Eliot, we see how crisis-consciousness places a constructional burden upon an ambitious, responsible novelist. In addition to the two crisis-utterances already cited, Eliot obliges her reader to attend to seven other *crisis*-images. Some characters initially seem merely to undergo the distress of crisis, whereas others variously resemble Esther Lyon (and Eliot herself) in devising life-scripts enabled by *crisis*-consciousness. Given Eliot's assumption of the role of sober instructor to her readers, a crisis-image signals the risk, even the likelihood, of some serious error in a character's judgment.

I need at this point to list the other *crisis*-passages in *Felix Holt*. Taken one at a time, they prove interesting enough, but unlike those in precursors such as *Clarissa* or *Emma*, they do not add up to a single structural effect. In being effectively scattered, they suggest more than anything the social disorder Eliot feels compelled honestly to represent.

(1) Taking a hint from popular journalism, Eliot generalizes the presumed link between *crisis* and manipulative language. Her epigraph for chapter 31, drawn from North's *Examen*, analyzes linguistic strategies used by fiercely partisan electioneers during the actual historical event. Whig and Tory use "factious language" in "the working of this crisis."

(2) *Crisis* can signal a swing back from many kinds of subjection. To a degree, *Felix Holt* explores the complexities of personal freedom as constrained by some form of determinism. Eliot's research during the 1860s for this political novel set in the 1830s would have turned up a radical journal, *The Crisis*. Edited by Robert Owen, this periodical flourished for several years after 1832, eventually merging with the *National Co-operative Traders' Union Gazette*. Owen's revolutionary motto: "The character of every human being is formed for, and not by, the individual." Owen's radical journal would have illustrated how *crisis* was becoming a concussive element in revolutionary rhetoric.[26] Eliot, although sharing Owen's positivistic optimism, would dialectically counter that the individual does to some degree form his own character. In partial agreement with Owen, she asserts a general principle to be tested by her characters: "there is no private life which has not been determined by a wider public life" (p. 51). As if acceding to a grim determinism, the self-pitying Mrs. Transome weakly concedes the necessity to "put up with all things as they are determined for me." By contrast, her son Harold perceives not only the dangers but also the opportunities provided by crisis, so he energetically seeks to impose his will upon the disorderly raw materials of life.

(3) The historical motif of determinism is amplified by Eliot's establishing two sorts of people: those who manipulate crisis (in deed and word) and those who only suffer crisis. In sharp contrast with the autodidact Felix Holt, the illiterate Tommy Trounsem illustrates the disadvantage of being unable to use grand language. Tommy is easily manipulated by Johnson and tricked by Philip de Barry's servant Christian into posting up the wrong advertising bills. He is also tricked into telling Christian the story of a further deception—by Mr. Johnson himself—which ensures that Tommy himself would never claim his share of the Transome estate. Tommy has only enough storytelling skills to know how to pause for a crude narrative effect. Lacking Mr. Johnson's vocabulary, he can only pause at the "crisis" in his story as his naïve enthusiasm shines only too patently in his face. Crisis-consciousness in this case resides not so much with the character but mainly within the governing consciousness of an implied author.

> *At this crisis in Tommy's story* the grey clouds, which had been gradually thinning, opened sufficiently to let down the sudden moonlight, and show his poor battered old figure and face in that attitude and with the expression of a narrator sure of the coming effect on his auditor. (p. 283; emphasis added)

I can not help thinking that here Eliot depicts all those millions of modern people who have been battered by manipulative crisis-exploiters. Tommy is the would-be manipulator being manipulated into deceiving himself. He has suffered the concussive effects of numerous crises but may never even have heard the Mr. Johnsons of this world twist the great trope. Eliot thus uses Tommy to reiterate a sobering crisis-logic. When the election-day riot ends, Tommy is dead, having been "trampled upon, doubtless, where he fell drunkenly, near the entrance of the Seven Stars" (p. 330). Like the deceased Tucker who suffered spinal concussion in the riot, Tommy literalizes the concussiveness of the great noun.

Within the rhetorical space created by the juxtaposition of naïve Tommy and sophisticated Mr. Johnson, the trio of Matthew Jermyn, Harold Transome, and Rufus Lyon enact a drama of consciousness, perception, and self-awareness as prerequisites of civilized life. Eliot obliges her reader to perceive these three fathers—a kind of rude triptych foreshadowing *Daniel Deronda*—as being enmeshed in a dialectic of perplexity and possibility. Eliot characterizes Jermyn, Transome, and Lyon in terms of their coping with the disorienting effects of crisis; they strive to compose or revise their own lives or other people's lives.

(4) A rage for metaphoric control marks the metonymic turn against turn between Jermyn and his illegitimate son Harold Transome. Jermyn anticipates coping with future problems arising from Harold's having returned from the Orient; his plan is simply to "prepare for any crisis" (p. 123). The worldly Jermyn is someone who, like Richardson's Lovelace, appropriates to himself the decision as to which moment may become charged with crisis-energy. Prudence equates roughly with preparedness for crisis, and the prudent man revises his script as he judges necessary. Eliot's superb characterization of the somber Jermyn integrates her dual crisis-motifs of manipulation and life-scripting.

(5) Unlike Harold's self-pitying mother, Harold himself possesses his father's tough-minded, ironical self-reflexivity. He desires domination over the perplexing raw materials of life. When he learns that another heir to the Transome estate has been discovered, he carefully wrings from Christian the crucial information that the heir is actually Esther Lyon, plus the crucial fact that his enemy (and his own undeclared father) Matthew Jermyn does not yet possess this information. Fearing a prolonged court action that could waste the estate, he nevertheless judges it best not to risk any suppression of the truth concerning Esther's claim on his property. Instead, he decides to inform Esther of her rightful claim. Eliot devotes a chapter to Harold's crisis and pointedly designates it as such. An "actual crisis" may, as it does in this case, provoke a tortured casuistry in a beleaguered mind, even a Radical who ostensibly represents the most advanced progressive or reformist spirit of the day.

> In fact, what he would have done had the circumstances been different, was much clearer than *what he should choose to do or feel himself compelled to do in the actual crisis.* He would not have been disgraced if, on a valid claim being urged, he had got his lawyers to fight it out for him on the chance of eluding the claim by some adroit technical management. . . . All the world would think the actual Transomes in the right to contest any adverse claim to the utmost. (p. 343; emphasis added)

Harold's driven personality complicates a strong desire for freedom with an intense psychological conflict. He judges it best to inform Esther Lyon that she is the true heir, to invite her to visit Transome Court, and, privately, to determine that he will in fact seek to marry Esther if necessary to retain his property (pp. 350-54). Like his father, though, he illustrates Paul de Man's belief that crisis-rhetoric may express deep-seated moral error and self-delusion.

(6) Many dimensions of Eliot's crisis-logic fuse in the Reverend Rufus Lyon. On two early occasions, he experiences ontological anxiety that

Eliot signifies as *crisis*. Early on, the young clergyman suffers intense stress when he falls in love with the pregnant Annette Ledru. Inflexibly pious, he resigns as pastor of a large Independent congregation. Eliot employs the metaphor of a raging, disorienting flood.

> *A terrible crisis had come upon him*; a moment in which religious doubt and newly-awakened passion had rushed together in a common flood, and had paralyzed his ministerial gifts. (p. 83; emphasis added)

His life-changing decision is to leave the ministry, marry Annette, and become the ostensible father of Esther.

After Annette's early death, Lyon resumes his ministerial career but continues to nurture Esther. For sixteen years relatively free of crisis-exigency, he becomes a fussy scholar. As Eliot structures the story, Lyon does not undergo a personal crisis again until he impulsively seizes an occasion to debate the Rector Philip Debarry on the constitution of the true Church. In Lyon's seeking for theological truth, Eliot literalizes the principle that crisis-rhetoric occurs in the context of truth versus error.

> To understand how these words could carry the suggestion they actually had for the minister *in a crisis of peculiar personal anxiety and struggle*, we must bear in mind that for many years he had walked through life with the sense of having for a space been unfaithful to what he esteemed the highest trust ever committed to man—the ministerial vocation. In a mind of any nobleness, a lapse into transgression against an object still regarded as supreme, issues in a new and purer devotedness, chastised by humility and watched over by a passionate regret.
>
> Now here was an opportunity brought by a combination of that unexpected incalculable kind which might be regarded as the Divine emphasis invoking especial attention to trivial events—an opportunity of securing what *Rufus Lyon had often wished for as a means of honouring truth, and exhibiting error* in the character of a stammering, halting, short-breathed usurper of office and dignity. (pp. 171-72; emphases added)

Ironically, Eliot devises a comic denouement, as Lyon's intention of "exhibiting error" in another person boomerangs against himself. The agreed-upon debate never materializes. Philip Debarry had wormed his way out of the debate by appointing a timid curate, Mr. Sherlock, to debate the Evangelical Lyon. An over-coffeed Mr. Sherlock runs away from the encounter with Lyon (p. 249).

Lyon's story poises between the serious and the comic. How will Eliot finally judge the nervous recluse? Happily, Lyon controls his anxiety by extending his crisis-consciousness into the life of his daughter Esther. A third and final event occasions Eliot's firm judgment that crisis-consciousness enables a test of one's moral fiber. If Esther's welfare is in jeopardy, the tremulous Lyon masters his nerves. When Harold Transome proposes to ensconce Esther at Transome Court, Lyon judges the moment to be a crisis. He agrees to inform her students of her departure, but he worries.

> "Doubt it not, my dear," said the old man, trembling a little under the *feeling that this departure of Esther's was a crisis*. Nothing again would be as it had been in their mutual life. But he feared that he was being mastered by a too tender self-regard, and struggled to keep himself calm. (p. 376; emphasis added)

Lyon's judgment proves correct. Esther becomes acquainted with Mrs. Transome's miserable isolation and eventually chooses to reject her inherited wealth so as to share a pious poverty with Felix Holt. His struggle for self-control in a crisis provides a viable model for Esther when she eventually faces her own perplexing impasse.

Some readers take Esther Lyon to be Eliot's nearest thing to a main character. And, in fact, the stolid Felix Holt is himself never singled out by any crisis-image. However, in light of the part/whole analysis enabled by my examination of these nine crisis-images (however scattered in their effects), it is clear enough that Eliot named her book *Felix Holt* for good reasons. Felix Holt is in fact her main character. Eliot's most radical critique in this book is a critique of radicalism itself, and Felix Holt provides the best definition of radicalism. A deep if autodidactic thinker, Felix explains to Rufus Lyon that he himself is truly, literally, a Radical, i.e., one who wishes to reform men by going deeper than merely shallow political changes such as extension of the franchise to certain property owners. Instead, he intends to pierce to the root (*radix*) of human nature where morals and politics are truly generated: "A Radical—yes; but I want to go to some roots a good deal lower down than the franchise" (p. 272).

Having taken note of Felix's own tropological understanding of the contents of consciousness ("what life thrusts into his mind"), we can now see that Eliot means for her reader to understand heightened consciousness itself—in something like Hayden White's sense of the term—to be the radical goal toward which Felix would, and all good men should, strive. Thus, Felix need not be identified with any single crisis-image because he has already passed through successive metaphorical identification (practicing and then giving up his father's bogus patent-medicine trade), metonymical and synecdochical relations (adopting new roles as watchmaker and schoolteacher), to arrive at an ironical stage that, in its turn, becomes the basis for a new metaphor (rejection of money) which equates the moral individual with responsible social action.[27]

Felix Holt, the Radical represents a paradigm case (admittedly inchoate) illustrating how a crisis-trope constitutes an essential part of a novelist's vision of modern consciousness. In elaborating a systematic account of human life as structured via turning points marked by incomprehension and ontological uncertainty but also marked by a strong yearning for freedom, it anticipates to a considerable degree both White's sequential tropes of consciousness and Brown's model of crisis as dialectical turning point. The historically vital noun *crisis* itself functions in many contexts as a kind of second narratorial voice, so to speak, within or underneath the main voice of Eliot's (or another's) implied author or narrator. If so, it resembles the process by means of which, as Mikhail Bakhtin urged, a dialogic form constructs both a subject and a truthfully complex narration. Historically, then, one value or function of *crisis* as a trope might reside in its being an ideological "voice" that lends itself to numerous ideologies but affixes itself exclusively to none.[28]

Given the lofty stature of *Middlemarch*, any rhetorical technique employed there automatically attains an honored place in the rhetoric of fiction. In another context, though without specific reference to the problem of consciousness, I have explained how Eliot used a *crisis*-trope in composing this majestic novel.[29] Historically, *Middlemarch* represents a moment in literary consciousness equal, I should think, to something as profound and permanent as Wordsworth's Immortality Ode.

The masterpiece of Eliot's mature realistic techniques, *Middlemarch*[30] represents an ambitious summary of English social classes during the same period (1830-33) covered by *Felix Holt*. In conception two distinct novels, *Middlemarch* incorporates historical data collected in elaborate notebooks. Eliot attempted a panoramic view of society from a position of judicious impartiality, and, as in *Felix Holt*, her ambitious plan posed severe compositional problems. She devised a structure in which numerous individual storylines would touch together briefly from time to time and then separate so as to suggest the social actualities of the class system. Although some traces of sensational fiction intrude, Eliot's effects derive mainly from such features as a genuine psychological complexity and a careful paralleling of themes in the various story lines. Major themes such as incompatibility in marriage and the impact of an outsider upon a closed society lend emotional substance and conceptual unity to her widely assorted materials.

The career of the *crisis*-trope takes an important turn as it comes under Eliot's magisterial intellect. Eliot's greatest gift was for psychological analysis. She used numerous devices to manage her unwieldy materials. In *Felix Holt*, she had distributed nine *crisis*-images evenly throughout the text. Presumably witnessing to a more widespread cultural usage or practice, as well as to her own unfolding sense of technique, in *Middlemarch* she employs *crisis*-images in fifteen contexts. Somewhat like Scott (and Forster later on), she distributes all fifteen *crisis*-signals after the halfway point of the story. Such concentration demonstrates again that any writer must adapt a crisis-trope to the unique requirements, aims, and overall decorum of each new book.

Narrative cruxes signalled by the great noun in the second half of *Middlemarch* include not only the Parliamentary elections associated with the Great Reform of 1832 but also social conflicts and personal predicaments experienced by a variety of characters: Dorothea Brooke, Edward Casaubon, Tertius Lydgate, Nicholas Bulstrode, Will Ladislaw, Harriet Bulstrode, and Rosamond Vincy. Via literal statement and figural suggestion, the cumulative trope certifies their importance to Eliot's intentional theme.

Human experience as rendered in narrative literature assuredly offers itself as the experience of moments.[31] In *Felix Holt*, Eliot had propounded a generalization on the subject: "Every minute that passes may be charged with some such crisis in the little inner world of man or woman." Nothing like Jane Austen's neat *crisis*-pattern in *Emma* (depicting the self-discovery undergone by Emma Woodhouse) informs Eliot's ambitious book. Even so, Eliot uses *crisis* to signal or enable character revelation and, in general, to focus the relative intensities of her various subplots. Like other novelists from Richardson to Bellow, she demonstrates how an individual human being may exploit crises for selfish reasons. She also uses *crisis* to signal dialectical turning points. Likewise (and here Eliot stands firmly in the main tradition beginning with Richardson), she singles out some of her characters as *crisis*-strategists, so that characterization results to some degree from one's lacking or possessing crisis-consciousness.

In the first half of the book, episodes that could plausibly derive critical signification from a *crisis*-signifier in fact do not. To name but a few: Dorothea's facing the decision whether to keep her jewelry or give it to her sister Celia; the problem faced by several people (Celia, her uncle Mr. Brooke, Sir James Chettam) whether to interfere in Dorothea's infatuation with the aging Edward Casaubon; Dorothea's dilemma whether to alter the lifestyle of her new husband Casaubon; Fred Vincy's financial blunders; the selection of a new chaplain for Nicholas Bulstrode's hospital; Will Ladislaw's first unsettling appearance at Casaubon's house; Ladislaw's untimely appearance in Rome where Dorothea honeymoons with Casaubon; Dr. Tertius Lydgate's ministering to the ailing Fred Vincy; Caleb Garth's failed effort to assist the unreliable Fred Vincy; Dorothea's difficulties with her husband over Will's attentions to her; Casaubon's own heart disease; Featherstone's prolonged dying, his rejected legacy to Mary Garth, and his subsequent legacy to Joshua Rigg; Mr. Brooke's founding of a liberal magazine; and so on. These and other occurrences might easily have been designated as crises, but they are not. What events, then, does Eliot stipulate for as crisis?

Eliot first uses the great noun to signal a dark turning in Dorothea's fortunes when the embittered Casaubon hardens his heart against his wife and his cousin Ladislaw. Dorothea's bitter pill results from her own willfully erroneous judgment of her husband.

> Pity was overthrown. Was it her fault that she had believed in him—had believed in his worthiness?—And what, exactly, was he?—She was able enough to estimate him—she who waited on his glances with trembling, and shut her best soul in prison, paying it only hidden visits, that she might be petty enough to please him. *In such a crisis as this, some women begin to hate.* (p. 417; emphasis added)

Eliot sets Dorothea apart as one who possesses crisis-consciousness. She perceives that "there had been some crisis in her husband's mind" (p. 423).

To contrast Dorothea's deepening crisis-consciousness with a seemingly more superficial kind, Eliot depicts the flighty Mr. Brooke as it were parodying Mr. Johnson's speech in *Felix Holt*. Excusing his own retreat from the unpleasant task of informing Dorothea about her husband's will, Brooke resembles Lawyer Johnson in exploiting the parliamentary crux triggered by the Great Reform Bill. He artfully dodges responsibility by declaring, "'Well, well, we shall see. But I must run away now—I have no end of work now—*it's a crisis—a political crisis, you know*'" (p. 479; emphasis added).

Almost immediately in the same chapter, however, Eliot refocuses on Dorothea's emergent crisis-consciousness. When Celia informs her sister that the deceased Casaubon had added a codicil to his will disowning Dorothea should she choose to marry his hated cousin Ladislaw, a "crisis" occurs in Dorothea's mind. The distressing effect on Dorothea, so noticeable that Dr. Lydgate detects her distress when he enters the room, is one of "convulsive change." She feels that her life is taking on a new form, that she is undergoing a metamorphosis "in which memory would not adjust itself to the stirring of new organs" (p. 481). She begins to feel toward the interdicted Ladislaw a "strange yearning of heart." The likeliest unifying plot in *Middlemarch* would be the Dorothea-Will romance; her epiphanic self-discovery, in combination with his defiant decision to remain in Middlemarch "as long as I like," represents a vital part of Eliot's intentional theme. Dorothea's new awareness of an anomalous attraction to Will has provoked a crisis, and, as a result, a violent paradigm shift, a new awareness of life.

Crisis-consciousness is never so much a final state as a developmental process, and a crisis-turn may take the form of an inward process. After Dorothea decides that she must not see Will again, a proposition to which he reluctantly agrees, they part under extremely painful circumstances ("like two creatures slowly turning to marble in each other's presence"). The narrator of *Middlemarch* expatiates at some length upon the erroneous understanding typical of callow youth. A *crisis*-passage occasions authorial wisdom.

> If youth is the season of hope, it is often so only in the sense that our elders are hopeful about us; for no age is so apt as youth to think its emotions, partings, and resolves are the last of their kind. *Each crisis seems final, simply because it is new.* We are told that the elder inhabitants of Peru do not cease to be agitated by the earthquakes, but they probably see beyond each shock, and reflect that there are plenty more to come. (p. 534; emphasis added)

The effect of this comment is to characterize Dorothea's outlook as being, at this stage, naïve but appropriate to youth. Yet it also holds forth hope that she will survive the current ordeal of separation.

Individuals may script their lives via a crisis-figure, but Eliot's crisis-language insists upon the sobering truth that some life-scripts turn out badly. The eventual happy marriage of Dorothea and Will is framed by two mismatched couples, the Lydgates and the Bulstrodes, whose distorted *crisis*-consciousness leads to unhappiness. Tertius undergoes a crisis when the extravagant Rosamond purchases precious stones he can ill afford. He irresolutely yields to the threat of losing her and dissimulates by telling her that "things were not coming to a crisis immediately" (p. 690). Uxorious weakness produces bad judgment which leads to financial and professional ruin. Even the light-minded, self-centered Rosamond proves capable of perceiving an event as a potentially benign crisis-enabled change. When Dorothea swallows her injured pride and displays genuine concern for Lydgate, Rosamond inwardly responds by undergoing a "new crisis," the "sharpest crisis" of her thoughtless life (p. 822). Ironically,

Lydgate himself regards his wife only as a light-headed doll and thus never glimpses her serious side.

A wife can assist her husband by acting upon her own *crisis-consciousness*. The Bulstrodes contrast sharply with the Lydgates on this score. Nicholas Bulstrode himself, faced with public exposure in the death of his co-conspirator Raffles, experiences "a crisis of feeling almost too violent for his delicate frame to support" (p. 715). When his wife correctly guesses that her husband has been guilty of some hideous crime, she responds not with condemnation or self-indulgent rationalization but with wifely support. Eliot provides her reader with her strongest authorial explication or definition of crisis-morality.

> That moment was perhaps worse than any which came after. It contained that *concentrated experience which in great crises of emotion reveals the bias of a nature*, and is prophetic of the ultimate act which will end an intermediate struggle. (p. 738; emphasis added)

Eliot understands rhetoric to mean both verbal strategies and behavioral strategies. If her earlier formulation ("the concussion of that great noun") perfectly expresses the manipulative effect of *crisis*, then this later formulation ("concentrated experience which in great crises of emotion reveals the bias of a nature") compellingly expresses the behavioral implication of the trope.

Historically, marriage underwent major changes as an institution in Eliot's day. The social problem of incompatibility in marriage figures prominently in poems, plays, tracts, novels, and other writings. So as to induce and highlight this historical problem as a major theme, she concentrates *crisis*-images in the second half of *Middlemarch*. Her own treatment of the incompatibility theme climaxes in Dorothea's decision to consider the welfare of Lydgate, Will, and Rosamond rather than her own bruised feelings. After discovering Will and Rosamond in what seemed a compromising situation, Dorothea must make an ethical judgment.

> And *what sort of crisis might not this be* in three lives whose contact with hers laid an obligation on her as if they had been suppliants bearing the sacred branch? The objects of her rescue were not to be sought out by her fancy: they were chosen for her. She yearned towards the perfect Right, that it might make a throne within her, and rule her errant will. "What should I do—how should I act now, this very day, if I could clutch my own pain, and compel it to silence, and think of those three?" (pp. 776-77; emphasis added)

In exploiting the three main implications of *crisis* (manipulation, dialectical change of direction, self-reflexive judgment), Eliot provides one of the most convincing moral appreciations of this seminally modern experience.

Lionel Stevenson discusses *Middlemarch* and *Daniel Deronda* under the heading "Recognition of Technique."[32] In 1870, Charles Dickens died, and his rough-and-ready style began to wane; by the end of the decade, Henry James had brought the English novel to a new aesthetic level. One element in the increasingly self-conscious rhetoric of fiction took the form of experiments in *crisis*-rhetoric. In some respects the first modern novel and among novels the favored example for deconstructive critics, *Daniel Deronda* represents a problematically special case.[33]

For some readers, *Daniel Deronda*[34] fails to meet the standards of Eliot's highest art. They find it over-intellectualized, or they object to Eliot's treatment of the Zionists' dream of a Palestinian homeland in terms of sensational mystery and sentimental romance. Some critics think that Eliot simply erred in choosing the Zionist subject. Some judge Daniel Deronda and Eliot's other Jewish characters as being too idealized or stereotyped. Likewise, Eliot is thought to have perversely rendered English society as insensitive and unrelievedly cruel. Only in the tormented Gwendolen Harleth do such dissatisfied readers find something to praise. F. R. Leavis considered *Daniel Deronda* to be a superb book, in some respects greater than *Middlemarch*, but only in the Gwendolen portions. In my history of the crisis-trope, this brilliant book represents a high point in its combination of three essential crisis-motifs (intense emotionalism, plot structuration, critical judgment).

Eliot's problematically broken-backed narrative required unusual strategies and techniques in its construction: retrospect and flashback, a subtle use of double plotting, and an extraordinary set of closural features. Shadowing the entire complex of substance and form, as Barbara Hardy notes, is a disturbing consciousness or "alien sensibility" that induces an unshakeable mood of "tension, mystery, dread, and strangeness."[35] I think that Eliot, in setting only this one of her novels in her own contemporary world, is here witnessing to the endless crisis (stress) of modern life. Much of the exacerbated Gothic sensibility that threatens to destabilize the book, plus much of the rational structuring that barely succeeds in holding the supercharged narrative together, derive from an innovative *crisis*-trope. In this connection, I have shown elsewhere, in psychoanalytical terms, how Freudian transference provides a linkage between the two major plots.[36]

Daniel Deronda opens as a novel depicting English life, marked by certain possibilities and perplexities, joys and sorrows; then it shifts to a depiction of anti-Semitism in Victorian England, together with a strenuous Zionist effort to establish a Palestinian homeland for Jews of the Diaspora. The novel is cut sharply into two parts, the English and the Jewish, but youthful Daniel Deronda links the two parts. Eliot provides the realistic details and psychologically acute analyses that have become her hallmark, and she manages a compelling panoramic view of many levels of English and European life. The complex story might be summarized as follows.

Gwendolen Harleth is espied feverishly gambling at Leubronn; she is watched intently by the "critical eyes" of Daniel Deronda. Deronda redeems a necklace Gwendolen had pawned and returns it anonymously to the reckless girl. Gwendolen leaves abruptly for England, where her mother has been suddenly impoverished by financial losses. In a flashback, Eliot depicts the high-spirited girl fleeing to Leubronn in order to evade the importunities of Mallinger Grandcourt, whose wealth and position made him a good catch but whose salacious past horrified the inexperienced Gwendolen. Daniel Deronda is the orphaned ward of Sir Hugo Mallinger, whose wealth not Deronda but Grandcourt stands to inherit. Yet Deronda is the favorite of Sir Hugo. Altruistically given to redeeming persons in distress, Deronda loses his own chances for success at Cambridge by helping his friend Hans Meyrick to win a scholarship. He also rescues a young woman, Mirah Lapidoth, from an attempted drowning. Discovering that she is a homeless Jew seeking her lost mother and brother in London, he shelters her with friends. Thus, when Deronda sees the fascinating Gwendolen at Leubronn, he has already promised to assist Mirah.

Desperate under the threat of impoverished dependence upon her relatives the Gascoignes, Gwendolen impulsively decides to marry Grandcourt, thus breaking a promise to his former mistress Lydia Glasher. In its ignorance, polite society approves of their marriage. Once married, though, Grandcourt proves to be sadistic and domineering. He breaks Gwendolen's spirit. Only in an occasional conversation with the sympathetic Deronda does Gwendolen find any solace. She pours out her anguish to him, and he listens without condemnation to her expressions of fear and hatred as well as her guilt over betraying Lydia Glasher and hating her own husband. Gwendolen heeds Deronda's advice to live unselfishly by assisting other people, but she achieves only the slightest relief from her anguish.

Meanwhile, Deronda assists Mirah to begin a singing career. In addition, he searches for her family in London's East End, becoming acquainted with one Ezra Cohen, a shopkeeper, who provides a home for a queer, learned man named Mordecai Cohen. Mordecai proves to be Mirah's lost brother as well as eventually a true friend and mentor to Deronda himself. Through Mordecai, Deronda becomes acquainted with Jewish history, culture, and religion, so that when he learns that he himself is in fact a Jew he is prepared to embrace Mirah and accept the vision of a Palestinian homeland as his own life's goal. Bidding Gwendolen farewell, he leaves England with Mirah to devote himself to founding a Zionist refuge.

As with *Felix Holt, the Radical* and *Middlemarch*, dozens of moments in *Daniel Deronda* might plausibly be designated *crisis*. Emergent predicaments and stressful events come so thick and fast that Eliot might well have followed Brontë's method in *Wuthering Heights* by decentering or even precluding *crisis* as being inadequate to characterize such exacerbated emotions. However, Eliot carefully builds into *Daniel Deronda* many crisis-images that effectively inform her unruly materials. From among the assorted themes which Eliot juggles, one compelling modern theme thereby takes on a special emphasis and value. Eliot had used fifteen *crisis*-utterances in the second half of *Middlemarch* to signal, structure, and valorize the theme of incompatibility in marriage. In *Daniel Deronda*, she uses sixteen *crisis*-signifiers to signal and structure the theme of incompatibility between generations, between fathers and children. In *Middlemarch*, the crisis-rhetoric had eventually focused upon Dorothea Brooke's happy marriage to Will Ladislaw, together with Will's success as a member of Parliament. In *Daniel Deronda*, the crisis-trope focuses attention upon Deronda's joyous acceptance of his parental origins, marriage with Mirah Lapidoth, and departure for Palestine.

Narrative passages highlighted or centered by a *crisis*-image in effect become like self-framing pictures. As such, they yield to the critical method that I think of as "reading frames."[37] Which moments does Eliot stipulate for as *crisis*, and how broadly do they permeate the surrounding diegesis? In the epigraph to chapter 7, Eliot cites a passage from Charles Lamb in which youthful love is humorously characterized as "the most alarming crisis in the ticklish state of youth." Alluding to Rex Gascoigne's infatuation with his cousin Gwendolen, Eliot highlights the idea that disoriented youth needs parental guidance. She then establishes a triptych of father-figures highlighted by *crisis*-images.

As a way of intensifying her critique of the cultural dislocations typical of her own day, Eliot makes of parental guidance a more explicit part of her story via two *crisis*-signals bearing upon the familial predicament triggered by Gwendolen's rejection of her cousin. In chapter 8, the worldly-prudent Rector Gascoigne rationalizes Rex's youthful despair by looking "beyond the crisis" so as to perceive the crisis itself to be the quickest way out of a bad situation (p. 75). The Rector's crisis-consciousness enables him to give his unhappy son a morsel of sensible advice, and Rex survives his disappointment. A darker episode in chapter 13, when Gwendolen initially rejects Grandcourt's offer of marriage, involves Rector Gascoigne's erroneous judgment of Grandcourt. This leads him to advise his confused niece to marry Grandcourt: "he did not conceive that he should do his duty in withholding directions from his niece in a momentous crisis" (p. 124). Eliot thus establishes in Rector Gascoigne a spectrum of parental advice—from adequate to wretchedly bad—that can issue even from a parent who possesses both *crisis*-consciousness and good intentions. In Chapter 16, Eliot depicts another father-figure, Sir Hugo Mallinger, who also possesses crisis-consciousness and who appears to his worshipful ward Deronda as possessing "an unquestionable rightness" in all his actions. Deronda admiringly studies Sir Hugo's numerous writings, on subjects such as travel and "things in general," in addition to "pamphlets on political crises." To Deronda, these writings become benchmarks of good sense by which other people's information can be judged (p. 156). For Deronda, crisis-judgment comes when Sir Hugo speaks. If Sir Hugo represents a nearly perfect father-figure, and if Rector Gascoigne represents a mixture of potentially good and potentially bad paternal guidance, then Eliot's third father-figure may be said to illustrate an unrelievedly bad sort. The disreputable father of Mordecai and Mirah—one Mr. Lapidoth—is depicted as a weepy sentimentalist who alternately neglects and exploits his children. While Mordecai teaches Deronda the mysteries of Jewish lore, the useless schemer Lapidoth "was at a crisis of discontent and longing that made his mind busy with schemes of freedom." In this impasse occasioned by his own undisciplined habits, Lapidoth decides to steal Deronda's ring and once again desert his children (p. 733).

The three father-figures thus highlighted by *crisis*-rhetoric make a compelling thematic triptych. On one side, while Deronda joins Mordecai in studying the crises of the Jewish people depicted in ancient writings, the rascally Lapidoth exploits a self-induced crisis so as to escape back to a dubious obscurity on the continent. On the other side, Sir Hugo's disciplined writing habits enable him to study crises as a normal part of human experience and to record his thoughts in writings that Deronda will deeply ponder. Sandwiched between this bad and good angel, Rector

Gascoigne exhibits a more typically mixed consciousness. From the confines of his study, he effectively applies trite formulae (e.g., this too shall pass) to his son's adolescent agony, but in a more serious predicament he yields to economic expediency and precipitates his niece into a hideous marriage. Eliot exhibits three possible responses to crisis in the behavior of these three father-figures, thus structuring an informing theme into her most intense, exhilarating book.

Welsh notes[38] that in Eliot's changing world fathers will be replaced by ideology. By understanding this major cultural development, both historically and aesthetically Eliot advances crisis-rhetoric by a quantum leap. Her strong theme witnesses to the proverbial wisdom that vices or virtues of the fathers will be visited upon the children. Her triptych of father-figures replicates itself in the crisis-consciousness of three younger people: Mordecai (Lapidoth) Cohen, Gwendolen Harleth, and Daniel Deronda. Eliot shapes their experiences to a considerable degree via crisis-language which implies that Mordecai turns to the utopian program of Zionism as a substitute for the parental care Lapidoth could not supply, that the fatherless Gwendolen endures in her own tormented life the same contradictions seen in her surrogate father Gascoigne, and that Deronda himself illustrates in his own destiny the composure induced by Sir Hugo's balanced crisis-consciousness.

The high-strung pitch of *Daniel Deronda* derives in no small degree from Eliot's rhetorical shaping of the Mordecai subplot. Two *crisis*-passages frame and animate Mordecai's most eloquent utterance, concerning a global Zionist vision, that arguably enables Deronda's eventual acceptance of his own Zionist destiny. Mordecai's *crisis*-trope brings the Longinian strain introduced into the novel by Scott to its highest pitch prior to the tormented twentieth century.

In chapter 42, during a meeting of "The Philosophers" at the Hand and Banner tavern, Mordecai utters his most sustained plea for Israel to become a unified nation and the spiritual salvation of mankind. Eliot redundantly but effectively signals as a "decisive crisis" Mordecai's reply to one of the debaters' insistence that a Jew's historical role must be not mystical but rational.

> "And so am I!" said Mordecai, quickly leaning forward with the *eagerness of one who pleas in some decisive crisis*, his long thin hands clasped together on his lap. "I too claim to be a rational Jew. But what is it to be rational—what is it to feel the light of divine reason growing stronger within and without? It is to see more and more of the hidden bonds that bind and consecrate change as a dependent growth—yea, consecrate it with kinship: *the*

past becomes my parent and the future stretches towards me the appealing arms of children." (pp. 490-91; emphasis added)

Eliot makes her crisis-theme of incompatibility between generations metaphorically explicit: "the past becomes my parent."

Between the two *crisis*-signals that alert Eliot's reader to Mordecai's special role in the debate at the Hand and Banner, Mordecai's great speech in effect defines crisis itself. Eliot reveals the compensatory nature of Mordecai's political vision by intensifying the literal meaning of *crisis* (choice) in Mordecai's perfervid insistence that Jews should enjoy freedom of choice in shaping their destiny. Mordecai harps upon the root meaning of the great trope.

"I say that the strongest principle of growth lies in human *choice*. The sons of Judah have to *choose* that God may again *choose* them. The Messianic time is the time when Israel shall will the planting of the national ensign. The Nile overflowed and rushed onward: the Egyptian could not *choose* the overflow, but he *chose* to work and make channels for the fructifying waters, and Egypt became the land of corn. Shall man, whose soul is set in the royalty of discernment and resolve, deny his rank and say, I am an onlooker, ask no *choice* or purpose of me? That is the blasphemy of this time. The divine principle of our race is action, *choice*, resolved memory. Let us contradict the blasphemy, and help to will our own better future and the better future of the world—not renounce our higher gift and say, 'Let us be as if we were not among the populations;' but *choose* our full heritage, claim the brotherhood of our nation, and carry into it a new brotherhood with the nations of the Gentiles. The vision is there; it will be fulfilled." (pp. 499-500; emphases added)

Even in his overwrought enthusiasm, Mordecai remains conscious that *crisis* is in fact a two-edged sword, simultaneously an opportunity and a risk, something that happens to someone but also something that one can choose and shape to his own ends.[39]

The main plot had taken a major turn earlier, in chapter 40, when Deronda leaves the security of the Meyrick home in Chelsea to begin his active search for Mirah's lost brother. The effects of Mordecai's impassioned speech at the Hand and Banner, to which Deronda carefully attends, will appear chiefly in Deronda's subsequent decision to embrace both his own Jewishness and Mordecai's Zionist dream. Following the speech, Eliot rounds off Mordecai's personal *crisis*-trope by once again explicitly signalling the moment as a "crisis which must be seized."

> The dawn of fulfillment brought to his hope by Deronda's presence had wrought Mordecai's conception into a state of impassioned conviction, and he had found strength in his excitement to pour forth the unlocked floods of emotive argument, with *a sense of haste as at a crisis which must be seized.* (p. 499)

Thus Eliot completes one of the most coherent and emphatic strands of her crisis-figure; indeed, one of the most compelling moments in the entire history of the revolutionary trope.

By the time Deronda hears Mordecai's exalted speech, his own consciousness of political and historical developments has been raised by Sir Hugo. Mordecai then becomes Deronda's new father-figure, and Deronda proceeds under his tutelage to confront the demands of his enlarging perception of human possibility. Gwendolen Harleth represents an opposite case. All readers of *Daniel Deronda*—detractors and admirers alike—acknowledge that the most blatant structural problem takes the form of a sharp contrast or cut between the Gwendolen plot and the Deronda plot. Given the standard rhetorical effects of climactic structure, according to which a rhetorician arranges elements of a text in increasing order of importance, the Gwendolen plot which dominates the first half of the book is relegated to a subordinate role when the Deronda plot becomes the main focus of attention in the second half. In Derrida's terminology, the Deronda plot deconstructs the Gwendolen plot. But Eliot links these plots by means of a crisis-trope that effectively measures the chief difference between her two major characters.

Eliot's announced intention was to delineate the "consciousness of a girl, busy with her small inferences," an inexperienced girl who is compelled to confront forces vastly more huge than her limited frame of reference is prepared to meet. The alien consciousness Eliot develops in this book is essentially an acute crisis-consciousness; moreover, the disturbing sensations of tension, mystery, dread, and strangeness derive considerably from Eliot's portrayal of the nervous Gwendolen. At three critical junctures in the first half of the book, plus one vivid moment in the penultimate chapter, Eliot characterizes the intense girl via a *crisis*-image. When Gwendolen seeks to avoid marriage by taking up a singing career, Eliot highlights her fear of being judged by the expert musician (and potential father-figure) Klesmer. The hysterical girl can not free herself from bondage.

> Poor thing! she was at *a higher crisis of her woman's fate* than in her past experience with Grandcourt. The questioning then, was whether she should take a particular man as a husband. The inmost fold of her questioning now,

was whether she need take a husband at all—whether she could not achieve substantiality for herself and know gratified ambition without bondage. (p. 233; emphasis added)

The fatherless girl, smarting from Klesmer's negative judgment of her prospects for a professional career, deludes herself by postponing her own decision.

By means of a superb irony, Eliot pictures Gwendolen as she proudly rides Grandcourt's horse named "Criterion." This loaded term, of course, like *critic* and *criticism*, shares a common etymological root with *crisis* itself. Gwendolen desires to be uncritically admired but comes to be critically judged not only from all sides but most intensively from within her own psyche. In chapter 26, when Gwendolen feels threatened with the despised duties of governess, she harshly judges a world that does not yield to her whims.

She was in that *first crisis of passionate youthful rebellion* against what is not fitly called pain, but rather the absence of joy—that first rage of disappointment in life's morning which we whom the years have subdued are apt to remember but dimly as part of our own experience, and so to be intolerant of its self-enclosed unreasonableness and impiety. (p. 268; emphasis added)

Gwendolen is spared from actually making this painful decision by a letter from Grandcourt. In effect, though, she cheats herself of an opportunity to make a consequential judgment and thereby develop adult responsibility.

Eliot literalized her *crisis*-motif by intensifying Mordecai's vocabulary of *choice* and related words. She also synecdochically characterizes Gwendolen in part by means of the titles of two of the eight sections of *Daniel Deronda*. Book 3 bears the title "Maidens Choosing"; book 4 bears the title "Gwendolen Gets Her Choice." However, Eliot also makes explicit the vast difference between Gwendolen and Deronda, the latter of whom follows Mordecai's urgent example by welcoming and even seeking out opportunities to make decisions and choices. Gwendolen desires the freedom to enjoy her destiny, but she also is said to desire, with one part of her divided mind, the contradictory fate of being "hastened" by exigencies for the reason that "hurry would save her from deliberate choice" (p. 272).

Ideally, one's father becomes internalized as a value system within one's own personality. One becomes one's own father and, potentially, a father-figure to less experienced persons. Mordecai found a surrogate father in Zionism, and he in turn became a father-figure to Deronda. By contrast, Gwendolen first rejects a stern but truthful father-figure (Klesmer) and then rejects an opportunity herself to serve as a parent-figure (governess). The key to Gwendolen is her ambivalence. As a climax to the early part of Gwendolen's experiences, Eliot establishes that one result of the girl's unfortunate upbringing is her continual "dread of crisis." Eliot makes this neurosis explicit as Gwendolen fantasizes about the power she expects to enjoy as Grandcourt's wife.

> Was it alone the closeness of this fulfilment which made her heart flutter? or was it some dim forecast, the insistent penetration of suppressed experience, mixing the expectation of a triumph with the *dread of a crisis*? Hers was one of the natures in which exultation inevitably carries an infusion of dread ready to curdle and declare itself. (p. 329; emphasis added)

Eliot has used *crisis* both to induce and signal Gothic effects, much like Scott's but with more serious artistic results. Gwendolen receives certain "poisoned gems" sent with a written curse on her marriage by the vengeful Lydia Glasher. Her hysteria is then triggered by the sight of her arrogant husband: "Gwendolen screamed again and again with hysterical violence" (p. 331).

The *crisis*-images centering on the "Spoiled Child" occur in the first half of the book. As if to suggest that Gwendolen's marriage so oppresses the girl's mind that hysterical makes rational judgment virtually impossible, Eliot provides no further signal until Gwendolen's final conversation with the Palestine-bound Deronda. At that point, Gwendolen has been freed from Grandcourt by a drowning accident that leaves her feeling more guilty for not saving her despised husband. Deronda's announcement triggers one final ordeal in Gwendolen's mind, an ordeal imaged by the continual falling away (turning) of the horizon.

> *That was the sort of crisis which was at this moment beginning in Gwendolen's small life*: she was for the first time being dislodged from her supremacy in her own world, and getting a sense that her horizon was but a dipping onward of an existence with which her own was revolving. (p. 748; emphasis added)

Gwendolen's failure as a crisis-strategist, which represents the key to her personality and fate, equates with a failure to free herself from a self-centered metaphor of womblike identity and embrace a more realistic metonymy and synecdoche involving common humanity.

Crisis-consciousness in *Daniel Deronda* reaches its culmination in Deronda's own highly developed consciousness. Eliot brings her theme of the complex relations between fathers and children to an optimistic if ironical closure by showing Deronda's own fine sensibility responding to Eliot's triptych of father-figures: Mordecai, Rector Gascoigne (via Gwendolen), and Sir Hugo. Earlier in history, Scott had structured *The Heart of Midlothian* via *crisis*-tropes in the second half of the narrative; in *Middlemarch*, Eliot followed Scott's example. Among the devices Eliot uses to shape her reader's responses in *Daniel Deronda* are five *crisis*-images in the Deronda plot, all occurring exclusively in the second half of the book. Taken together, they develop a clear premise: Deronda's critical awareness equips him for success in his personal life and also in the larger arena of global politics. Beginning in chapter 40, Eliot links critical self-reflexivity with moral responsibility when she establishes Deronda as himself a *crisis*-strategist. Mordecai's first appeal to his new friend to accept a Zionist destiny for himself, even before Deronda discovers that he himself is in fact a Jew, precipitates an ordeal: "The very sharpness with which these words penetrated Deronda, made him feel the more that here was a crisis in which he must be firm" (p. 468). Unlike Gwendolen, who would hide from the facts of life, Deronda defers judgment only in order to learn more about his own life before linking it with Mordecai's vision.

Eliot shows him as an introspective person able to "examine the grounds of his emotion" and also to look beyond his own limited experience. Sir Hugo's writings and personal example had taught him an acute crisis-consciousness.

> It was his characteristic bias to shrink from the moral stupidity of valuing lightly what had come close to him, and of missing blindly in his own life of to-day the *crises which he recognized as momentous and sacred* in the historic life of men. (p. 473; emphasis added)

In *Middlemarch*, Eliot had asserted that "crises of emotion" reveal the "bias of a nature." Deronda's bias or practice is to look synecdochically at many kinds of ordeals, and his own personal ordeals reinforce his critical habit. In Deronda, Eliot brings to a high point of development this type of consciousness that had interested serious novelists since Richardson.

Sir Hugo encouraged Deronda to recognize and evaluate crises; Deronda repays his mentor's generosity. In chapter 59, following Grandcourt's death in Genoa as well as Deronda's own being informed by his alienated mother that he himself is a Jew, the intense young man waits patiently in Genoa until Sir Hugo arrives from England. Deronda desires Sir Hugo's opinion of "the late crisis" triggered by his mother. In addition, from his position in Genoa the crisis-seasoned Deronda hopes to assist Sir Hugo in settling the affairs of the deceased Grandcourt. Similarly, Deronda temporarily sets aside his own grand design in order to pay close heed to Gwendolen's miseries. Before her husband's death, Gwendolen confessed to Deronda that she feared the deleterious effects on her own character of the hatred she bears her husband ("I am afraid I am getting wicked"). Worried that his nervous friend might in fact be undergoing "a new crisis" (p. 566), and ignorant of the depths of Grandcourt's corruption, Deronda urged her to confess her feelings to her husband. After Grandcourt's death, during Deronda's last visit to Gwendolen's home at Offendene, he thinks back upon the "old drawing room where some chief crises of her life had happened" (pp. 744-45). Deronda makes one final attempt to counsel the desperate young widow.

Deronda perceives stressful episodes as problems demanding judicious consideration, as entanglements needing to be cut but only with fine delicacy. If the distressed Gwendolen in fact has some chance in the future to redeem herself and achieve peace of mind, then undoubtedly she owes such a happy possibility not a little to Deronda and his intensively self-characterizing crisis-consciousness. On the whole, if Eliot herself is an authority among novelists who are *crisis*-rhetoricians, then Deronda represents a maestro, though not entirely free of error, among fictive characters who live by the great trope.

Eliot's special position in a critical history of *crisis* rests upon several claims. She confronts the trope's tripartite potential, as stimulant of unthinking responses, as marker of stressful turning points in an individual's strategy for constructing a life script, and as signifier necessitating self-scrutiny. In *Felix Holt, the Radical*, she foregrounds the ironically "great noun" and then attempts to show how a wide social range of individuals endeavor to shape their lives via the trope. The story of Felix Holt is essentially a story of emerging crisis-consciousness. In *Middlemarch*, she shows how some characters (Rosamond, Lydgate) remain arrested in metaphoric identification of self and other, whereas others (Dorothea, Will Ladislaw) advance into metonymic and synecdochic confrontations with otherness. These fortunate few may then reach the level of ironical self-reflexion so that they can engage dialectically with more advanced social challenges. In *Daniel Deronda*, Eliot raises all three functions of the crisis-trope to an extremely high level of art and intellect. Gwendolen never advances from narcissistic equation of self and other, but Mordecai moves to the stage of irony and new metaphor, whereas Deronda carries the burden of unifying plot by moving only from metaphor to metonymic and synecdochic engagement with large political schemes and real-world aspirations. Among novelists prior to Henry James, Eliot most intensely concentrates upon the synonymy of *crisis* and *criticism*. *Daniel Deronda* represents in several respects the most ambitious and successful of all crisis-narratives examined thus far.

Eliot's novels serve as crucial texts of reference in the present narrative. The sixteen crisis-passages in *Daniel Deronda* are the largest number employed in any novel prior to Bellow's *Humboldt's Gift* (1975) and Robert Coover's *The Public Burning* (1976). In subsequent chapters, I will examine Coover's and Bellow's scrutiny of and reliance upon the great noun, together with other writers who exhibit a wide range of agonized modern consciousness. In its intensity and its shrill psychology, *Daniel Deronda* anticipates the tortured vision of such seminal twentieth-century authors.

Each reader must judge whether Eliot's *crisis*-tropes constitute an element to be interpreted or whether the tropes themselves effect interpretation. In either case, no interpretation can ignore Eliot's *crisis*-philosophy in her two greatest books.

3

The Art of Crisis-Consciousness:
George Meredith, George Moore, George Gissing, and Henry James

I began this inquiry in order to determine what historical greatness we might reasonably attribute to George Eliot's putative "great noun." Or, from another angle, to determine the critical history—if any—of an odd narrative element I had encountered throughout Saul Bellow's oeuvre. What have I discovered or at least narratively represented so far? Given the variety of rhetorical purposes served by what I am calling the *crisis*-trope, and likewise assuming that literature manifests many forms of consciousness, I can at least tentatively conclude the following. The great noun indeed attains to greatness by its organic, functional association with grand ideas and theories, revolutionary aspirations, and ambitious literary works. It serves many writers in carrying out versions of cultural critique. The vexed modern self as confronted by Richardson, MacKenzie, Scott, Austen, and Eliot indeed derives its existence in part from consciousness of crisis. Likewise, crisis-consciousness seems indeed rooted (perhaps tropologically) in language and the human mind; crisis-behavior can be construed as moving dialectically from stage to stage by way of turning points (most schematically in narrative from metaphor to metonymy to synecdoche to irony to new metaphor). The great noun attains to greatness in part because of its extraordinary flexibility, so that it can at any moment function as a signifier variously of manipulation, of dialectical change, or of self-reflexive judgment. Ordering all of these functions are the artist's strategies, which can shift from one function to another as dictated by the decorum of a given text.

The human mind itself may indeed function narratively, and crisis-consciousness seems, in that case, to be one of the mind's essentially narrative strategies. The next chapter of this compelling story of a single word extends and deepens its range of relevance. More great names and theories (political, philosophical, economic, aesthetic) witness to the

96

centrality of crisis-consciousness in social change and related critical issues as the novel steadily becomes both more scientific and more artistic. I should note at this point a pertinent critical observation bearing upon my argument: "The relation of consciousness to matter and to other consciousnesses is the subtext of many late-nineteenth-century works."[1] In the second half of the nineteenth century, the great noun became increasingly serviceable in western culture. In socioeconomics, for example, theoreticians assumed its relevance to explanations and programs. The Marxist critique of capitalism, for example, included the description of a crisis-syndrome built into the very structure of capitalist economy. Marx's arcane explanation can be simplified as follows. The rate of profit is the ratio between surplus value and total investment of constant capital and variable capital. Whenever capital is greater than zero, the rate of profit is less than the rate of surplus value. The importance of this ratio derives from its ability to explain why capitalism is characterized by a tendency for the rate of profit to fall, why capitalism tends to experience profit-crunches, and why capitalistic systems regularly undergo economic crisis. Thus, economic crisis fundamentally expresses the inborn tendency of a commodity economy to witness a fall in the rate of profit as a result of the rising organic composition of capital.[2]

Benedetto Croce analyzed certain nineteenth-century theories as in themselves, for good or ill, error-prone crisis-rhetorics.

> But [communism] ended by recognizing that its accomplishment required as a *sine qua non* that the course of history should lead to the alternative of either injuring and reducing the production of wealth, preserving the capitalist system, that is, private property, or else guaranteeing and increasing production, thus abolishing private property. It believed it could confirm and prove this by the *economic crises and the destruction of wealth rendered from time to time necessary by the capitalist system in order to re-establish its equilibrium* by means of upheaval and bankruptcies.[3] (emphases added)

Croce's rhetorical query whether "things really do occur in this way" recalls Paul de Man's belief that any crisis-rhetoric states its own truth in the mode of error. In any case, the great noun itself begins to hover like a threatening cloud over an entire civilization.

Wherever the great noun appears, it frames or informs from within a context that thereby achieves a higher emotional pitch. *Crisis* lurks in the wings of European life and letters when it does not aggressively take center stage. Among French novelists, Balzac, Flaubert, and Zola would avail themselves of the word's concussive or semiotic effects. Balzac occasionally resorts to some specific crisis-image. For example, he momentarily presents the self-serving Eugène de Rastignac in *Père Goriot* as saying petulantly to his lover Delphine: "Considering the crisis I'm in at the present, I thought you would not be so cruel, but you never loved me."[4] In a different vein, Zola established the economic background for *Germinal* (1885) in terms of bourgeois economic struggle punctuated regularly by economic crisis.

> When the million rate had been touched, Monsieur Gregoire was advised to sell, but he refused with a superior smile. *Six months later there came an industrial crisis, and the denier fell* to six hundred thousand. But he went on smiling and had no regrets, for the Gregoires had an unshakeable faith in their mine.[5] (emphasis added)

Balzac and Zola thus define a range of possibilities from the private sphere to the public sphere. Balzac shows Eugène as a manipulative *crisis-rhetorician*, and Zola signals the Marxist concept of economic crisis. By contrast, Flaubert resorted to poetical language in providing a definition of *crisis* that anticipates Eliot's in *Middlemarch*. In the famous second chapter of part three in *Madame Bovary* (1857), he characterizes the apothecary Homais in a moment of anger:

> His rage had sent him into Latin: he would have spouted Chinese or Greenlandic had he been able to, for he was in the throes of *one of those crises in which the soul lays bare its every last corner*, just as the ocean, in the travail of storm, splits open to display everything from the seaweed on its shores to the sand of its deepest bottom.[6] (emphasis added)

In these classics, *crisis* functions as a moment of aporia or undecidability that challenges a reader to exert a complex critical effort.

The English Victorians wrote more than forty thousand novels.[7] How many of this huge number actually incorporate a crisis-trope may remain a question beyond investigation. Many books that do incorporate the word fit only peripherally into my own argument. In *Vanity Fair*, for example, Thackeray only once (chap. 66) designates a minor episode in Dobbins's relations with Amelia as a *crisis*. The rhetorical effects are hardly noticeable.

The central plot-energies of Dickens's *Great Expectations* have been described in terms of "the moment of crisis and reversal in the attempted escape from England."[8] On the whole, though, except for an unforgettable phrase such as one referring to Mr. Snagsby's undergoing a "crisis of nightmare" (*Bleak House*, chap. 25), Dickens makes little use of the great noun that would more substantially serve other writers.

Dickens seems to belong to the category of novelists for whom *crisis* is less a presence than an absence, as in *Oliver Twist* (1839), when young Oliver awakens from a feverish sleep, he discovers that he has recovered because the "crisis of the disease was safely past" (chap. 12). Only in *Our Mutual Friend* (1865) does Dickens use a somewhat developed *crisis*-image. At a crucial moment in book 4, chapter 6, Dickens depicts the opportunistic Eugene Wrayburn meditating upon a dilemma which he labels a crisis. Interestingly, he adopts the dialectical image of the river current which disorients by sweeping one off one's feet.

> The rippling of the river seemed to cause a correspondent stir in his uneasy reflections. He would have laid them asleep if he could, but they were in movement, like the stream, and all tending one way with a strong current. As the ripple under the moon broke unexpectedly now and then, and palely flashed in a new shape and with a new sound, so parts of his thoughts started, unbidden, from the rest, and revealed their wickedness. 'Out of the question to marry her,' said Eugene, 'and out of the question to leave her. *The crisis!*' (emphasis added)

On the whole, Dickens's grab-bag of rhetorical tricks and methods may not include to any significant degree a *crisis*-strategy.

Thomas Hardy's narratives abundantly depict stress and turmoil, crisis in the familiar sense of that loaded word, but Hardy relegates the trope itself to a relatively unimportant position. In *Jude the Obscure* (1895), the narrator delineates the intense sexual relation between Jude Fawley and Sue Bridehead in terms of their awareness of their own "mutual sensitiveness at emotional crises" (part 3, chap. 7). Sue sexually manipulates Jude via a self-serving rationalization.

> Even at this obvious moment for candor Sue could not be quite candid as to the state of that mystery, her heart. "Put it down to my timidity," she said with hurried evasiveness; "to *a woman's natural timidity when the crisis comes*. I may feel as well as you that I have a perfect right to live with you as you thought—from this moment. . . . But don't press me and criticize me, Jude!" (part 4, chap. 5; emphasis added)

Despite the shrill tone and the association of crisis with criticism, no large effect imposes itself on the story.

In *The Return of the Native* (1878), Hardy employed a rhetoric which, like that in *Tristram Shandy* or *Wuthering Heights*, effectively neutralizes any crisis-centered plot structure. Hardy uses his table of contents to insert a *crisis*-signifier.

Book Third: The Fascination.
    Chapter 5. Sharp Words Are Spoken, and a Crisis Ensues

The episode thus signalled comprises two related events. Clym Yeobright's worried mother complains to her son about his intimate relation with Eustachia Vye, and Clym impulsively proposes marriage to Eustachia. More important is a single *crisis*-passage, developed at some length in book 1, chapter 1, as part of the atmospheric opening sequence. In this famous beginning, Hardy establishes the deep history and symbolism of Egdon Heath as a natural force that dwarfs into insignificance any mere human ambition or enterprise. He carefully establishes that crisis-consciousness will involve not people but "things" and, moreover, that the only crisis which truly matters is some unimaginable "last crisis" or apocalyptic upheaval of nature.

> The place became full of a watchful intentness now; for when other things sank brooding to sleep the heath appeared slowly to awake and listen. Every night its Titanic form seemed to await something; but it had waited thus, unmoved, during so many centuries, *through the crises of so many things*, that it could only be imagined *to await one last crisis*—the final overthrow. (emphases added)

Beginning and ending with a metaphor (nature comprises reality), Hardy nevertheless decenters *Return of the Native* as effectively as Brontë decentered *Wuthering Heights*, not so much to dismiss an irrelevant Christianity (as in Brontë's case) as to emphasize an absolutely deterministic state of brute Nature. Thus he deflates human pretensions. Hardy's crisis-argument at the beginning of *Return of the Native* as it were obliquely urges that crisis itself may constitute for the most part not a human or cultural perception but a purely natural phenomenon. By contrast with such a naturalistic viewpoint, one of the most instructive examples of a human-centered crisis-rhetoric can be found in George Meredith's sophisticated comic novel *The Egoist*.

1. "a risky guess in the crisis of doubt and dispute"

Matthew Arnold decided that modernity would mean the mind's entering into dialogue with itself. Similarly, my argument is that a self-reflexive, *crisis*-centered narrative preeminently signals a discourse that doubles back in critical dialogue with itself, thus inducing a special form of literary consciousness. Novelists examined in the present study both underwent and witnessed to some sort of crisis, some anguish resulting from violent historical shifts of cultural materials and methods. Richardson witnessed to the traumatic process by which the English middle class strenuously engaged its own destinies with those of the aristocracy. Sterne witnessed to the powerful upwelling of a skepticism which challenged the confident logocentrism of his age. Lawrence would witness to the violence visited upon the human spirit by the mechanization of human life. The peculiar interest inhering in a study of the concussive crisis-trope derives in large part from the fact that the novelists themselves were acutely conscious that they were living through times of crisis in broad cultural and historical terms.

George Meredith suffered and witnessed to a literary crisis pertaining to the very ontology of authorship, a crisis that permeated his thinking and writing style. His novels thus anxiously enter into dialogue with themselves. Allon White notes:

> In Meredith we can find many such moments of obscure duality, splitting voices, inner and outer selves, schizoid representation and cleavages of subjectivity which reveal him as at times closer to Maurice Blanchot than to his Victorian contemporaries . . . . Meredith's 'dialogical novels' are full of the most unexpected eruptions and diversions which can be traced back to a conflict of domains and authority in the writing. *He is witness to a 'legitimation crisis'* in which the traditional, easily assumed mantle of single author/ity would no longer quite fit.[9] (emphasis added)

Meredith's agonized dialogues with his culture can be seen intensely focused in his own *crisis*-language.

The most potent image for crisis as dialectical turning point takes the form of Revolution.[10] This violent image bears directly upon Meredith's own *crisis*-speculations. Historically, the term "revolution" itself shifted from meaning a gradual change to meaning a rapid, violent disruption. A revolution is a turning point and a crisis; it suggests confusion (aporia), and the dialectical moment is one in which truth and error are inextricably mixed. As if to acknowledge this vertiginous principle, Meredith builds into *The Egoist* (1879) the dizzying, wit-driven, rapid-fire tempo of a Restoration comedy.

As a poet, Meredith must have acutely suffered the continual crisis described by Christopher Clausen. On two occasions he directly confronted the great noun in expressing his opinion of the revolutionary conflict between communism and capitalism. In the first of these poems, Meredith champions the communist system that promised to rid the world of economic crisis itself. In the second, he acknowledges that communism itself ironically forces upon Russia the judgment of a crisis. An undated manuscript poem, "The Capitalist" satirizes exorbitant and irresponsible power manipulated via purposive economic crises staged by the capitalistic overlords of production and consumption. Meredith champions the principle that engaged Zola's naturalistic attention in *Germinal* and which Croce skeptically questioned. A few lines from "The Capitalist" can suggest Meredith's purpose:

> A capitalist was I:
>   A mighty King of Cash:
> When Stock I would sell, or buy,
>   The nation ran close upon smash.
> . . . .
> *'Twas I begat that thing*
>   *Which men a Crisis call:*
> Likewise I pulled a string
>   And Panic o'ershadow'd them all.
>   (emphasis added)

Meredith's condemnation of the boom-and-bust cycles of capitalism derived in part from his sympathy with the Russian Revolution of 1905. In another poem, "The Crisis," he eschewed the satire and irony of "The Capitalist" for a somber exhortation to the Spirit of Russia on behalf of revolutionary uprisings against an outworn system of exploitation. A few lines adequately illustrate Meredith's hortatory tone.

> Spirit of Russia, now has come
> The day when thou canst not be dumb.
> Around thee foam the torrent tide,
> Above thee its fell fountain, Pride.
> . . . .
> Those rulers in all forms of lust,
> Who trod thy children down to dust
> On the red Sunday . . . .
> . . . .
> The countertides of hate arrest,
> Give to thy sons a breathing breast,
> And him resembling, in His sight,
> Say to thy land, Let there be Light.[11]

Among English poets, Meredith is perhaps unique in focusing a poetical crisis-rhetoric upon an historical revolution involving a system that seemed to depend upon systemic crisis. He thereby witnesses directly to the connection between crisis and consciousness.[12]

The crisis-rhetoric Meredith employs in his fiction concentrates not upon communism but upon a special form of capitalism, though with no less revolutionary an implication. He turns the *crisis*-trope in a new direction, linking it with high comedy by structuring *The Egoist*[13] via carefully thought-out narrative patterns. In order to achieve a strict discipline of form, the hyper-clever Meredith drew upon the formal resources of the neoclassical theater of Molière and Congreve. In his first chapter, he furnishes a summary of his influential essay on "The Idea of Comedy and the Uses of the Comic Spirit." Laughter, he insists, serves society as a form of intellectual clarification and emotional therapy. The perfect comedy will achieve a dispassionate and clear-sighted perception of folly, sentimentality, and conceit. Starting from these premises, Meredith then narrates a story with a potently modern crisis-theme: men harm themselves by repressing women's natural impulses and natural intelligence.

If *crisis* can serve the loose structures of a sentimental novelist like Richardson, it can also serve the more tightly controlled purposes of a novelist as disciplined as Austen. In the case of Meredith, a *crisis*-rhetoric functions together with other techniques: apothegms, scenic construction, figurative language, and recurrent symbols and metaphors, together with sharply contrasting passages of ornate description and lifelike dialogue. Admirers of Meredith praise these methods by which he makes art and intellect dance together in literary forms that approach aesthetic abstractions. Adhering generally to the strict laws of classical drama, he dazzles his reader while developing radical beliefs concerning sexual domination and the liberation of women.

Despite its fantastic language, *The Egoist* reduces to the simplest comic fable. Sir Willoughby Patterne, spoiled heir to Patterne Hall and foremost personage in the county, has been jilted by Constancia Durham; he in turn jilts Laetitia Dale so that he can marry Clara Middleton; subsequently, Willoughby is jilted by Clara; at the end, the Egoist is reduced to marrying Laetitia not on his own peremptory social terms but on her prudent economic terms. The entire story, despite its elaborate surfaces, thus boils down to a sobering Marxist fable and a tropological sequence. Willoughby moves from metaphor (rank egotism) to metonymy (courtship of one woman at a time) to synecdoche (the three women taken collectively as representing a hostile society) to irony (a fleeting moment of false self-criticism that actually leaves him mired in his original egotism).

Among the various perspectives which Meredith induces by positioning *crisis* at five crucial junctures in *The Egoist*, some have to do with scenic elaboration, character psychology, thematic ideas, narrative arrangement, and the operation of Meredith's punitive Comic Spirit. Within the context of the fifty chapters that comprise *The Egoist*, Meredith uses *crisis* to highlight and valorize five contexts contrasting the consciousness of the plodding Egoist Willoughby with that of quick-witted persons such as Clara Middleton. The five *crisis*-contexts thus form a symmetrical arrangement:

chap. 5   chap. 21   chap. 28   chap. 37   chap. 43

Such balanced emphasis can hardly be fortuitous.

Several of Meredith's personages possess the wit to perceive imbroglios as crisis, but he singles out only three: Clara Middleton, Horace de Craye, and (ironically) Willoughby himself. Meredith uses *crisis* to signal Willoughby's heedlessness as he precipitates crises in other people's lives; he also contrasts the Egoist's clumsiness with Clara's oppressed but graceful wit. Early on, Meredith establishes that Sir Willoughby Patterne has been reared to be selfish and insensitive. As a result of his insensitivity, Willoughby repeatedly causes trouble for other people. His forte is to exploit the readiness of other people to aid the "bettermost" among society's select few. By his impulsive proposal of marriage to Clara, he creates a dilemma for the eager but puzzled young woman and also manipulates her sinecure-seeking father.

> Willoughby aired his amiable superlatives in the eye of Miss Middleton; he had a leg. He was the heir of successful competitors. He had a style, a tone, an artist tailor, an authority of manner; he had in the hopeful ardour of the chase among a multitude a freshness that gave him advantage; and together with his undeviating energy when there was a prize to be won and possessed, these were scarce resistible. He spared no pains, for he was adust and athirst for the winning-post. He courted her father, aware that men likewise, and parents preeminently, have their preference for the larger offer, the deeper pocket, the broader lands, the respectfuller consideration. Men, after their fashion, as well as women, distinguish the bettermost, and aid him to succeed, as Dr. Middleton certainly did in the *crisis of the memorable question proposed to his daughter* within the month of Willoughby's reception at Upton Park. (p. 33; emphasis added)

At the outset, Willoughby appears as both willing to subject other people to his rule and also as being self-centered on the point of George Eliot's question as to what moment in a life should be regarded as a crisis. Much of *The Egoist* narrates Clara's agonized efforts, once she discovers how crudely egotistical her suitor can be, to break off their engagement.

Having established that the Egoist's problem is a crisis-problem, Meredith proceeds in chapter 21 to use *crisis* to shift Clara to center stage. The effect is, as it were, to reverse Richardson's shifting of crisis-management from Clarissa to Lovelace. Meredith contrasts Willoughby's obtuse assumption that other human beings should remain subject to his whims with Clara's "quick" temperament which seeks some degree of freedom to compose her own life-shaping crises. By way of intertextual analogy: in Richardson's *Clarissa*, following Clarissa's being raped by Lovelace, Clarissa writes and then tears into symbolic shreds a letter to her confidante Anna Howe; likewise, Clara Middleton writes and then tears up a desperate letter to her friend Lucy Darleton. Clara has been contemplating an escape to Switzerland but somewhat like Clarissa discovers that she is trapped at Patterne Hall.

Meredith posits the existence of "quick natures" who are ironically conscious of the crucial moment in human life which must plausibly be designated as a *crisis* and then seized as an opportunity for decisive action. He shows how such quick-minded persons structure their own lives around unavoidable crises. Meredith judges Clara's personality and character in terms of her fine crisis-consciousness:

> After a fall of tears, upon looking at the scraps, she dressed herself, and sat by the window and watched the blackbird on the lawn as he hopped from shafts of dewy sunlight to the long-stretched dewy tree-shadows, considering in her mind that dark dews are more meaningful than bright, the beauty of the dews of woods more sweet than meadow-dews. It signified only that she was quieter. *She had gone through her crisis in the anticipation of it.* That is how quick natures will often be cold and hard, or not much moved, *when the positive crisis arrives*, and why it is that they are prepared for astonishing leaps over the gradations which should render their conduct comprehensible to us, if not excuseable. (p. 169; emphases added)

To the general understanding of crisis as an enabling experience, Meredith adds the assertion that one's anticipation of crisis constitutes an element of moral consciousness. The "quick" Clara Middleton desires to be in love, even with Willoughby, but not at the price of her freedom. If not a room of one's own, Meredith suggests that a person entangled like Clara in the Egoist's manipulations ought at least to enjoy, as it were, a crisis of one's own.

Having established crisis-awareness as a key to moral awareness (Willoughby lacks it; Clara beautifully possesses it), Meredith goes on to center his account of Willoughby's oppression of Clara in explicit *crisis-terms*. He constructs chapter 28, recounting Clara's attempt to run away to London, so that a third party, Willoughby's Irish friend Colonel Horace de Craye, himself perceives Clara's plight in terms of crisis. Thus, a presumably neutral perception, distinct from Willoughby's and Clara's, enlarges Meredith's theme.

Meredith introduces complicated intellectual pleasure to the historical range of crisis-emotions. When the runaway Clara fetches up at the railway station and the concerned de Craye has guessed before anyone else at Patterne Hall where she might be, he confronts her there. Desiring to help Clara, he jauntily offers either to accompany her to London or to escort her back to Willoughby's house. Meredith emphasizes that the mercurial de Craye shares with Clara and other "quick natures" an acutely intellectual crisis-consciousness: "The bright illumination of his face was that of the confident man confirmed in a *risky guess in the crisis of doubt and dispute*" (p. 228; emphasis added).

Clara wearily judges it best to return to Patterne Hall and her Clarissa-like confinement. For the moment her quickness has been considerably diminished by a social system that encourages egoistic oppression, but Meredith has also established that more than one person possesses the crisis-consciousness that might countervail against egoism. Grounds for Willoughby's downfall have been prepared.

Meredith uses his crisis-trope to expose the Egoist's false valuation of things and people. He exposes Willoughby as a man who manipulates conventions for his personal ends but who in turn becomes imprisoned, through his own obtuseness, within his narrow social role. Obliquely, Meredith does provide some slight hints that Willoughby may in fact be capable of enlightenment. At the end of chapter 29, an anxious Willoughby resolves to change his conduct so as to cancel his "old world" and establish a "new one" (p. 248). However, Meredith's readers usually interpret such hints as ironic digs at an irredeemable Egoist. Appropriately skeptical readers remain unconvinced that the Egoist actually improves in wisdom despite his eventual adjustments to enforced restraints upon his marital options.

More convincing is Meredith's comic device, in chapter 37, of showing Willoughby's attempted expropriation of crisis-awareness from Clara and de Craye to himself. To Willoughby's narcissism, Meredith adds hypochondria, the medical equivalent of narcissism, as another of Willoughby's failings. Increasingly paranoid as his house of cards begins to totter, the Egoist mistakenly decides that de Craye is now his rival for Clara's hand. He then meanly decides "to do her intolerable hurt." Even so, when the witty Mrs. Mountstuart Jenkinson accuses Willoughby of using his scientific laboratory merely as a means of escape from social responsibility, Willoughby feels threatened: "The remark set him throbbing and thinking that a *prolongation of his crisis exposed him* to the approaches of some organic malady, possibly heart-disease" (p. 313; emphasis added). Meredith achieves a broad comic effect by ironically reversing the terms of medical crisis. In this case, a moral crisis threatens to trigger a medical crisis. The Egoist never looks more inanely self-absorbed than in this episode where Meredith parodies Richardson's originating device of having Lovelace expropriate from Clarissa the power of determining what moment is or is not a crisis, as well as in what a crisis will actually consist.

Meredith rounds out this part of his trope with a passage that depicts Willoughby, like Hamlet in the fifth act, surrounded by his enemies. Willoughby now appears as one who continues to conceive of crisis-experience not as an ensemble but as a solo. Superstitiously thinking that the stars have conspired against him, he spitefully seeks to "vanquish" Clara while she is in a beaten mood. With his intelligence "obscured," he is virtually defenseless in the "present crisis." Word having leaked out concerning his proposal to Laetitia while still engaged to Clara, the Egoist is finally to be exposed, punished, and, if redeemable, redeemed.

> He depended entirely on his agility to elude the thrusts that assailed him. Had he been able to believe in the treachery of the Powers above, he would at once have seen design in these deadly strokes, for *his feelings had rarely been more acute than at the present crisis*; and he would have led away Clara, to wrangle it out with her, relying on Vernon's friendliness not to betray him to her father: but a wrangle with Clara promised no immediate fruits, nothing agreeable; and the lifelong trust he had reposed in his protecting genii obscured his intelligence to evidence he would otherwise have accepted on the spot, on the faith of his delicate susceptibility to the mildest impressions which wounded him. (p. 369; emphasis added)

Willoughby avoids any enabling dialectical turn against turn vis-à-vis Clara that might make redemption possible. Having lost control of his entourage, Willoughby flounders helplessly and must at the last humble himself to the weary but willing Laetitia Dale. Meredith's tight structure in *The Egoist* represents a genuine advance in the history of the crisis-trope. He depicts in Willoughby a human being whose unhappy fate results from his failure to develop a mature crisis-consciousness. More correctly, perhaps, the Egoist's failure is that he never makes the effort.

2. "[she] guessed that her servant's life was at a crisis"

Approaching the problem from the opposite end of the economic spectrum, George Moore draws upon advanced aesthetic theories originating in France. He insists that crisis-consciousness is a property exclusively of the literary imagination. *Esther Waters* (1894) delineates the pathetic life of a scullery maid within the context of a society ruining itself by feverishly gambling away its economic and moral substance. Esther's sad story is a "long recital of isolated triumphs of integrity surrounded by long and discouraging wastes of insecurity and disappointment."[14] Like a drudge out of Zola's deterministic world, or like Defoe's Moll Flanders who never enjoys sufficient leisure for sustained reflection, Esther Waters never develops a distancing or ironical narrative perspective on her own drudging existence.

Moore echoes Eliot's belief that crisis-consciousness enables the possibility of restructuring a human life, but Moore both ironizes Eliot's idea and literalizes its metaphorical dimension. He shows Esther Waters herself as entirely unacquainted with the great noun. Only another character perceives Esther's experience in terms of crisis. Significantly, this unique personage is herself a novelist.

In chapter 22, Moore depicts Esther Waters's current employer, Miss Rice of 41 Avondale Road, London, as a genteel spinster who reads and writes novels. Like Esther herself a "quiet, instinctive" Englishwoman with a strong, warm nature "under the appearance of formality and reserve," Miss Rice shows genuine but unsentimental interest in her servant. Thus she represents both one of Moore's implied moral norms and a perfect example of metonymic objectivity. Esther inwardly labors to decide whom to marry—Fred Parsons or William Latch—while also yearning to visit her six-year-old son currently in the care of a certain Mrs. Lewis. The novelist Miss Rice perceives Esther's perplexity and acts upon her perception.

> And the desire to know what was happening became intolerable. She went to her mistress to ask for leave to go out. Very little of her agitation betrayed itself in her demeanour, but Miss Rice's sharp eyes had *guessed that her servant's life was at a crisis*. She laid her book on her knee, asked a few kind, discreet questions, and after dinner Esther hurried towards the Underground.[15] (emphasis added)

Moore's intention seems unmistakable. Like Eliot, he firmly establishes that some willingness to restructure human life originates in crisis-consciousness. In addition, rhetorical or tropological sophistication such as Miss Rice's authentic writerly perspective may be a requirement for such an outlook, at once privileged and privileging. Unlike the exhausted, stupified Esther Waters, Miss Rice can deliberately move from metaphorical identification with her pathetic servant to a distanced irony, from which point she can initiate social change.

Like other writers before and after him, Moore exhibits an interest in etymology, stipulating for the etymological meaning of *crisis* by specifying that Miss Rice's questions are *discreet*, a word that literally means in the Latin "to show good judgment." His plot dictates that a single appearance of the great noun occurs at the main turning point so as to point up a sharp contrast between Esther's hapless disorientation and Miss Rice's writerly sense of narrative order. By contrast with Eliot's Lawyer Johnson, Moore's Miss Rice employs *crisis* not to manipulate but to enable the desires of a less sophisticated person. Happily, she devises a crisis-strategy less exploitative and to all appearances more humane.

3. "a crisis which drew near might bring the favourable turn"

The philosophy of naturalistic determinism urges that experience in effect happens to victims rather than being invented or chosen by free moral agents. The writerly dimension of crisis-rhetoric, implicit from the first in Richardson's amateur playwright Robert Lovelace, receives explicit expression in *Esther Waters*. The drudging Esther never develops crisis-consciousness. Moore's economical linking of fiction writing with crisis-consciousness had been elaborated in different terms three years earlier in George Gissing's grimly naturalistic *New Grub Street* (1891).[16] Gissing's career based itself in an unflinching realism and honest psychological portraiture. His novels express the tensions and miseries of his own life, including extreme poverty and tuberculosis. His groundbreaking study of Dickens (1898) provides the rationale for his own adoption of Dickens's example in writing about London's poor people.

Gissing's abiding theme is grounded in the belief that misery is the keynote of modern life. To this end, he dwells upon the cultural bleakness of urban life. Commonplace and low-life themes in *Demos* (1886) took the form of a bitter portrayal of socialist agitators and proletarian rioters. *The Nether World* (1889) dwells upon urban squalor. Like Dickens, Gissing employed familiar devices from popular novels (improbable coincidence, multiple plot lines, explicit commentary on the action), but he lacked Dickens's energy and buoyant belief in social reform. Although Gissing escaped somewhat from his own miseries via writing a charming autobiography, *The Private Papers of Henry Ryecroft* (1903), his more typical stance expresses itself in *New Grub Street*, which unflinchingly describes the pathos and squalor experienced by struggling writers trying to maintain high literary standards despite public indifference. *New Grub Street* starkly contrasts an amateur and a professional, an imprudently aspiring artist and a cynical hack. The serious novelist Edwin Reardon dies in poverty because he lacks both the energy to overcome obstacles to success and the resilience to adjust his literary standards. By contrast, Jaspar Milvain adapts his small talent to the market place and uses his connections to secure not only financial and social advantage but also the deceased Reardon's widow.

Like Moore in *Esther Waters*, Gissing could have structured this story of the "power of money" shadowed by the "demon of failure" by arranging for some perceptive observer comparable to Moore's Miss Rice to stipulate for a crisis in Reardon's wretched existence. However, Reardon is himself a novelist who possesses at least a rudimentary (albeit not self-reflexive) crisis-consciousness and sense of narrative crisis. In this novel of thirty-seven chapters, Gissing structures Reardon's ordeal via four *crisis*-images (chaps. 9, 12, 29, and 32) that occasion judgment of Reardon's character while also signalling episodes in his sad decline from an artistic crisis to a financial crisis and finally a terminal medical crisis. His passage from metaphor (artistic preciosity) to metonymy (money as Other) arrests itself far short of reflexive irony or even synecdochic grasp of the economic facts of life.

Whatever intrinsic value a novel composed by Moore's Miss Rice might possess, it would presumably express her ability to project crisis-awareness into the organization of a narrative, thereby providing at least an artistic illusion of order. In chapter 9 of *New Grub Street*, Gissing elaborates an episode that reveals Edwin Reardon as a novelist who is unable to project his disoriented crisis-consciousness away from his own personal misery into the structure and meaning of his work-in-progress. In the throes of composition, the only crisis he anticipates would be the failure or drying up of his own "out-wearied imagination." Gissing's thoroughgoing literalization of the novelist as crisis-strategist is, in some respects, unique. Gissing writes:

> The title was always a matter for headracking when the book was finished; he had never yet chosen it before beginning.
>
> For a week he got on at the desired rate; then came once more the *crisis he had anticipated.*

A familiar symptom of the malady which falls upon out-wearied imagination. (emphasis added)

Gissing's narrator goes on to analyze certain ontological perplexities of Reardon's imagination. These include his being led astray by chimerical subject matter as well as his own excessive critical scrupulosity toward literary style. He experiences months of such frustration, which he construes as a sign of exhaustion. The crisis he inwardly dwells upon is not the imaginative crisis he might use to structure his novel but rather an impasse of the imagination itself: "The expected crisis came, even now that he was savagely determined to go on at any cost, to *write*, let the result be what it would. His will prevailed" (pp. 102-3; emphasis Gissing's).

Gissing continues to describe Reardon's stubborn working method in mechanical terms. Nevertheless, it is Reardon's friend Biffin who correctly characterizes Reardon's work at a deeper level: "the best things you have done are altogether in conflict with novelistic conventionalities" (p. 121). Reardon wishes to revolutionize the novel as a form. The negative aspect of his radical techniques, however, is that he can not follow Scott's or Eliot's example in building a structure of crisis-consciousness into his fiction. He can only (and perhaps as a result) undergo the anguish of crisis in his own bleak quandary.

In chapter 12, aptly named "Work Without Hope," Gissing shifts the emphasis as Reardon's stifling crisis-consciousness expresses itself in economic terms. Although enjoying a period of relative solvency, Reardon and his wife Amy nevertheless continually worry about money. In one scene, the anxious couple discuss Reardon's chances of marketing an essay on philosophy. Gissing urges his belief concerning the baleful power of money itself: "Blessed money! root of all good, until the world invent some saner economy" (p. 128). Like an embodiment of capitalism as condemned by Marx, manic-depressive Reardon becomes explicitly a crisis-strategist but one whose concern centers exclusively upon the threat of recurring financial insolvency: "a month or two more will see us at the same crisis again" (p. 130).

Gissing persists in this definition of crisis as economic disorder throughout the middle part of *New Grub Street*. A passage in chapter 29 refers to the loss of Amy's small inheritance because of "a crisis in affairs that were already unstable," but the emphasis then shifts to a medical meaning. Historically, the crisis-rhetoric that is part of the rhetoric of fiction includes episodes and scenes of illness, disease, and death. Notable examples would be Clarissa Harlowe in Richardson's *Clarissa*, Mr. Harley in Mackenzie's *The Man of Feeling*, Bazarov's death from typhus in Ivan Turgenev's *Fathers and Sons*, Hans Castorp's contraction of tuberculosis in Thomas Mann's *The Magic Mountain*, and the death of Asa Leventhal's nephew in Bellow's *The Victim*. The medical definition of *crisis* from the *OED* will bear repeating at this point. In pathology, *crisis* refers to that juncture in a disease when an alteration occurs leading either to recovery or death. *Crisis* may refer to any marked or sudden change occurring in the progress of a disease and also to the phenomena accompanying such change. The *OED* offers the following 1543 definition: "*Crisis* signifyeth iudgemente, and in this case, it is used for a sodayne chaunge in a disease." This ambiguous yoking of objective condition and subjective judgment partly characterizes the history of the trope.

Turgenev's *Fathers and Sons* (1862) provides a contrastive example that effectively throws light on Gissing's intention. In Turgenev's indictment of Nihilism, the nihilist Bazarov, even while reclining upon his deathbed, contemptuously scorns his pious father's solicitous hopes for his son's recovery. The old man manipulates his own responses via the great noun.

> "There, to think now!" murmured Bazarov; "what a word can do! He's found it; *he's said 'crisis,' and is comforted.* It's an astounding thing how man believes in words."[17] (emphasis added)

By contrast with Bazarov's confidence, in *New Grub Street* Reardon capitulates to a medical crisis. Unlike Robert Lovelace or Daniel Deronda, Reardon can not induce, seize, and shape crisis. He can only wait and hope, so that life merely happens to him.

> Another morning broke. It was possible, said the doctors (a second had been summoned), that *a crisis which drew near might bring the favourable turn*; but Amy formed her own opinion from the way in which the nurse expressed herself. She felt sure the gravest fears were entertained. (p. 373; emphasis added)

Reardon's tropological decline from an intense if frustrated concern with a crisis of the literary imagination, through a crisis of economic scarcity, terminates then in a medical crisis during which he no longer has the energy even to speak the word.

The qualitative differences between the defiant Bazarov and the spiritless Reardon can be comprehended by reference to a twentieth-century definition of *crisis* provided by a major crisis-theorist, the social scientist Jürgen Habermas. In *Legitimation Crisis*, Habermas provides a medical definition according to which any illness may seem objective, something contracted through external influences, but also problematically subjective, so that the patient's subjective awareness is not entirely excluded from the process:

> [The] patient experiences his powerlessness *vis-à-vis* the objectivity of the illness only because he is a subject condemned to passivity and temporarily deprived of the possibility of being a subject in full possession of his powers.
>
> We therefore *associate with crises the idea of an objective force* that deprives a subject of some part of his normal sovereignty. To conceive of *a process as a crisis* is tacitly to give it a normative meaning—the *resolution of a crisis effects a liberation of the subject* caught up in it.[18] (emphases added)

This startling definition carries serious implications for the present study, and Habermas will be discussed at some length in my chapter 7 as establishing an intellectual background for modern crisis-inducing anomie. In the case of Bazarov, Turgenev depicts a compelling if obnoxious human being undergoing medical crisis, one who nevertheless retains full possession of his subjective powers; by contrast, Gissing's Reardon does not achieve any such dignity but simply dies.

By comparison with an artist like Henry James, the desperate Gissing lacks the gift for recognizing or representing the gradual unfolding of self-understanding.[19] James himself, as his autobiography will reveal, cultivated a familiarity with Eliot's *Middlemarch* and *Daniel Deronda*, where he would have found a developed *crisis*-trope rendering the slow growth of self-reflexive wisdom. James records his affection for *Felix Holt, the Radical*, where he could have found Eliot's initial discovery of the concussive potential of the great noun. In the first chapter of *New Grub Street*, Gissing briefly establishes that Eliot constitutes a strong presence in the economic ordeal he depicts. The commercial writer Jasper Milvain expresses the prudent opinion that only "if [one] can be a George Eliot" can one expect to be simultaneously both a serious and a commercially successful novelist.

Ironically, Gissing's own critical intelligence surfaces in many places throughout *New Grub Street* in concepts (criticism, choice) that Paul de Man identifies with *crisis* itself and that Eliot uses to enrich the crisis-trope in *Daniel Deronda*. Repeatedly, Gissing analyzes Reardon's tormented psyche in terms not of Reardon's own critical imagination but of Reardon's sensitivity to criticism of his own performance as a man, husband, and author. Repeatedly, too, and as if parodying Mordecai Cohen's speech in *Daniel Deronda*, Gissing harps on the related words *choice* and *choose*. Reardon's most deep-seated problem as an artist and a husband may arguably be his inability to cope with the problematics inherent in freedom of choice, the root-concept inherent in *crisis*. But if Gissing lacked James's understanding of the slow growth of self-understanding, he could depict in compelling terms the dire consequences of such a deficiency. Gissing's characters decidedly lack the gift that had distinguished a certain type of novelistic character from Richardson's Lovelace to Moore's lady novelist, but Gissing himself proves to be a crisis-rhetorician worthy of study.

At about this same time, another novelist, one who inherited the mantle of high art which Eliot had passed down through Meredith, begins to compose ambitious narratives in which characters make splendid efforts to develop the valuable crisis-consciousness that Meredith's Egoist deliberately eschewed, Moore reserved exclusively to the literary imagination, Gissing's Reardon at best naïvely yearned for, and, as Matthew Arnold thought, strongly makes for humane culture.

4. "appreciation of the crisis"

Henry James extends the aesthetic richness of the figuration I am examining. Like Arnold and Eliot, James intensely admired the human ability (synecdochic competence) to remain calm and perceptive amidst turmoil. He lamented the scarcity of such aplomb in modern life and rejoiced when he found its active presence. Like Eliot, too, he found the great noun serviceable in his own personal life. In his autobiography he remarks that once, in an awkward situation involving men of public affairs, though being not quite adequate to the situation he yet managed to perceive "the crisis enriched by sundry other apprehensions."[20] James followed Eliot and Meredith in integrating the great noun into his major fictions, most notably *The Portrait of a Lady* and *The Ambassadors*. In the history of the trope, James represents that turning point where danger yields to opportunity, where emotional apprehension yields to aesthetic appreciation.

In examining the processes by which some novelists became crisis-strategists, I endeavor to remain curious but cautious about the question of sources and influences. Excepting that novelists presumably learn from reading novels, any writer's reasons for exploiting the great noun remain more than a little mysterious. No novelist has explained the practice. Novelists from Richardson onward incorporate the problematical trope into their fictions, but to what degree does a novelist take the device over from an admired or challenging precursor? Even those novelists who discuss the preconstructional stages of their work remain silent on this point. In the case of James, though, a novelist records his deep familiarity with the book where Eliot stipulated for the concussive noun's greatness.

James's admiration for Eliot's "applied and achieved art" is lovingly documented in his autobiography. He describes how he appreciated *Middlemarch* and *Daniel Deronda*, considering himself a "Derondist of Derondists." He writes of meeting Eliot herself and of the warm memories thereby stirred up of having read *Felix Holt* when it first appeared in 1866. For James himself, it became a major text of reference.

> Middlemarch [*sic*] had not then appeared—we of the faith were still to enjoy that saturation, and Felix Holt the radical [*sic*] was upwards of three years old; the impetus proceeding from this work, however, was still fresh enough in my pulses to have quickened the palpitation of my finding myself in [her] presence. I had rejoiced without reserve in Felix Holt—the illusion of reading which, outstretched on my then too frequently inevitable bed at Swampscott during a couple of very hot days of the summer of 1866, comes back to me, followed by that in sooth of sitting up again, at no great ease, to indite with all promptness a review of the delightful thing, the place of appearance of which nothing could now induce me to name, shameless about the general fact as I may have been at the hour itself: over such a feast of fine rich natural tone did I feel myself earnestly bend. Quite unforgettable to me the art and truth with which the note of this tone was struck in the beautiful prologue and the bygone appearances, a hundred of the outward and visible signs of the author's own young rural and midmost England, made to hold us by their harmony. The book was not, if I rightly remember, altogether genially greeted, but I was to hold fast to the charm I had thankfully suffered it, *I had been conscious of absolutely needing it*, to work. (*Autobiography*, pp. 574-75; emphasis added)

Undoubtedly, I believe, James derived from *Felix Holt*, at some level of artistic consciousness, an impetus toward using Eliot's methods, not excluding her *crisis*-figuration.

James anticipated the main principles of reader-response criticism. In his preface to the New York edition of *The Portrait of a Lady* (1881), he speaks of his "relation with the reader" and of the "artful patience," the "brick upon brick" and "little touches and inventions and enhancements," which ensure the desired relation with his audience. Preceding novelists had used *crisis* to establish a forceful if not precisely defined relation to the reader. The great noun is one means by which a given type of reader is inscribed into a text, and in *The Portrait of a Lady*, James carefully inscribes a reader who must become aware of a complex crisis-trope.

James composes the story of Isabel Archer, an imaginative American girl whose experience of Europe is intended to make possible a "free exploration of life." At the end, she deliberately returns to Italy where she has discovered that the freedom she anticipated may represent, in the form of a bad marriage, a prison of suppressive custom and even deadly restriction. James traces Isabel's transition from the elation of youthful freedom to the restraint of mature obligation. He does this by showing how Isabel, a curious mixture of naïve imagination and critical intelligence, attempts to structure her life as if it were a narrative. Somewhat like Eliot's Esther Lyon or the novelist Miss Rice in Moore's *Esther Waters*, who perceives as a crisis Esther's predicament with her child, Isabel imaginatively attempts to structure her own experiences as being, at one level, a narrative sequence.

The Portrait of a Lady consists of two plots, one made up largely of explicit crises, external actions, and public gestures; the other, enabled by and grounded in the first, consists of implicit crises, private meditations, and inward judgments. James requires his reader to respond to authorial emphases on selected episodes and also to recognize both naïvete and literary imagination as elements in Isabel's personal psychology. Following Meredith's example, he signals five separate crisis-contexts highlighting Isabel's relations to prospective husbands (Lord Warburton, Caspar Goodwood, Gilbert Osmond). As James manipulates his narrative point of view, *crisis*-images operate like informing narrative frames which enter into Isabel's own structuring of her life-script. Three of Isabel's five episodes make a cohesively tropological pattern. When Lord Warburton proposes to the penniless Isabel, the flustered girl recognizes the security such a union would provide but nevertheless puts Warburton off. She "deferred the need of really facing her crisis."[21] In the life-script she has initially imagined for herself, marriage to Lord Warburton would work against the "free exploration of life" she desires. Like Blake's Thel, she begins her adventure in a painfully confused state of timidity and boldness.

James reiterates and deepens Isabel's propensity to dramatize her own romantic attachments by means of Isabel's perceiving her confrontation with Caspar Goodwood as a crisis. At this point, Isabel feels more confident because she has inherited a significant fortune (sixty thousand pounds) from Ralph Touchett's father. She can remain strong in her resolve not to settle for second best. When the vigorous American youth Goodwood suddenly appears in Florence and insists that Isabel accept his proposal of marriage, Isabel's predetermined plan holds firmly enough so that she can resist even his insistence. Her crisis-imagination shapes their encounter: "His jaw showed the same voluntary cast as in earlier days; but a crisis like the present had in it of course something grim" (p. 276).

Shortly after her rejection of this second marriage proposal, Isabel performs the act that arguably represents the main critical juncture of an external plot of action. In recoil from Caspar Goodwood's hard importunity, she impulsively decides to marry Gilbert Osmond (p. 285). The qualitative differences between Isabel's frame of mind during her Warburton-crisis and her Goodwood-crisis, taken together, and her prolonged marital ordeal with her tyrannical husband Osmond, provide a measure of James's tragedy of awakening consciousness. Near the end of the novel (p. 445) the tyrannical Osmond forbids Isabel from journeying to England where she intends to comfort her ailing benefactor Ralph Touchett. Isabel forcefully exhibits her own powers of observation and her practice of dramatizing events as moments of crisis: "she was fully conscious of the weight of the occasion; *she knew that between them they had arrived at a crisis*. Its gravity made her careful" (emphasis added). In this ordeal of spoiled mutuality, Isabel discovers the depths of Osmond's tyranny. Her subsequent decision to flout her husband's prohibition by sailing for England expresses both desperation and courage. As in Isabel's two earlier romantic crises, James invokes the etymological meaning of the great noun by using it to denote not only a dire predicament but, of greater importance, an individual's judgment and action.

James reinforces Isabel's three-stage crisis-plot with two other contexts showing Isabel's awareness of the role of crisis in other people's affairs. When Ralph Touchett's father takes to his deathbed at Gardencourt, Isabel notes "throughout the house that perceptible hush which precedes a crisis" (p. 150). To be thus perceptive is to be, as Isabel aspires to be, one of the "finer natures" that, as James asserts in this same context, shine forth at "the larger times." James insists upon Isabel's possessing one requisite for the moral imagination, a quickened consciousness when other people are experiencing a crisis, together with a willingness to stand modestly aside. When Harriet Stackpole is momentarily flustered upon encountering Isabel in the company of Lord Warburton at a Roman excavation, Isabel quickly perceives the awkwardness of the moment. James depicts Isabel retiring into the shade while the other two people cope with their embarrassment. She thus gives Harriet time to establish "her relation to the crisis" (p. 250).

So much for Isabel's own *crisis*-centered plot. Obviously, such a framework may have helped the novelist to compose the novel. Likewise, just as it clearly aids the youthful Isabel herself as she attempts to structure her own life, it might also assist any perplexed reader in comprehending James's intricate narrative emphases. But James has yet another string to his bow. His purpose is deeper than mere external plot action. Co-terminous with and superior to the crisis-centered plot of decisive action is a plot of thought or consciousness. Two shocking revelations characterize Isabel's inner drama: her discovery that some mysterious, perhaps improper, relation exists between her husband and Madame Merle, and her discovery that Osmond's daughter Pansy is, in fact, the illegitimate child of Osmond and Madame Merle.

Almost as if echoing John Stuart Mill or as if anticipating T. S. Kuhn's description of the process by which the discovery of anomaly within a scientific system leads to crisis (which in turn may lead to the paradigm shift that constitutes scientific revolution), James describes Isabel's first hint of something wrong with her marriage as being her perception of an "anomaly" in the social behavior of Osmond and Madame Merle: "What struck Isabel first was that he was sitting while Madame Merle stood; there was an anomaly in this that arrested her" (p. 342). Shortly thereafter, Isabel meditates throughout an entire night and, in the turning point or crisis-judgment of this plot of consciousness, she reaches the dangerous conclusion that she must not yield to her husband's cynical plan to marry his daughter to Lord Warburton. She must attempt to free herself from Osmond's moral tyranny. James's tragic vision turns upon Isabel's heroical if erroneous crisis-trope.

All writers operate according to a certain parsimony of vocabulary. A writer may use a relatively few words some hundreds or thousands of times but also use many other good and useful words sparingly if at all. *Crisis* would seem to be a word that all serious novelists use with parsimonious care. James was a writer who with comparatively few words yet managed in *The Ambassadors* to create extraordinary literary effects, not excluding ontological disorientation. Hugh Kenner notes:

> The words he kept within easy reach, so to speak—say 20 per cent of them—were the ones he put to use some 80 per cent of the time. They're the same ones we all keep handy. When James did want something fancy he could always hesitate and grope. In an instance I happen to have handy—2,339 words, most of Book II, Chapter I of the authoritative New York edition of his 1903 novel *The Ambassadors*—there are just 665 different words, all told. With no more than those, James somehow managed atmosphere, and narrative, and dialogue, and several instances of psychic crisis—and how he did that is instructive.[22]

Kenner does not mention James's use of *crisis* itself in *The Ambassadors*, but he could have found it to be a significant trope in that superb book.

Like Richardson's *Clarissa*, Scott's *The Heart of Midlothian*, Eliot's *Middlemarch*, Meredith's *The Egoist*, Forster's *A Passage to India*, or Bellow's *Humboldt's Gift*, James's *The Ambassadors* is arguably the author's masterpiece. Both *The Portrait of a Lady* and *The Ambassadors* depict the initiation of a naïve American into the problematical sophistication of European culture, but in certain technical respects the latter book is so far advanced in theme and form that one might expect to find an entirely different set of structural principles there. This is not entirely the case. In composing Lambert Strether's experience in *The Ambassadors*, James avails himself of virtually the same structural schema—five judicially spaced contexts signalled by the great noun—which structures Isabel Archer's initiation into adult mysteries. The pattern by book and chapter:

III,2   IV,2   VIII,1   IX,3   XI,4

This five-stage structure also closely resembles Meredith's in *The Egoist* and thus suggests that something like a tradition, genre, or a typology is in the making.

Leaving aside the wealth of nuanced Jamesian details, the story of Strether can be neatly summarized. Lambert Strether voyages from Massachusetts to Europe in order to retrieve the wayward son of Mrs. Newsome, Strether's employer and fiancée. Exposed to the charms of Paris, by gradual stages Strether's somewhat puritanical attitudes change. He falls in love with the idea of Europe, and he begins to understand why Chad Newsome refuses to return to the Newsome mills, money, and humorless commercial duties. When Chad finally agrees to return home, Strether shocks everyone concerned by urging that both of them ought instead to remain in Europe. From America, Mrs. Newsome sends another delegation to retrieve the two runaways. During consultations with Chad, Strether advises him to stay with his beloved Mme. de Vionnet, but he judges that he himself must finally resist the charms of Paris and of Maria Gostrey and instead return to America to face Mrs. Newsome.

Crisis derives from the Greek *krinein*, to judge, and *krites*, a judge. James literalizes this meaning by having the wise and good Mme. de Vionnet put Strether's dilemma squarely to him as a task of judgment at once moral and aesthetic. Strether must decide about the true nature of Chad's relation with the French woman, particularly its possible effect on the young man's moral character.

"Ah that's as you'll think best. You must judge."

She had finally given him her hand, which he held a moment. "How *much* I have to judge."

"Everything," said Madame de Vionnet: a remark that was indeed—with the refined disguised suppressed passion of her face—what he most carried away.[23]

Strether recognizes that he himself has been sent to judge, to decide, to bring matters to a turning point and thus both bring Chad out of a crisis (embroilment) and into his senses (judgment) so that ultimately Strether himself can find his own way out of a personal crisis (impasse).

James stipulates for Strether's crisis-consciousness as a functional component of his moral consciousness. Shortly after Strether has first seen Chad Newsome in Paris, he bemusedly debates with himself whether to telegraph Mrs. Newsome that he had seen Chad ("Awfully old—grey hair") as, painful to contemplate, a "hoary sinner." James's increase in artistic maturity over *The Portrait of a Lady* manifests itself in a more richly ambiguous texture; likewise, in the fact that, whereas youthful Isabel Archer thrills to a crisis, Lambert Strether gradually develops or discovers a more sober "appreciation of the crisis" to which he had committed himself. The crisis-trope is here linked with a revolutionary episteme of nineteenth-century aestheticism.

As in Eliot's novels, a crisis-passage shows James at his most analytical. Within the space of a few lines James defines the prudent Strether, a cautious man who prides himself on keeping clear of "error" so as never to be required to explain himself to anyone. Strether prefers to keep "the ground free of the wild weed of delusion." Most importantly, as a closet aesthete he is able to remain aloof and appreciate a crisis.

. . . the wild weed of delusion. . . . easily grew too fast, and the Atlantic cable now alone could race with it. That agency would each day have testified for him to something that was not what Woollett had argued. He was not at this moment absolutely sure that the effect of the morrow's—or rather of the night's—*appreciation of the crisis* wouldn't be to determine some brief missive. (p. 92; emphasis added)

At this juncture, *crisis* valorizes Strether as the one among James's characters most crucially alive to the risks of modern crisis-consciousness.

James constructs his central consciousness in terms of fine moral and aesthetic discriminations. He explicitly empowers Strether to distinguish between two chief aspects of crisis, dangerous predicaments and consequential decisions. *Crisis* may have originally meant the decision one makes so as to solve a problem, but then it probably shifted its meaning to the problem itself (dire circumstance). James exploits both dimensions of this putative meaning. Strether announces to Maria that Chad has requested "that I shall oblige him by kindly not bringing our business to a crisis till he has had a chance to see [Mme. de Vionnet and her daughter] again himself" (p. 113). If Strether can appreciate the aesthetics of a crisis, he also recognizes as it were that a crisis (precarious situation) can be brought to a crisis (turning point or moment of decision). James presses full authorial emphasis upon Eliot's theme, namely, the process by which one attempts to arrange one's life. His second stipulation of a crisis occurs in a context where Strether acquires "almost a new lease on life."

Even in his preliminary plan for *The Ambassadors*, James resorted to a *crisis*-figure. His original project for the novel, as shown in his notebook, included his thinking through of Strether's experience as "a kind of crisis in his personal history." James contrives for Strether initially to perceive, while still in Massachusetts, that he himself is exhausted by overwork and fatigue. The mission to Paris, ostensibly concerning a crisis in someone else's experience, can only alleviate his exhaustion. For the straitlaced Strether, this sounds suspiciously like a holiday. James, however, goes on in the notebooks to describe how Strether, intending no more than to fetch Chad back to his mother, instead discovers that "the whole crisis" confronts him with a very personal truth.

During the middle part of the story, Strether defers to Chad's wish of "not bringing our business to a crisis." However, Strether happily "rambled largely alone" so that he not only enjoys his freedom but has time and occasion to discover or decide that the "present crisis" might in fact be, as it were, an ordeal for him alone to experience and appreciate. James contrives for Strether to measure his own new-found freedom against the narrow life of his hide-bound friend, the cabined and confined Waymarsh. Strether notes that "one of the marks of the crisis" was Waymarsh's studied lapse of interest in Strether's concern over Mrs. Newcome. In the same context (at the center of the novel in book 8), Strether wittily employs an image of relative movement that depicts to himself his "advance" over his stodgy friend, as a result of his increasing appreciation of what is now becoming his own crisis. Waymarsh had worriedly reported Strether's failure of responsibility, but Strether himself decides to remain coolly patient so as to enjoy a bit of innocent superiority over Waymarsh.

James uses *crisis* to thematize his story in two ways. Strether must be shown as perceptive in his relations with other people in a difficult situation. Also, he must be shown as competent to judge whether a crisis threatens to take a happy or unhappy turn. James accomplishes the former thematic end by showing Strether analyzing Waymarsh's behavior.

> However this might be, at any rate, *one of the marks of the crisis* was a visible, a studied lapse, in Waymarsh, of betrayed concern. As if to make up to his comrade for the stroke by which he had played providence he now conspicuously ignored his movements, withdrew himself from the pretension to share them, stiffened up his sensibility to neglect, and, clasping his large empty hands and swinging his large restless foot, clearly looked to another quarter for justice. (p. 200; emphasis added)

Considering himself a competent dialectical observer more flexible and less dogmatic than Waymarsh, Strether does not miss the implications of Waymarsh's pendulously swinging foot. He himself is becoming more pragmatically, more metonymically, receptive than Waymarsh to life's possibilities.

With reference to a second thematic thread, James provides Strether with a witty figure of speech suggesting the improvement, however slight, that he has made over Waymarsh.

> It was all very funny, he knew, and but the difference, as he often said to himself, of tweedledum and tweedledee—an emancipation so purely comparative that it was like the advance of the door-mat on the scraper; yet the *present crisis was happily to profit by it* and the pilgrim from Milrose to know himself more than ever in the right. (p. 199; emphasis added)

Strether begins as one half of a "tweedledum and tweedledee" set, but he advances from metaphoric dullness to ironic liveliness. James establishes Strether as an American provincial who, at age fifty, is either newly discovering or newly experiencing the pragmatic, dialectical principle that everything changes and everything is relative.

Just as James organized Isabel Archer's crisis-centered experience in *The Portrait of a Lady* by means of a double plot, in *The Ambassadors* he likewise keeps in play an outward plot and an inward plot. From one readerly angle, Strether's growing discovery of his own opportunity to catch up on the experiences he had earlier denied himself constitutes the appeal of the novel. From another angle, neither James nor Strether ever loses sight of the "huge collective life" of Paris and the larger world outside of Strether's personal perspective. Such references as "the present crisis" reveal Strether's concern with the large social questions, e.g., whether Chad will return home to Woollett to take up the family business, how things stand between Chad and Mme. de Vionnet, whether Mrs.

Newsome will overlook Strether's failure to carry out her orders and still consider him as a prospective husband, and so on.

Eliot had linked *crisis* with deliberate manipulation of naïve persons by oratorical (spoken) language in *Felix Holt*. Via a fourth crisis-image in *The Ambassadors*, James depicts Strether himself as it were manipulating or casting himself into a momentary anxiety when he sees a letter, left unopened, that Mrs. Newsome had sent to her daughter Sarah Pocock, the second ambassador sent to investigate Strether's failed embassy of retrieval. James emphasizes Strether's half-fear, half-hope that Mrs. Newsome will disown him by breaking their engagement and removing him from the editorship of the *Revue* which she finances. James thus uses *crisis* to signify another stage in Strether's enlarging consciousness, on this occasion with respect to the huge collective Parisian life teeming outside his own fastidious mind. When Strether sees the unopened letter, he recalls that Mrs. Newsome had ceased to write such instructive missives to him.

> In his own room, at his own hotel, he had dozens of well-filled envelopes superscribed in that character; and there was actually something in the renewal of his interrupted vision of the character that played straight into the so frequent question of whether he weren't already disinherited beyond appeal. It was such an assurance as the sharp downstrokes of her pen hadn't yet had occasion to give him; but they somehow *at the present crisis stood for a probable absoluteness* in any decree of the writer. He looked at Sarah's name and address, in short, as if he had been looking hard into her mother's face, and then turned from it as if the face had declined to relax. (p. 246; emphasis added)

James insists on Strether's realization that Mrs. Newsome has in fact manipulated him, has made him a "prey to anxiety." He then painfully breathes "an air that damnably requires clearing"; he hopes that Mrs. Newsome will herself come to Paris so that a head-on collision will clear the air. Eliot had noted the "concussion of that great noun." Similarly, at that part of Strether's story where one expects a major turning point, Strether virtually echoes Eliot by thinking that if Mrs. Newsome does appear in Paris, "a clarifying scene of some sort would result from the concussion."

One salient philosophical definition of consciousness boils it down to a complex of focal and subsidiary awareness. The entire tradition of crisis-consciousness in the English novel reaches a peak in Strether's extraordinary awareness in a final episode. In this climactic scene, James depicts a confrontation, potentially violent but eventually harmonious, not between Strether and Mrs. Newsome but between Strether, who has gone into the country for a day of pleasure, and the two lovers (Chad and Mme. de Vionnet), who quite independently of Strether have done likewise. James contrives for them coincidentally—"a chance in a million"—to arrive at the same pleasant inn on the same idyllic river. The concussive effect of their shock of recognition alarms Strether as potentially "horrible." Strether could be suspected of spying upon the pair, but his quick thinking turns the dangerous event into a delightful comic escapade in which, at the last, "everything found itself sponged over by the mere miracle of the encounter."

This confrontation is prepared for by Strether's painterly sense of a pictorial, idyllic scene he views from the river bank. Pleased to see a small pleasure boat containing two persons drift into his purview, he judges it to be the completion of a perfect picture. However, the boat contains Chad and Mme. de Vionnet. This crisis-passage, arguably one of the high points in the history of the novel, deserves to be cited at some length. It demands of the reader a crisis-consciousness both vivid and subtle.

It was a sharp fantastic crisis that had popped up as if in a dream, and it had had only to last the few seconds to make him feel it as quite horrible. They were thus, on either side, *trying* the other side, and all for some reason that broke the stillness like some unprovoked harsh note. It seemed to him again, within the limit, that he had but one thing to do—to settle their common question by some sign of surprise and joy. He hereupon gave large play to these things, agitating his hat and his stick and loudly calling out—a demonstration that brought him relief as soon as he had seen it answered. The boat, in midstream, still went a little wild—which seemed natural, however, while Chad turned round, half springing up; and his good friend, after blankness and wonder, began gaily to wave her parasol. Chad dropped afresh to his paddles and the boat headed round, amazement and pleasantry filling the air meanwhile, and relief, as Strether continued to fancy, superseding mere violence. Our friend went down to the water under this odd impression as of violence averted—the violence of their having "cut" him, out there under the eye of nature, on the assumption that he wouldn't know it. He awaited them with a face from which he was conscious of not being able quite to banish this idea that they would have gone on, not seeing and not knowing, missing their dinner and disappointing their hostess, had he himself taken a line to match. That at least was what darkened his vision for a moment. Afterwards, after they had bumped at the landing-place and he had assisted their getting ashore, everything found itself sponged over by the mere miracle of the encounter. (pp. 308-9)

This beautiful scene, rendering the complex moment (perception, judgment, action) when Strether accomplishes his personal shift from provincial puritan to authentic cosmopolitan, provides us with perhaps the most beautiful crisis-image in literary history. Additionally, it aptly depicts a turning point viewed from the inside, and it culminates Strether's experience, a virtual paradigm case of tropological development from metaphor (American provincialism) through metonymy and synecdoche (Parisian cosmopolitanism) to irony (higher aesthetic morality).

The dialectical turning point as revolution proved extremely pertinent to Willoughby's twistings and turnings in *The Egoist*. The turning point as disorienting river proves equally relevant to Strether's culminating crisis-experience. A river never stops changing in its twisting pauses and turns, it thereby symbolizes a consciousness marked by destabilization and even violence. As a symbol of time, the river illustrates reality as a turning point where we are swept off our feet.[24] This characterization describes Strether's "sharp fantastic crisis" by the river where, as he watched in horror, "Chad turned round" and Chad's boat "headed round," leaving Strether feeling a sense of potential violence but, happily at the end, of "violence averted."

With consummate skill, James advances toward a unifying closure. He depicts Strether's experiences unquestionably as a stage in crisis-consciousness. In his painterly treatment of the scene, he literalizes and deepens Strether's developing powers of "appreciation" of a crisis. He replaces Chad's attempts to establish rhetorical linkages between crisis and business by a linkage between crisis and aesthetics. Strether's final explicit crisis takes place under the "eye of nature" but a nature modified by a painterly impressionism. His crisis-trope expresses an ambiguous mixture of truth and illusion. James emphasizes Strether's sense of being essentially right in his judgment of human relations even while remaining acutely aware that one can be dismally mistaken in such judgments. Concerning the delicate question of the lovers' sexual entanglement, he contrives for Strether to revert to something like Waymarsh's "studied lapse" of attention. Strether's face, by sharp contrast with Mrs. Newsome's imagined stiff face, decidedly relaxes vis-à-vis the attractive lovers, whom he enables to safely pretend they did not have a room reserved and instead choose to travel with Strether on the same train back to Paris once their excited meal is finished.

The remainder of the book devotes itself to suggesting numerous metonymic effects on Strether of his metamorphic crisis-experience. On the whole, James exhibits Strether as a cogent example, in Brown's terminology, of "the wintry ignorance from which passionate knowledge springs."[25] Given the exceptionally high status of *The Ambassadors* among English novels, James's crisis-trope can arguably be judged to represent not only the culmination of a nineteenth-century tradition beginning with Austen and including other art-novelists such as Eliot, Meredith, and Moore but also a high point (perhaps the highest point?) in this rhetorical tradition.

As I prepare to enter the conflicted twentieth century in my pursuit of the historical facts and principles constituting a crucial modern trope, I wish to reiterate my belief in an intimate connection between crisis-consciousness and consciousness in general. The broad context within which I now wish my critical survey to be seen is a world where external sanctions and authorities have virtually disappeared. This world has been adumbrated by Benedetto Croce: "We no longer believe in anything of that, and *what we have alone retained is the consciousness of ourselves, and the need to make that consciousness ever clearer and more evident*, a need for whose satisfaction we turn to science and art" (emphasis Croce's).[26]

4

A Conflicted Trope for a Violent New Age:
D. H. Lawrence and E. M. Forster

Eliot's great noun comes into a full efflorescence in the conflicted twentieth century. Throughout western culture, it signifies both modern anxiety and responses to anxiety. *Crisis* will thus become increasingly functional in numerous forms of discourse, e.g., as a buzzword intended to trigger and manipulate unthinking responses in mass man but also as a sign of high seriousness, acute awareness, existential projection, and artistic design. But I am engaged in an act of literary criticism, so I am moved to inquire, how does the curious word serve a modern critic? Many writers employ the great noun solely for its concussive or electrifying effects without offering to define it. What problems complicate the responsible critic's attempts to formulate a definition? Paul de Man tried but failed to stipulate for a precise meaning. Alan Wilde also confronts this definitional task. His effort to define the slippery term appears in the essay "Modernism and the Aesthetics of Crisis," and it more than adequately prepares the ground for a violent new stage in this critical history.

Wilde discovers in the late modernism of the 1930s a prolonged cultural agony and an aesthetic that represents artists' response to such agony. He initially defines the modernist ordeal as an increasingly recessive and dissolving self struggling within an increasingly randomized world. Explaining how an "informing consciousness in a peculiar state of crisis" expresses itself as a "crisis of profound and radical indecision," Wilde characterizes the "difficult aesthetics of crisis" as consciousness heroically making art of its own uncertainty. Such aesthetic heroism occurs within the larger cultural context of a "crisis of consciousness in a state of radical indecision."

Wilde notes that "genuine crisis" should be understood as an intractable impasse. He interprets Joyce's *A Portrait of the Artist as a Young Man* as a narrative that

127

arrests its complexities and contradictions in one of modernism's variations on the basic, artistically perfected shape of paradox, inviting not the puzzle solver's ingenuity but the willingness to recognize, as at least a possible mode of response, the intractability of genuine crisis.

The aporia of modernist crisis is a matter of "blocked energies" calling for negative capability in writer and reader. Continuing this line of reasoning, Wilde resorts to the metaphorical expression of crisis as a dammed-up stream.

The dissatisfaction and frustration that are everywhere apparent in modernism progressively channel themselves into more and more rigid structures, which simultaneously externalize and turn inward the pressures that threaten to shatter them. For a moment—it is the *definition of crisis—the flow of an unresolved energy is dammed up*, arrested, before it breaks forth and floods the postmodern world, leaving in its wake a series of remarkable testimonies to the struggles of an age's consciousness which, despite themselves no doubt, predict a new, more haphazard conception of order and an end to the aesthetics of crisis. (emphasis added)

Wilde grounds the modernist crisis-aesthetic upon an historical definition of *crisis*, more rational than figurative but figuratively quite compelling.

I don't think it would be inaccurate to assert that, as the large, imposing structures that embody the modernist crisis become, from the thirties onward, increasingly modest and various, *crisis, redefined as an almost continuous response to a decentered or uncentered world*, turns, quite simply, into anxiety, that uneasy burden of contingent existence. (emphasis added)

Wilde's effort to define *crisis* can plainly serve to introduce the subject of the pervasive and at times violent rhetoric that dominates twentieth-century experience, thought, and literature.[1]

An equally strenuous critical attempt at definition has been made by Joseph Frank, who explores the modernist's obligatory task of asserting control (mastery) over the chaotic materials of destabilized modern life. In examining rhetoric in modern literature, Frank himself employs a complicated crisis-figure that meets the requirement of self-reflexivity laid down by Paul de Man. Frank's seminal essay, "Spatial Form in Modern Literature," initiates his main question: why and with what effect do modern artists reduce the flux of experience to linear or geometric (spatial) form? His answer requires him to reinterpret the conventional explanation that radical crises in modern culture have produced a dehumanization of art. Spatial form in literature, he counters, did not kill the sense of the sacred but instead conserved art's sense of the sacred *per se* without committing art's devotees to any specific doctrine. Frank himself uses the great noun judiciously to signal major intellectual junctures. He invokes one crisis-strategist (Ernst Cassirer) to expose the weakness of another (Ortega) so as to promote the conclusions of a third (André Malraux). In a brilliant finale, he critiques Lionel Trilling's crisis-speculations (in "Freud and the Crisis of Our Culture") in order self-reflexively to critique his own (Frank's) belief in the basic conservatism of modernist spatial poetics.[2]

These two critical efforts to understand the role of crisis-consciousness in modernist thought briefly but adequately demonstrate not only that modernist thinkers find it necessary to use a crisis-trope but also that the use of such a rhetoric inevitably induces certain kinds of consciousness. Something radically strenuous if not actually violent almost always characterizes such critical efforts.

The crisis-anxiety of the twentieth century has produced strong utterances in all areas of culture, including major statements by a theologian (Karl Barth), a philosopher (Edmund Husserl), a historian of science (T. S. Kuhn), and a social scientist (Jürgen Habermas). Such utterances might constitute materials for a separate study of crisis-rhetoric, but beginning with this chapter and in the next three chapters I will use them to contextualize the study of crisis-centered novels. Barth, Husserl, Kuhn, and Habermas have put their own distinctive coloration and stamp upon the great noun. Each one instructively pushes the trope well beyond its usual limits, displaying it as a pure verbal force and as a crucial invention of the human spirit. They compel *crisis* to serve not merely as a noun of substance or condition but to some degree as a noun of corporeality, a trope that bodies forth man's struggle for existence. All four witness to an agonized modern subjectivity transforming itself within an increasingly irrational but rationalistic, manipulative culture.

The German theologian Karl Barth intensified twentieth-century anxiety by insisting upon an inflexible principle: "the KRISIS of the conscious perception that we are under KRISIS." Barth understood crisis as a form of revolutionary dialectical violence. The most concentrated effort ever mounted to shock readers by means of a *crisis*-trope appeared in his revolutionary Pauline exegesis *The Epistle to the Romans* (1919; 1921).[3] With this shocking pronouncement, Barth exploded "a bomb on the playground of the theologians."[4] Hammering home the capitalized noun nearly one hundred times, Barth stunned his fellow Christians in 1921 with a virtual paradigm of the word's adaptability as a term of spiritual terror. His shock-tactics are doubly relevant to the rhetoric of fiction because he grounds his theology of KRISIS to a considerable degree upon the novels of Fyodor Dostoevsky.

Barth pursues a single theme: the infinite qualitative distinction between time and eternity, between man and God. Refusing to allow Christians to remain complacent in their own righteousness or possession of God's truth, he presses home one astonishing claim. Insisting that God's revelation will always take the form of judgment (KRISIS), he makes eschatology—together with paradox and dialectics—central to his radically destabilizing theology. Barth advances three principal ideas: (1) the voice of Paul the Apostle speaks relevantly to modern man, (2) Paul's insistence on the power of Christ's resurrection is a sign of judgment upon all temporal things but also a sign of hope regarding the world of God to come, and (3) regarded as temporal phenomena, Christian religion and morality themselves fall under judgment. The resurrection brings mankind to the ultimate limit of human experience, where men confront a Primal Origin that dissolves and reconstitutes all human expectations. The resurrection shakes the foundation of human enterprise and awakens in man the memory of eternity. Christ proclaims Himself at one with mankind and with God's purpose of erecting justice by means of a complete renewal of heaven and earth. Truth must always take a dialectical form: man and God, history and the Coming Day, weak religion and decisive Grace, and so on.

Barth's radical pronouncements are directed against organized religion itself. Through habitual use, religious forms become no more than dead forms, burned-out craters or empty canals. Man's task is to sustain religion without yielding to the temptation to become self-righteous about enjoying God's presence or approval. The Church and the Gospel must be held in tension. One citation suffices to indicate the style of Barth's shrill tone.

> Something of this KRISIS underlies all religion; and the more insistent the tension becomes the more clearly we are in the presence of the phenomenon of religion, whether or no we ourselves are conscious of it. . . . [The Old Testament prophets] make Him a thing in this world, and set Him in the midst of other things. All this occurs quite manifestly and observably within the possibility of religion. Now the prophetic KRISIS means the bringing of the final observable human possibility or of religion within the scope of that KRISIS under which all human endeavor is set. (pp. 243-44)

Endurance under KRISIS then becomes the first rule for true believers, and the church's one message should be simply that man exists in sin.

Barth develops an extremely wide range of problematical concepts signalled and judged by KRISIS: power, history, human character, God's law, good works, Abraham's exemplary status, election and rejection, affirmation and denial, Jesus Christ, obedience, religion, law, prophets, knowledge, dialectical thought, transformation of the world, eternity, Eros and Agape, revolution, complacency, ethics, death, Protestantism, freedom, and the like. The theology of crisis grows out of peculiar meanings and implications, all variously comprehensible or incomprehensible. The overall effect is that of a powerful explosion.

Barth acknowledged the impassioned seer-novelist Dostoevsky as a major inspiration for his own crisis-consciousness. Dostoevsky's acute awareness of contingency, stress, and angst constitutes his appeal. Barth presents a complex, battering image—at once both Pauline and Dostoevskian—of the ambiguity of human life. He concludes by linking the formal closure of Paul's epistle with the closural themes of Dostoevsky's novels.

> If the KRISIS be not pressed home to the end, all would be but sounding brass and a tinkling cymbal. Once again, therefore, at the end of the Epistle to the Romans—just as at the end of the novels of Dostoevsky—there is presented to us the impenetrable ambiguity of human life—even of the life of the Christians and of the Christian Community. Once again, it is the fact of the existence of our fellow men—the ethical problem—by which we are brought face to face with the great disturbance. (p. 505)

Barth's use of KRISIS to characterize nearly every manifestation of the modern Christian's mistaken direction leaves the great noun nearly emptied of all substance but capable of an overwhelming emotional impact. After this rhetorical tour de force, the word itself functions as an empty sign, an expostulation, a black mark, a stick to beat with, a mark of sin. Barth has placed his own agonized stamp permanently upon the great noun. Its original meaning has been permanently altered by its being seized, melted down, and shaped into a concussive weapon by this vehement theologian of crisis. By invoking Dostoevsky, Barth established a powerful linkage between the most extreme rhetorical use of *crisis* and the literary form of the novel. Thus he both exhibits this trope in its most emphatic form and also helps to prepare the ground for any study of the trope as part of the rhetoric of fiction.

Throughout the long history I am representing, one of the novelist's most difficult tasks, no less than the critic's, has been to define a metacritical term at once concussive and slippery. Within the historical context described by Alan Wilde and condemned by Barth, two major novelists—the prophetic enthusiast D. H. Lawrence and the tender skeptic E. M. Forster—labored assiduously to represent the modern age, in the process defining and enlarging the greatness of the great noun.

1. "crisis of falsity and dislocation"

Both *crisis* and *trope* signify a turning. No reader could plausibly deny the special if imprecisely defined status of these terms in critical inquiry. Even so, novelists who employ the great noun do not explain their reasons. No major novelist has composed an essay examining the linguistic, cultural, or historical implications of this extraordinary keyword. Few if any novelists even use the metacritical term in their expository writing. One exception is D. H. Lawrence. Almost ten years prior to *Lady Chatterley's Lover*, Lawrence published a book of travel essays, *Twilight in Italy* (1916), in which he employed *crisis* one single time as part of a philosophical generalization, brilliant in itself, on which he would then proceed to build his famous theory of "blood-knowledge."

In *Twilight in Italy*, Lawrence attempts a critique, at once outraged and saddened, of modern European life as being ruined by industrialization: "the same purpose stinking in it all, the mechanizing, the perfect mechanizing of human life." During 1912-13, Lawrence began his writing career in earnest with the first utterances of a redemptive mystique combining motifs of blood, flesh, and sexuality. *Twilight in Italy* advanced Lawrence's development by teaching him to observe and meditate upon people and objects, as well as how to glimpse the "dark god" in things and people, a belief that enabled him to hypothesize in mystical terms about man and nature. It surcharged his writing style with a harsh but compelling ring of truthfulness.

The philosophical center of *Twilight in Italy* grounds itself in the chapter "The Lemon Gardens." For one luminescent moment Lawrence becomes an eloquent crisis-philosopher, employing the electrifying trope as he elaborates his belief that Italian culture once possessed the secret of an integrated, organic, unmechanized life. Modern people choose to ignore the secret. Meditating upon the painterly reaction from medieval otherworldliness that characterizes the Renaissance, Lawrence rhapsodizes upon the Italian soul, "dark, cleaving to the night," which turned "back to the flesh" during the Renaissance and thus established the "Italian position." Lawrence insists that Aphrodite, "queen of the senses," rules this complex of "raucous, cat-like, destructive enjoyment." He imagines this fiery process as being at once an "ecstasy," a "transfiguration," and a "crisis."

> It is a lapse back, back to the original position, the Mosaic position, of the divinity of the flesh, and the absoluteness of its laws. But also there is the Aphrodite-worship. The flesh, the senses, are now self-conscious. They know their aim. Their aim is in supreme sensation. They feel the maximum of sensation. They seek the reduction of the flesh, the flesh reacting upon itself, *to a crisis, an ecstasy, a phosphorescent transfiguration in ecstasy.*[5] (emphasis added)

As a perceptive critic of anguished modern life, Lawrence preserved this apocalyptic understanding of *crisis* (ecstatic, transfiguring) and built it into his most revolutionary novel.

Consciousness itself may be at bottom a function of the dynamics of desire at war with the unconscious.[6] Likewise, crisis-consciousness. One of the oddest yet most compelling *crisis*-tropes undergirds Lawrence's revolutionary treatment of sexual desire and sexuality in general in *Lady Chatterley's Lover* (third version, 1928).[7] Lawrence structures the nineteen chapters of his story via five spaced contexts informed by the great noun.

chap. 3   chap. 5   chap. 12   chap. 16   chap. 19

In broad outline, this neatly balanced pattern recalls the patterns used earlier by Meredith and James. Even so, as an angry revolutionary, Lawrence surprises his reader in two distinct ways.

Previously, Gissing had structured *New Grub Street* by four crisis-images that exploit three different meanings of the great noun. He exhibited a sad declension in Reardon's fortunes from an artistic concern, through financial miseries, concluding with a fatal medical crisis. Similarly, Lawrence stipulates at first that *crisis* bears a purely sexual meaning; then, in two other contexts, he violently disorients his characters and his reader by changing the terms of his argument from the problematics of sexuality to sociopolitics and psychopathology. Even compared with Gissing's unsettling theme, the effects of Lawrence's changes upon the historically unfolding meaning of crisis are painfully concussive.

In *Lady Chatterley's Lover*, Lawrence presents a fierce critique of Western culture. At one level, his celebrated novel of sexual frankness reduces to a simple diegesis. Sir Clifford Chatterley had been crippled in Flanders in 1917. His frustrated wife becomes enamored of their game-keeper, Mellors, the misanthropic son of a coal miner. Constance (Connie) Chatterley becomes pregnant by Mellors and, at the end, plans to divorce Sir Clifford, desert her social class, and live out her life with Mellors. Lawrence affirms certain values (nature, sexuality) over against other values (machinery, intellect). He presents two basic kinds of scenes: explicit sexual acts in the woods (described in earthy language of bodily intuitions) and intellectual discussions in Wragby Hall. In one sense, Lawrence wished to show in Lady Chatterley's personal consciousness a shift conveying broad cultural implications. Artistically, his task was to make the planned union of Connie and Mellors seem plausible. The motif of a new life (or reborn self) had appeared from the beginnings of the English novel in association with crisis-tropes; Lawrence tempers this optimistic motif at the close by Mellors's apocalyptic warning: "There's a bad time coming."

Lawrence's rhetoric conveys a strong structural effect via a dialectical logic established by five crisis-images. Crisis defines potential human life, and actual human life defines crisis. Lawrence's most surprising innovation in this respect is to stipulate, at the outset, that *crisis* refers solely to sexual experience, specifically to orgasmic satisfaction. He is an extreme example of the necessity for each new user of a word to construct a rationale on which to erect his own peculiar usage. In *A Dictionary of Slang and Unconventional English*, Eric Partridge lists many sexual terms but none for *crisis*. According to conventional parlance, orgasm is regularly referred to by another term that perhaps not coincidentally also has a critical application, i.e., *climax*. Lawrence surprises his reader by referring to orgasm as *crisis*. He initially uses this surprising coinage when he depicts Connie Chatterley commencing an affair with the youthful playwright Michaelis (Mick) before she has become intimate with Mellors. In a vivid scene, Lawrence invokes his *ad hoc* neologism three times.

> [Mick] was the trembling excited sort of *lover, whose crisis soon came, and was finished.* There was something curiously childlike and defenseless about him. His defenses were all in his wits and cunning, his very instincts of cunning, and when these were in abeyance he seemed doubly naked and like a child, of unfinished, tender flesh, and somehow struggling helplessly.
>
> He aroused in the woman a wild sort of compassion and yearning, and a wild, craving physical desire, the physical desire he did not satisfy in her; he was always come and finished so quickly, then shrinking down on her breast, and recovering somewhat his effrontery while she dazed, disappointed, lost.

> But then she soon learnt to hold him, to keep him there inside her *when his crisis was over*. And there he was generous and curiously potent; he stayed firm inside her, given to her, while she was active. . . . wildly, passionately active, *coming to her own crisis*. And as he felt the frenzy of her achieving her own orgasmic satisfaction from his hard, erect passivity, he had a curious sense of pride and satisfaction. (p. 31; emphases added)

Lawrence establishes the extreme separateness of the lovers, particularly with reference to orgasm, which he defines almost entirely in physical terms. For a time, he will leave his reader in the dark as to his intention, in effect teasing the reader by the twist of referring to orgasm as *crisis*.

Lawrence makes the sexual dimension of his rhetoric somewhat clearer when Connie and Mick again engage in sexual intercourse (chap. 5). Lawrence elaborates his account so that *crisis* (sexual climax) curiously takes on an additional meaning over and above purely physical response. *Crisis* now is stipulated, by inference, to mean one's conscious decision at a given moment to experience one's own orgasm. In certain respects, this episode marks the end of the Connie-Michaelis affair, revealing as it does Michaelis's dissatisfaction with Connie's presumedly selfish control of her own orgasm as a private experience rather than as a mutual, simultaneous experience.

> He was a more excited lover that night, with his strange, small boy's frail nakedness. Connie found it *impossible to come to her crisis* before he had really finished his. And he roused a certain craving passion in her, with his little boy's nakedness and softness; she had to go on after he had finished, in the wild tumult and heaving of her loins, while he heroically kept himself up, and present in her, with all his will and self-offering, till *she brought about her own crisis, with weird little cries*.
>
> When at last he drew away from her, he said, in a bitter, almost sneering little voice:
>
> "You couldn't go off at the same time as a man, could you? You'd have to bring yourself off! You'd have to run the show!" (p. 61; emphases added)

The effect on Connie of Mick's "unexpected piece of brutality" is to harden her heart toward Mick and toward men in general as her whole sexual feeling "collapsed that night."

In general, Lawrence uses the Michaelis affair to affirm the sexological belief that simultaneous orgasm may be essential to authentic sexual love. More to the point, he urges that orgasm (*crisis*) should result from two lovers' deliberate choice. In a powerful turn against turn, the relation of the sexes thus reduces either to a battle or to a peaceful compromise of individual wills. Lawrence's crisis or willed orgasm reaches its fullest development at the main turning point of the story (chap. 12) when Connie, having taken Mellors as her lover, judges that she can "let go everything, all herself, and be gone in the flood" (p. 207). Lawrence describes Connie's decision to share mutual orgasm with the game-keeper in terms of rebirth. Connie "was born: a woman." This complex episode begins on the same negative note that marked Connie's love scenes with Michaelis. When Michaelis had derided her for selfishly enjoying her own orgasm separately, Connie felt humiliated. All the more important, then, that she recommences her sexual activity when she begins an affair with Mellors (chap. 10).

Lawrence constructs a famous love scene in Chapter 12 so that when Mellors reaches his climax (*crisis*), Connie is prevented by her "tormented modern-woman's brain" (p. 137) from joining him in orgasmic mutuality. Lawrence establishes Connie's viewpoint as selfish and resistant. As with Michaelis, she needs to feel superior to her lover, superior to *crisis* itself.

> And she put her arms round him under his shirt, but she was afraid, afraid of his thin, smooth, naked body, that seemed so powerful, afraid of the violent muscles. She shrank, afraid.
> And when he said, with a sort of little sigh: "Eh, tha'rt nice!" something in her quivered, and something in her spirit stiffened in resistance: stiffened from the terribly physical intimacy, and from the peculiar haste of his possession. And this time the sharp ecstasy of her own passion did not overcome her; she lay with her hands inert on his striving body, and do what she might, her spirit seemed to look on from the top of her head, and the butting of his haunches seemed ridiculous to her, and the sort of anxiety of his penis to come to its *little evacuating crisis seemed farcical*. Yes, this was love, this ridiculous bouncing of the buttocks, and the wilting of the poor insignificant, moist little penis. This was divine love! (pp. 204-5; emphasis added)

Lawrence has brought Connie and the reader to a low point from which recovery seems unlikely.

Nevertheless, as a crisis-strategist Lawrence has another intention in mind. He structures this complicated scene so that Connie, having contemptuously perceived Mellors's orgasm as a crisis, undergoes a crisis of her own. When Mellors calmly explains to Connie that she need not fret herself about her failure to reach orgasm—"There's no law says as tha's got to"—she relents and pleads with him to give her another chance. When he responds tenderly, she too responds and "let herself go," she "went all open to him." Lawrence urges that in deliberately choosing thus to respond she experiences one sort of crisis (decision) with the happy result that she is enabled to experience another sort of crisis (mutual sexual satisfaction) with her lover. Lawrence signals Connie's new status—"she was born: a woman"—in a passage containing some of his most poetical writing:

> and further and further rolled the waves of herself away from herself, leaving her, till suddenly, in a soft, shuddering convulsion, the quick of all her plasm was touched, she knew herself touched, the consummation was upon her, and she was gone. She was gone, she was not, and she was born: a woman. (p. 208)

Most importantly, when their mutual orgasm subsides, Connie views her detumescent lover not contemptuously in terms of a farcically "little evacuating crisis" but tenderly, being moved by the sight of "the small, bud-like reticence and tenderness of the penis." Lawrence regularly disparaged Freudian psychoanalysis, but here, almost as if to illustrate Freud's famous description of the orgasmically happy woman, he describes Connie curled on Mellors's breast, murmuring, "My love! My love!" Lawrence uses this powerful scene to complete the first major stage of his unique crisis-theme.

In the latter two-thirds of the book, though, Lawrence regretfully shifts to another premise and two other meanings of *crisis*. Mellors and Connie, having decided to establish a married life of their own, must leave their love-nest and cope with an indifferent, possibly hostile world. In this part of the book, Lawrence makes no further mention of sexual crisis. He now uses *crisis* to designate problems in two other arenas: politics and psychology. Lawrence's intention can be effectively measured by tracing his crisis-trope as it shifts from sexual to non-sexual activities. The metaphor of sexual union gives way to metonymic and synecdochic separation, multiplicity, and external danger.

Lawrence signals the lovers' problematical incursion into the larger world by means of a long symbolic episode in which they must push Sir Clifford in his symbolic wheelchair up a bumpy incline on his estate (chap. 13). In addition, Connie's responsibility to her father and sister Hilda necessitates a temporary separation from Mellors, whose child she now carries. When Connie is preparing Hilda to meet her lover, Lawrence signals a new nonsexual meaning that *crisis* will carry in the sociopolitical world at large. Assigning to the cynical Hilda the utterance of his new meaning, he attributes a certain dismal tone to the uncontrollable larger world by depicting Connie and Hilda sharing a "nondescript dinner" on a "nondescript evening" at a dreary hotel.

Connie's helplessness is contrasted with Hilda's tough-minded perception of her sister's predicament.

> There was nothing to be done with Connie. And anyhow, if the man had been lieutenant in the army in India for four or five years, he must be more or less presentable. Apparently he had character. Hilda began to relent a little.
>
> "But you'll be through with him in a while," she said, "and then you'll be ashamed of having been connected with him. One *can't* mix up with the working people."
>
> "But you are such a socialist! you're always on the side of the working classes."
>
> "*I may be on their side in a political crisis*, but being on their side makes me know how impossible it is to mix one's life with theirs. Not out of snobbery, but just because the whole rhythm is different."
>
> Hilda had lived among the real political intellectuals, so she was disastrously unanswerable. (pp. 289-90; emphasis added)

Lawrence uses Hilda's cynical or simply realistic utterance to contrast Connie's new sense of life's organic unity (metaphor) with Hilda's chopped-up view in which social life and political life are widely separated (metonymy). Her new definition of crisis, as a cut in the social fabric, stands directly opposite from the organic unity symbolized in chapter 12 by Connie's mutual orgasm with Mellors.

Hilda's use of *crisis* to signify a separateness threatens to obliterate Connie's hard-won sense of *crisis* as an enabling mutuality. It appears that Connie's joyous experience of the trope may not enjoy any currency in the larger world. Lawrence brings this grim possibility closer to home when he depicts Sir Clifford's response to Connie's letter announcing her departure. With a final crisis-image, Lawrence establishes a link between crisis and an ultimate form of metaphoric sameness, i.e., insanity.

Sir Clifford's companion, Mrs. Bolton, serves as the perceiving consciousness who judges Sir Clifford's infantile response to Connie's departure. Lawrence couches Mrs. Bolton's judgment of her employer's petulant behavior in quasi-technical language. She contemptuously decides that her employer actually had known that his wife loved another man and that he also deliberately uses hysteria as a manipulative ploy.

> Even, she was sure, Sir Clifford was inwardly absolutely aware of it, only he wouldn't admit it to himself. If he would have admitted it, and prepared himself for it! or if he would have admitted it, and actively struggled with his wife against it: that would have been acting like a man. But no! he knew it, and all the time tried to kid himself it wasn't so. He felt the devil twisting his

tail, and pretended it was the angels smiling on him. This state of falsity had now brought on that *crisis of falsity and dislocation, hysteria, which is a form of insanity.* (p. 350; emphasis added)

Lawrence's rhetoric here establishes that Sir Clifford's self-deluding "crisis of falsity" points toward the destabilizing future awaiting Connie and Mellors. Individual judgment such as had led Connie to her own fulfillment may no longer be effective once she has left the game-keeper's hut. A crisis of falsity and dislocation, being hysteria and therefore a form of insanity, threatens to preclude conscious choice. Connie and Mellors face a world, as represented by Sir Clifford's womblike wheelchair, where crisis means only a prolonged agony of self-centeredness or anomic isolation.

Lawrence's complex crisis-trope enables a coherent interpretation. In *Felix Holt, the Radical*, Eliot had described how one social class, represented by the lawyer Johnson, used crisis-language to manipulate the working class. Lawrence extends this historical motif of class exploitation, but he generalizes it to include equally all classes and subclasses of the English populace. Sir Clifford's financial fortune is based to a considerable degree upon his colliery, which paradoxically thrives the more he becomes dependent upon his "Magna Mater," Mrs. Bolton: "The wallowing in private emotion, the utter abasement of his manly self, seemed to lend him a second nature, cold, almost visionary, business-clever" (p. 352). He represents a model for the type of Englishman whom Mellors apocalyptically anticipates: "Mammon: which I think, after all, is only the mass-will of people, wanting money and hating life" (p. 363). Like *Felix Holt*, Lawrence's great book ends on a sour Marxist note, the bitterest of ironies: money.

Allowing for sharp differences of formal expression, Lawrence's crisis-figure expresses apocalyptic tonalities comparable to those in Barth's theology of KRISIS, published in the same decade as *Lady Chatterley's Lover*. Like Barth, Lawrence uses *crisis* to suggest, as Mellors puts it, that there is "a bad time coming" if people begin to think only of money. Like Barth, he implies by means of Mellors's rhetoric that *crisis* means a judgment upon materialistic people. Like Barth, he makes it clear that the individual powers of judgment invoked by *crisis* may be denied to individuals living inauthentic lives dictated by a de-natured culture.

Paul Valéry believed that the very act of reading a novel precipitates a reader into a crisis of confidence. Later in the twentieth century, Roland Barthes would distinguish between two kinds of texts—text of pleasure and text of bliss—the latter of which precipitates a reader into a crisis in his relation with language itself. Barthes's formulation bears upon Lawrence's rhetoric.

> Text of pleasure: the text that contents, fills, grants euphoria; the text that comes from culture and does not break with it, is linked to a *comfortable* practice of reading. Text of bliss: the text that imposes a state of loss, the text that discomforts (perhaps to the point of a certain boredom), unsettles the reader's historical, cultural, psychological assumptions, the consistency of his tastes, values, memories, brings to a crisis his relation with language.[8]

Barthes's radical assertion applies equally to the shock received by Lawrence's reader and to Lawrence's writerly methods. Lawrence precipitates a culture shock by radically twisting the great noun into a deconstructive trope signifying endangered meaning and value.

2. "At a crisis, the English are really unequalled"

Among critics of the novel, E. M. Forster holds a special place because *Aspects of the Novel* (1927)[9] provides a perennially enlightening discussion of the genre. Under headings of Story, People, Plot, Fantasy, Prophecy, Pattern, and Rhythm, Forster moves through specific technical concerns toward a generalization on the novel's crucial role in the development of human consciousness. In discussing plot, Forster notes how recalcitrant the novelist's people (characters) can be when they are required, as it were, to subserve the plot: "In vain [plot] points out to these unwilling creatures the advantages of the triple process of complication, crisis, and solution so persuasively propounded by Aristotle" (p. 85). Forster hints that a truly crisis-centered plot may actually be an infrequent, even undesirable, literary phenomenon. Nevertheless, when he comes to examine Joyce's *Ulysses* as a failed experiment in fantastic indignation or indignant fantasy, he employs the problematically great noun in one of his strongest commentaries on a single book. Forster understands *crisis* to be a figure of speech that—something like a myth—activates and centers other figures of speech.

> [Stephen] and Bloom meet half-way through in Night Town (which corresponds partly to Homer's Palace of Circe, partly to his Descent into Hell) and in its supernatural and filthy alleys they strike up their slight but genuine friendship. *This is the crisis of the book*, and here—and indeed

throughout—smaller mythologies swarm and pullulate, like vermin between the scales of a poisonous snake. (p. 179; emphasis added)

Forster judges *Ulysses* a failure, but he is not alone in under-valuing Joyce's great book. More to the point of my argument is Forster's detecting the traditional device of a plot-crisis in this radical modernist experiment. Turned away at the sensible front door, *crisis* enters the structure of his critical thought by Joyce's cellar door.

Coincidentally, Joyce is only one of fifteen novelists cited in *Aspects of the Novel* who also figure in the present critical history of the word-as-trope. The list includes Austen, Emily Brontë, Dickens, Eliot, Hardy, James, Lawrence, Meredith, Proust, Richardson, Scott, Sterne, Thackeray, and Woolf.

Forster could not function as a critic of the novel without resorting to Aristotle's problematical concept of crisis. Likewise, as a novelist he either could not or would not function without the great noun that had variously served illustrious predecessors, including his own special maestro Henry James. In *Howards End* (1910) and *A Passage to India* (1924), Forster elaborated a complex crisis-rhetoric which, if not as peculiarly shocking as Lawrence's, yet represents an equally high level of achievement.

Prior to *A Passage to India*, Forster's most fully realized novel was *Howards End* (1910).[10] A work of domestic realism that examines English society from the stance of an equable sympathy, *Howards End* displays subtle characterizations, deft irony, and careful plotting. Dealing generally with the contrast between illusion and reality, it endeavors to show the literary interest inherent in social misunderstandings and missed connections between ordinary people.

Historically, *Howards End* has been regarded as a prophetic book witnessing to and foretelling major disruptions, political and literary, in modern Europe. It is said to foreshadow "the crisis of liberal-humanism in the 20th century and, correlative to this, the crisis of realism in the novel." The sociopolitical crisis meant that Liberalism was being eroded away, with the resultant disappearance of such values as social improvement by reform and education, sanctity of the individual, tolerance, liberty, reason, generosity, freedom of speech, democracy, nonaggression, civil rights, personal relations, civilized discussion, regard for art and intellect, and the like. The composition of *Howards End* coincided with the Dreadnought Crisis in an atmosphere of international tension in which Germany was becoming England's nemesis. At the same time, a literary crisis also involved the failure of mimetic fiction (realism) and a concomitant shift to various modernist alternatives.[11]

Howards End narrates an answer to the familiar question, "Who shall inherit England?" The Wilcox family owns Howards End, a country house near London. Mrs. Ruth Wilcox bequeaths this symbol of continuity and fertility to her young friend Margaret Schlegel. After Mrs. Wilcox's death, Henry Wilcox keeps from Margaret the information that she owns the house. He wishes Margaret to become his second wife, a possibility complicated by Margaret's sister Helen's being attracted to Wilcox's younger son Paul. Further complications arise from Helen's brief sexual liaison with Leonard Bast, a young man already married to Henry Wilcox's former mistress. At the conclusion, Helen has given birth to Leonard's illegitimate son, Leonard is dead at the hands of Wilcox's elder son Charles, and a compassionate Margaret has brought her invalided husband, Helen, and Helen's son to enjoy a recuperative retreat at Howards End. The group begins "a new life, obscure, yet gilded with tranquillity."

Forster dialectically intertwines two major themes in *Howards End*. The imagination must be nourished, and (as Forster notes on his title page) individuals need "only connect" in order to live humane lives. I am convinced that Forster implicitly offers the imagination itself as the human power by which men can indeed connect with each other. More to the point of my argument, I believe he urges that imagination is in at least one important sense equivalent to crisis-consciousness.

Like Matthew Arnold's metaphor of crisis-consciousness giving access to the center of cultural reality, Forster's narrative culminates in an image of hay being harvested in the "sacred centre of the field" at Howards End (chap. 44). Forster depicts his main character Margaret Schlegel as winning through to the sacred center of English reality through the development of an acute crisis-consciousness. That is, Forster has internalized historical crises by using a crisis-trope. The imaginative connectiveness or connective imagination that alone promises redemption for Forster's disoriented characters depends to a considerable degree upon crisis-consciousness as an informing principle of humane culture. In a manner worthy of Eliot, Meredith, or James, he uses seven *crisis*-images (chaps. 2, 4, 10, 12, 24, 30, and 38) to develop Margaret Schlegel's characterization via a systematic and cumulative tropology.

In *Aspects of the Novel*, Forster would devote ten pages of commentary to James's *The Ambassadors*. From James's superb crisis-strategies there, Forster could have learned the method he employs in *Howards End*. Like James, Forster takes pains to establish the status of important characters in terms of their grasp of the complicated role of crisis in human affairs. In a narrative strategy somewhat reminiscent also of Eliot's triptych of fathers in *Daniel Deronda*, a grouping of three characters (Mrs. Juley Munt, Helen Schlegel, Henry Wilcox) contrast sharply with one other character (Ruth Wilcox) on the score of their inadequate or distorted understanding of crisis as a structuring principle. Margaret Schlegel will win her way to the sacred center of English social reality by virtue of her decision to follow the example of her benefactress, Mrs. Wilcox, a more finely tuned crisis-consciousness.

In Mrs. Munt, Forster offers a comic "Auntie" who misinterprets social facts and then vanishes from the story early on. During an early episode involving Helen's romantic contretemps with Paul Wilcox at Howards End, Aunt Juley Munt had thrust herself officiously into the melee, made a fool of herself, retreated ignominiously back to London, and then proceeded to rationalize her own absurd behavior as altruistic and even heroic.

> *Even at the crisis* she had cried: "Thank goodness, poor Margaret is saved this!" which during the journey to London evolved into: "It had to be gone through by someone," which in its turn ripened into the permanent form of: "The one time I really did help Emily's girls was over the Wilcox business." (p. 21; emphasis added)

The ridiculous Mrs. Munt does not come under heavy moral censure, but her mindless exploitation of crisis must be regarded as a failure of the connective imagination. Forster's irony dictates that Mrs. Munt attempt to shield Margaret from the very sort of wisdom that, once accepted and coped with, will enable the salvation of two families.

In Helen Schlegel, Forster again depicts a confused person who distorts a crisis to serve her own narrow aims. A dazed Helen informs her brother Tibby how she had led the déclassé couple Leonard and Jackie Bast to Evie Wilcox's wedding at Oniton Grange in Shropshire. Helen dimly perceives the episode as having been a crisis. She impulsively decides to compensate the humiliated Basts with a gift of five thousand pounds, and she also decides to inform Margaret of Henry Wilcox's former sexual liaison with Jackie Bast. Forster depicts Helen's recollection of the episode to Tibby as alternately malicious and confused. She remains unaware of Tibby's astonishment at her bizarre story.

> Helen, rehearsing her commission, noticed nothing: the Basts were in her brain, and *she retold the crisis in a meditative way* which might have made other men curious. She was seeing whether it would hold. (p. 252; emphasis added)

As a crisis-manipulator, Helen fails miserably in both word and deed. Like Mrs. Munt, she provides a benchmark by which to measure Margaret's eventual achievement of connective imagination.

In Henry Wilcox himself, Forster situates a crisis not in a character's narrative reconstruction of an event but in the event itself. Wilcox stubbornly refuses Margaret's request that the pregnant Helen be allowed to spend one night at Howards End before taking up residence in Germany. Ironically, Henry's quandary occasions a display of Margaret's sensitivity to human crises of many kinds.

> *It was the crisis of his life.* Again she would have recalled the words as soon as they were uttered. She had not led up to them with sufficient care. She longed to warn him that they were far more important than he supposed. She saw him weighing them as if they were a business proposition. (p. 302; emphasis added)

In this "crisis of his life," Henry's callous refusal ("I do not give you and your sister leave to sleep at Howards End") illustrates two important principles. First, the mentality typical of an acquisitive business ethos proves self-hurtfully inflexible. Second, Forster in effect embraces one of Eliot's definitions of *crisis*: "that concentrated experience which in great crises of emotion reveals the bias of a nature, and is prophetic of the ultimate act which will end an intermediate struggle."

In these three crisis-passages involving Mrs. Munt, Helen Schlegel, and Henry Wilcox, Forster represents distinctly moral deficiencies (weakmindedness, obsessiveness, inflexibility). By contrast, he presents in Ruth Wilcox another sort of crisis-consciousness, one in whom the active imagination operates effectively in the real world of manners, morals, and money. The first Mrs. Wilcox realizes that crisis can be deliberately induced and benignly managed. Forster contrives for Margaret to desire the sensible Mrs. Wilcox as a personal friend but for the older woman herself to orchestrate in explicit crisis-terms the tropological stages of their growing friendship. With true sophistication, Mrs. Wilcox makes certain that "when the crisis did come all was ready."

> But the elder woman would not be hurried. She refused to fit in with the Wickham Place set, or to reopen discussion of Helen and Paul, whom Margaret would have utilized as a short-cut. She took her time, or perhaps let time take her, and *when the crisis did come all was ready.*
>
> The *crisis opened with a message*: would Miss Schlegel come shopping? (p. 77; emphases added)

Like Richardson's Lovelace, though with a different purpose and result, Ruth Wilcox uses a letter to initiate a crisis. By contrast with Mrs. Munt's weakmindedness, Helen's debilitating obsessiveness, and Henry's rigidity, Ruth Wilcox's grasp of the social utility of *crisis* seems all compound of Arnoldian intelligence, flexibility, and freedom. In Jane Austen's *Emma*, the young heroine learned from an older woman the importance of crisis-consciousness; similarly, in *Howards End*, Margaret Schlegel will prove herself worthy to inherit the symbolic house simply by connecting with her older friend.

Forster's theme of the connective imagination, intimately associated with and perhaps constitutive of crisis-consciousness, supports another theme operating at another level: the rightful heir of England will be one who sanely prepares for the role of inheritor. Forster keeps this belief squarely before the reader as he unfolds Margaret Schlegel's developing crisis-consciousness. His first signal of something special about Margaret appears early on when her sister Helen sends a message from Howards End concerning her romantic entanglement with Paul Wilcox. Before being preempted by Aunt Juley Munt, Margaret judges it best to go to her sister's aid ("I love my dear sister; I must be near her at this crisis of her life"). Margaret displays extraordinary fluency in the "voiceless language of sympathy" concerning another person's ordeals (p. 6). Forster thus stipulates for her delicately unfolding awareness of the life-shaping possibilities afforded by crisis.

Margaret's own life-shaping point occurs in chapter 33, when she decides to visit Howards End alone so as to take spiritual possession of the place. Before she can perform this symbolic act, Forster must make it clear that she understands life in terms of crisis. He provides Margaret with the occasion for an extended meditation upon the English tendency to waste energy preparing for crises that never materialize. Margaret's meditation equals in effect Isabel Archer's famous night-long meditation in James's *The Portrait of a Lady*, which also centers upon the heroine's exfoliating crisis-consciousness. Like Isabel herself, Margaret (and/or the narrator) notes the presence of anomalies in human affairs.

Actual life is full of false clues and sign-posts that lead nowhere. *With infinite effort we nerve ourselves for a crisis that never comes.* The most successful career must show a waste of strength that might have removed mountains, and the most unsuccessful is not that of the man who is taken unprepared but of him who has prepared and is never taken. On a tragedy of that kind our national morality is duly silent. It assumes that preparation against danger is in itself a good, and that men, like nations, are the better for staggering through life fully armed. The tragedy of preparedness has scarcely been handled, save by the Greeks. Life is indeed dangerous, but not in the way morality would have us believe. It is indeed unmanageable because it is a romance, and its essence is romantic beauty.

Margaret hoped that for the future she would be less cautious, not more cautious, than she had been in the past. (pp. 104-5; emphasis added)

Life, Forster enigmatically suggests, is a "romance"; fortunately for Margaret Schlegel, it proves to be, in Marshall Brown's dialectical terminology, an "escapable romance."

Forster follows the practice of earlier novelists by signalling important passages of character psychology and authorial philosophy with a crisis-image. Margaret invokes the image of historians composing recalcitrant human life into manageable written units. Forster thus reiterates that crisis-rhetoric takes two basic forms: a rhetoric of manipulative or decisive action and a rhetoric of manipulative or strategic utterance. Like the crisis-tropes of Lovelace or Lambert Strether, Margaret's language shapes a script which she herself will act out.

Writing out of a firm Arnoldian context with its injunction to "see life steadily and see it whole" (p. 266), Forster rounds off the stages of Margaret Schlegel's crisis-consciousness when he describes how she forgives and pities her husband for his previous affair with Jackie Bast. This final *crisis*-passage depicts Margaret as in some respects an ideal woman. Forster emphasizes Margaret's adherence to her earlier decision to be less cautious (albeit not less sensible) in dealing with other people.

> *Pity was at the bottom of her actions all through this crisis*. Pity, if one may generalize, is at the bottom of woman. When men like us, it is for our better qualities, and however tender their liking we dare not be unworthy of it, or they will quietly let us go. But unworthiness stimulates woman. It brings out her deeper nature, for good or for evil. (p. 240; emphasis added)

Following immediately upon this account of her adroit crisis-management, Margaret "felt herself at one with her future home." Stipulating for Margaret's ironical reward (increased joy but increased responsibilities), Forster rounds off his crisis-trope, even though it continues to radiate effects until the end of the story.

Subsequently, in chapter 43, following the arrest of Paul Wilcox for the inadvertent killing of Leonard Bast, Margaret's compassion dictates that she take her helpless husband, together with Helen and Helen's illegitimate child, to recuperate at Howards End. At the conclusion, in one of the happiest closures in any English novel, Helen can exuberantly declare after a day in the harvest fields, that Howards End will produce "such a crop of hay as never!" On the whole, Forster has employed a crisis-trope somewhat resembling Austen's, Eliot's, and Arnold's. His main character carries a double thematic burden of alertness to the necessity for connective imagination coupled with an acute awareness that crisis-conscious imagination functions as an informing principle of civilized life, or, in Arnoldian terms, humane culture. Crisis-imagination overrides many other considerations, including the gap between social classes.

In *A Passage to India*, Forster replaces the happy affirmation of *Howards End* with a grim rejection of any possibility that the English governing class can ever be fast friends with England's subordinates in India. Whereas Joyce will conclude *Ulysses* with the most important word in the English language (*Yes*), Forster's final opinion is *No*. He concludes: "'No, not yet,' and the sky said, 'No, not there'." Moreover, just as James's *The Ambassadors* became deeper than *The Portrait of a Lady* by reason of its incorporating a more ambitious crisis-trope, *A Passage to India* is a greater book than *Howards End* to some degree because Forster employs there a more anguished crisis-rhetoric.

A Passage to India[12] consists of two very large elements. First, sociopolitical tensions between Indians and imperialist English in India, together with comparable tensions between Hindus and Moslems, combine to produce an acutely disorienting impasse. Second, Indian mysticism, with its transcendent aspirations to infinite realms of being, calls attention to illogical and inexplicable strains in the ostensibly cooler English temperament. Massive dichotomies between English and Indian, between organized religion and raw nature, as well as between the noumenal and the phenomenal, find formal expression in Forster's external organization of the book into three sections: Mosque (chaps. 1-11), Caves (chaps. 12-32), and Temple (chaps. 33-37).

Forster's story in *A Passage to India* is less focused than *Howards End* upon one main character. In a tributary plot, Dr. Aziz the Moslem surgeon befriends an English woman, Mrs. Moore, but is disappointed when the English colony at Chandrapore continues to discriminate against him on the basis of his race. In another subplot, Mrs. Moore's companion Adela Quested becomes hysterical during a visit to the Marabar Caves and wrongly accuses Aziz of attacking her in the dark. By means of a third narrative thread, Forster presents Cyril Fielding, principal of the Government College, as a friend of Dr. Aziz and a would-be mediator between the aloof English and the excluded Indians. Forster connects these and other threads at the trial of Dr. Aziz, where Adela finally blurts out the truth that Aziz is in fact entirely innocent of her original charge.

A few years later, during the Khrishna Festival, Fielding returns to India with a new bride. Aziz and Fielding are not able to resume their former friendship and, at the end, they are shown to be divided in a way that foreshadows India's separation from England at midcentury.

Throughout the book, Forster's third-person narrative is marked by strong dialectical turning points, poetical nuances of substance and style, richly textured renderings of Indian local color, and acute psychological insights into human behavior. A terrifying episode at the Marabar Caves justly ranks as a masterpiece of symbolic writing. Additionally, as in *Howards End*, Forster builds into his text seven crisis-images that shape the story distinctively so that the book represents a technical advance in the history of the trope. In *Howards End*, seven *crisis*-figures were distributed fairly evenly throughout. By contrast, all but one of the seven crisis-images in *A Passage to India* appear in the second half of the book. In this respect, Forster's technique from novel to novel resembles Eliot's as she moved from *Felix Holt, the Radical* to *Middlemarch*, where all crisis-references concentrate in the second half. Eliot herself, of course, could have found the model for such an emphasis in Scott's *The Heart of Midlothian*. Such a delayed and concentrated placement of the images cumulatively induces strong climax-effects and truth-effects.

Several of Forster's crisis-contexts in *A Passage to India* are commonplace plot signals. Thus, after Adela Quested's ordeal at the Marabar Caves, her fiancé Ronny Heaslop informs her of "one or two things which they had concealed from her during [her medical] crisis, by the doctor's orders" (p. 186). Then, as Adela agonizes whether to testify against Aziz or tell the truth and acquit him, she is said to be "in a nervous crisis" (p. 193). Likewise, Forster explicitly signals a main turning point during the trial of Aziz when Adela will have, finally, to decide how to testify. Forster notes: "But the crisis was still to come" (p. 216). This passage does indeed prepare the reader for Adela's subsequent declaration to the court ("I'm afraid I have made a mistake") that clears Aziz of all charges, but like the other crisis-signals already cited it is unaccompanied by the sort of profound commentary Forster triggered via such signals in *Howards End*.

Several other crisis-passages reveal that in *A Passage to India* Forster intends a function for *crisis* in certain respects more specialized than any employed by preceding English novelists. Forster's own definition makes explicit a meaning only implicit from Richardson to Lawrence. Historically, English writers from Richardson onward clearly believed that crisis-consciousness constitutes an element of moral consciousness itself. This tradition prompts the question whether some peculiar variation of crisis-consciousness might represent a peculiarly English trait. From the cosmopolitan vantage point of an international novelist, Forster responds to this question. He uses a crisis-image to formulate, or at least to hypothesize, a definition of *crisis* as being, in some minds at least, an essential component of the English temperament sufficient to differentiate the English from other cultures. Forster insinuates that crisis-consciousness might indeed figure in a distinctively English moral outlook when his narrator notes that even though crises are stressful yet "English people are so calm at a crisis" (p. 82). This hint of a national dimension to crisis-consciousness undergoes considerable elaboration in a series of four crisis-passages beginning in chapter 19 with the preparations for Aziz's trial.

In chapter 19, as Cyril Fielding discusses Aziz's defense with the Indian lawyer Hamidullah, the Indian responds (perhaps ironically?) to Fielding's appeal for patience with a theme-setting remark: "'At a crisis, the English are really unequalled'" (p. 166). At this point, Forster could plausibly have cited the lawyer's opinion of the unflappable English as a simple means for distinguishing Indians from Englishmen. Such would in fact seem to be Forster's intention when his narrator asserts, during the trial, that the generic native Indian by contrast does not know how to prepare for a crisis: "There is no stay in your native. He blazes up over a minor point, and has nothing left for the crisis" (p. 216). Forster also depicts Adela Quested facing her own personal crisis (decision) during the trial and then individually, even heroically, deciding in favor of truth rather than merely personal or English convenience. Forster thus appears to have used *crisis* to define Englishman and Indian as clear opposites and to provide a simple rationale for his sobering closure.

Even so, his crisis-language functions in a still more complex fashion. The generic Indian is next shown to possess a crisis-consciousness but of a relatively more collective rather than individualistic kind. Following the acquittal of Aziz, the mob outside the courtroom rampages in a twisting procession to numerous points in the city, ending at the Minto Hospital. As a contrast to Adela's individual decision, Forster describes the mob's disorientation largely in terms of a collective response. Forster depicts this literal turning point decidedly from the outside.

> When Neruddin emerged, his face all bandaged, there was a roar of relief as though the Bastille had fallen. *It was the crisis of the march*, and the Nawab Bahadur managed to get the situation into hand. Embracing the young man publicly, he began a speech about Justice, Courage, Liberty, and Prudence, ranged under heads, which cooled the passion of the crowd. He further announced that he should give up his British-conferred title and live as

a private gentleman, plain Mr. Zulfiqar, for which reason he was instantly proceeding to his country seat. *The landau turned*, the crowd accompanied it, *the crisis was over*. (p. 225; emphases added)

Excepting the behavior of the Nawab Bahadur, which plausibly can be understood as either the result of English influence or political pressure, Forster achieves a vivid effect in showing the irrational mass-mind juxtaposed over against the cooler, more individualized English national type.

This would seem to be the extent of Forster's satirical intent. Thus far, his premise could be stated as follows: a measurable difference between the Englishman and the Indian takes the form of a crisis-consciousness and a crisis-ethos operating either as rational judgment or irrational mass response. Put thus baldly, Forster's crisis-rhetoric could be understood to contribute both to his compelling portrayal of cultures in conflict and to his satire of the English. His final word, then, ought to be either one final *crisis*-passage depicting an Englishman (most plausibly Fielding) faced with some last crucial decision affecting his friend Aziz, or, one final *crisis*-image highlighting a collective action by Indians (most plausibly during the Birth Festival of Shri Khrishna) acting out some group impulse. Forster does indeed give the final word to an individual, but he surprises his reader by depicting an Indian faced with a final decision.

At the end of chapter 34, Forster depicts the festival both for its own cultural interest and as a context for a personal crisis facing Dr. Aziz. When Fielding has returned to India with his new bride, the daughter of the deceased Mrs. Moore, Aziz erroneously thinks his former friend to be married to the hated Adela Quested. A friendly note from Fielding seeking to renew an old acquaintance provokes a negative response from Aziz. Forster carefully distinguishes between the mass behavior (crisis) of the festival crowd and the personal turmoil experienced by Aziz, who now undergoes "a crisis of a very different sort." He provides an intertextual reference back to the origins of novelistic crisis-rhetoric in Richardson's *Clarissa*.

Aziz tore the note up. He had had enough of showing Miss Quested native life. Treacherous hideous harridan! Bad people altogether. He hoped to avoid them, though this might be difficult, for they would certainly be held up for several days at Mau. (p. 286)

Aziz's personal response of tearing Fielding's note into metonymic shreds recalls a similar act by Clarissa Harlowe (repeated by Meredith's Clara Middleton). It also enables and symbolizes the final split between Aziz and Fielding, between England and India, that Forster brilliantly depicts on the last page when, during a ride together, the two men's horses swerve apart. In effect, Aziz tragically shapes his life by a crisis-cut. So to speak, he violently rejects a metaphoric consciousness of experience (racial equality), preferring a metonymic mode of separation and isolation.

In *Aspects of the Novel*, Forster urges that the novel as a discursive and narrative form represents a crucial stage in the development of human consciousness. A crucial role in this historical process was the role played by metaphor and other figurative language, including the crisis-trope that initiates and centers crisis-consciousness itself. Aziz's individualized act in the final crisis-passage in effect ironically blurs the crude demarcation between Indian and English, thus enabling or even necessitating an unspecified new political metaphor. Forster has used a tropological crisis-rhetoric first to distinguish between and then to confuse and oppose the two national groups he lovingly depicts. *A Passage to India* proves at the last to utilize a crisis-trope as technically intricate and poetically moving as any in the history of the English novel.

5

A Trope to be Avoided:
Joseph Conrad and James Joyce

Any history of the crisis-trope will reveal the device to be a kind of index to one feature of development within the main tradition of representation. The explosion of Karl Barth's terrifying theology of KRISIS reverberated throughout western culture and conditioned the ground for all subsequent crisis-consciousness. Barth established once and for all the extreme Longinian impact, the devastating concussion, of the great noun as a term of spiritual terror. A major work of philosophy assuredly enabled by Barth's theological crisis-bomb was Edmund Husserl's book *The Crisis of European Sciences and Transcendental Phenomenology* (1936).[1] Later in the century, Paul Valéry would characterize the novel reader as one who enters a state of pure subjectivity amounting to a *"crisis of credulity."*[2] Husserl's main goal in the *Crisis of European Sciences* was to elucidate the *"enigma of subjectivity"* precipitated by a scientific enterprise which claimed for itself a purely rationalistic objectivity (p. 16). Once and for all, Husserl establishes a philosophical link between crisis-consciousness and the ineluctably subjective modern self.[3]

Crisis of European Sciences culminates one of the most strenuous careers in modern philosophy. Insisting that philosophy held the only meaning in life, Husserl initially aspired to establish objective and indisputable truths upon a scientific basis. He insisted on constant self-reflection as a requirement for philosophy, but he also urged that all mental activity is fallible.

At the core of phenomenology, Husserl placed a methodological device, a transcendental reduction, which enables the transition from an ordinary stance toward the world to a self-reflexive stance. This reduction gives the transcendental individual an access to a pure consciousness or transcendental ego, making the entire world exist only as an object for contemplation. A new realm of being can thus be explored and described.

Not empiricism but only phenomenological description ("eidetic intuition") can cope with this new realm of being. Only near his death in 1938 did Husserl moderate his extreme opinion. In *Die Krisis der europäischen Wissenschaften und die transcendentale Phänomenologie* (1936), he conceded that the transcendental ego might not be absolute but only "correlative" to the world. The world is not determined solely by the views of the transcendental individual but by an intersubjective community of individuals. Such criteria as coherence and adequacy of experience came to condition Husserl's world view. The first task of phenomenology would henceforth be to study the existential or lived world (*Lebenswelt*).

I have already cited how, from an analysis of Husserl's tortured reasoning in the *Crisis of European Sciences*, Paul de Man drew a startling premise: "The rhetoric of crisis states its own truth in the mode of error." De Man urged:

> The point, however, transcends the personal situation. Speaking in what was in fact a state of urgent personal and political crisis about a more general form of crisis, Husserl's text reveals with striking clarity the *structure of all crisis-determined statements*. It establishes an important truth: the fact that philosophical knowledge can only come into being when it is turned back upon itself. But it immediately proceeds, in the very same text, to do the opposite. The *rhetoric of crisis states its own truth in the mode of error*. It is itself radically blind to the light it emits.[4] (emphases added)

Husserl in effect provided de Man with the dialectical concept of an ambiguous crisis-vocabulary.

Unlike Barth, Husserl employs the great noun sparingly, a total of only thirteen times. His *Crisis of European Sciences* consists of three main divisions. In the second part (pp. 21-100), Husserl elucidates the modern opposition between scientific objectivism and transcendental subjectivism. He takes his reader on a mental journey from Galileo's pioneering mathematics through Descartes's idealistic speculations and finally to Kant's revolutionary conception of a transcendental philosophy. Nowhere in this long survey of his forerunners does Husserl mention crisis as such. Likewise, in the third part (pp. 103-265), Husserl makes no use of the loaded word signified in his title. Instead, he explains how an inquirer may find his own way from the pre-given life-world to a privileged phenomenology.

Husserl's sixteen-page introduction carries a self-explanatory title: "The Crisis of the Sciences as Expression of the Radical Life-Crisis of European Humanity." He does not cite any novelist such as Barth's exemplary Dostoevsky, but the general cultural malaise he describes resembles the European aporia described at length by Thomas Mann in *Der Zauberberg* [*The Magic Mountain*] (1924). Granting science its marvelous accomplishments, Husserl insists that he objects only to the "positivistic reduction of the idea of science to mere factual science," such reduction itself constituting the "crisis" of science. Husserl adopts a theme from existentialism by identifying the crisis of science as being "the loss of its meaning for life."

Husserl's crisis is as radical as Barth's: "After all, the crisis of a science indicates nothing less than that its genuine scientific character, the whole manner in which it has set its task and developed a methodology for it, has become questionable" (p. 3). Moreover, if the crisis-problem goes to the heart of science, it also applies broadly to all of Western, or at least European, culture. Husserl intends to investigate the "deepest motives of this crisis" that involve psychology and the "*enigma of subjectivity*" within a "crisis which developed very early in modern philosophy and science and which extends with increasing intensity to our own day" (p. 16).

Husserl's insistent *crisis*-rhetoric, confined to the brief first section, announces his subject and emphasizes its emergent seriousness.

> But this is to say that, ultimately, all modern sciences drifted into a *peculiar, increasingly puzzling crisis* with regard to the meaning of their original founding as branches of philosophy, a meaning which they continued to bear within themselves. This is a *crisis which does not encroach upon the theoretical and practical successes of the special sciences*; yet it shakes to the foundations the whole meaning of their truth. This is not just a matter of a special form of culture—"science" or "philosophy"—as one among others belonging to European mankind. For the primal establishment of the new philosophy is, according to what was said earlier, the primal establishment of modern European humanity itself--humanity which seeks to renew itself radically, as against the foregoing medieval and ancient age, precisely and only through its new philosophy. Thus the *crisis of philosophy implies the crisis of all modern sciences* as members of the philosophical universe: at first latent, then a more and more prominent *crisis of European humanity itself* in respect to the total meaningfulness of its cultural life. (p. 12; emphases added)

Husserl's cultural critique emphasizing the need for renewal is as radical as Barth's, albeit less florid.

Husserl's translator notes that the main argument, directed toward the very idea of a "true crisis of man, with the fate of the human spirit undecided and hanging in the balance," expresses Husserl's belief that this crisis should be understood as a turning point for mankind.[5] But

Husserl's unfinished three-part text never circles back self-reflexively, never returns after the sixteen-page introduction to any explicit concern with crisis as *crisis*.

Husserl might have concluded his unfinished book on the model of the Vienna Lecture (7 and 10 May 1935) that de Man cites in "Criticism and Crisis." Husserl's thirty-page lecture, preparatory to the eventual book itself, carries the title "Philosophy and the Crisis of European Humanity."[6] It opens with specific references to *crisis*, stipulates for *crisis* twice in the lecture, and concludes with a magnificent peroration in which *crisis* rings out alarmingly and concussively. He begins the lecture modestly by citing "the frequently treated theme of the European crisis" that he intends to elucidate, but he quickly employs a *crisis*-image in a bold medical analogy: "The European nations are sick; Europe itself, it is said, is in crisis." For Europe's dire malaise only a comprehensive humanistic philosophy can provide a cure. Twice in the body of the lecture Husserl returns to his crisis-image. He agrees with other culture critics that "the European crisis has its roots in a misguided rationalism" (p. 290). He insists that his own task will be to show, "in connection with our problem of the crisis," how Europe fell into its "European distress."

Husserl closes with a grand peroration, a piece of pure rhetoric, a pure gesture of persuasion, and one of the high points in the European history of the great noun. It deserves to be quoted at some length.

The "crisis of European existence," talked about so much today and documented in innumerable symptoms of the breakdown of life, is not an obscure fate, an impenetrable destiny; rather, it becomes understandable and transparent against the background of the *teleology of European history* that can be discovered philosophically. The condition for this understanding, however, is that the phenomenon "Europe" be grasped in its central, essential nucleus. In order to be able to comprehend the disarray of the present "crisis," we had to work out the *concept of Europe as the historical teleology of the infinite goals of reason*; we had to show how the European "world" was born out of ideas of reason, i.e., out of the spirit of philosophy. The "crisis" could then become distinguishable as the *apparent failure of rationalism*. The reason for the failure of a rational culture, however, as we said, lies not in the essence of rationalism itself but solely in its being rendered superficial, in its entanglement in "naturalism" and "objectivism."

There are only two escapes from the crisis of European existence: the downfall of Europe in its estrangement from its own rational sense of life, its fall into hostility toward the spirit and into barbarity; or the rebirth of Europe from the spirit of philosophy through a heroism of reason that overcomes naturalism once and for all. Europe's greatest danger is weariness. If we struggle against this greatest of all dangers as "good Europeans" with the sort of courage that does not fear even an infinite struggle, then out of the destructive blaze of lack of faith, the smoldering fire of despair over the West's mission for humanity, the ashes of great weariness, will rise up the phoenix of a new life-inwardness and spiritualization as the pledge of a great and distant future for man: for the spirit alone is immortal. (p. 299; emphases Husserl's)

Husserl's lofty rhetoric not only recalls Eliot's exploitation of the "uncomprehended," manipulative function of the great trope but also anticipates Lawrence Durrell's linking of crisis with the "reborn self."

Paul de Man insisted in "Criticism and Crisis" that the crisis-philosophy employed by Husserl offers its truth in the mode of error. In practical terms, de Man meant simply that whenever the crisis-rhetoric emerging from the structuralist controversy failed in self-reflexiveness it thereby failed as true philosophical criticism. In the present critical history of crisis-rhetoric in the novel, de Man's insistence on its tendency to err translates into a broad, general meaning at once relevant and compelling. Novels exist as seamless narrative movement, marked by signs of chronology and causality, directed toward some definite closure of content and form. Nothing must be allowed to impede pure narrative movement. However, by insinuating a crisis-image into the rhetoric of a narrative, the novelist obliges a reader to stop, to question, to examine, to reflect. A crisis-trope obliges a reader to judge as he reads. The effect is to interrupt the crisis of credulity experienced by the engrossed novel reader. Perhaps more so than any other narrative device, the crisis-trope destabilizes narrative flow. The rhetoric of fiction, when it transforms itself even momentarily into a crisis-rhetoric, utters the narrative's truth in a new mode, a mode of self-criticism and potentially a mode of error.

Twentieth-century novels variously parallel Husserl's fanatical concern with the agonizing dialectics between objectivity and subjectivity. Modern novels desperately acknowledge the fact that crisis-rhetoric replicates or even produces both self-orientation and disorientation. Perhaps more so than any other device, the crisis-trope introduces "judgment" into a discourse and thus activates and literalizes inherent powers of criticism and self-criticism. Novels selected for the present study may or may not represent the best possible selections. Certainly they do not represent the only possible examples. The English Victorians alone produced tens of thousands of novels. Only by means of some super computer could the total body of fiction be scrutinized for every occurrence of the great noun. Happily, such thorough coverage is not necessary. The fifty or so novels I cite constitute if not an exhaustive repertoire at least an adequate sampling. As was the case in the nineteenth century, in national traditions other than the English (Italian, French, German) many important twentieth-century novelists resort to the word that was becoming a major keyword in the western world. A few foreign examples can serve to contextualize relevant English-language novels by suggesting how crisis-consciousness was becoming a characteristic of European literature at large.[7]

One of the most brilliant crisis-tropes in a novelist's examination of subjectivity in the modern world occurs in Italo Svevo's *Confessions of Zeno* (1923). This ironical comedy represents the first important narrative of psychoanalysis as well as an analysis of the addiction to tobacco. Svevo builds into Zeno's first-person narrative several turning points (Zeno's problems with cigarettes, his father's death, his troubled marriage, his complicated relations with a mistress, his laughable business career, his abortive psychoanalysis), but he defers the crisis-trope until his final pages. Like Husserl, via a grand peroration Zeno himself becomes a powerful crisis-rhetorician as he draws an ambitious analogy between a poisoned human environment and a diseased human body.

> I am not so naïve as to blame the doctor for regarding life itself as a manifestation of disease. *Life is a little like disease with its crises and periods of quiesence*, its daily improvements and setbacks. But unlike other diseases life is always mortal. It admits of no cure. It would be like trying to stop up the holes in our body, thinking them to be wounds. We should die of suffocation almost before we were cured.[8] (emphasis added)

Zeno then concludes his unsettling narrative by imagining a severe environmental crisis, an apocalyptic ontology of industrialized human existence ending on a note of "disease."

> When all the poison gases are exhausted, a man, made like all other men of flesh and blood, will in the quiet of his room invent an explosive of such potency that all the explosives in existence will seem like harmless toys beside it. And another man, made in his image and in the image of all the rest, but a little weaker than them, will steal that explosive and crawl to the center of the earth with it, and place it just where he calculates it would have the maximum effect. There will be a tremendous explosion, but no one will hear it and the earth will return to its nebulous state and go wandering through the sky, free at last from parasites and disease. (p. 398)

Just such an apocalyptic image looms behind much of the thinking in the troubled twentieth century.

By contrast with Svevo, the French-Algerian novelist Albert Camus composed the existentialist classic *The Plague* (1947) without once resorting to *la crise*, even though his narrative contains numerous emergent predicaments including a bubonic plague as well as a strong turning point at the moment when the main character Rambert decides to remain in Oran and assist in the fight against the plague.[9]

Earlier in the century, Marcel Proust and André Malraux availed themselves of the great noun. In *Swann's Way* (1913), Proust establishes in "Combray," the second of four sections, that his characters may structure their own lives in terms of crisis. Proust's narrator, the budding author Marcel, composes his first novel, "Swann in Love," as the crisis-centered third part of *Swann's Way*, a shift (so to speak) from metaphor (subjective first person) to metonymy and irony (objective third person). "Swann in Love" constitutes a problematically objective interruption of a basically subjective narrative. Charles Swann attempts to project crisis-consciousness away from himself onto his love-object Odette de Crécy. However, Proust contrives for Swann himself at a turning point to lose all self-respect by capitulating to his obsession with Odette. Swann himself then figuratively undergoes a medical crisis ("as surgeons say, his case was past operation").[10] Similarly, in *Man's Fate* (1933), André Malraux signifies *crisis* in three contexts so as to single out three characters from among an extraordinarily varied *dramatis personae*. In this narrative account of the 1927 Chinese Revolution, Malraux tropologically characterizes Ch'en Tu Erh the terrorist (metaphor), Kyo Gyors the organizer (synecdoche), and Ferral the troubled French executive (irony). In all three, Malraux stipulates for a problematical crisis-consciousness.[11]

Earlier, three masters of international modernism (Mann, Kafka, Hesse) likewise inscribed the great trope into major novels. Mann managed the overwhelming mass of narrative and expository materials in *The Magic Mountain* (1924) partly by signalling via *crisis* a precise turning point in Hans Castorp's adventures at a metamorphic sanatorium high in the Alps. At the end of the chapter "An Attack, and a Repulse," Mann describes young Castorp's rejection of his uncle's request that Hans give over his infatuation with romantic indolence at a sanitorium and instead take up a normal bourgeois routine.

> Thus ended the campaign of the flat-land to recover its lost Hans Castorp. Our young man did not conceal from himself that *the total failure of this embassy marked a crisis* in the relations between himself and the world below. It meant that he gave it up, finally and with a metaphorical shrug of the shoulders; it meant, for himself, the consummation of freedom—the thought of which had gradually ceased to make him shudder.[12] (emphasis added)

Like Jürgen Habermas and Joyce Cary, Mann associates crisis-consciousness with the ordeal of human freedom.[13] Given the lofty status of *The Magic Mountain*, Mann's traditional use of a crisis-figure, at once Aristotelian and eminently practical, constitutes an exemplary case.

The career of the great noun takes many weird turns in the modern period. In Franz Kafka's enigmatic masterpiece *The Castle* (1926), at the halfway point of the story (chap. 13), the servant Frieda directly accuses the main character K. of being, in effect, a crisis-manipulator.

> You have no tenderness to spare for me, you have hardly even time for me, you leave me to the assistants, the idea of being jealous never comes into your mind, my only value for you is that I was once Klamm's sweetheart, in your ignorance you exert yourself to keep me from forgetting Klamm, so that when the decisive moment comes I shan't make any resistance; yet at the same time you carry on a feud with the landlady, the only one you think capable of separating me from you, and *that's why you brought your quarrel with her to a crisis*, so as to have to leave the Bridge Inn with me; but that, so far as I'm concerned, I belong to you whatever happens, you haven't the slightest doubt.[14] (emphasis added)

Kafka's harrowing scene recalls Richardson's structuring of the conflict between Clarissa Harlowe and Robert Lovelace in terms of a struggle over crisis-management. Within the numerous enigmas of this strange book, Kafka's momentary crisis-trope, with its implications for traditional narrative logic, provides a momentary stay against modernist confusion.

A special case among modernist crisis-tropes informs Hermann Hesse's *Steppenwolf* (1927). Only once does the narrator Harry Haller invoke *crisis* in recounting his own unhappy experience as the neglected artist in conflict with bourgeois materialism. However, this one instance achieves a powerful effect.

> I had no motives, no incentives to exert myself, no duties. Life tasted horribly bitter. I felt that *the long-standing disgust was coming to a crisis* and that life pushed me out and cast me aside. I walked through the grey streets in rage and everything smelt of moist earth and burial.[15] (emphasis added)

Hesse's spare crisis-rhetoric takes on additional interest because Hesse also composed a poetical counterpart to *Steppenwolf*, published the next year in 1929 under the title *Krisis*.

Among the great novelists, Virginia Woolf occupies a solid position, and her importance in exploring new ranges of consciousness is undeniable. Yet her books are lyrical novels that submerge narrative beneath layers of imagery and portraiture. Instead of plots with strong turning points, the lyrical novel constitutes itself from patterns of language selected according to a peculiar theory of knowledge. Woolf was thoroughly familiar with the main tradition of English fiction that since Richardson had included a tradition or sub-genre based on crisis-images. She was acquainted, for example, with Austen's *Emma*, where she could have found a strong pattern. Even so, in her own books she depicts a modern self, a progressively depersonalized and formalized consciousness. Like Eliot, she realized that any specific moment can plausibly be construed as a crisis, but she utilizes a non-Eliotic theory of the "moment." For Woolf, the moment appears chiefly an internalized phenomenon consisting of an analysis of pure consciousness. Her commitment to a plotless lyrical form meant that she must reject any Aristotelian crisis-structure.[16]

In *A Room of One's Own* (1929), explicit references suggest Woolf's rejection of crisis as a structuring device: "But the effect was somehow baffling; one could not see a wave heaping itself, a crisis coming around the corner."[17] Even more typical of Woolf's modernist experiment would be a narrative such as *Mrs. Dalloway* (1925), where Woolf glides over problems and simply ignores the great noun. This omission takes on a special interest because Woolf drew the name of her main character, Clarissa Dalloway, from Richardson's sentimental masterpiece in which Clarissa Harlowe vies with Robert Lovelace in a struggle to the death over the management of crisis-strategy.

Consciousness in and of itself may be nothing more than the experience of subjectivity.[18] On the basis of these numerous examples from various national literatures, one would expect that no serious novelist would attempt to render conflicted modern subjectivity without some recourse, however ambivalent, to Eliot's rich figure of speech. At a time when the great noun appears increasingly in numerous types of discourse, two great masters of modernism—Conrad and Joyce—provide an enlightening spectacle of artists who wish to portray extreme forms of acute crisis-consciousness but who would prefer to avoid the increasingly familiar word itself.

1. "obscure sense of an impending crisis"

Studies of keywords reveal that individual words can convey doctrines and value judgments in subtle ways. As Empson notes, a concentrated richness of individual words can provide a writer with valuable resources for his art. Or, as Trilling puts it, keywords can furnish a writer with a dark source of art. So many writers use crisis-images in order to treat a subject, conduct an argument, sway a reader, or construct a narrative, that we might understandably expect every writer to use the great noun in various interesting and significant ways. Among novelists, a kind of minor great tradition of crisis-rhetoricians can be identified, ranging from Richardson through Scott and Austen to Meredith and James, then proceeding through Lawrence and Forster to Durrell and Bellow. In a careless moment, one might assume that any individual novelist seeking a place within this tradition will inevitably and ambitiously use *crisis* in establishing a rhetoric of fiction within a single text or throughout an oeuvre. That such universality proves not to be the case constitutes part of the interest raised by my own study of this metacritical figure.

In a thirty-year career stretching from *Almayer's Folly* (1895) to *Suspense* (1925), Joseph Conrad composed narratives that depict strenuous adventures and romantic hazards combined with anguished moral decisions but which depend little, if at all, on any crisis-figure. Even so, Conrad's novels regularly elicit critical commentary that includes designations of crises or turning points in his plots. Faithful to the artistic principles of Henry James, Conrad yet managed to avoid James's subject of the London drawing room, choosing instead to write about perilous adventures in exotic settings in the Malayan islands or on shipboard. His favorite subject was the degeneration of a white man in the tropics. He composed variations on this subject under the influence of sensational writers including Sir Walter Scott. A consummate stylist who first thought out his stories in Polish before translating them mentally into French and then writing them in English, Conrad concentrated on analytical subtlety in providing his reader with meticulous dissection of mental states enriched with poetical overtones and symbolism.

Three of Conrad's acknowledged masterpieces—one early, one middle, one late—show how sparingly and even dismissively this modernist master used the noun that had been a crucial element in the rhetoric of preceding novelists. In *Lord Jim*, *Nostromo*, and *Victory*, Conrad used *crisis* a total of only four times, and (unless absence be considered as forceful as presence) he induces no significant patterns or effects via the word. In *Lord Jim* (1900),[19] Conrad employs an impressionistic method to tell the story of a young Englishman who desperately seeks to redeem his lost honor by performing heroic deeds for the underdogs fighting a civil war in the remote jungles of Patusan. Using an onlooker-narrator (the philosophical Marlow), Conrad constructs a tale in which abrupt and intricate departures from ordinary chronology test the reader's powers of attention and comprehension, thereby complicating but enriching the story. Despite the unconventional arrangement of episodes, a strong turning point structures the story via Jim's decision to become Stein's trading-clerk in faraway Patusan, thereby enabling his own moral redemption. Even so, Conrad does not signal this act as a crisis-decision. Nor does he thus signal any of several important passages of philosophical observation by Marlow and Stein. His single crisis-image in *Lord Jim* resembles, if anything, the dismissive type seen in *Wuthering Heights*. Emily Brontë stipulated for one of Lockwood's violent dreams at Wuthering Heights as a *crisis*, thus effectively decentering crisis away from presumably more crucial parts of her complicated narrative. Conrad likewise stipulates that a bizarre early episode represents the only explicit crisis in Jim's tormented story. Interestingly, like episodes in *The Heart of Midlothian* and *A Passage to India*, this judicial trial centering on a point of maritime law itself literalizes the root meaning of *crisis* (judge).

Following Jim's trial for deserting his sinking ship, a trivial misunderstanding occurs as the principals and spectators leave the courtroom. A man standing near Marlow points at a pathetic animal in the street ('Look at that wretched cur') with the unhappy result that the disgraced Jim mistakenly thinks he himself to be insulted. Jim confronts Marlow and attempts to face down the older man who ironically will prove to be his friend and benefactor. He addresses Marlow threateningly, "in a tone suggestive of a crisis" (p. 45). Admittedly a crucial scene for establishing Jim's hot-headed pride, as well as for advancing the crucial relation between Jim and Marlow, this single passage nevertheless resembles not at all the more systematic *crisis*-figurations employed by other novelists of equal stature and that would seem entirely appropriate to Jim's story. Tropologically, of course, Jim does indeed move dialectically from metaphor (naval duty) through metonymy (jumping ship) and synecdoche (carrying the white man's burden throughout Stein's commercial empire) to the ultimate irony (suicide). Even so, Conrad signifies the overwrought "cur" scene as a *crisis* only to set aside the great noun as irrelevant to his more stoical and perhaps more subtle intentions.

Historically since Richardson, crisis-images signify anomic or alienated individuals attempting to achieve self-identity by joining the human race on new terms, as it were as reborn selves. In *Nostromo* (1904), Conrad recounts the attempt by an alienated man to reconnect with a human community. As Robert Penn Warren notes: "the crisis of this story comes when the hero recognizes the terms on which he may be saved, the moment, to take Morton Zabel's phrase, of the 'terror of the awakening.'"[20] Yet even less than in *Lord Jim* does Conrad take pains with an explicit crisis-language. In this romantic adventure of political intrigue, political revolt, purloined treasure, and sexual involvement in a South American setting, only twice and in the most casual ways does Conrad resort to the great noun itself. In chapter 8, part 1, of *Nostromo*,[21] Conrad's narrator alludes to some prominent man's private ridicule of "the line of action taken by the Sulaco authorities at a time of political crisis"; in chapter 4 of part 3, the narrator refers to Dr. Monygham as someone possessing a "special conception of this political crisis." Although Conrad regularly investigates the problem of crisis-consciousness that appealed so strongly to other novelists, he judged it best to do so without recourse to the problematical keyword, regarding it as perhaps too conventional. The two crisis-references in this long, difficult book remain at the level of casual observations. In *Nostromo*, Conrad was doubtlessly a crisis-rhetorician but not a *crisis*-rhetorician.

An equally spare but very different attitude toward the great noun appears later in Conrad's career. In *Victory* (1915),[22] Conrad narrated the story of a lonely white man, the scholarly recluse Axel Heyst, who violates his own rule of noninvolvement by rescuing a beautiful girl from a tyrannical employer and fleeing with her to a remote island in the Malay Archipelago. For a time he enjoys a prelapsarian bliss until his enemies send a trio of thugs to punish him. These villains track him to the island and precipitate a Grand Guignol finale of conflagration and death. Conrad built a subtle turning point into the story (p. 196) by having the naïve Heyst innocently invite his exhausted and vulnerable enemies ashore ("But hadn't you better land?"). When the unholy threesome has landed safely ashore, Conrad surprises his reader by invoking *crisis* in its most conventional form, almost like a device in a sensational novel: "A silence fell on that group of three [Heyst and two of the villains], as if every one had become afraid to speak, in an obscure sense of an impending crisis" (p. 198). The phrase "obscure sense of an impending crisis" rings on the ear less like serious fiction than like crude melodrama. Ironically, of course, Heyst's disorienting crisis or turning point is already past, the damage already done, so that the reader can only surmise that at best Conrad intended this single *crisis*-signifier either to contribute to his delineation of Heyst's naïvete or perhaps to test his reader's responses to a popular narrative cliché. At the worst, an aging Conrad sadly fell back upon a weak device unworthy of his art at its finest.

On the whole, Conrad's parsimonious use of *crisis* resembles the decentering enterprise of experimental novelists such as Sterne and Emily Brontë. Perhaps because of his of Stoic idealism, he is one major novelist who clearly managed to construct an outstanding critique of solipsistic subjectivity using only the faintest hint of a sustained crisis-trope. Similarly, other novelists usually associated with Conrad as radical innovators contributing to the broad epistemic shift from realism to modernism confronted the problematically concussive noun in complicated ways. An extreme case appears in the career of James Joyce, who used *crisis* even more sparingly than Conrad but with fanatical care and amazing results.

2. "a queeleetlecree of joysis crisis"

Perhaps the most sheerly intricate episode in this history of a problematical word occurs when James Joyce puts his literal stamp, his own surname, upon the keyword of his age. Among major novelists, Joyce committed himself most fully to the extreme tenets of modernism, in the process revolutionizing the techniques of characterization, plot, and the rhetoric of fiction in general. In preempting this unique position in literary history, Joyce would inevitably set himself in opposition to any traditional crisis-trope. If the writerly practices and readerly responses associated with the Richardson to Forster line of development is basically conservative, then Joyce's radical experimentation might well preclude any use whatsoever of Eliot's metacritical keyword. Yet as an ironist and a parodist, he might feel obliged to offer an oblique opinion of an established practice.

Joyce was himself preeminently a man and a writer in crisis. In *Crisis and Criticism*, the Marxist critic Alick West concludes his argument with an essay urging that *Ulysses* (1922) resulted from Joyce's unresolved dependence upon the Catholic Church and resultant inability to criticize western capitalism. West thus accords to Joyce a place in the Marxist "crisis of capitalism" viewed as a "crisis of humanity." So, *Ulysses* is paradoxically a work in which formal experimentation acknowledges a new post-bourgeois consciousness in and of society, even though the content of the work betrays Joyce's dependence upon older social forms and values. The reborn self in *Ulysses* is said to work at the level not of the individual but of social change and of novelistic consciousness. West's essay on *Ulysses* concludes by urging that Joyce was a writer fixated in cultural crisis.

> Resentment and weariness seem to me the fundamental mood of *Ulysses*. The social activity embodied in the content, to which the social energy awakened in us by the form of expression is directed, is partly destruction, partly exploitation of forms of intellectual and emotional life, created by society, at

a lower level of activity than that which created them. Consequently the book does not organise social energy; it irritates it, because it gives it no aim it can work for.[23]

West's essay on Joyce focuses on crisis in a generalized Marxist sense rather than on crisis-rhetoric as foregrounded in Eliot's *Felix Holt, the Radical* or analyzed by Paul de Man in "Criticism and Crisis." Even so, had West examined Joyce's novels for the presence of the great noun, he would have found it used distinctively in *A Portrait of the Artist as a Young Man* and *Finnegans Wake*.

Joyce's development into the maestro who gave the world *Finnegans Wake* covered more than thirty arduous years of experimental writing. His first novel, *A Portrait of the Artist as a Young Man*,[24] presented both a careful study of the artistic temperament and a self-portrait. This *Bildungsroman* depicts a boy's discovery of the realities of his own life and his revolt against familial limitations. Using a narrative point of view discovered by Henry James in *The Ambassadors*, this third-person narrative keeps strictly within the consciousness of one main character, Stephen Dedalus. An overall pattern grows out of Stephen's unfolding personality, including his revulsion from nationalistic bigotry and Roman Catholic theology, brief bursts of religious fervor, the discovery of his own sexuality, and his developing literary sensibility. Foregoing traditional plot structure, Joyce constructed only one scene potentially marked by dramatic tension, the climactic moment when Stephen not only rejects his dying mother's request that he return to the Catholic faith but also decides to pursue an artistic career. Joyce spent ten years composing and revising this short novel, so that a reader can easily imagine (as Joyce himself claimed to be the case) that the author could justify every single word.

Historically, Joyce occupies a unique place in the present survey, but in one respect he fits in neatly with other writers. Among novelists who employ crisis-structures, one tendency is to follow Eliot's example and to use it within a single text in various ways, sometimes numerous and elaborate ways, and according to the special aesthetic decorum of each book. For such writers, the great noun presumably seems indispensable. Another category includes novelists who, presumably with great care, use the word a single time in a given text. Henry Mackenzie initiated this practice in *The Man of Feeling*, adding the structural fillip of using *crisis* both for its medical analogy and as a signal for a main turning point. In the next century, George Moore would use the same device a single time to signal both a perception and a turning point. In the twentieth century, William Golding would structure *Lord of the Flies* by means of a single judiciously placed crisis-figure. Another sort of novelist uses *crisis* one single time in a text but with a different intention. In this category belong Sterne, Emily Brontë, and Conrad, who decenter or debunk any narrative centering upon a clear crisis (turning point) or any blatant use of the word itself. A poetical equivalent of this debunking practice would be T. S. Eliot's poem "The Love Song of J. Alfred Prufrock," where Eliot satirizes his hero Prufrock as both a crisis-addict and a crisis-coward. He wittily debunks the great noun itself by means of a famous comic rhyme.

> Should I, after tea and cakes and ices,
> Have the strength to force the moment to its crisis?

As if to prove that a serious writer may invoke the great noun with careful forethought but then dismiss it as irrelevant, Eliot's debunking of *crisis* represents the one and only time he ever used the word in his poetry. Joyce fits into this last category, writers who use *crisis* one dismissive time in a major text.

The crisis-ridden modernistic imagination operates upon a complex of blocked cultural energies. Joyce's *Portrait of the Artist* perfectly illustrates this point. Alan Wilde notes:

> *A Portrait of the Artist as a Young Man* arrests its complexities and contradictions in one of modernism's variations on the basic, artistically perfected shape of paradox, inviting not the puzzle solver's ingenuity but the willingness to recognize, as at least a possible mode of response, the intractability of genuine crisis.[25]

At several points in Stephen Dedalus's experiences in *Portrait of the Artist*, Joyce might plausibly have invoked *crisis* for its affective, self-reflexive structuring effects. Such episodes as a Christmas dinner ruined by political dispute, a brutal football game at school, a wrenching sermon at college on the subject of mortal sin, a lingering illness that wastes his mother—these and other turning points might understandably have been *crisis*-signalled. Undoubtedly, within the context of his mother's illness, Stephen's decision to pursue an artistic career could have yielded a crisis-formulation both realistic and compelling.

Joyce's actual strategy can be elucidated by comparison with a precursor's strategy. Ivan Turgenev's powerful episode in the penultimate chapter of *Fathers and Sons* (1862) depicts the nihilist Bazarov's adamant rejection of his parents' outdated value system even as he reclines on his own deathbed. It has already been discussed in connection with Gissing's *New Grub Street*. Did Joyce adapt Turgenev's famous scene to his own purposes? Joyce's grudging admiration of Turgenev's works has been documented in the Richard Ellmann biography, and he could have found in *Fathers and Sons* an ironical model for his depiction of Stephen's ordeal at his mother's deathbed.

Turgenev depicts Bazarov's humble parents helplessly watching their arrogant son die of a typhus contracted while treating a peasant. Distracted by grief, and hoping against hope for his son's recovery, old Vassily Ivanovich declares: "Thank God! the crisis is coming, the crisis is at hand." He refers only to his son's medical predicament. The sarcastic intellectual Bazarov, ever the rational nihilist, scorns his father's desperate optimism and ridicules the old man. He satirizes his father as a self-deluded crisis-strategist given to deluding himself via loaded words. Ironically, such biting sarcasm in fact brings hope to the anxious father who regards it as a sign of renewed energy in his son. Turgenev's rhetoric drives home the pathos of Bazarov's refusing his father's plea that his son receive extreme unction from a priest. Bazarov sarcastically torments his father by asking, "is the crisis over, or coming?" Even so, as a physician he fully realizes the seriousness of his plight. Eventually he declares, "I agree with you that the crisis has come," though he never gives in to his father's plea. Shortly thereafter he dies.

In *Portrait of the Artist*, Joyce places his own youthful nihilist Stephen Dedalus not on his own deathbed but at his mother's deathbed. Yet his predicament is ironically similar to Bazarov's. Within an atmosphere fraught with human mortality but faintly alleviated by the pathetic hope of immortality, an ambitious young revolutionary, upon being asked to embrace his parents' faith, adamantly refuses. The critical issue here is not a question of crudely mechanical sources or influences. Joyce could in fact have followed Turgenev's example by employing an explicit crisis-image in constructing his own unforgettable scene, but perhaps he had good reasons for not doing so. In his subsqent revolutionary books *Ulysses* and *Finnegans Wake*, Joyce's mythic thought and technique would express not chronological form but spatial form. Here, in *Portrait of the Artist*, Joyce still wavered somewhat between the older mode and a newer mode. During the years Joyce worked on his first novel, the great noun was becoming more current in Western culture, a fact he would surely notice. Its currency might plausibly have challenged him to confront the problematical word. Moreover, Joyce's unmatched knowledge of the main tradition in English fiction could have provided him with numerous warrants for a literary use of *crisis*: Austen's sober character development of Emma Woodhouse, Meredith's contrasting of characters on the basis of their lacking or possessing crisis-consciousness, Moore's self-conscious literary device of having a novelist designate as a crisis another character's disorientation, James's building an aesthetic philosophy out of Strether's fine crisis-sensibility, and so on. Even at the outset of his career, the author of "The Dead" might be expected to produce a crisis-trope as daring as Lawrence's or as profound as Forster's. We would not be surprised if Joyce had achieved an aesthetic mastery of cultural crisis by adapting, if only to satirize, the familiar noun.

Joyce's one actual use of *crisis* as part of Stephen's interior monologue proves to be both innovative and puzzling. Near the beginning of the final section of *Portrait of the Artist*, Joyce depicts Stephen taking a walk while meditating upon two topics, his Latin text book and his plan to invent his own aesthetic philosophy. By this time, Stephen has heard Father Arnall's fervent wish that any lost soul among the students may use the religious retreat as a "turningpoint" toward repentance and grace (p. 110). Likewise, he has attended to the priest's suggestion that Stephen himself might entertain a vocation to the priesthood. Stephen ruefully rejects this seductive offer, judging it best to follow the path not of an otherworldly priest with "secret knowledge and secret power" but the path of an artist of the secular world, the world of "kitchengardens." Joyce establishes as Stephen's main turning point the self-conscious moment when the young man "turned his eyes coldly" toward a shrine of the Blessed Virgin but "bending to the left" turned his feet toward his father's home and the lowly scenes of his boyhood: "He smiled to think that it was this disorder, the misrule and confusion of his father's house and the stagnation of vegetable life, which was to win the day in his soul" (p. 162).

During this epiphanic walk with its literal turning of eyes and feet, the solitary Stephen crosses a small bridge over a stream. By contrast, a little while later Stephen observes a squad of Christian Brothers marching "two by two" in unison across another bridge so that the cadence of their tramping feet sets the bridge "trembling and resounding" (p. 165). Only lockstep marching will cause a bridge thus to vibrate, so that Stephen's solitary turning across a bridge becomes symbolic of his heroic turn toward a lonely artistic destiny. But what has all this to do with the history of *crisis*?

Arguably the most famous personal crisis in modern literary history, Stephen's turning point is signalled not as itself a crisis but as occasioning Stephen's attempt, while meditating upon ancient Rome, explicitly to project crisis itself away from himself and onto a large, impersonal, collective, dead historical past. Joyce accomplishes this depersonalization of crisis during his young artist-hero's meditating upon the names of previous owners of his Latin text ("noble names on the dusky flyleaf") as well as upon the book's historical account of Roman history.

> The *crises and victories and secessions in Roman history* were handed on to him in the trite words *in tanto discrimine* and he had tried to peer into the social life of the city of cities through the words *implere ollam denariorum* which the rector had rendered sonorously as the filling of a pot with denaries. (p. 179; emphasis added)

Stephen's ambivalent meditation succinctly expresses his simultaneous attraction toward and repulsion from traditional high culture. At one level, Joyce wishes to show Stephen's growing awareness that by drawing upon "monkish learning" (Aquinas) for his aesthetic theories he dooms himself always to be "but a shy guest at the feast of the world's culture" (p. 180). Clearly, though, Joyce's intention at another level is to show Stephen's decision to forego any florid crisis-rhetoric in representing the turning point of his own life. Stephen projects Eliot's complexly life-shaping noun, in its plural (hence, synecdochic or impersonal) form, onto the remote "crises and victories and secessions" in Roman history, so that crisis becomes merely one element among many in the nightmare of history from which he is trying to awake. Although used sparingly, the ironical trope thus proves if not central at least somewhat crucial to Joyce's structuring of Stephen's experience. By its association with orthodox literary practice, the crisis-trope could threaten to turn Stephen away from the high road of art. More correctly, perhaps, it might block his turn from the high road of conventional life into the devious side road of art.

In any case, Joyce here offers one of literature's most intricate crisis-figurations. It fully exploits several of the word's traditional and etymological meanings, even though the overall effect finally proves to be debunking or deconstructive. By contrast, in *Ulysses* Joyce has another story to tell, and he forgoes the great trope entirely. Admittedly, Alick West's analysis of *Ulysses* portrays Joyce as an artist in crisis. Likewise, E. M. Forster writes compellingly that *Ulysses* is strongly marked by a crisis (turning point) of the familiar kind when Dedalus and Bloom meet in Night Town.[26] Joyce, however, following out the logic of his decentering and rejection in *Portrait of the Artist* of the concussive noun as being irrelevant to his own strenuous modernism, omits the word entirely from his ambitious Homeric redaction. One might expect, then, that this intractable artist might never again use the tainted word. Nevertheless, he does actually use it in one unique, startling way in his final masterpiece *Finnegans Wake*.

Some writers not only possess a keen nose for keywords but also manage to color these words in their own way. Eliot certainly put her stamp upon *crisis*, by defining it as great, concussive, and manipulative; also by systematically using it to center and complicate characterizations, plots, and themes in her two greatest novels. Lawrence put his own special stamp upon the word by stipulating a new sexual meaning at once daring and compelling. Later in the twentieth century, by means of a cloacal anecdote, Lawrence Durrell will radically satirize the novelist's dependence upon the curious metacritical term, but Saul Bellow will make the great noun his own by using it developmentally through his ongoing oeuvre. Numerous other novelists, poets, critics, philosophers, and the like have put their own stamp upon the malleable word.

In the case of *Finnegans Wake*, an author literally puts his stamp—his name—upon the great keyword. In *Dubliners*, Joyce had highlighted contexts via the related words *critic*, *criticism*, and *critical*; however, he never resorted to their root word *crisis*. In *Portrait of the Artist*, he used it once as a means of signalling Stephen Dedalus's self-determined distance from cultural institutions which threaten to distract him from his artistic destiny. Joyce's final confrontation with the word appears in *Finnegans Wake*, arguably the most daring experiment in English literature, where Joyce forcefully uses *crisis* in a trope that puns upon his own surname.

More daring even than *Ulysses*, the virtually incomprehensible *Finnegans Wake*[27] is said to depict the dream-existence of one human being during one single night's troubled sleep. Joyce invented a new vocabulary that posits multiple meanings for many individual words. Instead of rational communication via traditional linguistic form and style, he provides an endlessly jumbled grammar, syntax, and narrative style. Guided by hints from Jung (collective unconscious and archetypes) as well as Freud (Oedipal family romance), plus Viconian cycles of history (divine, heroic, human), Joyce attempts to render the experience of the human race in terms of minor episodes from Irish history and culture. Beneath the nightmare fantasies, half-conscious dream sensations, and verbal quibbling, Joyce's behemoth develops a shadowy story. The dreamer is Humphrey Chimpden Earwicker, a pub-keeper in Dublin, who once accosted another person in Phoenix Park and now lives in fear of public exposure; who stands in complex relations to his own daughter Isobel, two sons Shem and Shaun, and wife Ann; and who spends a tormented night dreaming about his own troubles in a style calculated to recapitulate man's creation, fall, and redemption. To treat *Finnegans Wake* in familiar terms of narrative plot is to misjudge its decorum, since it is a book of mercurial transformations. H.C.E. and his wife undergo repeated metamorphoses until they embody change itself. Joyce offers a constant renewal of language via multi-levelled puns, portmanteau words, and parodies.

Finnegans Wake dramatizes modern consciousness, which grew out of social alienation and anomic isolation experienced by individuals "alone in the city." As a cultural and linguistic phenomenon, the new consciousness that steadily came to distinguish serious English fiction included the development of "a universal isolated language." Raymond Williams identified Joyce's last book as having a special role in this process: "*Finnegans Wake* is the crisis of the development we have been tracing: of the novel and community; the novel and the city; the novel of 'acting, thinking, speaking' man."[28] Not surprisingly, perhaps, Joyce himself conceived of *Finnegans Wake* as an anomic crisis-experience within which he must cannily provide himself with a name. His desperate strategy is symbolized by his having inscribed into this unconventional narrative the conventional word *crisis* at a major turning point.

I am convinced that Joyce's key phrase—"queeleetlecree of joysis crisis"—both parodies and pays homage to Lawrence's designation of Lady Chatterley's orgasm as a "crisis, with weird little cries." Broadly speaking, *Finnegans Wake* consists of four numbered parts. Near the end of part 2, Joyce depicts, under the guise of an athletic contest, a sexual union between a man and a woman. The woman eagerly joins their genitals in the nick of time to receive the man's seed. Joyce uses this episode to insinuate his own name, thus metonymically to connect the sign of his own artistic identity with the great noun he might prefer to ignore.

> For it was then a pretty thing happened of pure diversion mayhap, when his flattering hend, at the justright moment, like perchance some cook of corage might clip the lad on a poot of porage handshut his duckhouse, the vivid girl, deaf with love, (ah sure, you know her, our angel being, one of romance's fadeless wonderwomen, and, sure now, we all know you dote on her even unto date!) with a *queeleetlecree of joysis crisis* she renulited their disunited, with ripy lepes to ropy lopes (the dear o'dears!) and the golden importunity of aloofer's leavetime, when, as quick, is greased pigskin, Amoricas Champius, with one aragan thrust, druve the massive of virilvigtoury (flshpstshe) both lines of forwards (Eburnea's down, boys!) rightjingbangshot into the goal of her gullet. (pp. 395-96; emphasis added)

This intricate passage occurs at the three-fifths point where one expects the main turning point of a traditional novel. The explicit but spare crisis-trope may be construed to signal, however ironically, a turning point in an informing plot.

With Joyce, one must always begin with the punning language itself, with a discourse which extends significance not laterally but downwards into levels of meaning. How should the bizarre locution "joysis crisis" be construed? In its immediate context, "joysis crisis" imitates the joyous cries uttered by the woman in sexual ecstasy. With joyous cries she fuses herself to her lover and accepts his "massive of virilvigtoury" and his seed. Additionally, "joysis crisis" yields such permutations as "joy(s) is crisis" and the obverse corollary "crisis is joy(s)." We already know both that and how Joyce smuggled his own name into *Finnegans Wake* under more than two dozen guises.[29] Now, I believe, we can see that a heretofore unnoticed self-reflexive pun constitutes a special case of Joyce's subliminal and sublime egotism. The phrase itself can be construed as "the queer little cry of Joyce's crisis." It also can yield "Jesus Christ" or even "Jesus's crisis." Joyce could have found in the Middle English Dictionary an entry (*crise*) adjacent to the entry *cris-* (having to do with Christ). He may be echoing, perhaps parodying, Karl Barth's theology of KRISIS in which Jesus Christ is characterized as follows: "In Christ the KRISIS breaks forth." Intertextually, too (I believe), this curious phrase recalls Connie Chatterley's self-defining orgasmic utterance.

These verbal possibilities provide a clear warrant for conceptually construing the passage as follows: (1) sexual intercourse is a joyous crisis, (2) sexual intercourse is Joyce's crisis, (3) sexual intercourse is Jesus's crisis, (4) sexual intercourse is Jesus Christ, i.e., divine, (5) Jesus Christ is sexual intercourse, i.e., an in-breaking into the world such as Barth emphasized, or (6) sexual intercourse occasions Joyce's own cries of joy, i.e., *Finnegans Wake*. In any case, the "joysis crisis" passage establishes Joyce as a noteworthy, and in some respects unique, crisis-thinker. One further level of meaning—crisis as turning point—suggests that Joyce used the great noun not only for verbal and conceptual effects but, like novelists before him and since, for plot structure and character elaboration.

The turning point I choose to connect with the *joysis crisis* passage occurs in book 2, chapter 4 (the "joysis crisis" chapter). Narrated by a composite of the four Gospel writers (Mamalujo), this section insinuates and elaborates Joyce's main theme: youth supplants age. Joyce uses the chapter to bring to a climax the seminal love affair between Tristan and Isolde, whose cosmic coupling outstrips the efforts of the middle-aged Earwicker and his wife Ann. Via the frantic sexual union of Tristan and

Isolde, Joyce establishes a revolutionary cosmic or mythic time-scheme that supplants the more usual chronological time-scheme of western culture.[30] Historically, too, "joysis crisis" signals the main paradigm shift from the dead narrative of the gospels toward a Viconian scheme of mythic time. Joyce's major symbols are simply the male and female sexual organs of the human body.[31] By means of this one startling crisis-trope, I wish to urge, *Finnegans Wake* signifies its status as a huge, explosive dirty joke but a healthy joke validated by human experience and joyfully endorsed by its author. In several senses, it thus constitutes one of the memorable turning points in English literature.

Confronted with the numerous difficulties of *Finnegans Wake*, one lays down one's arms. Suffice it in the present context to say that one of the most daring modernists apparently discovered that he could not compose even his most revolutionary book with its largely incomprehensible rhetoric without resorting at least once to the great noun that had served English novelists since the invention of the form. Joyce goes George Eliot one better by actually making uncomprehended words in effect entirely incomprehensible as he contributes a brilliant chapter and an extremely personal dimension to the history of the crisis-trope as part of the rhetoric of narrative fiction.

In the process of putting his stamp, his own great name, upon a metamorphically great noun, he single-handedly wrought a permanent change in crisis-consciousness and literary consciousness itself.

6

A Trope to be Exploded:
Lawrence Durrell

The history of consciousness represents a drama of being and, even more so, of becoming human. The history of crisis-consciousness intensifies the awareness of one's thoughts, beliefs, impressions, desires, and existential predicament. To confront consciousness is a hard-to-define calling and task. Crisis-consciousness peculiarly resists definition, although the history of the crisis-trope thus far makes clear that it can be construed variously as focal and subsidiary awareness, experiential subjectivity, symbolization, hermeneutics, dynamics of desire, or incarnate subjectivity. In every case, it structures itself in terms of sharp polarities: rational and irrational, subjective and objective, sameness and difference, active and passive, self and other, intellectual and spiritual, horizontal and vertical, and the like. Each new generation of writers tries but fails to pin it down, in the process elaborating Eliot's great noun into a great cultural tale.[1]

Every crisis-trope in one of its effects guarantees that a writer will, in Hans Kellner's paradoxical phrase, inadvertently or purposively "get the story crooked."[2] Modern individualistic subjectivity informed by crisis-consciousness takes many a twist and turn. If Barth and Husserl variously and heatedly appeal to the emotions, the historian of science T. S. Kuhn constructs an influential study, *The Structure of Scientific Revolutions* (1970), which employs the great noun almost exclusively as a rational keyword in describing processes of scientific change. Recalling Thomas Paine's or George Meredith's linking of *crisis* with revolution, Kuhn's chapter headings signal his intention:

VII. Crisis and the Emergence of Scientific Theories
VIII. The Response to Crisis

Like J. S. Mill and Thomas Hardy, Kuhn builds *crisis* overtly into his skeletal outline. Kuhn invokes no literary figure such as Barth's exemplary Dostoevsky, but he is more sympathetic to literature than Husserl. His theory of paradigm shift has itself played a role in literary theory.[3] Likewise, his elucidation of how crisis within a scientific community necessitates ontological change bears specifically upon narrative turning points as well as generally upon cultural climates or mind-sets.

Kuhn's crisis-figure derives from a history-of-ideas method employed in non-scientific fields, as he himself explains:

> To the extent that the book portrays scientific development as a succession of tradition-bound periods punctuated by non-cumulative breaks, its theses are undoubtedly of wide applicability. But they should be, for they are borrowed from other fields. Historians of literature, of music, of the arts, of political development, and of many other human activities have long described their subjects in the same way.[4]

Kuhn's exposition of dialectical paradigm shift could be applied, *mutatis mutandis*, to the crisis-signals by which novelists internally formalize their representations of human life. His argument goes as follows. Historically, science moves from paradigm to paradigm in large, fateful revolutions (Copernicus to Newton to Maxwell to Einstein). A paradigm is a scientific achievement providing model problems and solutions for a community of practitioners (p. viii). At key moments, whenever anomalies seriously disrupt a paradigm, a major shift in consciousness and practice may occur. A condition of crisis may ensue, and when a researcher ends a crisis, a scientific revolution has occurred.

Science moves from one perception of the world to another, in a process involving not only steady data-gathering but also random accident (arbitrariness). Normal science usually does not suppress novelty for long. An unexpected discovery means that the scientist's world view has been "qualitatively transformed as well as quantitatively enriched." Normal science enacts ingenious "puzzle solving." An expert puzzle-solver aims to achieve not so much a new result but an anticipated result in a fresh way (p. 36). Kuhn initiates a crisis-trope when he elucidates two stages of research that enable paradigm shift. Revolutionary discovery commences with the awareness of anomaly (p. 53). When the awareness of anomaly reaches a certain intensity, the scientist sees nature in a different way. This predicament Kuhn labels *crisis*. Within the context of growing crisis, any failure of existing rules may necessitate a search for new rules (p. 68). When an established theory becomes vague and useless, competing theories may proliferate and compete: "The significance of crises is the indication they provide that an occasion for retooling has arrived" (p. 76). *Crisis* thus functions as a sign within a sign system.

An existing theory will be declared invalid only if an alternate theory is offered in its place. Creative scientists, like artists, must be able to tolerate the state of crisis ("the essential tension") implicit in research. Crisis loosens the rules of normal puzzle-solving in ways that ultimately permit a new paradigm to emerge (p. 80). Two principles explain the variety of responses to crisis. A paralyzing malaise accompanies the awareness of acute crisis, but once faced, crisis enables a significant "switch of gestalt" or new way of seeing the world. A crisis-induced paradigm shift means the adoption of a new world view or "gestalt switch" (p. 122). Paradigm shift necessitates deep epistemological and ontological processes, and after the switch has occurred scientists "work in a different world." Paradigm shift carries two basic meanings: group commitment and shared example. Kuhn's crisis-trope signals, first, "the common awareness that something has gone wrong" and, second, "a self-correcting mechanism which ensures that the rigidity of normal science will not forever go unchallenged" (p. 181). These two meanings equate roughly with meanings I have assumed throughout this book, including dire situation, dialectical turning point, and self-reflexive critical judgment. I also believe that Kuhn would not deny that some degree of manipulation via *crisis* will characterize a scientific revolution, given that careers and economics are at stake.

By contrast with Barth's fearsome rhetoric of KRISIS or Husserl's anxious warning to rationalistic Europeans, Kuhn's rhetoric remains reasoned and cool. One excerpt can illustrate both his thought-style and his own grasp of the complexities of scientific crisis-consciousness.

> Such explicit recognitions of breakdown are extremely rare, but the *effects of crisis* do not entirely depend upon its conscious recognition. What can we say these effects are? Only two of them seem to be universal. *All crises begin* with the blurring of a paradigm and the consequent loosening of the rules for normal research. In this respect *research during crisis* very much resembles research during the pre-paradigm period, except that in the former the locus of difference is both smaller and more clearly defined. And *all crises close* in one of three ways. Sometimes normal science ultimately proves able to handle the *crisis-provoking problem* despite the despair of those who have seen it as the end of an existing paradigm. On other occasions the problem resists even apparently radical new approaches. Then scientists may conclude that no solution will be forthcoming in the present state of their field. The problem is labelled and set aside for a future generation with more developed tools. Or,

finally, the case that will most concern us here, a *crisis may end with the emergence of a new candidate for paradigm* and with the ensuing battle over its acceptance. (p. 84; emphases added)

Kuhn's vocabulary has become a standard component of the history of science.

Kuhn's crisis-speculations bear indirectly upon the dialectical changes constructed by novelists. Fictive choices and transformations in effect represent paradigm shifts. In James's *The Portrait of a Lady*, Isabel Archer notices in the behavior of her husband an "anomaly" which she broods upon, thus precipitating a crisis leading to a shift in the value system by which Isabel chooses to compose her own life. Likewise, John Stuart Mill's personal crisis included his recognition of anomalies in an existing cultural system: "the anomalies and evils characteristic of the transition from a system of opinions which had worn out, to another only in process of being formed." Like Barth and Husserl, Kuhn powerfully witnesses to the widespread reliance upon George Eliot's great noun.

A novelist may structure a narrative as a *crisis*-determined paradigm shift. William Golding's *Lord of the Flies* (1954)[5] is regularly praised for its consummate control of the novel form and deep insight into the human condition. In its portrayal of a regression from civilized order to primitive violence experienced by a group of boys on a deserted tropical island, Golding's superb allegory compellingly elaborates a theme expressible variously (in phrases drawn from the book itself) as a "breaking up of sanity" or a "liberation into savagery" or simply an "end of innocence."

Much of the popular and critical appeal of *Lord of the Flies* results from its being an extraordinarily controlled narrative. Underneath Golding's superb descriptions, dialogue, episodic excitement, and atmosphere of terror, the novelist also built a firm intellectual structure based on a traditional schema of human nature. The major characters Jack, Ralph, Piggy, and Simon represent, respectively (and, so to speak, tropologically) the elements of passion, will, reason, and conscience (Simon's acute consciousness of ambiguity). In the story itself, under pressure of isolation and freedom, the boys grow ever more violent. Golding's remarkable achievement results from his depiction of dialectical paradoxes operating between rationality and irrationality. In addition to the rational four-part schema of passion, will, reason, and conscience, Golding also incorporates another pattern, based on irrational but powerful Jungian symbolism.[6] His fable-like novel depicts one of the most acute fears of the twentieth century: what would happen to human life after a nuclear holocaust? His lucid control can be seen in part in his becoming, at a main turning point, a confident crisis-rhetorician.

In chapter 8, Golding constructs a scene in which a red-haired, hot-headed boy named Jack, having earlier deserted the other boys by asserting that "I'm going off by myself," now returns to the group only to impose his dominant personality and lead them down the path to violence. Jack promises the mob not only positive rewards but also some relief from their fears. Golding signals this fateful moment as a revolutionary but muted dialectical turning point. A paradigm shift occurs, from rational to irrational (group) behavior.

> "We'll hunt. I'm going to be chief."
> They nodded, and *the crisis passed easily*.
> "And then--about the beast."
> They moved, and looked at the forest.
> "I say this. We aren't going to bother about the beast."
> He nodded at them.
> "We're going to forget the beast."
> "That's right!"
> "Yes!"
> "Forget the beast!"
> If Jack was astonished by their fervor he did not show it.
>
> (p. 159; emphasis added)

Although not using the manipulative keyword itself, Jack nevertheless uses a sophistication enabled by crisis-consciousness to exploit the boys' fears so as to pierce them in the "depths of their tormented private lives." He thus terrorizes and tyrannizes them into submission. In this story that is arguably one prolonged crisis, and in an age when the exploitative word was being exploded in all quarters, Golding constructed a crisis-trope as economical of means as Henry Mackenzie's or George Moore's and with comparable success. One single occurrence of crisis splits the narrative in two and thus radically challenges any unity-effects.

Golding's parsimonious use of the increasingly exploited keyword by no means represents the sole or even the chief type of crisis-trope during this period. Only three years after *Lord of the Flies*, a less traditional writer began to publish a four-volume novel that as radically as Joyce's books critiques the question whether such a metacritical term deserves any place in imaginative works which attempt to advance beyond traditional literary form and literary truth.

"The crisis in the drama precipitates . . . the reborn self"

One response to the spreading influence of the great noun as a mere buzzword or too-convenient ploy has been various attempts to neutralize it by ridicule and laughter. T. S. Eliot's brilliant couplet in "The Love Song of J. Alfred Prufrock" ("Should I, after tea and cakes and ices, / Have the strength to force the moment to its crisis?") may be taken as representing this type of response. But the problem remains complex. George Eliot's crisis-tropes illustrated how human beings use words both to manipulate other people and to script their own lives. The possibility of becoming one's true and best self by passing through a crisis-experience informs many other writers' work. This complex formation of the self via crisis-consciousness and an appropriate rhetoric stands in sharp contrast to all simplistic interpretations of crisis as merely an external turning point in a plot of action.

Aristotle himself in effect may have oversimplified the problem by emphasizing external action and external change of circumstance. Paul Goodman urges that the crisis in a Greek tragedy involved not so much external action as a character's realizing himself by achieving subjective wholeness.

> The error of the *Poetics* is to put in the foreground the complex plot, here plot and counterplot: the scheme to abduct Philoctetes and his unerring bow, and the contrary effort of Philoctetes to go home. But, if we think of this as the main structure, the characters are not even serious (as defined above). *In the crisis Neoptolemus simply gives up the scheme and agrees to something else*; and, as Philoctetes is presented, his desire to get home is only a small part of his need, it is not the essential thing, to be rid of his wound. Yet it is a serious play. What *is* serious for these characters? It is for Neoptolemus to be himself and fulfil himself, the honest young man thirsting for glory, and for Philoctetes to become whole. This, as it is handled, they cannot possibly achieve, and yet they achieve it.[7] (emphasis added)

In effect, Goodman's theory puts an intensively subjective twist upon Eliot's implied definition of *crisis*.

Lawrence Durrell similarly redefined crisis as a factor bearing upon an inward change or "reborn self." In a letter to Henry Miller, Durrell rejected Sartrean existentialism as lacking "CRISIS" and hence as lacking the potential for rejuvenative change. Coincidentally, the awareness of subjectivity that Goodman denied to Aristotle, Durrell presumably would generously and more properly restore.

> Apropos the existentialists—there is, it seems to me, one terrible metaphysical flaw in the whole Sartre thesis. The lack of CRISIS. The only justification for the art of *stasis* which is XXth century art is in the precipitation of crisis. The

crisis in the drama precipitates the crisis in the audience—and thus the cathartic principle of change of stance—*the reborn self*.[8] (emphasis added)

Like Kuhn's crisis-triggered paradigm shift, the crisis-enabled "reborn self" represents a crucial ideal in the modern world, from Carlyle and Mill through James and Lawrence to Bellow. Lawrence has already been cited as a writer who took pains to define the great noun (ecstatic, transfigurative, rejuvenative) before employing it in an ambitious novel. In *Twilight in Italy*, Lawrence proclaimed a perfervid belief in a reborn self. He then elaborated an innovative crisis-trope in *Lady Chatterley's Lover*. Durrell follows this powerful example. Any reader might expect that a novelist taking such pains to define *crisis* might also grapple with it in his fiction, and Durrell in fact does so in *The Alexandria Quartet*.

Throughout the *Alexandria Quartet* (1957-60),[9] Durrell uses *crisis* in eight contexts, ranging from the routine to the unusual and finally to the unique. In general, he urges the principle of the reborn self, but he ultimately treats the great noun with comic disdain.

A self-questioning text that thus induces a dizzying sense of aporia and doubt, *The Alexandria Quartet* consists of *Justine*, *Balthazar*, *Mountolive*, and *Clea*. The first, second, and fourth volumes express an intensely subjective point of view, whereas the third volume jolts the reader by being cast as an objective third-person narrative. Durrell sets the *Alexandria Quartet* in Egypt around the time of the second World War. Heavily influenced by Joyce and Proust, he narrates an involuted story shot through with complex ideas and experimental techniques. He subjects his narrator and major character L. G. Darley—a schoolteacher and aspiring writer—to a strenuous education in emotion and experience so that ultimately Darley masters his self-doubts and confidently begins to write his book. Intertextually (as I have shown elsewhere) the quartet derives its ontological structure from Proust's four-part *Swann's Way*.[10]

Within the historical context of a disruptive war, Darley's adventures involve him politically with a Coptic minority scheming against a Moslem majority. He also becomes sexually involved with three women (Justine, Melissa, Clea) who enable him to grow in humane understanding. The *Alexandria Quartet* also plays with complex ideas such as Einsteinian relativity, dimorphism, and cyclism. Providing a matchless evocation of an exotic international city, Durrell's ambitious enterprise develops major cultural themes. He wishes to refute fashionable clichés about alienation, dissociation of sensibility, and dehumanization as twentieth-century man's ineluctable fate and only subject for art.

Durrell's subject and style overwhelm the reader with a torrent of images, descriptions, impressions, ideas, reflections, and tropes. In such a torrent, no single word would likely stand out above the rest. Yet from the first page of *Justine*, Durrell's narrator demonstrates a self-reflexive awareness of his own vocabulary ("I do not know why I use the word 'escape'"). For Durrell to use *crisis* in only eight contexts—but at least once in each of the four volumes—seems niggardly enough but still more than fortuitous. At one point he signals an important philosophical speculation via *crisis*, and in closing, he takes pains to debunk crisis-rhetoric itself.

In this *Künstlerroman*, Darley undergoes his apprenticeship to life and art by becoming, to some degree at least, a crisis-strategist. Durrell shares the reader's amusement at the spectacle of Darley's attempting to construct in English a narrative about Egyptians using crisis-terms familiar to readers of James or Forster. Consistent with the historical moment, a prolonged entanglement of wartime danger and stress, Darley renders his characters as, from time to time, seeking to avoid the disorienting effects of crisis itself. Darley characterizes them in terms of crisis-consciousness. In *Justine*, Darley portrays himself as Justine's lover, almost in sight of her husband the Coptic banker and political conspirator Nessim Hosnani. During a summer retreat from the city to the Hosnani country home, while describing Nessim's laboring at common tasks in order to soothe his nerves, Darley ironically renders Nessim's crisis-consciousness in terms of quotidian reality: "There is always time for spiritual crises, he thought, as he doggedly mixed cement and dry sand in a wooden mortar" (p. 165).

In *Balthazar*, Darley violently deconstructs the story he told in *Justine*. Accepting Percy Pursewarden's belief that human beings enact "lives based upon selected fictions" (p. 14), Darley uses numerous writings by various of his characters as the basis for his own subjective account of events—social, political, sexual—in Alexandria and its environs. When a minor character named Amar has been acquitted of charges that he murdered the homosexual French agent Toto de Brunel, Darley goes on to write that Clea Montis expresses her sense of relief afforded by the verdict because she has thus been spared an ethical crisis: "'It has saved me from a *crise de conscience*'" (p. 228). Her reasoning is based upon her own privileged knowledge that Narouz Hosnani, brother of Nessim, had in fact accidentally killed Toto. In the event of Amar's conviction, she would feel compelled to testify so as to save Amar. Now she can keep her illicit knowledge from the authorities. Only in terms of a presumed crisis-motif does this muted passage carry much thematic weight. It valorizes Clea as a special character in Darley's system of values, demonstrates that under prolonged stress Durrell's (and Darley's) characters attempt to avoid crisis, and shows Darley himself resorting, albeit sparingly, to the great noun in composing his experimental narrative.

In another letter to Henry Miller, Durrell described the objective third volume, *Mountolive*, as the key to understanding the quartet of novels: "This big novel [*Mountolive*] is as tame and naturalistic in *form* as a Hardy; yet it is the fulcrum of the quartet and the rationale of the thing. With the fourth I can plunge back into the time-stream again as per *Justine*."[11] *Mountolive* jars the reader's consciousness and sensibilities by taking the form of a novel of Balzacian objectivity. It is a medium-length fiction of sixteen chapters containing powerful symbols (trap, whip) and strong themes (memory, entrapment, futility). It begins with an unforgettable "fish drive" on Lake Mareotis, in which the English visitor David Mountolive participates, and it ends with an equally memorable Coptic wake, from which Mountolive is absent. In between these vivid episodes, a detailed narrative focuses on Mountolive's role as the English Ambassador to Egypt. A complicated set of personages and circumstances make up Egyptian politics just prior to the second world war. Egypt has its independence from England, and a difficult transfer of power is underway. The Arab majority threaten to obliterate a Coptic-Christian minority, but the Copts scheme to ensure their future safety by secretly shipping guns to the Jews in Palestine. While still a junior diplomatic officer, Mountolive becomes romantically drawn toward a mysterious Coptic group, the Hosnani family. He is seduced into a love affair by Leila Hosnani, mother of his friend Nessim. Posted away to Prague and other capitals, he corresponds with Leila, who tries unsuccessfully to broaden his education with poetry and art. Returned to Egypt as ambassador (chap. 6), he is vexed by Leila's refusal to receive him and by rumors of a Coptic conspiracy involving his friend Nessim. At a key moment, he must decide how to respond to Pursewarden's revelation that Nessim smuggles guns to Palestine. Mountolive's dilatory behavior prevents his carrying out any official action until a British intelligence officer stationed in Palestine confronts him with evidence.

By this time, chaos reigns. The Coptic community is scattering to Kenya and other refuges. Mountolive is summoned to a final confrontation with the secluded Leila, now a hideously pock-marked, grotesque, "fattish Egyptian lady with all the marks of eccentricity and age written upon her appearance." When she begs him to protect her son Nessim, he curtly refuses her plea and takes to his heels (p. 280). The book closes with a detailed account of a Coptic wake for the fanatical Narouz Hosnani, Nessim's brother, who had been assassinated by other, less rabid, Copts.

Durrell's minimal use of *crisis* in both *Justine* and *Balthazar* would hardly justify their inclusion in the present study. Likewise, *Mountolive*, despite its undeniable interest, could only be taken to represent a negative exemplum. Only once in the objective story of David Mountolive will Durrell include any crisis-signal. *Mountolive* is regularly taken to be Durrell's insertion, for unaccountable reasons, of a naturalistic novel in which the narrator of the other three volumes participates as a character and thus becomes not so much a narrating subject as a narrated object. It thus provides the beleaguered reader with a momentary stay against confusion by offering true-seeming facts that clarify Darley's perplexing subjectivity in volumes one, two, and (eventually) four. Durrell's readers welcome the unexpected if only temporary feeling of certitude that comes with *Mountolive*. However, a more consistent reading of this book of solid specificity urges that it represents an ontologically distinct division of the *Alexandria Quartet* by virtue of its being Darley's unannounced first effort at composing a novel proper. Consistent with the principles of the Proustian *Künstlerroman*, this third book of the quartet enacts a crucial metonymic stage in Darley's maturation and thus proves to be, as Durrell asserted to Miller, the ironical "rationale of the thing."[12]

In any case, Darley makes little explicit use in *Mountolive* of any crisis-trope. The story contains a strong turning point of the sort other novelists (Mackenzie, Conrad, Golding) judge it best to signal via *crisis*. This turning point is the agonized moment (p. 187) when David Mountolive must decide what to do about Nessim Hosnani's smuggling of guns to Palestine, where they are used to undermine the peace by killing British soldiers. His dilemma replicates the evidentiary crisis-dilemma facing Clea Montis in *Balthazar*, but Darley narrates the moment without recourse to the great noun.

Darley signifies the electrifying keyword only when Nessim himself must decide whether to disown his extremist brother Narouz, whose violent temper threatens their secret conspiracy: "Ideally, then, he should be prepared in such a crisis to disown Narouz, to depose Narouz, even if necessary to . . . him!" (p. 228; ellipsis Durrell's). However, Nessim concludes: "'I shall never harm him.'" Given that Narouz will eventually be assassinated, perhaps with Nessim's tacit approval, this crisis-moment in Nessim's experience certainly counts heavily in Durrell's overall thematic purpose. Yet, given that not Nessim but David Mountolive functions as the main character in *Mountolive*, it proves to be of only peripheral importance.

In a special sense, Durrell does confront the rhetorical question historically present from Richardson's time onward in connection with Eliot's concussive, electrifying, manipulative, structuring noun. Granted that this word which means "judgment" will plausibly serve critics who must judge literary performances, one wonders if it will also serve the imaginative requirements of Darley the artist? In *Clea*, Durrell uses the great noun but finally judges it to be laughably inadequate to life's exigencies. With *Clea*, Darley resumes his subjective narration, and his crisis-rhetoric here transcends the random gestures in the first three books. Four crisis-images in *Clea* not only advance the artist's coming-of-age theme that informs the entire quartet but also culminates in one of the most memorably self-critical crisis-tropes in the history of the novel. Dividing *Clea* into three numbered books, in book 1 Darley narrates his return to Alexandria—after a temporary escape from that feverish city—and his love affair with the artist Clea Montis. He concludes Book I by citing a radical idea uttered by his mentor Pursewarden: "'There is no Other; there is only oneself facing forever the problem of one's self-discovery!'" (pp. 98-9). The motif of self-discovery ("reborn self") thenceforth becomes Darley's major consciousness theme. In book 2, Darley renders the hysterical atmosphere of wartime Alexandria, the "passions and profligacies" of the numerous soldiers. He floridly signifies the chaotic atmosphere as a violent if temporary paradigm shift from "old harmonies" to new discordances.

> Their furious gaiety tried hard to match the *gravity of the crisis* in which they were involved; at times the town was racked by the frenetic outbursts of their disguised spleen and boredom until the air became charged with the mad spirit of carnival; a saddening and heroic pleasure-seeking which *disturbed and fractured the old harmonies* on which personal relationships had rested, straining the links which bound us. (p. 104; emphases added)

Here, Darley writes like a conventional novelist about wartime noise and disorientation.

Like *Justine* and *Balthazar*, the first-person *Clea* is not informed by any single turning point. Where one expects a turning point in a more traditional novel, Darley contrives for the English journalist Johnny Keats, while dizzied with fatigue and champagne, to utter a radical crisis-theory as an explanation of the human tendency to wage war. As Durrell lays the groundwork for Darley's intellectualized debunking of the crisis-trope itself, he allows Keats to define crisis as being part of a Darwinian survival mechanism designed to force inert human beings to acknowledge the reality of death.

"I believe the desire for war was first lodged in the instincts as a biological *shock-mechanism to precipitate a spiritual crisis* which couldn't be done any other how in limited people. The less sensitive among us can hardly visualise death, far less live joyfully with it. So the powers that arranged things for us felt they must concretise it, in order to lodge death in the actual present. Purely helpfully, if you see what I mean!" (p. 183; emphasis added)

Durrell both gives and takes away. Crisis-consciousness is exalted as a strategy for the survival of an entire species, but the species itself is composed at least in part of individuals so inert that they must be violently jolted into consciousness. Keats's tipsy hyperbole might provide Darley with a reason for changing his mind about the value of the metacritical word *crisis* itself. Keats in effect reduces to absurdity the principles of the *Bildungsroman* and the *Künstlerroman* by egotistically asserting his ironic belief that the horrifying spectacle of crisis-inducing war has one main function: "'All this had to be brought about so that poor Johnny Keats could grow into a man'" (p. 182). Keats might be satirizing the solipsistic Darley himself. His ludicrous crisis-motif encroaches upon Darley's own personalized theme of self-discovery and might cause a negative reaction in the solemn young author. Durrell may thus be satirizing his priggish young hero in parodying the convention by which *crisis* inwardly shapes a narrative, in this case by signalling a philosophical reflection. Darley's most acute discovery could then be that he can now hope to function as an artist without resorting to any traditional device like the explicit image insinuated by the drunken Johnny Keats.

Durrell accomplishes Darley's aesthetic paradigm shift by a curious but effective logic. Darley narrates one further crisis-episode in complete seriousness before satirizing the trope itself. Late in book 2, while describing how he liberated himself from dependence upon Clea and became his own man, he erroneously tries to characterize Clea herself by means of the great noun: "But now she was standing by the window listening, her whole body stiffened into an attitude of attentive interrogation so acute that it suggested *something like a crisis of apprehension*" (p. 233; emphasis added). Darley confuses two ideas that ironically enable his maturation. First, he learns that what he mistakenly perceived as a "crisis of apprehension" proves to be merely a symptom of Clea's physical illness (which reaches its own properly medical crisis and can then be treated by a physician). Second, he is shocked into recognizing the deep relation between *crisis* and *criticism* (judgment). Informing Clea that he plans to write a "book of criticism," he humbly accepts from his intense lover a monitory slap in the face (p. 237). He thereby receives an insight into the self-reflexive nature of crisis-consciousness itself. He must now acknowledge that his own perceptions may prove erroneous; more importantly, he learns that not the critic's but the artist's judgment must inform an artist's work. In a complex way, Darley becomes, like Eliot's Daniel Deronda, one of literature's most properly instructed crisis-rhetoricians but one who must paradoxically distrust a trope that enables his own self-defining and self-constituting literary activity.

Now able self-reflexively to apply critical thought to a presumed crisis, Darley culminates his crisis-trope near the end of *Clea* by inserting an exuberant comic story told him by the Egyptian magistrate Nimrod. Wishing to pay a tribute to his deceased friend Joshua Scobie, Nimrod recounts how Scobie had once invented a mechanical contraption (Bijou Earth Closet or "old mud-slinger") designed to provide a method of cloacal sanitation by simply throwing a shovelful of dirt over each occurrence of fecal waste. In one instance, as Nimrod recalls, the contrivance went awry, precipitating a "crisis" and providing Nimrod with a superb anecdote with which to regale his friends.

> "It looks queer, I admit. In fact it looks arcane. But it's a wonderful contrivance the little Bijou. *Once there was a crisis* while I was home on leave for a month. I called in to see Budgie. He was almost in tears. The chap who helped, Tom the carpenter, used to drink a bit and must have misplaced the sprockets on one series of Bijous. Anyway complaints started to pour in. Budgie said that his closets had gone mad all over Sussex and were throwing earth about in a weird and unwholesome way. Customers were furious." (p. 262; emphasis added)

Rube Goldberg machines gone mad and "throwing earth about in a weird and unwholesome way" in respectable English homes. Darley has thus attempted ultimately to judge his own and perhaps any writer's use of the florid trope. In tropological terms, Darley's inset story ridicules the very idea of crisis by depicting a shift from metaphor (the body) to metonymic otherness (feces) to synecdochic part/whole systematics (the berserk machine).

Durrell thus seems to laugh at the widespread practice of using *crisis* as a covering word for all emergencies, real and imagined. Then, too, he also may be laughing at himself and his impertinent narrator. Darley and the shadowy implied author judge any Aristotelian crisis to be an anomaly in modernist aesthetics. They attempt to explain, explode, or simply laugh out of existence a problematical word associated with Mill, Newman, Barth, Husserl and other influential thinkers but also linked intimately with Durrell's theme of the reborn self struggling with the dialectics of objectivity and subjectivity.

The splendid, vexing *Alexandria Quartet* resembles Proust's masterpiece in which, at the end, the artist-hero Marcel has learned to order the intensities of human existence via narrative prose fiction. Both Proust's Marcel and Durrell's Darley can now take up the pen and compose, as it were, a story that begins "once upon a time." Paradoxically, however, the book each neophyte will compose is in fact the book each one has already finished writing. The very crisis-trope Darley wishes to forswear by means of his anecdote about Scobie's Rube Goldberg machine already constitutes part of his narrative. In the present critical history, such formal wit and intricate authorial dependency have been matched only by another self-consciously high-modern strategy, Joyce's punning phrase "joysis crisis" in *Finnegans Wake*.

The *Alexandria Quartet* represents an important stage in the career of the great noun. Durrell provides a memorable crisis-trope, as serious in its cultural critique and revolutionary aesthetics as that elaborated by Eliot or Lawrence. Paradoxically, he illustrates in an intricate but convincing way the cogency of his belief in a crisis-enabled reborn self that contributes to the survival of the human race. Crisis-consciousness enables men to contemplate the ineluctable fact of their impending physical death. When does the judgment come? Durrell answers resoundingly. With courage and wit, he urges that Eliot's problematical trope ought to occasion nothing but cloacal humor. Ironically, given the Proustian circularity of the *Alexandria Quartet*, this ostensible last word is one the reader must finally reject. The great noun unarguably serves Durrell's constructional and thematic intentions, never more so than when he ridicules it.[13]

7

An Extremist Crisis in Crisis-Consciousness:
Robert Coover

As modern individuals become more deracinated and anomic, the great noun becomes more widespread as an effective figuration, keyword, and buzzword in numerous departments of life. In such a circumstance, certainty and legitimacy grow acutely problematical. In literature, Flaubert and Conrad had demonstrated that writers themselves may experience disorienting shifts in readership so their artistic innovations represent a source not only of subversive freedom but also of anomic desperation. As revolutionary artists, they desperately required some sign of legitimation.[1] In this context, the social scientist Jürgen Habermas is a major crisis-analyst. As much as Barth, Husserl, and Kuhn provide intellectual context for Lawrence, Joyce, and Durrell respectively, the German Habermas provides a viable framework or cross-reference for my next major example. Habermas's *Legitimationsprobleme im Spätkapitalismus* (1973) has been rendered as *Legitimation Crisis.*[2] Habermas reconceives old theories of crisis in new ways and thus provides an alternative to Marx's crisis theory by explaining problems in advanced capitalism. As was the case with J. S. Mill and T. S. Kuhn, his table of contents announces his intention:

Part II Crisis Tendencies in Advanced Capitalism

Chapter 3   A Classification of Possible Crisis Tendencies
Chapter 4   Theorems of Economic Crisis
Chapter 5   Theorems of Rationality Crisis
Chapter 6   Theorems of Legitimation Crisis
Chapter 7   Theorems of Motivation Crisis

Habermas uses *crisis* as insistently as Barth and as rationalistically as Kuhn.

188

The most influential contemporary German thinker, Habermas has handled thorny concepts in hermeneutics and social theory, adapted systems-theoretic approaches to social inquiry, and speculated about the relations between communicative competence and the philosophy of social theory. On the whole, he illustrates how deeply the loaded word *crisis* has rooted itself in advanced social-science thought and terminology. By contrast with Barth, Habermas makes little direct mention of literature, but indirectly he provides one of the clearest pictures of modern literature as being grounded in an acute crisis-consciousness. As a social scientist interested in questions of social control, he labels human experiences lived outside of the category of administration as "uncontrolled societal processes." Literature thus falls under the category of "world-maintaining interpretive systems" that belong to the past. Habermas relinquishes the unruly contingencies of human life (Husserl's life-world) that make grist for the novelist's mill. In the process, though, he aptly describes the existential realm belonging to the serious novelist who would alter the reader's consciousness.

> Considering the risks to individual life that exist, a theory that could interpret away the facticities of loneliness and guilt, sickness and death is, to be sure, not even *conceivable*. Contingencies that are irremovably attached to the bodily and moral constitution of the individual can be raised to consciousness only *as* contingency. We must, in principle, live disconsolately with them. (p. 120)

By contrast with Habermas, a novelist such as Iris Murdoch follows Sartre's example by founding her entire oeuvre on the uncontrollable contingencies bracketed by Habermas.

Sociocultural life is not subject to arbitrary definitions, consisting as it does of inner environments that are "paradoxical from the point of steering" (p. 8). By contrast with George Eliot, who could value uncomprehended words for their usefulness in scripting one's life, Habermas regrets that individuals can use words to evade social control. He laments the "splendor and poverty of bourgeois subjectivity." Habermas's unflinching (and appalling) last word is to insist that social control must be achieved at any cost: "at the price of—so be it! old European human dignity!" (p. 143). By contrast, the present study shows that novelistic crisis-rhetoric since Richardson has enabled novelists to critique and thereby sustain "old European human dignity." Historically, then, *crisis* has served the most diametrically opposed rhetorical purposes. Far from invoking novelists and novels to support his argument,

Habermas sets his face against any such "narrative production of an illusion of order" (p. 119).

Habermas provides a sustained definition of the great noun (pp. 1-31). He treats of four areas of experience: medicine, dramaturgy, history, and social science. As profoundly as Husserl, but regretfully, he acknowledges the challenge to rational objectivity residing in personalized subjectivity. He also extends the range of meanings. In medicine, although an illness may seem objective, something contracted through external influences and accessible to analysis, yet the patient's consciousness is not entirely excluded from the total process: "the resolution of a crisis effects a liberation of the subject caught up in it." Subjectivity proves equally important in dramaturgical crisis. Thus classical aestheticians, writes Habermas, define *crisis* as "the turning point in a fateful process that, despite all objectivity, does not simply impose itself from outside and does not remain external to the identity of the person caught up in it." In drama, both action and personality express objective and subjective contradictions during the catastrophic culmination of the plot. Similarly, a complex meaning of crisis figures in the idea of history as salvation. Beginning with eighteenth-century philosophers of history and continuing into nineteenth-century evolutionary social theories, history as salvation reaches a plateau in Marxism. Finally, a systems-theoretic meaning of crisis is a familiar tool in the social sciences. There, *crisis* means "persistent disturbances of *system integration*."

Habermas writes a notoriously dense jargon yet one adequately self-reflexive to suit even Paul de Man. His style can be seen in a passage such as the following:

> Crises in social systems are not produced through accidental changes in the environment, but through structurally inherent system-imperatives that are incompatible and cannot be hierarchically integrated. Structurally inherent contradictions can, of course, be identified only when we are able to specify structures important for continued existence. Such essential structures must be distinguishable from other system elements, which can change without the system's losing its identity. The difficulty of thus clearly determining the boundaries and persistence of social systems in the language of systems theory raises *fundamental doubts about the usefulness of a systems-theoretic concept of social crisis.* (pp. 2-3; emphasis added)

Social systems can blur their own identity. The analogy to disease in this case would be the modern condition of rootless anomie. Crisis-states assume the form of a disintegration of social institutions, but mere "crisis ideologies" must be logically distinguished from "valid experiences of crisis."

Crisis, including identity crisis, results from "unresolved steering problems" (p. 4). Strict social controls will govern until some "steering problem" precipitates change. Habermas's explanation somewhat resembles Kuhn's account of a researcher's discovery of an anomaly, which triggers crisis, which in turn may trigger scientific revolution. Habermas glimpses the mechanisms by which *crisis* comes to be an important capitalistic trope.

> No previous social formation lived so much in fear and expectation of a sudden system change, even though the idea of a temporally condensed transformation—that is, of a revolutionary leap—is oddly in contrast to the form of motion of *system crisis as a permanent crisis*. (p. 25; emphasis added)

Like Barth, Habermas thinks of *crisis* as a sign ("crisis designates") within a sign system. His vocabulary likewise resembles Barth's ringing changes upon a variety of phrases: "crisis manifestations," "system crisis," "crisis tendencies," "economic crises," "permanent crisis," "crisis management," and the like. In its own way, Habermas's use of the great trope is as rhetorically varied, logically incomprehensible, and emotionally persuasive as Barth's.

As if systematizing Eliot's example in *Felix Holt, the Radical*, in "Theorems of Legitimation Crisis" (pp. 68-75) Habermas acknowledges an administration's securing of legitimation for itself by manipulating "expressive symbols that release an unspecific readiness to follow." Eliot's Mr. Johnson manipulated his illiterate audience merely by exploding the concussive word; administrations employ such crisis-strategies as symbolic hearings and "juridical incantations" so as to exploit cultural prejudices. On the whole, Habermas uses *crisis* as a rhetorical term alternately rational and irrational, comprehensible and incomprehensible. Concerning the realm of life carved out by novelists, he asserts that, given the powers of scientific analysis to regulate human life, the traditional bourgeois class no longer exists or need exist. Likewise, the "end of the individual" is necessitated by the fact that modern life is too complex to tolerate traditionally individualistic democracy. In social planning, even at the price of "old European human dignity," scientific reason must prevail.

Paradoxically, Habermas's bracketing of the novel as outmoded social thought proves uniquely valuable in my survey of *crisis* as a great noun. He clearly perceives the cultural ontology and value of the novel. The novel, a "narrative production of an illusion of order," constitutes a "world-monitoring interpretative system."   As if he were thinking of Richardson's depiction of the *crisis*-conflict between the bourgeois Clarissa Harlowe and the aristocratic Robert Lovelace, he expresses a pity bordering on contempt for the "splendor and poverty of bourgeois subjectivity" that he would replace with scientific "crisis-management." Habermas would willingly sacrifice the novel, with its unruly contingencies flourishing outside of administrative controls. He accedes to administrative deceptions such as juridical incantations being used to manipulate a populace. His account of anomic alienation in effect foregrounds in critical consciousness the fact that anomie constitutes a central motif in modern literature. Ironically, he thus calls attention to the possibility that novelists using a crisis-trope actually enable beleaguered individuals (characters, readers, and, presumably, novelists) to overcome or at least alleviate the pain of anomic modern life.

Habermas's dismal but sobering view must be balanced over against the traditional view that the novel has guaranteed the survival of "old European human dignity" as well as the lonely, struggling individual. Crisis-conscious novels have enriched human life, and crisis-figurations have not only enriched literature but continue to guarantee the existence of critical thought itself. An acid test of this hypothesis is provided by Robert Coover's scathing account of anomic alienation in mid-century America.

"the fack can't be no longer disgised that a Krysis is onto us"

Lawrence Durrell attempted to ridicule *crisis* into submission or oblivion. Another novelist making a comparable attempt is Robert Coover, who bases an ambitious satire on the historical crisis-rhetoric of Richard M. Nixon. Given my own governing trope, consisting (I think) of my belief that a single word can in fact be shown to achieve a form of greatness, Coover's novel proves to be a godsend for my argument.[3]

Human reality truly structures itself as an endless dialectical series of error-riddled turning points. Likewise, each such turning point is a crisis or point of peril.[4] The beleaguered individual undergoing endless perilous moments, stressful decisions, and desperate judgments assuredly may be swept off his feet. Indeed, historical accounts of twentieth-century existence testify that life seems like a torrent of disorienting crisis after crisis after crisis. A proper culture hero for such a world would be one as tormented and heroic as Charles Baudelaire, whose "perpetual moral crisis" expressed a deep commitment to an intense anguish and doubt associated with a tortuous metaphysical inquiry.[5] But the average man is no Baudelaire. If mankind's embroilment in endless crisis makes for spectacular literary effects, yet for the majority such a prospect seems decidedly repugnant if not literally unbearable. The actual effect of endless crisis on mass man produces a painful condition of rootlessness or anomie, with no relief in sight.

> Man in middle-class mass society has doubts about his significance in the community; and, no less painful, doubts about his significance in his own eyes, within his mental universe. This loss of stature is potentially dangerous: fascism is a disease of people who feel insignificant. Yet "crisis" is not a proper word for the situation. It suggests a limited problem, and specific solutions applied over a finite period. This is not the challenge. *If there is a crisis, it is one which (in the twentieth century, at least) is likely to be without end*. It will be more like adjusting to a new way of life than solving a problem.[6] (emphases added)

To doubt one's place in the human community is to suffer alienation and anomic dread.

The category of crisis-discourse that includes writings by Husserl, Barth, Kuhn, and Habermas might well include Richard Nixon's famous self-examination in *Six Crises*.[7] Following Nixon's defeat in 1960 as a Republican candidate for the presidency of the United States, the former vice-president composed *Six Crises* in order to "distill out of my experience a few general principles on the 'crisis syndrome'" (p. xii). Nixon's lengthy book represents a more extreme use of the great noun than any other, excepting perhaps Barth's *Epistle to the Romans*. Nixon's content and form derive almost entirely from his analysis of a "crisis syndrome." In a six-page "Introduction" he employs *crisis* and *crises* no fewer than twenty-eight times, including such phrases as "major crisis," "crisis situation," "crisis syndrome," "conduct in crisis," "crisis behavior," "reaction and response to crisis," "Confidence in crisis," "minor crisis," "meeting crises," and the like. Guided in part by suggestions from political scientists engaged in studying crisis behavior, Nixon asks questions and lays down operative guidelines for a study of his own public career in terms of a crisis syndrome.

Almost as if Nixon were anticipating Marshall Brown's meditation upon dialectical turning points or constructing a rationale for the present study of crisis-tropes, he asks numerous rhetorical questions. Is it possible to be rational in crisis situations? Do crises have elements in common? Does the "participant" learn from one crisis to the next? Does a feeling of exhilaration or enjoyment accompany crisis? Did Nixon himself discover personal strengths or weaknesses from a crisis-experience? Does a crisis trigger unsuspected resources of energy and strength? What feelings of tension or anxiety might one expect to feel during a crisis or when a crisis has passed? Can one assemble a set of rules or guidelines by which to direct one's behavior in a crisis?

Historically, the six chapters in *Six Crises* deal with problems and entanglements such as Nixon's prosecution of Alger Hiss on charges of being a communist, the charge that his own political career was secretly funded by illegal monies, President Eisenhower's heart attack in 1955, Nixon's ordeal in Venezuela involving mob violence, his confrontation with Premiere Kruschchev, and the election campaign of 1960 when he was defeated by John F. Kennedy. These events were in fact major episodes in American history during the 1950s, but Nixon insists (p. 230) that "this is a story of a crisis, primarily as it affects an individual, rather than government policy." He concerns himself almost exclusively with his own crisis-experience as a general model:

> "*reaction and response to crisis is uniquely personal* in the sense that it depends on what the individual brings to bear on the situation—his own traits of personality and character, his training, his moral and religious background, his strengths and weaknesses." (p. xiii; emphasis added)

Nixon puts many twists upon his narrative, as in his self-reflexive assertion that the composition of the book itself "turned out to be the seventh major crisis of my life" (p. xii).

Relations between Nixon's style and that of other intellectuals are themselves problematical. His shrill voice conveys an anxiety comparable to Barth's but none of Barth's Christian humility. On the other hand, Nixon perfectly illustrates Husserl's insistence on the impossibility of attaining an objective view of reality untainted by solipsistic subjectivity. Nixon endures and even enjoys self-doubt and anomic anguish, so that his crisis-experience, on which he dwells at unwearying length, never achieves any sense of "paradigm shift" comparable to the process described by Kuhn. Of considerable interest and relevance, Nixon's rhetoric expresses a social-science mentality similar to that voiced by Habermas. Ironically, the crisis-syndrome Nixon seeks to elucidate resembles in microcosm the persistent syndrome said by Marxists to characterize the capitalistic economy.

My study of crisis-tropes climaxes in an electrifying novel by Robert Coover. Curiously, and as if to turn the tables on both Habermas and Nixon, the quantitatively most extreme crisis-trope among my novelistic examples appears in a narrative which explores the painful reality of anomie and crisis-manipulation in the life of R. M. Nixon, the highly placed American governmental official. Coover's controversial novel *The Public Burning* (1976)[8] is not as well established in literary history as works by James or Forster, but it aims at a high place among serious novels, and it has been the subject of serious critical study. It amply rewards such study. Four essays in the journal *Critique: Studies in Modern Fiction* (1982) examine Coover's hilarious and shocking indictment of mid-century America from four critical perspectives: as a "novel of excess" (other such books being written by Thomas Pynchon, Joseph Heller, and John Barth); as a historical novel with metafictional dimensions; as a novel in which an emblematic episode provides a compelling metaphor for the entire work; and, as an apocalyptic book which explains how and why the American dream has been corrupted.

Examining Nixon as a prime example of the perverse modern thirst for angst and aporia, Coover re-creates the ambivalent atmosphere of the United States during the Eisenhower years, the 1950s. This atmosphere consists largely of two elements, peaceful conformity and communist-baiting hysteria. Couched in an exacerbated rhetoric, *The Public Burning* narrates an account of the execution at Sing Sing Prison in 1953 of two "atomic spies," Ethel and Julius Rosenberg. Fussily over-determined in its external form, the book includes a prologue and epilogue; major divisions labelled Parts 1, 2, 3, and 4; twenty-eight numbered chapters; and, intermezzos following parts 1, 2, and 3.

Coover also provides a good deal of rhetorical steering in the form of titles for each part, so that a peculiarly insistent rhetoric of control shapes the narrative. The book begins with a "Groun'-Hog Hunt" alluding to the ferreting out of real or imagined communists from the dark corners of American society, and it ends with Richard M. Nixon, sitting alone at home, remembering his role in the events surrounding the Rosenbergs' execution. Like Melville's *Moby Dick*, which furnishes Coover with one of his major symbols, *The Public Burning* oscillates violently between objective and subjective perspectives. Even-numbered chapters are narrated by an omniscient third-person voice, a variation of the official or journalistic voice of American orthodoxy; odd-numbered chapters are narrated by Coover's version of Vice-President Richard Nixon. In addition to re-creating the sociopolitical atmosphere of the times, the book also incorporates an informing plot in which Nixon attempts to rescue the Rosenbergs. In this plot, Nixon moves anxiously from metaphor (delusion of belonging to the Washington club), through metonymy (sense of being excluded) and synecdoche (numerous "street" adventures culminating in a visit to Sing Sing prison), to the final irony of being at home alone in his kitchen from where he sadly reprises his failed effort to save the Rosenbergs.

Karl Barth used Paul's Epistle to the Romans as a source; George Eliot would have found a clue for *Felix Holt* in the radical journal *The Crisis*. Coover also used a source for his fiction. He took his cue directly from the historical Richard Nixon's own elaborate crisis-trope in *Six Crises*. Nixon's personalized keyword electrifies Coover's story fifty-two times (effectively like an irresistible leitmotif) as part of a complex pattern worthy of the other rhetorical intricacies of *The Public Burning* as a whole. Coover produces crisis-perspectives of considerable importance for his purpose and for my history of the trope. In Coover's rhetoric, something narratively approaching to Barth's overwhelming purpose and effect has been attempted. He distributes fifty-two uses of the great noun as follows. On ten occasions, the word signifies special effects in passages narrated by the third-person omniscient narrator. The other forty-two occurrences rise repeatedly in the narration by Vice-President Nixon. By such distribution, Coover establishes several broad patterns of rhetorical emphasis. He omits the word from three intermezzos, where he develops President Eisenhower's complacent Manichean vision of reality as well as the dignified pathos of the Rosenbergs as they face a certain death. Then, too, every crisis-image except one uttered by the omniscient third-person narrator occurs before the end of Part 2 (Chapter 14), after which turning-point this official voice modulates to an imperturbable tone. By contrast, Nixon begins his narration as an opportunistic politician quick to designate and exploit an occurrence as a crisis, and he steadily increases and internalizes such strategies right up to and including the epilogue. Nixon's voice throughout becomes generally more shrill in its self-delusive crisis-consciousness.

The crisis-images employed by the third-person narrator modulate through several modes, including comic impersonations of Uncle Sam and Winston Churchill, as well as journalistic voices such as the *New York Times* and *Time* magazine. In chapter 2 ("A Rash of Evil Doings") this voice circles the globe cataloguing problems in Brazil, Cambodia, Alaska, and so on. A note of comic absurdity pertaining to American claims of omnipotence intrudes when the official voice designates as an "international crisis" a fiasco in Nepal over the question whether Edmund Hillary dragged his Sherpa guide to the top of Mount Everest or the guide actually dragged Hillary: "An international crisis develops, and America seems unable to do anything about it" (p. 38). As this journalistic voice drones on, it labels one other circumstance out of many as a crisis: "The French, facing the most serious crisis in the dismal history of the Fourth

Republic, are losing their nerve in Indochina, and everybody from President Auriol on down is protesting the Rosenberg executions" (p. 41). Thematically, excepting for implications of random absurdity, no strong pattern emerges at this stage.

In chapter 6, though, the omniscient narrator darkens the tone. In describing the situation of the Rosenbergs at Sing Sing Prison, he urges that the entire world itself is involved, and the cause is the Phantom: "For make no mistake: that *the world is tonight in crisis*, that the Phantom is afoot with rare favor and authority, is largely due to the persistent agitation of Julius and Ethel Rosenberg, who will not talk and will not be silent" (p. 101; emphasis added). In chapter 8, Coover shows how Uncle Sam quickly expropriates crisis-rhetoric so as to manipulate crowds of people who have been attracted by the preparations for the Rosenberg executions. Deploring the street violence and robberies that occur at times of public stress, Uncle Sam closely echoes Eliot's Mr. Johnson when he attempts to stir up and exploit the aimless mobs. Eliot's suave lawyer announced to a gang of colliers: "It's a crisis—I pledge you my word it's a crisis." Uncle Sam begins a long harangue similarly: "Yes, friends, the fack can't be no longer disgised that a Krysis is onto us" (p. 169). Historically, crisis-rhetoric promises in Coover's book to turn full circle. Coover manipulates crisis-oratory as late as chapter 24 ("Introducing: The Sam Slick Show!") when Uncle Sam depicts Winston Churchill blustering his famous Iron Curtain speech to the mob in Times Square: "'Cor blimey! the crisis is upon us, an iron curtain has descended on the broad sunlit uplands'" and so forth (p. 422). He also uses journalistic voices to advance the public dimension of his trope. Two references in chapter 10 establish that the *New York Times* deliberately over-stimulates and hence manipulates the American people by publishing "crisis tabulations" (p. 194) and by stipulating randomly, as if by means of a lottery, which of numerous public problems should be regarded as crises: "the French crisis enters its 5th week" (p. 196).

More importantly, the third-person narration reaches a climax in chapter 14 ("High Noon") when *Time* magazine, "America's Laureate Balladeer," sings a parody of the theme song from the cowboy film *High Noon*. Coover uses two devices already identified as part of the present history. Like Scott in *The Heart of Midlothian*, he valorizes the great noun itself by calling attention to it in an inset poem (song); like Joyce in *Finnegans Wake*, he calls attention to the concussive keyword by punning upon someone's name (Alger Hiss):

high noon united artists creeping

on hadleyville pop four oh oh
one hot sunday morning is the
   moment of crisis
   of crisis for the
the little western cow-ow town

                    (p. 236; emphasis added)

. . . .

throughout the action dmitri tiomkin's
plaintive high noon ballad sounds
a recurring note of impending doo-oom
   as the heat and drama
   mounts relentlessly to
to the *crisi-hiss* of high noon . . .

                    (p. 237; emphasis added)

Scott had used a passage from a poem to highlight the dissolution of George Robertson. Coover uses a filmic theme song with its melodramatic "moment of crisis" to establish that the midwesterner Eisenhower must confront the Red Phantom on the streets of Washington. Historically, too, Joyce literally stamped his name on the great noun by means of the intricate phrase "joysis crisis" in a multi-levelled pun. Coover inscribes "crisi-hiss" not only to satirize Americans who regard the Phantom as a proper melodramatic villain but also to satirize Nixon's prosecution of Alger Hiss. Coover thus prepares the ground for his narrative premise that Nixon embodies the central crisis-mentality in this version or perversion of the American dream. Ironically, not Eisenhower but a hapless Nixon himself will play the would-be hero who confronts the shadowy villain.

As a general introduction to twentieth-century rhetoric, I have already cited Alan Wilde's strenuous efforts to define *crisis* in modernist aesthetics. His crisis-aesthetics bears upon Coover's delineation of Nixon's crisis-consciousness. Within the prolonged cultural agony of modern life, the modernist crisis involves an increasingly recessive and fluid self struggling to find certainty within an increasingly chaotic environment. In this state of radical indecision, modern consciousness attempts heroically to create art from its own perplexities. Modern culture takes the form of dispersed and thwarted energies. Modernist crisis, being an unending response to a decentered world, finally transposes itself into mere anxiety. Wilde's definition of crisis might be describing Coover's central character.

Coover elaborates an extremist crisis-rhetoric via Richard Nixon, in the process depicting Nixon as an amorphous or anomic personality undergoing a painful indecisiveness concerning cultural disruptions lurking behind the bland surfaces of the Eisenhower decade. At the end, Coover vividly depicts the consequences of Nixon's nail-biting existence. Having failed to rescue the Rosenbergs, Nixon has returned home after their ritualistic execution. In an ironical moment, he recalls the event:

> I'd just sat there amid all those beaming fatsos, part of the waxworks, feeling ugly, very lowdown and smarmy and ugly, *deep in post-crisis fatigue,* suffering their smirks and grimaces and thinking: Ah, fuck, I've done it again. No matter how many times I warn myself, no matter how many goddamn notes I write myself or how many quotations I copy out, I always forget: the point of greatest danger is not in *preparing to meet the crisis* or fighting the fucking battle—it occurs *after the crisis of battle* is over. It is then, with all his emotional resources shot to shit and his guard down, that a guy can easily, if confronted with another battle, even a minor skirmish, blow it. (p. 522; emphases added)

Although couched in secular terms appropriate to Coover's subject, Nixon's vocabulary ("post-crisis fatigue," "meet the crisis," "crisis of battle") recalls in effect Barth's KRISIS-diatribe. The process by which Nixon reaches this burnt-out state of mind can be tracked by one's following the numerous images that inform Nixon's excitable narration in Coover's symbolically odd-numbered chapters. Nixon is the oddball or odd man out.

Nixon first appears as a hustling Quaker anxiously floundering amidst the power brokers in Washington, one who glibly lumps together (p. 46) "the Korean and German and Rosenberg crises" but who proudly recalls his own "Fund Crisis last fall" that provided the occasion for his manipulation of the American public via his infamous Checkers speech on television. Meditating upon the dilemma precipitated by Justice Douglas's judgment prohibiting the scheduled executions, Nixon anxiously recalls that "Uncle Sam had actually prepared me for this crisis during our last match at Burning Tree Golf Club, but I had not understood" (p. 53). Further reference (p. 60) to the Fund Crisis, seemingly an egotistical obsession, occurs in this early meditation. Coover ironically deepens Nixon's superficial thoughts by providing the compulsive hustler with a compelling metaphor that links Nixon's mid-century hysteria with symbols propounded in the nineteenth century by Matthew Arnold and in the early twentieth century by E. M. Forster.

Arnold has already been cited as believing that crisis-consciousness represents an essential element of culture and that only by remaining alert to crisis can one reach the center of humane culture. Forster developed Margaret Schlegel's unfolding consciousness in *Howards End* so that her developing crisis-consciousness leads her ultimately into a "sacred center" which represents as much of self-identity and happiness as one may hope to find in disoriented modern England. Early in *The Public Burning*, Coover nimbly contrives for Nixon to echo both Arnold and Forster (in particular the latter) when Nixon concludes his early crisis-meditation with a reference to "crisis occasions" and "America's sacred center." While presiding over the Senate, Vice-President Nixon daydreams of becoming the newest Incarnation of Uncle Sam. Nixon's powers of self-reflexiveness are judged and found wanting.

> I had the conviction Uncle Sam preferred Republicans for this process: somehow he never seemed to fit just right in Democrats, and he had even left a number of them in pretty bad shape after. We Republicans were closer to *America's sacred center* than the Democrats, which was what made it easier in a way to be a "good" Republican: the catechism belonged to us. But the people, living their day-to-day profane lives, were closer to the crude worldly pragmatism—the bosses, boodle, buncombe, and blarney—of the Democrats, and so, except on *ritual or crisis occasions*, tended to vote for them. Who listens to his conscience unless he must?   (pp. 60-61; emphases added)

Coover depicts Nixon as an anomic modern self desperately seeking some mythic or sacred center where he hopes to receive his identity and true name. In Nixon's wildly decentered mind, the many crises he will either perceive, precipitate, or concoct represent a *rite de passage* giving access to a centered selfhood.

Eliot asserted in *Felix Holt, the Radical* that any moment in an individual life may be "charged with" crisis. In Coover's account of two infamous electrocutions, Nixon specifies that for him successfully to reach the putative sacred center of American life would mean "everything," particularly the power that he imagines to exist throughout the universe "like electricity" (pp. 175-76). By contrast, the third-person narrator characterizes the same imagined center not as a sacred center but as "the terrible center, the edgeless edge" (p. 195). Coover thus complicates and judges a crisis-trope that links his novel even further back than Forster and Arnold, all the way back perhaps as far as Jane Austen's *Emma* and perhaps as far back as Richardson's terrifying depiction of Lovelace's anguished attempt to establish his own identity. Nixon's agonizing crisis of anomic alienation intensifies a self-naming motif essential to historical crisis-rhetoric. James Joyce's naming himself at a critical juncture of *Finnegans Wake* represents an aesthetic high point in this process.

Coover's treatment of Nixon is satirical, so Nixon's *crisis-consciousness* must be trivialized. In chapter 5, during a golf match with Uncle Sam, Nixon foolishly confuses his strenuous efforts to persuade Uncle Sam that the Rosenbergs should not be executed with the trivial problem of deciding which golf club to use. He attempts to calm his twitching nerves by reasoning them away.

> "I do not believe that *some men are just naturally cool, courageous, and decisive in handling crisis situations*, while others are not. I chose a number two wood for a change. I knew this was a mistake and put it back." (p. 87; emphasis added)

Coover further trivializes Nixon's crisis-mentality in several pages of dialogue with the arrogant, pragmatic Uncle Sam. The anxious Nixon can barely tee up his golf ball but goes on feverishly rationalizing his predicament in terms of crisis: "But life for everyone is a series of crises, I cautioned myself; it's not just you, and with that I finally got the ball on the tee" (p. 87).

Much of Nixon's cumulatively self-defining crisis-trope consists of his self-reflexive meditation upon the enabling conditions and consequences of crisis. He rationalizes his own exhausting work habits as "preparing to meet a crisis" (p. 113) rather than in terms of his Quaker conscience, escapism, or simple anxiety. He glibly analyses other people in terms of their own presumed crisis-consciousness. Fretting over his lack of success at the crucial age of forty, Nixon spitefully reasons that the boy-wonder Judge Kaufman "must have been going through his own fortieth-birthday crisis at the time of the trial two years ago" (pp. 117-18). Coover's reader remembers, if Nixon does not, that in its root meaning "crisis" signifies "judge." For Nixon, crisis at times represents nothing more than one item in a litany of onerous tasks: "I was tired. It had been a long day. Crisis conferences, world tensions, chairing the Senate, fear for Uncle Sam, phone calls, the Rosenberg affair" (p. 139). All through part 1 of *The Public Burning*, Coover trivializes and deconstructs Nixon's personality by depicting the self-important hustler as himself a crisis-ridden, crisis-exploiting trivializer.

Throughout part 2 ("Friday Morning"), Coover continues to denigrate Nixon as a petty, self-centered crisis-consciousness. In chapter 9 ("The Vice President's Beard"), as Nixon prepares to attend a cabinet meeting at the White House, Coover depicts him reducing his own self-importance to the level of situation comedy: "I hoped that Pat grasped the fact that I was in a major crisis and was fixing corned beef hash for me with an egg on it" (p. 186). In chapter 11 ("How to Handle a Bloodthirsty Mob"), Nixon compulsively reads the *New York Times*, where he notes among thousands of details a reference to "the government crisis in France" (p. 199). He is thereby provoked spitefully to judge his own "fund crisis" as a "trial by press" conducted by his Democratic enemies (p. 200). Coover shows Nixon's desperate belief that he has arrived "at the center of things" to be steadily disintegrating as Nixon perceives a surprising congruence between his own plight and that of the Rosenbergs: "The range and scope of this crisis began to fall into a pattern" (p. 209).

During "The Cabinet Meeting" (chap. 13), President Eisenhower rambles so incoherently that Nixon can not follow his reasoning: "Whichever crisis the President had been talking about, Foster [Secretary of State John Foster Dulles] now resumed his briefing on the one in Korea" (p. 222). When the talk turns to the government's plan for staging an elaborate spectacle in Times Square at the time of the scheduled execution, Nixon cynically personalizes the occasion: "I tried to tune into this because I knew that a man was at his best in a crisis when he was not thinking of himself but of the problem at hand" (p. 225). He continually reverts to a tone of pompous self-reflection masking a paranoid insecurity.

Following an intermezzo depicting a dialogue between Eisenhower and Ethel Rosenberg, Coover intensifies Nixon's crisis-rhetoric. In Chapter 17 ("The Eye in the Sky"), Nixon initiates a reasoning process that will peak at the main turning point of the plot when he decides to prevent the executions. He recalls his own childhood and adolescence, in the process highlighting the school plays he performed in, as well as the extempore debates which taught him verbal agility and "coolness in crisis situations" and in general how to "manipulate ambiguities." In order to be prepared for life's adversities, one must be prepared to confront crises: "confidence in crisis depended in great part, I knew, on the adequacy of preparation—where preparation was possible. The Boy Scouts were right about this" (p. 303). Recalling his earlier decision not to be forced off of the Eisenhower ticket, he perceives the ordeal as a "crisis of unbelievably massive proportions" in which he needed to be combative and daring: "In any crisis, one must fight or run away, but one must do something." In Nixon's disoriented mentality, any learning experience whatsoever may represent a crisis: "I had learned from my experience in the Hiss case that what determines success or failure in handling a crisis is the ability to keep coldly objective when emotions are running high" (pp. 308-9). But lest the reader take too seriously Nixon's own mock-sincere Poor Richard style of rationalization, Coover dictates that in the Fund Crisis Nixon's most momentous decision was whether to make the Checkers speech following the Lucille Ball Show or the Milton Berle Show.

In chapter 19, Coover exhibits Nixon as a pathetic soul who can not rise above his own comic pathos. Coover's rich intertextuality recalls D. H. Lawrence's sexual crisis-theme by having Nixon literally manipulate himself. When Uncle Sam discovers Nixon masturbating during Nixon's fantasized coitus with Ethel Rosenberg, the abashed Nixon can only think: "This crisis is worse even than the fund" (p. 331). On a larger scale, Nixon decides that the Fund Crisis had truly been a turning-point in his personal life. He feels annoyed by the "total isolation I'd been feeling since the fund crisis, like maybe Checkers had given me rabies or something" (p. 345). Repeatedly, he attempts to strike the note of reflexive seriousness. During his train ride to Sing Sing Prison, he grumbles to himself that "the real crisis of America today is the crisis of the spirit" (p. 348). In actuality, though, he continues to worry about petty matters such as his clothing and physical comfort.

Throughout *The Public Burning*, Coover judges his main character as himself an ambitious if laughable crisis-strategist. Coover thus follows the example of predecessors as varied as Richardson, Scott, Austen, Meredith, James, Lawrence, Forster, and Durrell, to name but a few. Like Richardson's Lovelace, Nixon attempts to manipulate other people by expropriating to himself the right to designate which events should be thought of as crises. Like the self-dramatizing Lovelace, Meredith's hapless Egoist, or James's Lambert Strether (as well as eighteenth-century playwrights such as Colley Cibber and Richard Cumberland), the playwriting Richard Nixon attempts to script a better existence for himself via Eliot's concussive, electrifying, delusive, life-shaping noun. Nixon as it were constructs his own plot with a strong turning point which he signals as a *crisis*. Early on in the final chapter of part 3 (chap. 21, "Something Truly Dangerous"), Nixon arrives in Ossining, New York. He literalizes two allied popular meanings of crisis when he thinks of the "promise and danger" inherent in his sudden decision to confront the Rosenbergs in Sing Sing Prison. Literalizing another meaning, he dwells upon his belief that his decision, being made in a "critical situation," had to be followed to its logical conclusion. In a recollection dominated by theatrical images, he again refers to the "fund crisis last fall" as if it were the "climax" of a theatrical production. Now, having decided that his own career was "atrophying" and that "only a wild and utterly unprecedented action will save it," he trudges through the streets of Ossining while making his final major decision: "to step in and change the script!"

Nixon reaches this decision via a meditation upon his own analysis of a predicament which he identifies as "my crisis." Perhaps more so than any of my other examples, Coover's version of Nixon perceives that *crisis* functions something like a disruptive *mise en abyme* which places one over the abyss of terror.

> This then was my crisis: to accept what I already knew. That there was no author, no director, and the audience had no memories—they got reinvented every day! I'd thought: perhaps there is not even a War between the Sons of Light and the Sons of Darkness! Perhaps we are all pretending! I'd been rather amazed at myself having thoughts like these. Years of debate and adversary politics had schooled me toward a faith in dénouement, and so in cause and consequence. The case history, the unfolding pattern, the rewards and punishments, the directed life. Yet what was History to me? . . . . In a lawless universe, there was a certain power in consistency, of course,—*but there was also power in disruption.* (pp. 362-63; emphasis Coover's)

At precisely the point where one expects a major paradigm shift in a protagonist's fortunes, Nixon the dramatist provides himself with a rationalization in the form of a carefully-scripted crisis-image. Both Richardson's pioneering method in *Clarissa* and Eliot's narratorial premise in *Felix Holt* at this point come to their literal fulfillment.

Having casuistically judged that he can save the Rosenbergs by persuading them to admit to the charges against them, Nixon enters the prison. He continues to trivialize himself by reifying and parodying self-reflexiveness itself: "When a man has been through even a minor crisis, he learns not to worry when his muscles tense up" and so on (p. 365). And further: "making the decision to meet a crisis is far more difficult than the test itself" (p. 365). To some degree, Coover shows his main character attempting to rise above his own pettiness and examine larger geopolitical issues: "at the heart of this worldwide conflict and crisis lay a simple choice: who was telling the truth, the Federal Bureau of Investigation or two admitted Reds?" (p. 368). For reasons alternately selfish and altruistic, Nixon decides that the Rosenbergs are innocent, that he himself must expose the FBI as part of a conspiracy against the truth. But if Nixon wavers, Coover's intention is steady. Near the end of this crucial chapter with its clear turning point, he depicts Nixon donning a fake moustache as he approaches the prison still anguishing over "the most difficult period in a crisis situation, the period of indecision: whether to fight or run away" (p. 374).

After the flurry of passages near the end of part 3, Nixon moderates his rhetoric. During his interview with Ethel Rosenberg, he decides that he need not fear her wrath because the "worst of the crisis, I knew, was past. This was the creative phase now!" (p. 435). In the final part of Nixon's narrative (chap. 27, "Letting Out the Dark: The Prodigal Son Returns"), Coover depicts Nixon posing a series of rhetorical questions the general effect of which is to leave the outcome very much up in the air. On the stage in Times Square confronting the mock-up of an electric chair, Nixon in effect asks himself how a crisis looks from the inside.

Is it possible to be rational at all in *crisis situations*? Do *crises* seem to have many elements in common? Does the participant seem to learn from one *crisis* to another? (p. 470; emphases added)

Nixon's electrifying crisis-trope literalizes Eliot's assertion that any moment in a human life may be "charged with" the energy of crisis. Coover's hilarious Nixon proves to be the ultimate self-deconstructor. Nixon himself is not only an artist who would employ a crisis-rhetoric but also the critic who will analyze such a device. The presumed answer to his rhetorical questions about the inner reality of crisis is, in each case, an emphatic No! Coover's Richard Nixon can not behave rationally in a crisis, or learn from a crisis, because each crisis is unique, and his powers of memory are in any case perverted. Nixon goes on to urge upon the listening mob his own conviction that this is "one of those critical moments in history that can change the world." His "inspired rhetorical ploy" of asserting that not only he but all Americans have been caught with "our trousers down" is itself plagiarized from his own "famous crisis speech last fall." As always, Tricky Dick succeeds in tricking both the rabid mob and himself.

When Nixon would generalize most confidently about his own moral character, he thinks in terms of crisis. In reconstructing his long speech to the mob, Nixon reasons to himself that he conceives of history "in terms of tragedy." As a playwright he should realize that crisis, at least as described by Aristotle, represents merely one element of tragedy, yet he never ceases to interpret history in the narrowest of egotistical terms, as egocentric opportunity. Nixon thus coincidentally illustrates Paul Goodman's opinion concerning the objective and subjective dialectics of tragedy.

On the whole, Coover's *crisis*-trope in *The Public Burning* represents the most extreme example of characterization by *crisis* as well as the most overdetermined novelistic anatomy of a society by means of the great noun. Coover skillfully brings Nixon to an exhausted frame of mind in the

Epilogue, where he reexamines his recent adventure in terms of "post-crisis fatigue" and the "crisis of battle." In a real sense, Coover's Nixon represents a culmination or climax of anomic crisis-consciousness, a process that Raymond Williams thinks began with *Felix Holt, the Radical*, where the deracinated modern individual first is compelled to invent his own socio-moral history. Right to the end, Coover's self-inventing Richard Milhous Nixon is an extremist among crisis-rhetoricians and, together with Richardson's Lovelace, one of the most energetically engaging of the type.

Coover's and Durrell's ingenious attempts to explode or ridicule the great noun out of existence did not succeed. In 1987, the article "Crise du Jour" in the *National Review* explained how the manipulative trope had come to serve political programs. The article asserts that the strategy of declaring a "crisis" had become a tactic in a systematic effort to concentrate power in Washington. Each alleged crisis leaves a permanent residue of bureaucracy. This has been true since the Great Depression: "No crisis ever seems to warrant a *diminution* of federal power." The article complains that casual and induced hysteria threaten to undo the principles of constitutional government.[9]

Coover's premise concerning Nixon's crisis-mongering would thus prove generally true of American society. Any undesirable condition can be exploited as a crisis, so Eliot's trope has achieved a millionfold the manipulative power she attributed to it in the England of 1832.

The great noun has become a keyword in many jargons. Jonathan Green's *Newspeak: A Dictionary of Jargon* (1984) lists four terms (crisis communications management, crisis intervention, crisis theory, crisis management) employed in public relations, social work, and the military. "Crisis Communications Management" recalls the manipulative legitimation strategies described by Habermas. In order to relieve pressure on a corporation or administration when a blunder spoils a public perception or image, public-relations specialists induce a more favorable perception. In social work, "Crisis Intervention" necessitates the involvement of a social worker with a client who is suffering a breakdown of adequate mechanisms for coping with stress. In the military jargon peculiar to foreign relations, "Crisis Management," having been coined by Secretary of State Robert McNamara during the 1961 Cuban Missile Crisis, retains McNamara's meaning: "There is no longer any such thing as strategy, only crisis management."[10]

8

Career of a Crisis-Watcher:
Saul Bellow

"Under pressure of public crisis the private sphere
is being surrendered"

This book began in one sense as an inquiry into George Eliot's provocative assertion that by 1832 *crisis* had become a uniquely important word in English culture. In another sense, it began as an effort to comprehend the historical foreground leading up to Saul Bellow's confrontation with this unique signifier in the second half of the twentieth century. My historical survey amply rewards both motives and also uncovers many other dimensions of the problem. The word Eliot singled out proves to be one of the most characterizing single words in the modern world, shading and deepening into a master trope. Beginning with the invention of the novel, the extraordinary career of the *crisis*-trope constitutes an essential element in literary history and also modern consciousness. By means of its tropical twistings and turnings under the hands of major authors composing their masterpieces—within cultural contexts including theology, philosophy, social science, psychology, and the like—the great noun forcefully proves its special potency and greatness.

My survey might have ended with Coover's Nixonian extravaganza in *The Public Burning*. That corruscating satire appeared within one year of Saul Bellow's masterpiece *Humboldt's Gift* (1975). Coover's book is indeed a fitting climax to my story, but Bellow's oeuvre of ten crisis-ridden novels is a more fitting culmination—to date—of an enlightening historical narrative of unfolding consciousness. I derive my own consciousness of Bellow's stature from a careful study of his books and a large body of Bellovian criticism. In particular, I derive a powerful reinforcement of my own impression of the knowledge-effects and truth-effects conveyed by Bellow's work from a collection of essays on the philosophical dimensions of Bellow's fiction (1984). These essays place Bellow securely, if conservatively, within the main tradition of western literature, so that he finds a place in major cultural categories such as romanticism, transcendentalism, skepticism, Freudianism, Judaism, and nihilism.[1]

Bellow's subject matter includes a "crisis mentality" in the American psyche, and his rhetoric measures up to its tortured ancestry.[2] Even so, none of Bellow's critics confront the issue of his confrontation with the great keyword itself, though he uses it regularly. A list of his ten novels to date showing the frequency of use can provide an enlightening statistical framework.

Dangling Man (1944)	(2)
The Victim (1947)	(3)
The Adventures of Augie March (1954)	(6)
Seize the Day (1956)	(3)
Henderson the Rain King (1959)	(6)
Herzog (1964)	(9)
Mr. Sammler's Planet (1970)	(8)
Humboldt's Gift (1975)	(16)
The Dean's December (1982)	(6)
More Die of Heartbreak (1987)	(13)

A strong pattern emerges as Bellow's novels become generally longer, more complex, and more ambitious.

George Eliot had asserted that every minute in a human life can be a crisis, which is to say that every minute can be a dialectical turning point. Such an assertion may read like a mere truism: ranging upward from the level of the phoneme to the largest macro-element, any novel can plausibly be viewed as a constant metamorphosis from word to word, sentence to sentence, episode to episode, character to character, and chapter to chapter. To designate any one point as a crisis or turning point might seem arbitrary in the extreme. Even so, Marshall Brown has convincingly demonstrated that a worthy critical enterprise can be initiated by heuristic designations of narrative turning points. As Bellow repeatedly attempts to imagine how a transition appears from the inside, his formulations resemble those urged by Brown, who imagines turning points variously as change, passage of time, trial, judgment, regression, progression, avoidance, changing of the guard, paradigm shift, new broom, disorientation, paradoxical combination of balance and imbalance, radical alteration, new path, or, most comprehensively, as dialectical moment.³ Many of these possibilities animate turnings and twistings in Bellow's fictions. In his latest novel, *More Die of Heartbreak*, the narrator speculates in explicit terms on the existential implications of crisis-enabled turning points in existential life-scripts.

During the forty-three years from *Dangling Man* (1944) to *More Die of Heartbreak* (1987), Bellow inscribed a crucial turning point or paradigm shift into most of his novels. Each such shift illustrates, though variously, a tropological movement from metaphoric sameness to other tropological states of being. In *Dangling Man*, the narrator's muted or implied decision to resist his own anesthetic attitude toward himself is framed and enabled by two crisis-images. A very different sort of turning point structures *The Victim*. In that grim book, Asa Leventhal redirects his own life by the fateful act of opening his apartment door to his nemesis Kirby Allbee. In the more expansive *Adventures of Augie March*, Bellow places his main character on the road. Augie's disorienting turning point takes the form of his impulsive decision to travel with an adventurous woman to Mexico. Two years later, in the short novel *Seize the Day*, Bellow attempted a narrative of filial frustration, a seamless story containing no unmistakable turning point. Subsequently, though, in *Henderson the Rain King*, he returned to his basic type of structure. Eugene Henderson's daring entrance into a lion's cage so as to "act the lion" constitutes an informing turning point. Bellow's most intricate experiment in fictional form, *Herzog* depicts a depressed intellectual in whose experiences no vivid turning point signals a structure of the before-and-after kind. Next, however, Bellow structured *Mr. Sammler's Planet* by means of Sammler's decision to travel from New York City to New Rochelle so as to retrieve Dr. Lal's stolen manuscript. In *Humboldt's Gift*, Bellow insinuates a forceful turning point via Charles Citrine's deciding to postpone his pleasure trip to Milan in order to journey to New York City and accept Humboldt's posthumous gift. In 1982, Bellow inscribed into *The Dean's December* a subtle turning point in the form of Dean Albert Corde's decision to write a series of articles for *Harper's* magazine, thereby triggering an unexpected change in his career. Finally, in *More Die of Heartbreak*, the narrator Kenneth Trachtenberg explicitly expresses the view that "our existence was worthless if we didn't make a turning point of it." In narrating an account of his admired uncle's marital ordeal, Kenneth stipulates for a clear turning point, his Uncle Benn's agreeing to pursue a legal action against his own uncle, Harold Vilitzer. On the whole, Bellow decrees that his main characters themselves will be, in word or deed, crisis-rhetoricians in word and deed, and in most of his novels, the turning point of the main plot takes on its fullest resonance as part of a crisis-trope.

Bellow's dialectical narratives might be fulfilling a program laid down by Paul de Man in "Criticism and Crisis." Bellow offers literature as a primary source of knowledge but knowledge potentially flawed by error. He derides "safe, comfortable people playing at crisis" (*Herzog*), but his protagonists at various depths of being shape their souls via the very sort of vocabulary that de Man seriously questioned. Their *crisis*-signalled turning points generally represent regrettable fallings-away from existential sources but in some cases they also signify the onset of reborn selves. By and large, Bellow offers an authentically self-critical critique of modern culture. As I have shown elsewhere, his vision offers its truth convincingly because he anchors it in the ambiguities of Husserl's error-ridden lived world.[4]

Bellow's first novel renders the turmoil of an introspective young man waiting to be inducted into the army in late 1942 and early 1943. Alienated from his family, friends, and spouse, Joseph waits helplessly in a boarding-house room, snarled in red tape, simultaneously both loving and hating his transient freedom. By means of flashbacks, Joseph reconstructs his life, in the process exhibiting tension, bad temper, selfishness, and confusion. A work of Flaubertian pessimism, *Dangling Man*[5] convincingly depicts a private individual's pessimism in contrast with an official public patriotism. At the end, Joseph will insist upon being inducted and conclude his story with a sardonic anticipation of Orwell's *1984*: "Long live regimentation!"

Bellow uses two crisis-images to signal Joseph's shift from an anesthetic mood to a mood at least ironically vibrant. The journal entry for 15 December 1942 identifies in sadly deterministic terms Joseph's backwater existence during the months he awaits induction: "And so I am very much alone, I sit in my room, anticipating the minor crises of the day, the maid's knock, the appearance of the postman, programs on the radio, and the sure, cyclical distress of certain thoughts." Bellow induces an atmosphere of quietism, even of despair. Happily, though, he then allows his protagonist at a crucial moment (6 January 1943) to reflect upon a predicament once faced by his radical friend Morris Abt. Joseph describes Abt's youthful high jinks in relation to three revolutionary geniuses of politics, art, and psychology:

"That winter he was Lenin, Mozart, and Locke all rolled into one. But there was unfortunately not enough time to be all three. And so *in the spring he passed through a crisis*. It was necessary to make a choice." (p. 87; emphasis added)

Like George Eliot and Henry James, Bellow literalizes the etymology of his tropological keyword.

Bellow insinuates two rhetorical principles via Joseph's two crisis-images: first, a gloomy deterministic tendency to perceive crisis as mere external quotidian circumstances, beyond one's control but also a source of mental pain; and, second, a gradual perception (initially projected onto another person) that external problems both proceed from one's own character and also necessitate or enable personal judgment or choice. Joseph's own sarcasm toward Abt's youthful overreaching in effect makes imaginatively more accessible to him several historical revolutions. His recollection of Abt's dilemma positions him to face his own dilemma. Consciousness of revolutionary models (Lenin, Mozart, Locke) ushers Joseph into his own authentic life. Bellow's low-keyed framework prepares the reader for Joseph's own muted decision (26 January 1943) to the effect that he must counteract defensive impersonalization. Tropologically, as it were, Lockean association of ideas reminds Joseph that he himself can reject the dead end of "cyclical distress" and instead adopt a revolutionary stance, even if Bellow does not specify whether Lenin's political rigidity or Mozart's musical generosity will win the young man's spirit. His closing salute to regimentation remains decidedly Lockean, albeit decidedly ironical. What matters finally is that he chooses to accept and examine his own personal existence: "But I must know what I myself am." Although not as pronounced as the existential shifts in later novels, Joseph's adoption of a new consciousness of his metonymic (relational) existence functions consistently, within a mordant decorum, as a paradigm shift triggered or enabled by a muted crisis-trope. Bellow thus initiates his career by raising serious issues concerning the problematics of the crisis-conscious modern self.

The Victim[6] extends but puts a twist upon this initial line of inquiry. Bellow shifts his focus as follows: what would happen if a person trapped in metaphoric self-centeredness did not recognize and seize a window of opportunity such as Joseph's recalling Morris Abt's emulation of Mozart? In a minor plot, Asa Leventhal attempts to evade responsibility for his sister-in-law Elena and her ailing son Mickey. In a major plot, Leventhal undergoes a frustrating struggle to find meaningful employment in New York City. During one interview, his stubbornness and sullen temper alienate both a prospective employer and the friend Kirby Allbee who had arranged the interview. Leventhal unsuccessfully attempts to stave off Allbee's efforts at revenge. His victimization by Albee triggers a tortuous self-examination in Leventhal's obtuse mind. Bellow experiments by placing Leventhal's crucial crisis-images closer to the turning point than in *Dangling Man*.

The Victim illustrates the perplexing contrast between naturalistic determinism and self-determinism. In general, Bellow presents a dumb-ox, on the order of Rodin's *The Thinker*, clumsily engaged in painful self-scrutiny. Leventhal fixates upon real or imagined anti-Semitic slights. He recalls how Benjamin Disraeli achieved success despite being a Jew, but he then misinterprets Disraeli's accomplishments in negative terms of paranoid Jewish defensiveness. Self-perplexed, he fails to take advantage of a potential role model. Instead of admitting the great Disraeli into his imaginative consciousness, Leventhal literally admits Allbee into his home, where he is dominated by his vindictive friend. Only by resorting to violence does he finally rid himself of this incubus. At the end, Leventhal has attained some worldly success, including the promise implicit in a pregnant wife, but he never perceives himself as being in control of his destiny. Bellow thus presents the spectacle of a dumb-ox undertaking a painful self-scrutiny.

More ambitious than *Dangling Man*, this second novel yet incorporates a similar crisis-pattern. Leventhal begins by distancing himself from his sister-in-law when she insists that her son Mickey is dying. Via a clumsy crisis-rhetoric, Leventhal projects his own metaphoric self-centeredness upon the woman: "So that was the crisis. He might have guessed it was something like that" (p. 8). Bellow thus again observes that crisis-rhetoric may facilitate an avoidance of intimacy. At this point, for Leventhal crisis functions either in its medical sense or as someone else's manipulative strategy. Eventually, though, judgment becomes available to Leventhal. He becomes somewhat less self-centered, so that, like Joseph, he perceives crisis as simultaneously more than a medical problem, variable as to cause and seriousness, and an existential part of his own being.

Leventhal reveals a bias of his nature and becomes a problematical crisis-thinker during a meditation on the "showdown" in Mickey's worsening illness. He admits to himself that more is involved than only the boy's medical plight:

> "But what he meant by this preoccupying 'showdown' was a crisis *which would bring an end of his resistance* to something he had no right to resist. Illness, madness, and death were forcing him to confront his fault." (pp. 157-58; emphasis added)

Bellow so to speak replaces "medication" with "meditation," so that Leventhal begins to reflect upon his own alienation. He overcomes his bad habit by opening his door (p. 165) so as to allow Allbee to spend the night with him. Ironically, of course, Allbee then temporarily dominates Leventhal's life.

Revolution (as Thomas Paine demonstrated) may be the master image for crisis-induced dialectical turning points. In *Dangling Man*, Joseph invokes Lenin; in *The Adventures of Augie March*,[7] Bellow's picaro will briefly encounter, at several removes, the exiled revolutionist Leon Trotsky. More than twice the length of *The Victim*, the rambling *Augie March* required twice as many crisis-signifiers in its management of unwieldy narrative materials. Following Scott, Eliot, and Forster, Bellow places most of these six images in the second half of the book and elaborates a startling new meaning.

Bellow drives home Eliot's point concerning the manipulative potential of the great noun, as when Augie analyzes his brother Simon's aggressive manipulation of routine business crises. At Simon's coal-yard, after a fracas with a customer: "For Simon wanted to show me how justly he handled such crises, and how badly, by contrast—because of chicken-heartedness—I did" (p. 248). After Thea Fenchel deserts Augie in Mexico, the wretched Augie is consoled by a friend: "Iggy knew I was in a crisis and didn't want me to be alone." Ironically, Augie thinks that Iggy desired to avenge himself by offering such compassion (p. 399). On another occasion, Augie sarcastically judges a Spenglerian gloom-and-doom attitude to be merely another instance of *crisis*-manipulation. He parodies Robey's complaints thus: "We were facing the greatest crisis in history" (p. 441). Augie also analyzes the marital discord between Simon and Renee as mutual manipulation, deriding their constant bickering: "And during the day, every hour nearly, there were crises when they shouted and screamed at each other" (p. 463).

At a deeper level, Bellow uses another set of two crisis-images to introduce a new motif. They insinuate implications of adult sexuality and thereby recall Lawrence's radically *ad hoc* meaning in *Lady Chatterley's Lover*. Lawrence had stipulated that orgasmic sexual fulfillment should be thought of not as *climax* but as *crisis* (decision or choice). In *Augie March*, Bellow likewise assigns a sexual meaning to *crisis*. Early on, when the virginal Augie escapes from the sexual clutches of a predatory woman, the young man voices an ambiguous sense of relief: "I was bitter about that but reckon I felt freed, too, from a crisis" (p. 79). Subsequently, Bellow tropologically shifts this motif of sexual crisis by having Augie himself become a homely crisis-philosopher. Lawrentian undertones resonate throughout Augie's crisis-statement (his strongest to date) during his Mexican adventure.

> I thought that *in the crisis that seems to have to occur when a man and a* *woman are thrown together* nothing, nothing easy, can happen until first one difficulty is cleared and it is shown how the man is a man and the woman a woman; as if a life's trial had to be made, and the pretensions of the man and the woman satisfied. I say I thought, and so I did. A considerable number of things. But I was terribly hot for this woman. As, suddenly, with a breathless impulse toward me, she was for me too. (p. 390; emphasis added)

To the question "when does the judgment come?" Bellow replies that it comes during the sexual trial. Bellow specifies a sexual dimension both to Augie's personal growth and to Augie's (and his own) crisis-thought. In that Augie's impetuous decision to travel to Mexico with Thea Fenchel constitutes a turning point, Bellow effectively dissolves Augie's original hang-up, a Sophoclean reluctance to be born. Like Lawrence and Durrell, Bellow valorizes the crisis-enabled reborn self.

Eliot's *Daniel Deronda* enacted an historic crisis of paternal authority. In *Fathers and Sons*, Turgenev's nihilist Bazarov ridicules his aged father's desperate manipulation of crisis. In Bellow's next novel, a father in effect ridicules his son's desperate reliance upon a similar verbal strategy. *Seize the Day*[8] rings changes upon the conflict between generations. It depicts a hapless young business man condemned by an indifferent father to ignominious dependency. Tommy Wilhelm's failure as a son and a person takes its shape from three crisis-signals which effectively distinguish Tommy from Joseph, Leventhal, and Augie March. Bellow initiates this trope in Chapter 2, emphasizing Tommy's dependency and bad habit of regarding crisis not only as external to himself but also as single dimensional (monetary) and as someone else's fault. When Tommy begs for assistance, Bellow notes: "He meant that his father knew how deep the crisis was becoming; how badly he was strapped for money; and that he could not rest but would be crushed if he stumbled; and that his obligations would destroy him" (p. 39).

Bellow intensifies Tommy's inability or refusal to mature by offering a vivid image of adult infantilism. Being rejected by his cold-hearted father, Tommy has turned to the devious speculator Dr. Tamkin, who, he decides, must be a master of crisis. Tommy is a crisis-strategist attempting to compose his own life by projecting responsibility off onto another person or, more literally, by inscribing his own impasse into the script of another person:

> [Tommy] appeared to have worked it out at the back of his mind that Tamkin for thirty or forty years had gotten through many a tight place, that *he would*

get through this crisis too and bring him, Wilhelm, to safety also, and Wilhelm realized that he was on Tamkin's back. (p. 96; emphasis added)

Bellow drives home the point that crisis-consciousness may be taken as a sign and measure of the moral imagination. Tommy's desperate strategies finally signal his habitual hysteria as being a self-induced delusion. He is a crisis-addict who unconsciously delineates himself by inventing predicaments that postpone his coping with adult responsibility. His dread is self-fulfilling, so that when Tommy's adventures in the stock market fail, Bellow writes: "His heart, accustomed to many sorts of crisis, was now in a new panic. And, as he dreaded, he was now wiped out."

Tommy Wilhelm's characteristic utterance is to insist that he can not survive without employing the avoidance mechanism of one crisis after another. In Bellow's next novel, the main character explicitly complains about suffering "crisis after crisis." The distance between *Seize the Day* and *Henderson the Rain King* can be estimated by the fact that, unlike Tommy, Eugene Henderson manages to endure and mature through crisis-consciousness. *Seize the Day* is variously devoid of crisis (turning point) or devoid of crisis (personal judgment) or is simply one prolonged crisis (entanglement). In *Henderson the Rain King*,[9] Bellow returned to a dialectical or Aristotelian model. He employs a crisis-figure possessing intellectual and aesthetic interest but also some oddness in relation to his other novels. *Henderson*, approximately one-half the length of the exuberant *Augie March*, incorporates the great noun an equal number of times (six). In *Augie March*, Bellow had placed the majority of crisis-images after Augie's liberating decision to journey to Mexico. In *Henderson*, he distributes all *crisis*-signifiers except one in the first third of the novel, the sole exception being reserved for the precise moment of Henderson's dialectical decision to enter a lion's cage armed only with a newly conceived if heuristic trust in a metonymic Other. As one element of Bellow's expressive form, this inventive new structure induces compelling paradigm shifts from faith to doubt and again to faith.

Henderson makes three revolutionary decisions: to journey to Africa, to destroy a pestilence of frogs at a well, and to enter a lion's cage. He initially specifies that crisis is a mark of hysteria, and for him traveling to Africa means leaving despicable crisis-mongers behind in America. At this metaphoric stage, he denigrates his second wife Lily because of her hysterical response to his social behavior: "The reason is not that she is afraid of me, but that it starts some new crisis in her own mind" (p. 7). Like Joseph, Asa Leventhal, and Augie, he attributes crisis-manipulation not to himself but only to other people. Of his first wife Frances, he recalls: "Well, she was in one of these mental crises when we went to that party, and in the middle of it she recalled something she had to do at once and so she took the car and left, forgetting all about me" (p. 9). Only when Henderson reaches Africa does he link crisis to his own motives: "At this moment I was too tired even for a drink (we carried a few canteens filled with bourbon) and was thinking only of the crisis, and how to destroy the frogs in the cistern" (p. 62). Even so, in this bizarre episode of the frogs, Henderson still tends to project crisis away from his own existential self. He would prefer that the Arnewi tribe find another person to resolve their predicament: "Anyway, I was thinking that a more useful person might have arrived at this time among the Arnewi, as, for all the charms of the two women of Bittahness, the crisis was really acute" (p. 78).

For much of the story, Bellow suspends explicit signs of any crisis-trope. Nevertheless, before he concludes Henderson's adventure with the frogs, he establishes that Henderson not only acknowledges crisis in his own personal psyche but, like Leventhal, provides at least a rudimentary definition of the manipulative trope. As a point of contrast, in *The Public Burning* Robert Coover literalizes the electrifying effect that Eliot attributes to the great noun by vividly describing the electric chair in which Richard Nixon momentarily sits. In his turn, Bellow literalizes Eliot's concussive effect by depicting Henderson carrying a bomb at the precise moment when he defines himself in crisis-terms.

> In the dead of the heat we reached the cistern and I went forward alone into the weeds on the edge. All the rest remained behind, and not even Romilayu came up with me. That was all right, too. *In a crisis a man must be prepared to stand alone*, and actually standing alone is the kind of thing I'm good at. "By Judas, I should be good, considering how experienced I am in going it by myself." And with the bomb in my left hand and the lighter with the slender white wick in the other—this patriarchal-looking wick—I looked into the water. (p. 107; emphasis added)

Henderson's comic heroism in this instance must fail, so the bomb actually destroys the cistern rather than the frogs. Nevertheless, triggered by his looking at himself in the water, his self-discovery in this concussive experience enables one crucial stage in his spiritual growth.

The process of this growth is fairly intricate. Following Henderson's failed romantic gesture at the well, Bellow might be expected to depict Henderson, like Coover's self-lacerating Nixon, stipulating for crisis after crisis as opportunities either to prove his manhood and selfhood or further to lacerate his wounded sense of self. Henderson instead now follows some stoical principle, eschewing further reference to crisis until the main turning point of his experience. Bellow decrees that Henderson's vanity, expressed via crisis-consciousness, must be humbled in terms of crisis-consciousness. In Chapter 16, when Henderson first enters the lion's den where, according to his mentor King Dahfu, some spiritual release or fulfillment awaits him, Bellow illustrates the existential difficulty of "standing alone." Henderson, in the cage for the first time, nearly dissolves in terror: "I was all broken up. I couldn't take crisis after crisis, like this" (p. 225). Happily, though, learning humbly to undergo crisis for the sake of personal growth changes him into the new man depicted at the end, galloping across the ice, gleefully, with a child in his arms, in Newfoundland. The new crisis-consciousness integrated into his soul gives him a new lease on life.

By the end of the 1950s, forceful patterns have emerged in Bellow's experimentation with the great noun. In his first five novels, he has used *crisis* in each novel, with relatively increasing frequency, complexity, and rhetorical ambition. His generic main character neurotically projects crisis-consciousness and its corollary moral responsibility onto other people and only gradually accepts its recoil back upon himself. *Crisis*-signals highlight and amplify Bellow's major themes: exploitation, confrontation, human sympathy, dependency, sexuality, obsession, and self-reliance. Bellow experiments with various positionings of *crisis* so as to enable major turning points. In his first five books, he positions *crisis* differently in each novel, such variable emphases both contributing to character psychology and also enabling or signalling existential paradigm shifts. One wonders if Bellow will use some such pattern as he advances toward the mature novels of the next decade?

W. H. Auden complained in person to Bellow that *Herzog* (1964) suffered from being "too well written." Auden's point, with which Bellow agreed, was that a novel ought to be more rough around the edges in depicting real life.[10] *Herzog* doubtlessly represents Bellow's most over-determined experiment in novelistic form. Like Melville's *Moby Dick* or Coover's *The Public Burning*, his sixth novel alternates between emphatically distinguished objective and subjective elements. Whereas Coover exhibited the dichotomy by means of alternating chapters, Bellow insinuates into an objective narrative certain of Moses Herzog's inner thoughts under the guise of letters Herzog composes in his mind. Both books formally witness to the root meaning of *crisis* as a "cut" in the flux of experience.

Like Freud, Bellow wishes to protect men from the onus of total vulnerability to cultural determinism. Freud believed that if man is even partly a biological creature then to that degree he may live free of cultural manipulation. Bellow believes that men can indeed resist cultural determinism simply because of a stubborn tendency toward moral indeterminacy.[11] In *Herzog*, within a pronounced oscillation between objectivity and subjectivity, a crisis-effect informs Herzog's moral indeterminacy in its dialectical collision with powerful forces urging cultural determinacy.

Lacking a clear plot line, *Herzog*[12] proves the most difficult of Bellow's novels to summarize. It narrates the story of a man's attempting to rid himself of a debilitating resentment against his former wife. Having retired to his country house, during a nine-day period Herzog analyzes the dissolution of his marriage and finally reaches an exhausted state of tranquillity. He also examines his own failure as a literary intellectual and professional scholar. Episodes in his mental life establish parallels to the lies, adulteries, and bickerings of his failed marriage. Herzog's large ambition, to produce a study of the revolutions and mass convulsions of the twentieth century, fuses with his failed marriage so that they can be wrung out only by means of a single, supine catharsis. He ends up on a Récamier couch, entirely talked out as it were, with not a "single word" left on any subject.

A formalistic problem facing Bellow's reader is whether to take the objective and subjective components of Herzog's story as parts of one sequence. To remain true to Bellow's own laborious technique, I choose to treat the two main formal components separately. Thus I discover a peculiar method to Bellow's (and Herzog's) mad figurations. In nine contexts, Bellow establishes that Moses Herzog is both objectively and subjectively a disoriented but inventive crisis-strategist. Four signals inform the third-person account of his tribulations, and five others structure the first-person utterances expressed in his unsent letters to personages living and deceased.

In the third-person narrative, Herzog begins by projecting crisis-exploitation off onto other people. Near the end of chapter 1, Herzog derides Madeleine as a narcissist:

> "And she had told Moses during one of their crises that she had had a new look at herself before the bathroom mirror. 'Still young,' she had said, taking inventory, 'young, beautiful, full of life. Why should I waste it all on you?'"

Subsequently, while discussing Madeleine with the psychiatrist Edvig, Herzog complicates his perspectives by complaining that Nietzsche, a vituperative critic of Christianity, was in spite of himself a crisis-thinker:

"I don't agree with Nietzsche that Jesus made the whole world sick, infected it with his slave morality. But Nietzsche himself had a Christian view of history, *seeing the present moment always as some crisis,* some fall from classical greatness, some corruption or evil to be saved from. I call that Christian, and Madeleine has it, all right." (p. 54; emphasis added)

Viewing crisis-consciousness objectively in another philosopher, Herzog views it contemptuously.

A few pages later, he moderates his contempt of Madeleine, but only very slightly: "'I know,' said Herzog, 'she's going through a long crisis—finding herself. And I know I have a bad tone, sometimes'" (p. 59). As if to intensify Herzog's self-righteous contempt for crisis-mongers, Bellow concludes this sequence of passages with a *reductio ad absurdum.* Herzog recalls how a friend, Lucas Asphalter, had undergone an unusual mid-life crisis triggered by the death of his pet monkey. Asphalter had replied to Herzog's queries by citing a certain popular psychotherapy: "Have you read the book by that Hungarian woman Tina Zokoly about what to do in these crises? . . . She prescribes certain exercises. . . . You pretend you have already died" (p. 269). In context, this solemn utterance renders the subject ludicrous. Herzog's judgment of crisis-rhetoric has oscillated through topics such as other people's exploitation, self-exculpation, Nietzschean gloom, and self-obsession, ending finally on a note of comic absurdity. In effect, Herzog's error-ridden crisis-strategies insulate him temporarily from doubts as to his own authenticity.

Subjectively, Bellow and Herzog elaborate a different sort of language. Bellow distinguishes Herzog's thought-letters from the objective narrative by means of italics. Bellow has stated that in writing *The Dean's December* (1982) he was dealing not so much with a literary form as with a type of mind. In *Herzog,* Bellow anticipates this method, delineating a peculiar type of personality: "An eager, hasty, self-intense, and comical person" (p. 110). Herzog complicates Bellow's intention in his private or epistolary attitude toward crisis. Herzog's own five crisis-images in his "thought letters" illustrate an intricate and forceful range of implication. In a letter to the psychiatrist Edvig, he discusses Madeleine in terms that inadvertently reveal his own manipulative motives: "*I might have won back her love. But I can tell you that my meekness during these crises infuriated her, as if I was trying to beat her at the religious game*" (p. 57). A few pages later, while meditating upon the decline of the West, a cultural topic entirely proper to his type of literary intellectual, he reveals that he is indeed a neurotic rationalizer or escapist. The phrase "*crisis of dissolution"* signals Herzog's most powerful utterance on the subject of consciousness.

> *Are all the traditions used up, the beliefs done for, the consciousness of the masses not yet ready for the next development? Is this the full crisis of dissolution? Has the filthy moment come when moral feeling dies, conscience disintegrates, and respect for liberty, law, public decency, all the rest, collapses in cowardice, decadence, blood? . . . I can't accept this foolish dreariness.* (pp. 74-75; ellipsis added)

Herzog's linking of *crisis* and *consciousness* recalls Eliot's program in *Felix Holt, the Radical*, where the great figuration is first explicitly foregrounded. Herzog's lofty concerns and moral percipience may be entirely valid, but carping criticism remains one key trait in this diatribe. He continues for some time to employ his self-serving grasp of crisis as a means of evading responsibility for completing tasks such as his own scholarly book.

> *I was present also when Premier Khrushchev pounded on the desk with his shoe. Amid such crises, in such an atmosphere, there was obviously no time for the more general questions of the sort I have been concerned with.* (p. 161)

Herzog's abiding concern with general questions precludes direct action. No vivid decision or action (hunting lizards, journeying to Africa) signals an Aristotelian turning point in a major plot. Herzog's plot is not a plot of action but at most, in R. S. Crane's familiar terminology, a plot of character or even a plot of thought.

Except in a lethargic Oblomovian sense, Herzog avoids any possibility of fully accepting crisis as being existentially related to himself. In the last chapter, which presents Herzog's last week of letter writing, Herzog attempts one final time to project crisis-manipulation exclusively onto other people's irresponsible "playing at crisis." Writing to his successful rival Professor Marmelstein, he insists that they both should *"remain loyal to civilization"* and thus reject all merely fashionable pessimism. Bellow uses a crisis-signifier to bring Herzog's moral adventure to its supine closure. Herzog urges upon Marmelstein a Kierkegaardian view that modern man can achieve truth only by acknowledging, but not yielding to, the reality of pain and evil.

> *Let us put aside the fact that such convictions in the mouths of safe, comfortable people playing at crisis, alienation, apocalypse, and desperation, make me sick. . . . We love apocalypses too much, and crisis ethics and florid*

extremism with its thrilling language. Excuse me, no. I've had all the
monstrosity I want. (pp. 316-17; ellipsis added)

In one sense, Herzog has undergone a paradigm shift from despair to an
ironical Nietzschean optimism. Herzog's diatribe against crisis-mongers
could be construed as a critique of the mentality represented by Richard
Nixon's *Six Crises*, published two years earlier in 1962. By means of
structural intricacies and psychological perplexities that make this
Bellow's most difficult book, Moses Herzog represents an unforgettable
version of the paralyzed intellectual in explicit terms of a manipulative
rhetoric that petulantly seeks to repudiate others who resort to similar
defenses. Bellow reiterates the principle that the "thrilling language"
peculiar to a crisis-trope does indeed speak its truth in a paradoxical mode
of error.

Following *Henderson the Rain King*, Bellow writes novels that render
a certain type of mind or personality. *Herzog* initiated this enterprise, and
Mr. Sammler's Planet[13] continues the effort. Unlike *Herzog*, though, it
incorporates a key decision, dialectical turn, and consequential action.
Seventy-two-year-old Artur Sammler, as Bellow's center of consciousness
or "registrar of madness," might seem as passive as Moses Herzog.
Initially no more than a mature if mordant version of Bellow's original
device (the defensive person who views crisis as someone else's problem),
he comments upon the "unbearable agitation" evident everywhere in
American life during the turbulent 1960s, an agitation obvious to anyone
who reads the paper or watches television and thus witnesses the
"collective ecstasies of news, crisis, power" (p. 73). Sammler could easily
lose himself in observing such collective crises, but Bellow intends that
Sammler define himself otherwise.

As in earlier novels, Bellow reiterates both that crisis carries a familiar
medical meaning and that some people deliberately choose to exploit
crisis. Wallace Gruner describes one unsavory aspect of his admired
father's medical practice.

"Now and then, as a favor to highly placed people, Papa performed
operations. Dilatations and currettage. Only *when there was a terrific crisis*,
when some young socialite heiress got knocked up. Top secret. Only out of
pity. My dad pitied famous families, and got big gifts of cash." (p. 101;
emphasis added)

Presumably, whereas "collective ecstasies" of crisis signifies blatant
public behavior, "terrific crisis" refers to private or even secret behavior,

and crisis thus may function as a potent mechanism for self-induced, manipulative hysteria that permits the cynical bending of moral rules.

Bellow links public and private crisis by means of two images that focus on the problematics of communication. In describing Sammler's wartime excursion to Israel in 1977, he establishes that crisis can occasion the expression of divisive character traits: "The last time he was in Israel, and that was very recent, he had wondered how European, after all, Jews were. The crisis he witnessed there had brought out a certain deeper Orientalism" (pp. 116-17). Such deeper Orientalism alludes not only to presumedly distinguishing features of Jews collectively but also to Sammler's own quietism. Bellow reemphasizes that human communication may in fact be impossible and that crisis literally tests this gloomy premise. Within a context of technological failure, complicated by overtones of disease occasioned by Elya Gruner's fatal illness, Sammler ironically notes: "'There's a telephone crisis, anyway, all over New York. The experts are working on it'" (p. 258). Like other novelists as diverse as Gissing, Turgenev, Proust, and Italo Svevo, Bellow reminds his reader that medical crisis provides both occasions for and compelling analogies for crisis of the spirit.

Bellow intensifies the dialectics between public life and private life by means of five references to the "Aqaba Crisis" that led to the Six-Day War in 1967. Sammler had been stirred by the reports of the war: "from the start of the crisis, he could not [merely] sit in New York reading the world press" (p. 142). Later, Bellow offers an explanation of "why, during the Aqaba Crisis, Mr. Sammler had had to go to the Middle East" (p. 247). Sammler's motive includes his desire to gain some relief from his own perplexity, that is, his failure to cope with intimate relationships. Yet Sammler reveals that he too exploits crisis. Happily, during a further exploration of Sammler's consciousness, Bellow writes that Sammler, while visiting wartime Israel, admits to himself the relative impracticality of his being there: "An odd person to be rushing to this war. . . . who did not seem very useful in a crisis" (p. 249; ellipsis added). In Sammler's rhetoric, crisis may call forth one's adventurism or one's escapism, two very different enabling motives. Sammler's varied judgments establish a forceful context for his own crucial decision to travel to New Rochelle so as to retrieve Dr. Lal's stolen manuscript from Sammler's daughter. Coming from an inveterate reader of the mystic Meister Eckhart, his precipitate action can be thought to represent comparatively as bold a gesture and turning point as Henderson's entering the lion's cage. Bellow has thus used a *crisis*-trope to connect and judge the mutually exclusive spheres of public life and private life. He thereby prepares the ground for his major theme, the main premise of his greatest book, *Humboldt's Gift*.

Contrasted with Coover's *The Public Burning*, any one of Bellow's first seven novels employs *crisis* as parsimoniously as a novel by Austen, James or Forster. By contrast, Coover followed the example of an overpowering rhetorician like Karl Barth or a feverishly egotistical polemicist like Richard Nixon in using a superabundant *crisis*-vocabulary. From *Dangling Man* through *Mr. Sammler's Planet*, Bellow uses a total of only thirty-four *crisis*-images. Even so, his large ambitions as a novelist decreed that with each new book he resort increasingly to the great noun. From novel to novel, he experimented with various rhetorical positionings and meanings. While exploring a variety of motifs, he was patiently developing a major cultural theme that finds its fullest expression in *Humboldt's Gift*. Prior to *Humboldt's Gift*,[14] Bellow had triggered a rich assortment of motifs by means of *crisis*-images. Among these concepts: anxiety, practicality, routine, responsibility, violence, illness, communication, responsiveness, and sexuality, as well as a set of self-reflexive ideas such as self-examination, self-confrontation, self-expression, self-reliance, and self-definition. Which of these ideas, if any, or which new ideas, if any, would Bellow develop in his eighth novel?

George Eliot had used the great concussive noun fifteen and sixteen times in *Middlemarch* and *Daniel Deronda* respectively. Bellow's use of the figure quantitatively reaches its peak in *Humboldt's Gift*, where he also uses it in sixteen places. He centers these sixteen figurations in the consciousness of various personages: Von Humboldt Fleisher, Abraham Lincoln, Charles Citrine, George Sweibel, Denise Citrine, Julius (Ulick) Citrine, Charles Citrine's mistress Renata, Pierre Thaxter, Kathleen Fleisher, and, in general, the American public.

Bellow initiates a new practice by beginning on a high note. His main character Charles Citrine discusses the poet Von Humboldt Fleisher's citing Abraham Lincoln as someone who knew how to cope with crisis: "Lincoln knew Shakespeare well and quoted him at the crises of his life" (p. 27). Preceding novelists had linked *crisis* with literature in its potential as a model for life-scripting; such strategists include Richardson, Moore, and Durrell. Bellow's linking of *crisis* with literary composition and self-definition, carried over from *Herzog*, proves crucial to his portrayal of a strange American poet. Even so, he balances off Humboldt's portrait of Lincoln as a crisis-survivor by showing another type of person, one who not only can not "use" literature constructively but who is numbed by an overdose of literary culture. Of Humboldt's wife, Citrine writes: "Kathleen was a somnambulist. Humboldt had surrounded her with the whole crisis of Western culture. She went to sleep. What else could she do?" (p. 28). Citrine confesses that he himself had slept through many problems. Bellow thus establishes a new set of parameters within which his main character faces the dilemma of either integrating literature into real life or, as it were, falling asleep over a book. Hysteria in effect neutralizes consciousness itself, as Bellow thus broadens and complicates modern life.

Yet Bellow regularly brings his theme down to earth again, reminding his reader that many people not only exploit crisis but even perversely enjoy the spectacular imbroglios of other people undergoing crisis. That is, crisis-consciousness in its trivializing forms satisfies a desire or kinky need in the American psyche. Of the businessman George Sweibel, Citrine notes that "George's average day, as he and his people saw it, was one crisis after another." Citrine extrapolates from Sweibel's workaday consciousness: "I hung up thinking of the crisis-outlook in the USA, a legacy from old frontier times" (p. 47). Citrine's speculations concerning the western genesis of an endemic American "crisis-outlook" represents another innovation in Bellow's sustained meditation on the great noun.

Citrine advances in specific crisis-terms from snide criticism to enlarged sympathy. Like Henderson and Herzog, Citrine begins by sniping at his wife Denise as being a glib manipulator. He trivializes crisis-consciousness by harping on his wife's scheming practices, recalling the time when they were preparing his play for stage presentation: "When she came to ask a question she had the script to her chest and spoke to me in a condition of operatic crisis. Her voice seemed to make her own hair bristle and to dilate her astonishing eyes" (p. 56). Likewise, after they were married: "I could always tell from her dinner conversation whether she'd been to the hairdresser that afternoon, because she was a speed reader and covered every detail of world crisis under the hair dryer." In this same passage (p. 57), Citrine cites an intense occasion at Kennedy's White House. Here, Bellow indicates his awareness that the jargon term "Crisis Management" in fact originated at Kennedy's White House with Secretary of State Robert McNamara during the 1961 Cuban Missile confrontation. Recounting a public ceremony in Washington, Citrine ridicules his wife's cynically arming herself with conversational ammunition: "On the flight to Washington we reviewed the Bay of Pigs and the Missile Crisis and the Diem problem." At the outset, then, Citrine seems merely one more petty carper with a low opinion of other people's crisis-consciousness.

To offer a gift means to cut oneself loose from the given object. Bellow's intention in *Humboldt's Gift*, as suggested by the title, is to celebrate the spirit of human generosity. He insinuates hints of such generosity even into Citrine's critique of his wife's crisis-mongering. As Citrine analyzes Denise's intellectual maneuverings at the White House, he sympathetically judges her inability to distinguish between her own private crises and larger public crises.

> After dinner she got hold of the President and spoke to him privately. I saw her cornering him in the Red Room. I knew that she was driving urgently over the tangle of lines dividing her own terrible problems—and they were all terrible!—from the perplexities and disasters of world politics. *It was all one indivisible crisis.* (p. 57; emphasis added)

Bellow propounds an ultimate paradox: *crisis* means "cut" or "divide," but a disoriented individual may entangle all perplexities into one "indivisible crisis." In this crucial part of Bellow's ambitious trope, the novelist links three major motifs: the terror that crisis can induce in an individual, the confusion between private and public spheres of experience, and the necessity for critical judgment (literally *crisis*) in any unknotting of seemingly indivisible crisis. Both the generosity of spirit and the enlarged imaginative appeal of *Humboldt's Gift* derive in part from Citrine's widening understanding of crisis-consciousness. The ventilating effects of *Humboldt's Gift*, following upon the more confined atmospherics of *Herzog* and *Mr. Sammler's Planet*, parallel the earlier effects of Bellow's following *Dangling Man* and *The Victim* with the expansive *Augie March*.

Fortunately, Citrine's self-chastening produces a new mood. In referring to his editorship of a highbrow journal, he equates crisis-consciousness very nearly with consciousness itself. Also, he notes that he himself, like Kathleen Fleisher, had avoided or evaded crises by sleeping: "I have snoozed through many a crisis (when millions died)" (p. 108). Bellow goes on in this passage to introduce into Citrine's experience the theosophical ideas of Dr. Rudolf Steiner, whose theories concerning the curative powers of a "sleep-soul" offer him some consolation. Citrine's escapist sleeping habits recall Moses Herzog reclining upon his Récamier couch. Bellow urges that modern life, with its excessive future shock and continual overexcitation of the senses, in effect overwhelms the beleaguered individual. Such a line of thought positions Citrine to state his (and Bellow's) major theme, at once analytical and moralistic, in the form of a crisis-utterance. This theme judges and denounces a presumed modern threat to the traditional individual, to what Habermas calls "European man." Bellow establishes a clear turning point when Citrine decides to travel to New York in order to hear the reading of Humboldt's will. Just prior to this fateful decision, he expresses Bellow's major theme: "Under pressure of public crisis the private sphere is being surrendered" (p. 250).

Bellow indicts the appalling modern tendency not so much to exploit or obliterate as simply to ignore the individual person. His novels, reaching a climax in the joyful utterance that is *Humboldt's Gift*, set their collective face against the obliteration of the unique human person with his desire to structure his life according to the principles of crisis (dialectical judgment). Historically, Bellow extends and complicates Eliot's theme in *Felix Holt* by illustrating how even sophisticated people risk divesting themselves of personhood or selfhood.

Bellow writes realistic fictions rather than transcendental romances, so that Citrine's personal turning point effects no general reformation of morals or manners. He himself remains all too human. Other characters also continue to flounder within a historical context of crisis-mongering. At one point, during a conversation with Pierre Thaxter, Citrine explains that popular psycho-therapeutic information concerning stress has itself contributed to a public hysteria: "We read about identity crisis, alienation, etcetera, and it all affects us" (p. 268). Such hysterical personal response to manipulative public agitation might be termed the crisis of the knowledge explosion or more radically the crisis of crisis. The great noun itself has taken on a constitutive function in human behavior.

Various characters in *Humboldt's Gift* succumb to the seductive and reductive appeal of popular or merely personal crisis. The intellectual adventurer Thaxter plans to interview notorious dictators like Qaddafi and Amin ("I intend to analyze the crisis of values") until Citrine warns his glib friend against meddling with such dangerous men. Citrine's brother Ulick stipulates for crisis-exploitation (p. 401) when he plans to make a profit from current economic problems ("Only railroads can move the coal, and the energy crisis is bringing coal back strongly"). Lest Citrine seem to have undergone some radical transformation by his generous response to Humboldt's gift, he himself is again shown (p. 403) self-righteously rebuking Renata for enjoying a crisis ("You've spent weeks fretting about your identity crisis"). Consistently, Citrine's entire narrative exhibits his own existential identity crisis.

Citrine's speculations about the structure and function of crisis in human life continue almost to the last page. Two moments in the next-to-last chapter prove noteworthy. Citrine displays signs of his earlier cynicism or despair when he excuses himself from helping to rescue the abducted Thaxter by replying to Thaxter's publisher to the effect that "for forty years during the worst crises of civilization" he had kept abreast of affairs without such effort doing any good. Yet, later in the same chapter, during a conversation with Kathleen Fleisher, Citrine begins despairingly but concludes by proposing an alternative to despair. He explains to Kathleen that human beings have too easily and too deeply immersed themselves in the "false unnecessary comedy of history" such as politics. But, he concedes:

> "*The common crisis is real enough.* Read the papers—all that criminality and filth, murder, perversity, and horror. We can't get enough of it—we call it the human thing, the human scale." (p. 479; emphasis added)

In reply to Kathleen's query "What else is there?" Citrine offers a vague but appealing Steinerian alternative based upon the "existence of a soul" situated within "a great hierarchy that goes far far beyond ourselves." Thus Bellow tracks Citrine from metaphoric selfishness to ironic self-awareness. Such a generous view derives from Steiner but also from Humboldt's own soulful view of the larger realities, and—in the form of a film script—it constitutes Humboldt's essential gift to Citrine and the world.

Bellow refuses to accept death, neutralization, or cultural absorption of the individual. His crisis-philosophy grounds itself in an assumption somewhat akin to Keats's powers of negative capability, an ability to dwell in the midst of doubts and mysteries without any nervous grasping for arbitrary certainties but with an ability to act when necessary. He witnesses to a severely disruptive crisis mentality in Western culture, and he frequently laments the public's pleasure in such violent spectacles as race riots and sex scandals to the neglect of serious reflection upon underlying causes. Bellow's concern over this endemic zeitgeist climaxes in *Humboldt's Gift*. Humboldt never reaches his goal of living the poet's life because in an unpoetical culture many people enjoy the spectacle of his prolonged anguish. As Judie Newman points out:

> The audience prevent Humboldt's winning his battle with madness, delighted by Humboldt's drama, much as they would be by war, or any other *crisis as a relief from their dull lives*. His narrative has moreover a sexual theme, titillating to the psychiatrists. His evasion is therefore two-fold, like Citrine, who takes refuge from later events in the arms of both 'crisis mentality' and a sexually gratifying woman.[15] (p. 168; emphasis added)

Bellow epitomizes the long tradition of novelistic crisis-rhetoric beginning with Richardson by anatomizing the sad spectacle of human beings who deliberately forfeit their own responsible selves by exploiting crisis as entertainment.

Historically, George Eliot initiated a modern form of crisis-trope in *Felix Holt, the Radical*, where she urged (chap. 13) that "there is no private life which has not been determined by a wider public life." Bellow's own conservative imagination elucidates the consequences, alternately malign or benign, of Eliot's revolutionary principle. In Bellow's vivid final depiction of Citrine attending Humboldt's reburial in the Valhalla Cemetery, he offers a muted but persuasive closure to his celebration of beleaguered soulfulness. In elaborating a crisis-rhetoric through eight novels climaxing in *Humboldt's Gift*, Bellow finally hit upon a formulation for his master theme or complaint: "Under pressure of public crisis the private sphere is being surrendered." His thesis or solution accordingly would be that the private sphere must not be surrendered, the individual (*contra* Habermas) must be continually supported and defended at all costs.

Paul de Man defined crisis as an "apocalyptic tempest," but Bellow distinguishes between crisis and apocalypse. With *Humboldt's Gift*, Bellow's long crisis-meditation passes a watershed as he works through implications and possibilities of the great trope. When he came to write *The Dean's December*, his meditation upon this problem must have seemed completed, so that his spare account of Dean Albert Corde's experiences in Chicago and Bucharest did not depend seriously upon a highly developed crisis-figure. Whereas Durrell and Coover attempted to ridicule the fashionable word into irrelevance, Bellow appeared simply to have exhausted its usefulness.

In *The Dean's December*,[16] Bellow mainly foregoes *crisis* in favor of "different terms." He employs *crisis* five times, as Henry James did in *The Ambassadors*, but with no comparable structural purpose or effect. Instead, he humorously trivializes the trope as a minor domestic problem. As Dean Corde packs his luggage for his visit to Bucharest, he notes: "Item: his pots of African violets. What good would it do to let the rods of ultra-violet light burn on? A crisis—how to save his plants!" (p. 17). Another implication, less trivial than pathetic, appears when Corde explains to Dewey Spangler his motivation for writing a series of professionally ruinous *Harper's* articles on slum conditions in Chicago. Bellow renders Corde's thoughts on the subject of an "American moral crisis" that required a special kind of perception in order to be understood. Yet in the same context, Spangler complains that Corde had scooped him with a *New Yorker* article about Stalin, Churchill, and Truman at Potsdam (pp. 123-124). Bellow thus signals an egotism appropriate to a half-jocular confrontation between *macho* journalists playing oneupmanship.

In two subsequent passages, Bellow attributes crisis-consciousness to minor characters. Corde recalls that a Chicago lawyer, Wolf Quitman, had described "hustlers around who live off the black crisis" (p. 153). Later, Corde distinguishes between communism and capitalism on the basis of a kind of "rational citizen's courage," an ability to "keep our heads in crisis" in a "cold steady way" (p. 277). Yet when Corde and Minna discuss Dewey Spangler, they both recall that the ambitious journalist differed from Corde in that he employed a different sort of vocabulary: "different terms—crisis, catastrophe, apocalypse" (p. 264). Spangler's progressively exacerbated vocabulary suggests that Eliot's keyword is yielding its place of relevance to a less rationalistic word such as *apocalypse*.

The Dean's December is a book of compelling power and relevance. To say that Bellow in composing it has foregone the sort of crisis-trope that exfoliated in *Humboldt's Gift* is not to denigrate its literary value. In this conceptually pure, cold narrative Bellow continues to develop a sustained examination of revolutionary violence but with only a minimal use of the great noun itself. Certainly, Dean Corde's unforgettable closing scene at the Mount Palomar Observatory (p. 311), depicting Corde aloft in the viewer's cage confronting a sky "tense with stars" that possibly "had to do with your existence," thus links Bellow's closing vision with one of its forgotten astrological usages. At the end of *The Dean's December*, Bellow resorts at least to one ancient meaning of the great noun with its powerful implications for man's fate.

Subsequently, Bellow discovered that he in fact could not further elaborate his vision of contemporary life without a more systematic recourse to the great noun. *More Die of Heartbreak*,[17] a book of ten unnumbered chapters, is at present of too young a vintage for any substantial critical judgment to have been formed, but in Bellow's last novel to date he raises crisis-consciousness to one of its highest levels.

Like skepticism, the apocalyptic mode must be difficult to sustain. Bellow's apocalyptic tone, expressed in *The Dean's December*, absents itself from *More Die of Heartbreak*. Here he adopts a comic tone that parodies many of his own stylistic quirks. His story is simple but in some key respects unique. His narrator Kenneth Trachtenberg, a student of Russian literature, tells of his experiences with his brilliant, erratic uncle (Benn Crader), a world-class botanist but an inept womanizer. Kenneth narrates a story in which the widower Crader's recent marriage results in a complicated attempt by his new in-laws to retrieve millions of dollars out of which Crader had been cheated by his own uncle, the rapacious politician Harold Vilitzer. Given the relative brevity of *More Die of Heartbreak*, the fact that the narrator employs *crisis* thirteen times represents Bellow's relatively fullest use of the great noun and a return to the strong tropological pattern which culminated in *Humboldt's Gift*.

Kenneth criticizes the sexual mores of his father's generation in terms of exploitation: "The world crisis was everybody's cover for lasciviousness and libertinage (two little words you seldom see)" (p. 41). Bellow's comic tone exhibits itself unmistakably here in Kenneth's bantering wordplay. Throughout, Kenneth uses the great noun to enable an analysis of Uncle Benn's symbolic adventures. A structural similarity to *Augie March* appears in Bellow's placing a majority of Kenneth's crisis-signs near and after the main turning point of the plot, namely, Uncle Benn's painful decision to meet at a hospital with his manipulative father-in-law Dr. Layamon (p. 220) and his subsequent agreement to prosecute his Uncle Vilitzer. A more important similarity to earlier books is that Bellow characterizes crisis as occasioning or enabling critical self-scrutiny (pp. 11-12). Kenneth evokes the great name of Emanuel Swedenborg, whose own turning point consisted of a religious conversion in middle age. This allusion enables a crucial hypothesis concerning Uncle Benn's problematical sensualism.

> The private diary kept by *Swedenborg during the years of his crisis* records dreams that go from "angelic sexuality" to erotic earthiness. I wondered whether this was what Uncle was talking about when he spoke of interesting dreams. I suspected that he was, or once had been, a sensualist. Foolish to say "once had been." If you were that, you continued for life to be it in some degree—no, exaggeratedly, like Balzac's Baron Hulot or Stravinsky's centenarian grandfather. Benn wouldn't have been sexually abused by women if he hadn't had the carnal strength to attract abusive types or to endure (perhaps to invite?) the abuses. (p. 95; emphasis added)

This Swedenborgian allusion harks back to *Dangling Man*, with its paradigm shift enabled and signalled by the great revolutionary names of Lenin, Mozart, and Locke.

Uniquely, *More Die of Heartbreak* stipulates for *crisis* on the first page and in the first sentence.[18] Kenneth begins thus: "Last year while he was passing through a crisis in his life my Uncle Benn (Benn Crader, the well-known botanist) showed me a cartoon by Charles Addams." This opening gambit, in which a character is merely "passing through a crisis," together with the reference to a mordant *New Yorker* cartoonist, guarantees at the outset a comic tone. Bellow's narrator continues to project crisis onto another character (Uncle Benn) until near the end (p. 329), and Bellow's crisis-trope is both strung out to unusual length and also used for new effects.

In addition to *crisis* being used in the opening sentence, another innovation proves even more noteworthy. Almost as if Kenneth were reflecting upon Bellow's dialectical turning points, or as if he had studied Marshall Brown's representation of turning points "from the inside," he identifies his own personality type as one "obscurely motivated by the conviction that our existence was worthless if we didn't make a turning point of it" (pp. 246-47). This comment reinforces his earlier observation concerning the practice of structuring one's life via real or imagined turning points. In reply to his former mistress's assertion that he is self-sufficient, Kenneth launches into his most extensive analysis of his own character. He might be echoing Husserl.

> There she was right on the nail. Particularly in this day and age, you have no reason to exist unless you believe you can make your life a turning point. *A turning point for everybody—for humankind.* This takes a certain amount of gall. One would call it ambition, another effrontery. Explain it in a hall to the employees of the VA and they would vote me a straitjacket. Still, if you think that historical forces are sending everybody straight to hell you can either go resignedly with the procession or hold out, and hold out not from pride or other personal motives but from admiration and love for human abilities and powers to which, without exaggeration, the words "miracle" and "sublimity" can be applied. (pp. 68-69; emphasis added)

Kenneth's optimistic outburst represents Bellow's fullest statement on the subject, as well as a major statement on the subject in general. Bellow subsequently signals a strong turning point in *More Die of Heartbreak.* Kenneth notes that his Uncle Benn was "in a rapidly developing crisis" (p. 198) as he recalls Benn's account of his own fateful interview at the hospital with his father-in-law Vilitzer: "This was the onset of his crisis" (p. 220).

Five crisis-images in Bellow's penultimate chapter create his most concentrated effect. Kenneth confronts his Uncle Benn with the fact of Benn's emotional disorientation: "You're having an anxious crisis about confronting Uncle Harold" (p. 260). Kenneth accommodates his own behavior to Uncle Benn's predicament: "he was in a crisis and it would be unforgivable to ride him" (p. 264). Concerning a public hearing, dealing with a rape case, which they attend in order to confront Harold Vilitzer: "This hearing at such a time of crisis was hell on him" (p. 275). He even becomes spiteful toward his uncle in terms of crisis.

No, *he had entered the present crisis under his own power*, kept his decision to marry a secret from me, opting for the Layamons' penthouse, for the silks and satins, the eiderdown duvet of Matilda's bed, the carpets deeper than forest moss, the tremendous force of the taps in the bathroom, the whirlpool tub, the great view of the slums (like Sodom and Gomorrah the day after). Uncle had made love to his employment. Nevertheless I didn't want to see his head on the headsman's block. (pp. 277-78; emphasis added)

With Kenneth's intertextual glance at *Hamlet* ("Uncle had made love to his employment"), Bellow reinforces a motif of "critical consciousness" announced explicitly a few pages earlier (p. 265).

Bellow's crisis-images in the ninth chapter permit the reader a glimpse of a selfish motive behind Kenneth's concern for his uncle. Kenneth exploits his uncle's agonies in order to avoid confronting his own anxieties. When Uncle Benn flees from his marital problems by joining a scientific expedition in Brazil, Kenneth pretends to worry about Benn's "persistent and sharpening crisis, and nobody for Benn to talk to—how would he manage without me?" (p. 294). Like Richardson's energetic but desperate Robert Lovelace or Coover's Richard Nixon, Kenneth is both instinctively and by design a crisis-manager.

Early on (p. 20), Bellow announces a "primary modern theme" by alluding to Admiral Richard Byrd's book *Alone*, in which Byrd notes that during long polar nights individuals reveal themselves to each other, in the process discovering that there will be "no escape" from one's "inadequacies." Such painful self-consciousness might well lead to despair, but Kenneth subsequently decides that "love" must be invoked against the dangers of "critical consciousness" which otherwise "reduces all comers to their separate parts" and "disintegrates them" (p. 265). Modern life in Western culture results in "decisions" becoming increasingly problematical: "Personal freedom is beset by choice-torments" (p. 61). Hence, critical consciousness should be economically focused directly upon human problems. In a strong turn against turn, Bellow echoes but rejects the sort of crisis-manipulation espoused by Habermas in *Legitimation Crisis*, with its theme of "Man at the End of History." Kenneth desperately attempts to visualize man as "illuminated man," a microcosm "incorporating universal Being in himself, with the proviso that he be on top of the edifice of universal knowledge" (p. 36). Bellow rejects the world view espoused by abstracting social scientists.

Kenneth's apparently high-minded sentiments remain unexamined until his final crisis-reference signals a long meditation as he lies awake thinking of his uncle self-exiled in Brazil. In this meditation, reminiscent of similar ordeals undergone by crisis-adepts such as Eliot's Daniel

Deronda, James's Isabel Archer, and Forster's Margaret Schlegel, Kenneth self-reflexively bends analysis back upon himself. While for the first time admitting his own personal experience of "crisis nights," he again harshly critiques modern life in terms reminisicent of Habermas's view of the death of the individual. Happily, though, Kenneth resists such a grim view by linking crisis-consciousness with human freedom itself.

> Beauty rest can't always be had in this era, described by an intelligent lady in a magazine as "post-human." Therefore *crisis nights should be faced with maximum composure* [emphasis added]. You can't be worrying about haggard looks and rings under the eyes. You have to think, when so many supports and stabilities are removing themselves from you, about the possible advantages of removing yourself from *them*—the human being, preserving himself humanly, may find a channel which brings him to liberty. (pp. 329-30)

Despite his unsettling sense of aporia, Kenneth resists the end of man, but Bellow in effect has provided a radically ironical critique of his self-contradictory narrator who sips cheap brandy throughout this long meditation. In keeping with the long history of the trope, Bellow ultimately portrays Kenneth in ambiguous terms, as an infantile exploiter and manipulator of other people's crises but as one who nonetheless faithfully, even heroically, renders an authentic account of another person's conflicted existence.

Bellow's prolonged meditation upon the great noun confirms Eliot's prophecy in *Felix Holt, the Radical* that in the modern world human experience would structure itself via this concussive word. Eliot's dual themes, manipulation and self-scripted destiny, coalesce in Bellow's diligent oeuvre, but he both personalizes and broadens Eliot's theme so as to produce a master *crisis*-theme appropriate to his own times: "Under pressure of public crisis the private sphere is being surrendered" (*Humboldt's Gift*). Like Eliot, Bellow has remained alert to widespread exploitations of the great noun, ranging from the street to the White House. By his sensitivity to nuances of modern life, as well as his confronting the more blatant expressions of crisis-haunted modern consciousness, he has been able to show how life-strategies now consist largely of crisis-management.

In *Humboldt's Gift*, Charles Citrine resembles not only Coover's Richard Nixon but also Richardson's Robert Lovelace. More broadly, the generic Bellow protagonist variously enacts crucial dialectical principles uncovered in my historical survey, being alternately disoriented by the dizzying flux of raw experience, desperate under some form of oppression, wandering on the periphery of some kind of revolution, mired in disorder and sorrow, inwardly torn by the dialogue or dialectic of the mind with itself, and, in general, either overwhelmed or exalted by the permanent mystery of dialectical turnings. At each twist and turn, as Paul de Man would urge, error dogs his steps.

Bellow might reject Karl Barth's theology of KRISIS as a floridly thrilling language which encourages behavior such as "safe, comfortable people playing at crisis." Yet Barth singled out Dostoevsky as the writer who most compellingly depicts the crisis-anguish of souls in pain. Dostoevsky also provided for Bellow an irresistible model.[19] The creative tensions in Bellow's novels derive in considerable part from his uncanny ability, like Dostoevsky himself, to balance his characters precariously between serious attempts to invent their own moral histories and certain merely trivial pursuits. As Judie Newman discovered, Bellow both depicts and judges a peculiarly modern crisis-mentality.[20]

Bellow's example may demonstrate some inherent conservatism in the tradition or genre I have been representing. Early on, Bellow consciously made himself the heir to the great moralistic and realistic tradition that included Richardson, Scott, Austen, Eliot, James, and Lawrence. One clear sign of his anti-modernist intention emerges in his metamorphic and metaphoric attempts to shape a given text via crisis-tropes. His inquiry into experiential meanings of the great noun culminates in Kenneth Trachtenberg's definition of a "turning point for everybody—for humankind" (More Die of Heartbreak). Bellow thus fulfills a program initiated by Richardson, sustained by Mackenzie and Scott, moralized and psychologized by Austen, and finely honed in the art of Eliot, Meredith, Moore, and James. He drives home the point that a high degree of crisis-consciousness, albeit perplexed and perplexing, accompanies all self-consciousness. More Die of Heartbreak brings to its fullest expression to date all explicit efforts to define crisis as social turmoil, as manipulation, as existential turning point, and as critical self-reflexion.

Bellow's sustained meditation upon crisis-experience gathers up numerous threads reaching back into the eighteenth century and connecting with many kinds of discourse. In book after book, like Richardson he depicts a battle of the sexes between an earthbound individual and a transcendent individual. The outcome of his novels often hinges upon which character expropriates the power to dominate a relationship by determining moments of decision. Bellow likewise recalls Henry Mackenzie in depicting a weak hero (Tommy Wilhelm) who betrays his own lack of moral stamina via a crisis-trope. In The Victim he uses the great noun in its familiar medical sense as Sterne had done in

Tristram Shandy, but in *Henderson the Rain King*, along lines laid down by Scott in *The Heart of Midlothian*, he exploits a wider range of emotional extremes inherent in the enabling figure. Both *Augie March* and *Henderson the Rain King* enact a self-discovery similar to the kind depicted in Austen's *Emma*. In *Humboldt's Gift*, Bellow manages an unwieldy set of narrative materials via sixteen *crisis*-images, a strategy recalling Eliot's method in *Middlemarch* and *Daniel Deronda*, at once systematic and rational. The progression from James's *Portrait of a Lady* to *The Ambassadors*, in the latter of which mere crisis-exuberance is replaced with a mature "appreciation of the crisis," is approximated in the movement from Bellow's early novels to the mature *Mr. Sammler's Planet* or *More Die of Heartbreak*.

Historically, at least up to and including Lawrence and Forster, the rhetoric of fiction includes books to which Bellow's texts stand in relation as a kind of fulfillment or extension. *Augie March* hints that authentic sexual expression represents a Lawrentian life-determining principle. In general, Bellow's work offers the spectacle of a crisis-quest to reach a place, a sacred center, where a meaningful reality dwells as in the Arnoldian *Howards End*. On the other hand, with quirky modernist works such as *Finnegans Wake* and *The Alexandria Quartet* Bellow's novels formally have little in common, even if Bellow indirectly puts his own stamp on the great noun only less literally than Joyce. Historically, Coover's *The Public Burning* represents a special case. Bellow's ten novels taken together contain only slightly more crisis-signals than Coover's tour de force, but Bellow's intention, spread out over a career, adds up to a satirical indictment of crisis-mentality at least equal to Coover's.

Bellow brings to its fullest expression the novelists' judgment that the valuable word *crisis* threatens to become a merely fashionable gesture. At one level, Moses Herzog's complaint about "safe, comfortable people playing at crisis" can be taken to refer to novelists themselves and to their characters as crisis-strategists. A novelist distances himself or herself from raw human experience and, in effect, "cooks" raw material into digestible or manageable portions. Not only a supposedly aloof rhetorician such as Austen, James, or Forster but any novelist, even as heated a polemicist as Lawrence, distances himself somewhat from and manipulates experience by rhetoric, including crisis-tropes. Richardson's manic Robert Lovelace manages occasionally to compose his turbulent mind by means of the tightening dramatic structure of a crisis-strategy. Meredith's Willoughby Patterne protects himself at one point from comic exposure by imagining a crisis of heart disease. Lambert Strether's fine "appreciation of the crisis" at a moment of disorientation illustrates Strether's own exploitation of an impressionistic aesthetic in coping with disturbing intensities. Richard Nixon, both historically in *Six Crises* and fictionally in Coover's novel, masochistically enjoys his own self-distancing, self-dramatizing maneuvers as he shapes his crisis-centered narrative. Even Coover's nail-biting Nixon thus ironically represents what Bellow derides as comfortable people playing crisis-games.

No less relevant are other similarities between Bellow's strenuous book-by-book experiments and certain earlier experiments, novelist by novelist and book by book, from Richardson to Golding. Bellow extends Eliot's three-pronged effort in *Felix Holt, the Radical* simultaneously to satirize political manipulation via an emerging buzzword, to depict both satirically and seriously individual efforts to shape a life-script or moral history via the great keyword, and also to structure an ambitious book via the trope. Earlier authorial strategies reappear in Bellow's constant experimentation with this figure of speech. In *Dangling Man*, Joseph's crisis-experience with historically attested cultural paradigm shifts resembles Harley's crisis with Shaftesbury's philosophy of benevolence. The tight structure of both books expresses the authors' visions of the effects of emotional deprivation. In *The Victim*, Bellow echoes *Middlemarch* by providing Leventhal with a hasty *ad hoc* definition of the great noun during a moment of self-discovery. In *Augie March*, Bellow follows the example of Scott, Eliot, and Forster by deconstructively positioning the trope in the second half of the book so as to induce the theme of Augie's reborn self. Crisis-enabled rebirth in *Augie March* and *Humboldt's Gift* recapitulates a crisis-theme projected by Lawrence and Durrell. In *Henderson the Rain King*, Bellow foregoes climactic pattern, instead placing emphasis in the first third of the novel as if to decenter crisis away from any position of structural importance. Even so, he thereby achieves a brilliant effect, comparable to Golding's in *Lord of the Flies*, by using *crisis* one more time precisely at the hectic moment when Henderson fearfully enters the lion's cage. An echo of Richardson's epistolary crisis-rhetoric appears in Moses Herzog's stillborn thought-letters.

Bellow's acknowledged masterpiece, *Humboldt's Gift*, with its fully elaborated crisis-trope in sixteen contexts, epitomizes how novelist after novelist has depended upon the great figure in producing a great book. It makes explicit a sobering principle implicit from the beginning of the novel: human beings enjoy the spectacle of other human beings undergoing embarrassments and even agonies. This grim principle underlies not only the tragic view of life but also much serious literature.

To describe Saul Bellow's accomplishment is very nearly to approximate the agonized history of the modern world's most highly wrought figure of speech. His career-long agonizing over the nuances of crisis-consciousness in the rhetoric of literature and life strongly validates the historical importance of the trope but leaves us to face serious questions about the future of this dark source of art.

Historically, then, such has been the career of the great noun. Following George Eliot and Paul de Man, I have foregrounded and represented one version of a rich trope but one which may threaten at any moment to become merely a technical device, both banal and exhausted. Is the revolutionary episteme that it helped to initiate and in which it has participated now near completion, or will the trope connect afresh with new materials and methods of life, literature, and rhetoric? Will it simply disappear as being unable to serve changing artistic programs and intentions? Kant believed that any history, being a specific version of the past, ineluctably posits questions about the future.[21] What is yet to come in the story of the strangely twisting *crisis*-trope? In rhetoric generally and specifically in literature, is its future to be the future of an illusion or will it continue to enjoy the career of a potent intertextual allusion?

Notes

Introduction: A Model for a Critical History

1. George Eliot, *Felix Holt, the Radical*, intro. George Levine (New York: Norton, 1970), 42. References to page numbers refer to this edition.

2. Walter F. Ong, "The Writer's Audience is Always a Fiction," *PMLA* 90 (1975): 9-21.

3. Ferdinand de Saussure, *Cours de linguistique générale* (Paris: Payot, 1973), 174. Of course, to insist upon the figurativeness of any figure would be, as Lucien Dällenbach thinks, futilely "dogmatic and casuistic." *The Mirror in the Text*, trans. Jeremy Whiteley and Emma Hughes (Chicago: University of Chicago Press, 1989), 108.

4. I understand *crisis* in its historical development to become something like what Kenneth Burke characterized as a "god-term." At the risk of trivializing my topic, I will occasionally refer to *crisis* as a buzzword. A buzzword is simply a word (or phrase) used by members of some in-group, having little or imprecise meaning but sounding impressive to outsiders. *Crisis* will prove to be a peculiarly consequential buzzword for the modern world, and it will be seen to be used by individuals to dazzle not only others but also themselves. Thus, I hope to demonstrate that as a trope it hovers uncertainly—and productively—between sameness (metaphor) and difference (metonymy); that is, it both induces unthinking emotional intensities and necessitates reflexive judgment of such intensities. In *Felix Holt, the Radical*, Eliot's Lawyer Johnson clearly uses the great noun as a buzzword.

5. Hayden White, *Tropics of Discourse: Essays in Cultural Criticism* (Baltimore: Johns Hopkins University Press, 1978), 1-25. In establishing an ontology of consciousness, White argues for a consciousness-determining tropology in all discourse. Not even the most logical of syllogisms or most mimetic of texts evade the necessity for some degree of figurativeness. Such figurativeness originates in and as a mind-set. The relations between description (mimesis) and argument or narrative (diegesis) must undergo interpretation (diataxis). We can not hope to make sense of experience without tropes. Such tropes fall into an "archetypal pattern" which, historically, informs influential systems elaborated by, e.g., Vico, Nietzsche, Hegel, Marx, Freud, Piaget, Foucault, and E. P. Thompson. White's privileged form of this four-stage pattern is rendered as four post-Renaissance master tropes: metaphor, metonymy, synecdoche, and irony. In plain language, these four types embody experiential principles of identification, separation, classification, and self-awareness. Piaget, for example, identifies four stages of genetic epistemology in the child: sensorimotor, representational, operational, and logical. Earlier, Vico described four historical ages: gods, heroes, men, and decline (*ricorso*). Freud

describes four stages of dream work: condensation, displacement, representation, and secondary revision. Thompson traces the development of working class consciousness in four stages: relative obliviousness, self-willed apartheid, new sense of society as a whole, and final division of the working class into workers and intellectuals. In all of these examples, the dialectical movement is from naïve consciousness (metaphor) to sophisticated self-consciousness (irony). For White, tropology offers a valuable model both of discourse and of consciousness itself. Ontologically, though, he wavers between believing that the four-stage process in Piaget and others is merely analogous to or is actually an outgrowth of and essentially the same as figures of speech.

6. In a sense related to but somewhat different from White's tropology, the search for master tropes that powerfully but subtly activate ambiguities of psychology and language itself has been one constant effort of modern critical thought. Not only Vico and Nietzsche but Kenneth Burke, Paul de Man, and Harold Bloom have identified master tropes. In rhetoric, a trope is simply any figure of speech that effects a twist or turn in sense and meaning, a shift from a literal to a figurative sense. As practiced by such critics as Burke, Angus Fletcher, Francis Fergusson, and John Hollander, tropology mounts a critical effort to identify and interpret tropes in literary discourse. Unquestioned master tropes include metaphor, metonymy, synecdoche, and irony. Other candidates put forward include aporia, hyperbole, litotes, and metalepsis. For the rhetorician, whether an author or a fictive character, one chief purpose of a trope is to achieve self-expression and self-definition. By means of a trope, a rhetorician achieves an implicit formal critique of his material or of his basic form. Traditionally, then, tropes function in narratives as techniques of indirect argument. I am indebted for this succinct definition (and much more in the way of lively critical thinking) to Henry Louis Gates, Jr., *The Signifying Monkey: A Theory of Afro-American Literary Criticism* (New York: Oxford University Press, 1988).

7. At least one major philosophy (Hegelianism) grounds itself in the definition of man as essentially a form of self-consciousness. See Andrew Feenberg, *Lukács and the Sources of Critical Theory* (New York: Oxford University Press, 1986), 50. For other philosophical dimensions of this problem, see Eugene Webb, *Philosophers of Consciousness: Polanyi, Lonergan, Voegelin, Ricoeur, Girard, Kierkegaard* (Seattle: University of Washington Press, 1988), who sees forms of self-knowledge such as consciousness and self-consciousness as at once social and conflictual (5). Webb discusses consciousness as awareness, operation, symbolization, hermeneutic field, desire, and subjectivity. In my own view, the *crisis*-trope reduces to a special form of skeptical or ironical self-consciousness in writer, reader, and discursive form itself. The general belief that a literary form induces new stages in human consciousness can be seen, e.g., in Paul Oppenheimer, *The Birth of the Modern Mind: Self, Consciousness, and the Invention of the Sonnet* (New York: Oxford University Press, 1989). For a survey of many theories of consciousness, together with an application of such theories to a body of literary works, see Howard W. Fulweiler, "Gerard Manley Hopkins and the Evolution of Consciousness," in *Centenary Revaluation of Gerard Manley Hopkins*, ed. Eugene Hollahan, *Studies in the Literary Imagination* 21 (Spring 1988): 91-108.

8. I hasten to add that I am not, strictly speaking, "doing tropology" or writing a tropological history of *crisis*. But in ways obvious and perhaps not so obvious I am influenced by two recent books that do base themselves in White's tropology. At the level of practical criticism of novels, I am indebted to James M. Mellard, *Doing Tropology* (Urbana: University of Illinois Press, 1987), which starts, as I start, with Hayden White's tropology of consciousness but which uses phenomenology to ground White's abstract

categories and thus to enable practical criticism of actual narratives (i.e., the interpretative "doing" of tropology). Like Mellard, I narrow and apply White's categories. Essentially, I avail myself of White's most fundamental premise, that structures of consciousness, regarded as tropes or mind-sets (lamps rather than mirrors) can be studied in actual language utterances (concrete *parole* rather than abstract *langue*). On the other hand, whereas Mellard confines himself to a nonchronological (defamiliarizing) reading of four American classics, I range over several dozen narratives in order more broadly to examine the history of one important modern word. My general purpose is different from Mellard's, but I will frequently draw upon *Doing Tropology*. In addition, as a historian of a trope, I am also indebted to Hans Kellner, *Language and Historical Representation: Getting the Story Crooked* (Madison: University of Wisconsin Press, 1989). Kellner assists me in my effort to remain aware of my own tropological procedures throughout, and I frequently draw upon his witty principle of "getting the story crooked." Both Mellard and Kellner acknowledge the difficulties created by White's assumptions (see Kellner, 208-9), but they make White's ideas accessible to literary criticism and historical representation. Both display an appropriately healthy "fear of tropology's explanatory power" (Kellner, ix).

9. For this idea, derived from C. S. Peirce, see Michael Cabot Haley, *The Semeiosis of Poetic Metaphor* (Bloomington: Indiana University Press, 1988), 96. Haley also supports my argument by agreeing with C. S. Lewis's equating of *conscious* and *conscience* as illustrative of the growth of metaphor and in the "actual development of human consciousness" (166-67). I should point out here that in *Felix Holt*, Eliot similarly develops character psychology and motivation by repeatedly collocating *conscious* and *conscience*, frequently in the same contexts where she elaborates her subject of crisis-consciousness. All such propositions reinforce my belief that the crisis-trope at the very least conditions modern consciousness itself.

10. J. Hillis Miller, *Fiction and Repetition: Seven English Novels* (Cambridge: Harvard University Press, 1982), 20.

11. Kellner, *Language and Historical Representation*, vii-xi.

12. See Michel Foucault, *Power/Knowledge: Selected Interviews and Other Writings, 1972-1977*, trans. Colin Gordon and others, ed. Colin Gordon (New York: Pantheon, 1980), 231.

13. The *Dictionary of Philosophy and Psychology* notes how *crisis* was carried over from physical ailments to mental disorders. Meaning an attack or spell, it formed an essential feature in the earliest doctrines of Mesmer, the purpose of whose "magnetic" treatment was to aid nature in calling out the crisis and thus to quicken recovery. The room in which Mesmer's cures were performed was called the "salle de crises." Large conceptual categories to which *crisis* stands in strong relationship, as listed in *Roget's Thesaurus of English Words and Phrases* (1962), include the following: juncture, degree, eventuality, limit, important matter, danger, predicament, and excitation. Foreign phrases include the French *crise de adolescence*, *crise de coeur*, *crise de combat*, and *crise de nerfs* (hysteria). *Webster's New Dictionary of Synonyms* (1978) identifies two sets of synonyms. The first set pertains to the structure of any process. *Crisis* thus indicates turning point, critical juncture, climax, climacteric, decisive turn, acme, height, vitally important stage in the course of anything, critical occasion, hinge, and contingency. The second set conveys a different sense, not of chronological process but of dire circumstance or danger:

Emergency, exigency, conjuncture, strait, pass, pinch, rub, push, extremity, crux, trial, entanglement, pickle, uncertainty, muddle, mess, perplexity, kettle of fish, hot water, stew, deadlock, quandary, dilemma, predicament, scrape, imbroglio, fix, plight, hole, corner, impasse, difficulty.

By contrast, a prescriptive usage guide such as *The Right Word at the Right Time* (1985) condemns one large category of usages—*crisis* as emergency—as being carelessly non-standard. Relating *crisis* to *crucial*, it notes:

Careful users avoid the word in the loose sense it has recently acquired—'a serious, urgent, worrying, or dangerous state of affairs':

It looks like England has a crisis on its hands—the first three wickets have tumbled within the space of two hours.

It is interesting to note that the currently popular phrase *mid-life crisis* does actually use *crisis* close to its etymological sense of 'turning-point'. Ironically, this source also mistakes the true etymology.

A witty rationale for such censure of the widespread practice of making *crisis* chiefly mean "emergency" appeared earlier in Eric Partridge's *Usage and Abusage* (London: Hamish Hamilton, 1957):

crisis, in the two years preceding the Second World War, during it, and since, has been used with nauseating frequency. The Munich Agreement ('the peace that passeth all understanding', as a journalist called it) was only the first of a series. Without a crisis, preferably a *grave crisis*, we should feel lost. There seems to be little danger of our getting lost. (360; emphasis Partridge's)

Despite such cavilling, individuals and societies continue to feel lost without this seductive word.

In literary studies, *crisis* has generally been a useful word with a clear meaning.

Crisis: In a FICTION or a DRAMA the point at which the opposing forces that create the CONFLICT interlock in the decisive ACTION on which the PLOT will turn. *Crisis* is applied to the EPISODE or INCIDENT wherein the situation of the PROTAGONIST is certain either to improve or worsen. Since *crisis* is essentially a structural element of PLOT rather than an index of the emotional response that an event may produce in a reader or spectator, as CLIMAX is, the *crisis* and the CLIMAX do not always occur together. (*A Handbook to Literature*, 5th edition, edited by William Harmon [New York: Macmillan, 1986])

Some handbooks, however, vary this definition, attesting to a checkered history. In one source, *crisis* in a literary plot is said not to effect a "cutting" or "breaking" but rather as itself being cut or broken.

This point of maximum instability is called the *crisis* (a technical term here, not to be confused with "crisis" in the ordinary sense of "any emergency"). As in a disease, the crisis breaks—owing, in the novel, to some climactic discovery, moral assertion, rescue or catastrophe. (Richard Eastman, *A Guide to the Novel* [San Francisco: Chandler, 1965], 11)

Such definitions raise the philosophical question whether crisis is something which merely happens to an individual or whether the individual deliberately enacts the experience. *A Handbook for the Study of Fiction* links *crisis* chiefly with an older type of narrative. Concerning Stephen Crane's naturalistic short story "The Open Boat": "The approach to land and the waning of the men's strength force the crisis, the attempt to reach shore through the surf." Consistent with Crane's naturalistic assumptions, a reader is thus invited to see the crucial event as being determined by uncontrollable natural forces. (Lynn Altenbernd and Leslie L. Lewis, *A Handbook for the Study of Fiction* [London: Collier-MacMillan, 1966], 66-67).

One of the discoveries in the present study will be that serious novelists, depicting moral ordeals in a culture where moral responsibility appeared to be steadily eroding, attempt as it were to restore the import of *crisis* to its etymological base of "judgment" or "decision." Handbooks regularly ignore this meaning, but the *Concise Dictionary of Literary Terms* hints at the motif of judgment.

> The term can refer to a point of time when it is decided whether a course of action or an affair shall be stopped, be modified, or proceed and also applies to an emotionally significant event or radical change of status in an individual's life.

In the example given, the most crucial judgment would be Claudius's presumedly hectic decision to flee the scene rather than brazen out Hamlet's audacious ploy (the play-within-the-play) (Harry Shaw, *Concise Dictionary of Literary Terms* [New York: McGraw-Hill, 1972], 71).

14. Christopher Clausen, *The Place of Poetry: Two Centuries of an Art in Crisis* (Lexington: University of Kentucky Press, 1981).

15. Poem #889 ("Crisis is a Hair") and poem #948 ("'Twas Crisis—All the length had passed—") in *The Poems of Emily Dickinson*, ed. Thomas H. Johnson, 4 vols. (Cambridge: Harvard University Press, 1955).

16. Frequently, critics and scholars exploit *crisis* as an empty signifier—like a "Danger" sign—mainly to attract attention. Yet in some studies, *crisis* may signal a type of subject matter or a critical methodology. It may refer to a stressful transition in a cultural period, mode, style, or taste (nineteenth century, symbolism, realism). It may signal an ordeal in the life of a writer, such as a decline in reputation of an artist, an individual work, or an oeuvre. Sometimes it refers to a disruptive change in a mode or genre (lyric, tragedy, novel). It may range in application from an author's agonized selection of a persona to a dilemma troubling a national literature. It may refer to subject matter such as economics, politics, religion, aesthetics, or language. It may refer to stages in an artist's life (middle age, retirement, ill health). Grammatically, critic and scholar use *crisis* either as a noun modified by an adjective (witchcraft crisis); or, in an "and" phrase (crisis and the reconstruction of the self); or, in an "in" phrase (crisis in the humanities). Rhetoricians also use *crisis* in a prepositional phrase signalled by "of" (crisis of self-identity). The MLA Database demonstrates that in scholarly discourse, as in popular parlance, every conceivable human activity has been characterized as undergoing or representing a crisis. Such widespread usage, when it reduces the word to the lowly if endemic status of a buzzword, is condemned—as will be seen—by prescriptive lexicologists such as Eric Partridge.

17. Bellow's position in Anglo-American literary history is effectively suggested in *Philosophical Dimensions of Saul Bellow's Fiction*, ed. Eugene Hollahan, *Studies in the Literary Imagination* 17 (Fall 1984). Also, see my essay "'Crisis' in Bellow's Novels: Some Data and a Conjecture," *Studies in the Novel*, 15 (1983): 249-63.

18. See Haley, *Semeiosis*, 96.

19. Paul de Man, *Blindness and Insight: Essays in the Rhetoric of Contemporary Criticism* (New York: Oxford University Press, 1971), 3-19.

20. Christopher Norris, *Deconstruction: Theory and Practice* (New York: Methuen, 1982), 100.

21. Raymond Williams, *Culture and Society: 1780-1950* (New York: Columbia University Press, 1958; reprint, 1983) and *Keywords: A Vocabulary of Culture and Society*, rev. ed. (New York: Oxford University Press, 1983).

22. Other studies of complex keywords include William Empson's brilliant if quirky commentaries on "magnificent rich words" such as *wit*, *honest*, and *sense* in masterpieces

by Shakespeare, Pope, and other major authors (*The Structure of Complex Words* [Norfolk, Conn.: New Directions, 1952]). Likewise, C. S. Lewis examines specific keywords (*nature, sad, wit, free, sense, simple*) in texts such as *Macbeth, The Beggar's Opera, Essay on Criticism, The Merchant of Venice, Measure for Measure,* and *All's Well That Ends Well* (*Studies in Words* [Cambridge: Cambridge University Press, 1960]). Some keyword studies concentrate more intently upon a single word. Norman Knox devotes a book to *irony* (*The Word "Irony" and Its Context, 1500-1755* [Durham, N. C.: Duke University Press, 1961]). P. N. Furbank directs a spirited polemic at critics' abuse of *image* (*Reflections on the Word "Image"* [Boston: David R. Godine, 1976]). Lionel Trilling describes radical disruptions in European moral development by tracing the history of *sincerity* (paired with *authenticity*) (*Sincerity and Authenticity* [Cambridge: Harvard University Press, 1971]). Susie Tucker makes a readable narrative of the vicissitudes of *enthusiasm* (together with *enthusiast* and *enthusiastic*) via an extended commentary on the *Oxford English Dictionary*'s notes on this set of words; Tucker also provides a chapter on metaphors associated with *enthusiasm* and its congeners (*Enthusiasm* [Cambridge: Cambridge University Press, 1972]). William Gass impressionistically enacts a complicated rhapsody celebrating every possible meaning and nuance of the adjective *blue* (*On Being Blue* [Boston: David R. Godine, 1976]). Finally, Richard Gilman indignantly complains of numerous departures from root meanings of *decadence* (*Decadence: The Strange Life of an Epithet* [New York: Farrar, Straus, and Giroux, 1979]).

23. For example, qualitatively, a *crisis*-trope embedded but perhaps scattered in a discourse will be a subtle figuration requiring deft or bold analysis; quantitatively, it may consist of anything from one single occurrence of the word to more than fifty (Coover's *The Public Burning*) or one hundred (Karl Barth's *Epistle to the Romans*, which thereby establishes a scandalous theology of KRISIS).

24. Nowhere does the word appear in Dante, Boccaccio, Cervantes, Racine, Jean de la Fontaine, or the Baudelaire of *Les Fleurs du Mal*. Nowhere do we encounter it in Horace or Ovid; nowhere in Garcilaso de la Vega, Kant, Lorca, or Rimbaud. Among English-language poets, many who wrote after the date of the first *OED* entry (1543) likewise eschew the word. Chaucer, Spenser, Shakespeare, and Milton ignore it. An extensive list can be compiled: Sir Thomas Wyatt, Samuel Daniel (sonnets), Sir Phillip Sidney, Michael Drayton (sonnets), Thomas Traherne, John Donne, Ben Jonson, Robert Herrick, Andrew Marvell (English poems), George Herbert, Henry Vaughan, William Collins, Oliver Goldsmith, Alexander Pope, Robert Burns, Samuel Johnson, Thomas Gray (English poems), William Blake, John Keats, Matthew Arnold, Gerard Manley Hopkins (English poems), A. E. Housman, Alfred Tennyson, William Butler Yeats, James Joyce, and Dylan Thomas. In America, a similar phenomenon presents itself. Poets who avoid *crisis* include Edward Taylor, R. W. Emerson, Sidney Lanier, Stephen Crane, Hart Crane, Ezra Pound, Marianne Moore, Theodore Roethke, and Langston Hughes. Some poets do use the great noun. Important figures such as Cowper, Coleridge, Byron, Shelley, and D. H. Lawrence did not entirely shrink from it. Even so, and as if to complicate even further this problematical history, five important poets (Dryden, Wordsworth, Coleridge, Shelley, Eliot) each use it only one single time. A puzzling tale indeed. Such absence surely represents a challenge to any critic or historian, but such a study would necessarily follow the present introduction to a history of a presence.

25. Lionel Stevenson, *The English Novel: A Panorama* (Boston: Houghton Mifflin, 1960). In order to attach my own heuristic history of the *crisis*-trope to a conservative history of the novel, I regularly draw upon Stevenson's summaries and commentaries.

26. Stevenson traces the form from its beginnings in pastoral and picaresque; its divigations into romance, allegory, and scandal; the discovery of realism and the first masterpieces by Richardson, Fielding, Smollett, and Sterne; the establishment of a tradition based on the assimilation of such revolutionary masterpieces; a decline into didactic sentimentality and Gothic excess; the recovery of the novel's prestige by Scott and Austen; the expansion of scope via new content and form; Dickensian humor and melodrama; an awakening social consciousness; serious treatment of domestic matters such as marriage and family; intellectual maturity with George Eliot; a period of dominant or pure realism; recognition of technique via the art novel; concern with ethical problems and exotic (imperial) adventures; the anatomy of society; and, after 1915, the psychological exploration of the psyche. A subsequent volume chronicles novels appearing in the second half of the twentieth century, an account that must eventually include the post-modern novel. Novelists of importance and interest have been arbitrarily excluded from the present study. Not only important lesser names such as Daniel Defoe, Charlotte Brontë, and Ford Madox Ford but also possibly greater names such as Henry Fielding, Anthony Trollope, and Evelyn Waugh have been omitted here from consideration. Dozens, perhaps hundreds, of other names and titles could be adduced as potentially relevant to this study of a putative *crisis*-trope in the development of the novel.

27. Miller, *Fiction and Repetition*, 4.

28. For an impassioned expression of the principles involved in the New Historicism, see Frank Lentricchia, *Criticism and Social Change* (Chicago: University of Chicago Press, 1983).

29. Floyd Merrell, *Pararealities: The Nature of Our Fictions and How We Know Them* (Philadelphia: John Benjamins, 1983), 123.

30. For a Marxist approach to this problem, consult the chapter "Culture and Consciousness" in Feenberg, *Lukàcs*, 133-71.

31. Lucien Dällenbach's magisterial study *The Mirror in the Text* defines the *mise en abyme* as "an original unit determined only by the reflexive function it has in the narrative" (206 n. 38) and also as "*any aspect enclosed within a work that shows a similarity with the work that contains it*" (8). From time to time, I will urge that the *crisis*-trope works as a whole-reflecting part something like the *mise en abyme*. My general principle in that case is that the narratives I choose to examine in detail depict massive and prolonged crises in the usual sense of dire circumstances and emergent predicaments. The *crisis*-trope thus has an internally mirroring role to play along with its constitutive role.

32. See Mellard, *Doing Tropology*, 20, and Kellner, *Language and Historical Representation*, 232.

33. Marshall Brown, "'Errours Endlesse Traine': On Turning Points and the Dialectical Imagination," *PMLA*, 99 (1984): 9-25. Confronting the Mill and the River, Brown meditates upon George Eliot's *The Mill on the Floss* as a narrative which "twists and turns." In an uncontrollable turmoil of feeling, Eliot's characters tragically make a "turn back rather than a turn ahead." Brown's principle here—"Rivers never stop changing"—suggests an obscure violence because the present is fully experienced as turning point only when "we are swept off our feet." Reasoning from the eddying and flooding river, he hypothesizes that time and human life constantly turn but that their meaning "lies beyond all possibility of awareness." Moreover, literary art constantly literalizes that turning point where "actions outstrip comprehension." Even more broadly, history perplexes because it is always made "without our awareness, or at least without our comprehension."

Meditating upon the Wheel and the Swing, Brown unpacks texts by Yeats, James, Zola, Conrad, Mallarmé, and Socrates in uncovering the principle that crisis or the turning point occurs as "a point of disorientation." Viewed from the inside, crisis is variously a turbulent flow, a moment of balance and unbalance, aporia or perplexity, and a dialectical switch from path to pathlessness. Brown links such dizziness to the desire for freedom: The moment when one swings back from subjection—whether under a dogma or a public leader—to independence is a period of turbulence when the movement of the soul and the movement of the world are no longer in alignment, a period of blindness and floundering before the new path is illumined.

At the crisis or turning point an old order vanishes but a new order may not yet have arrived. Such inchoate paradigm shifts will be seen repeatedly in my own historical account. In Kant's *Critique of Pure Reason* Brown discovers crisis as Revolution. He derives another premise: "the notion of speed . . . central to all revolutionary dialectic." Historically, the astronomical term "revolution" lost its gradualist and conservative implications and took on connotations of violent progressivism: "Turning has always suggested disorder and violence." Revolution functions as a dark force that ineluctably drives individuals. At the moment of a turning or crisis, "error and truth, confusion and clarity, labor and delivery are inseparably mixed." Plato, Hegel, and Nietzsche provide Brown with evidence for the turning point as Dialectic. Crisis can be linked with the notion of progress, as for example the paradigm shift distinguishing scientific revolution described by T. S. Kuhn. Brown urges a bold Nietzschean assertion: "Truth is not a place (*topos*) but a way, and the way is not a road (*hodos*) but a turning (*tropos*) off that deadly high road."

Contemplating Sir John Davies's *Orchestra: A Poem on Dancing*, Brown discovers that even an orderly dance combining motion and fixity in fact depicts human reason endlessly attempting to "unweave the fabric of thought the mind has woven." Brown concludes, *pace* E. M. W. Tillyard, that "turning and dancing were never fully imaged as a principle of order." Most radically, perhaps, Brown notes that the Greek word for judgment or decision is *krisis* and that every turning point involves a judgment which is a "point of peril." Individuals knowingly or unknowingly turn events and conflicts against the counterturns of other persons. From Keats, Milton, Yeats, Wordsworth, and Derrida, Brown assembles numerous figures of turning, in both nature and culture, turnings which illustrate that the "melancholy train of error has no end." Human experience expresses a trajectory toward an unspecified goal. Even so, the moment of turn against turn depicts an authentic openness to human possibilities because of the dialectical character of knowledge itself.

In Escapable Romance, like a true Socratic dialectician Brown self-consciously questions the very ontology of his own speculations. He inquires if the topic he chose to meditate upon—how a turning point or crisis appears from the inside—actually exists: "is there anything in our heads?" Or, is revolution a permanent mystery with no solution?

34. Norris, *Deconstruction*, 133-34.

35. See Wolfgang Iser, *The Act of Reading: A Theory of Aesthetic Response* (Baltimore: Johns Hopkins University Press, 1978) and *The Implied Reader: Patterns of Communication in Prose Fiction from Bunyan to Beckett* (Baltimore: Johns Hopkins University Press, 1974). Also, the introductory essays in *Contemporary Literary Criticism: Literary and Cultural Studies*, 2d ed., ed. Robert Con Davis and Ronald Schleifer (New York: Longman, 1989).

36. Foucault, *Power/Knowledge*, 237.

37. Peter Brooks, *Reading for the Plot: Design and Intention in Narrative* (New York: Alfred A. Knopf, 1984), 7.

38. Howard Felperin, *Beyond Deconstruction: The Uses and Abuses of Literary Theory* (Oxford: Clarendon Press, 1986).

39. Paul Valéry, *The Art of Poetry*, trans. Denise Folliot, intro. T. S. Eliot (New York: Vintage, 1961), 210-11.

Chapter 1. Revolutionary Roots of Modern Crisis-Consciousness

1. In 1986, during a conversation at her home in Jerusalem, the critic Shlomith Rimmon-Kenan expressed to me the opinion that I could not possibly carry out my project because in the contemporary world *crisis* is, in effect, everywhere and everything. In rising to Rimmon-Kenan's challenge, I repeatedly resort to concepts and terminology spelled out in her excellent summary in the New Accents series, *Narrative Fiction: Contemporary Poetics* (New York: Methuen, 1983). Assuming that textual segments are always conjunctions of compositional principles, and consolidating many influential theories, she divides narrative poetics into Story, Text, and Narration. Story is a matter of Events and Characters; Text is a matter of Time, Characterization, and Focalization; Narration is a matter of Levels or Voices and Speech Representation. Rimmon-Kenan's own governing trope seems to be her convincingly argued belief that the writer places effects which the reader must strenuously cope with if any understanding is to unfold. *Narrative Fiction* is a gold mine of critical terms and intelligent commentary.

2. E. M. Forster, *Aspects of the Novel* (New York: Harcourt, Brace, 1927), 129.

3. W. K. Wimsatt, Jr., *The Verbal Icon: Studies in the Meaning of Poetry* (Lexington: University of Kentucky Press, 1954), 28-29 passim.

4. Longinus, *On the Sublime*, in *Criticism: The Major Statements*, 2d edition, ed. Charles Kaplan (New York: St. Martin's Press, 1986), 87.

5. Howard W. Fulweiler provides a cogent study of the development of consciousness in terms of mankind's growing away from an "original participation" in the natural world. Drawing upon Owen Barfield, Mircea Eliade, T. S. Kuhn, and Erich Neumann, among others, he identifies "special moments of transition": Hellenic philosophy, medieval scholasticism, Baconian science, the Enlightenment, Victorian industrialism, and the like. I think that the novel's emphasis on increased freedom and alienation from the natural world results in its being crucially a part of the Enlightenment's trope of crisis-consciousness. For Fulweiler's moments of transition, see "Gerard Manley Hopkins and the Evolution of Consciousness," 92-93.

6. Richard D. Altick, *The Art of Literary Research*, rev. ed. (New York: Norton, 1975), 33-37.

7. Thomas Paine, *The American Crisis*, in *The Writings of Thomas Paine*, intro. Moncure Conway, 4 volumes (New York: AMS Press, 1967). References to page numbers refer to this edition.

8. Moncure Conway, "Introduction" to *The Writings of Thomas Paine*, I, vi.

9. Colley Cibber, *An Apology for the Life of Mr. Colley Cibber, Comedian, with an Historical View of the Stage During His Own Time, Written by Himself*, ed. and intro. B. R. S. Fone (Ann Arbor: University of Michigan Press, 1968).

10. Samuel Richardson, *Clarissa, or the History of a Young Lady*, intro. Philip Stevick (San Francisco: Rinehart, 1971).

11. That is, the hermeneutical circle, which I understand as follows. A reader can not hope to understand any part of a discourse until the whole is grasped, at least impressionistically. Likewise, the whole can not be grasped until the parts are comprehended. One reads provisionally, tentatively, accommodating one's sense of the whole as one perceives the parts; these parts are viewed in light of an unfolding perception of the whole. As W. W. Holdheim puts it: "human perception and understanding always proceed from foreknowledge of a (however dimly apprehended) totality that is gradually modified and clarified in a mutual approximation of the one and the multitude, the comprehensive and the subordinate, the whole and its parts." *A Handbook to Literature*, 5th ed., ed. C. Hugh Holman and William Harmon (New York: Macmillan, 1986), 234.

12. Monroe C. Beardsley has assimilated Austin's concepts to literary criticism in *The Possibility of Criticism* (Detroit: Wayne State University Press, 1970), 51-65.

13. Eugene Webb, *Philosophers of Consciousness*, 317.

14. Philip Stevick, "Introduction" to *Clarissa, or the History of a Young Lady*, p. xvii.

15. Dorothy Van Ghent, *The English Novel: Form and Function* (New York: Harper & Row, 1953), 56.

16. Lionel Stevenson, *The English Novel*, 148.

17. Henry Mackenzie, *The Man of Feeling* (New York: Norton, 1958). References to page numbers refer to this edition.

18. Laurence Sterne, *The Life and Opinions of Tristram Shandy, Gentleman*, ed. James Aiken Work (New York: Odyssey, 1940). References to pages numbers refer to this edition.

19. Marian Cusac, *Narrative Structure in the Novels of Sir Walter Scott* (The Hague: Mouton, 1969).

20. Sir Walter Scott, *The Heart of Midlothian*, intro. David Daiches (New York: Holt, Rinehart and Winston). References to page numbers refer to this edition.

21. John Lauber, *Sir Walter Scott*, Twayne's English Authors Series (New York: Twayne, 1966), 106-14.

22. Webb, *Philosophers of Consciousness*, 6.

23. Hans Kellner, *Language and Historical Representation*, 192. However, lest I become over-confident in my own perceptions, I must remind myself what Dällenbach says of a certain kind of *mise en abyme*: "Given that virtually all commentators have ignored it, we should not be too confident that it exists." Lucien Dällenbach, *The Mirror in the Text*, 47.

Chapter 2. Ideology and Crisis-Consciousness

1. Tony Bennett, *Formalism and Marxism* (New York: Methuen, 1979), 155.

2. Matthew Arnold, "My Countrymen," *Culture and Anarchy, with Friendship's Garland and Some Literary Essays*, ed. R. H. Super, in *The Complete Prose Works of Matthew Arnold* (Ann Arbor: University of Michigan Press, 1965). V, 3-31.

3. Hans Kellner, *Language and Historical Representation*, urges the existence of such a governing or Over-Trope: "a trope that shapes and regulates the tropic differences and combats within it" (214). Given the self-reflexive properties of *crisis*, I think that crisis-consciousness functions as such an over-trope.

4. Thomas Carlyle, *Sartor Resartus: The Life and Opinions of Herr Teufelsdröckh*, ed. Charles Frederick Harrold (New York: Odyssey, 1937).

5. John Stuart Mill, *Autobiography and Literary Essays* (Toronto: University of Toronto Press, 1981). References to page numbers refer to this edition.

6. John Henry Newman, *Apologia Pro Vita Sua*, Norton Critical Edition, ed. David Delaura (New York: Norton, 1968). References to page numbers refer to this edition.

7. Stuart Tave, *Some Words of Jane Austen* (Chicago: University of Chicago Press, 1973).

8. David Cecil, *A Portrait of Jane Austen* (New York: Hill and Wang, 1979), 160.

9. Jane Austen, *Emma*, Norton Critical Edition, ed. Stephen M. Parrish (New York: Norton, 1972), 49.

10. Wayne Booth, *The Rhetoric of Fiction* (Chicago: University of Chicago Press, 1961), 116.

11. Michael Riffaterre, *Text Production*, trans. Terese Lyons (New York: Columbia University Press, 1983), 6.

12. Lionel Trilling, *Sincerity and Authenticity*, 67.

13. See my essay "'Of Course the Whole Thing Was Couéism': *The Heart of the Matter* as a Critique of Emile Coué's Psychotherapy," *Studies in the Novel* 21 (1989): 320-31.

14. Emily Brontë, *Wuthering Heights*, Norton Critical Edition, ed. William E. Sale, Jr. (New York: Norton, 1963). References to page numbers refer to this edition.

15. Hayden White, *Tropics of Discourse*, 13-15.

16. I derive this idea of a "charter" from Lucien Dällenbach, *The Mirror in the Text*, 7-8. Dällenbach cites Gide's original statement about the trope now known as the *mise en abyme* as being like a charter or fixed point of reference for a critical history of the device. Like Dällenbach's study of the *mise en abyme*, my study of the "great" crisis-trope discovers that historically the figure goes off in many different directions only faintly hinted at by the originating charter.

17. David Williams, *Mr George Eliot: A Biography of George Henry Lewes* (New York: Franklin Watts, 1983), 281-82.

18. Raymond Williams, *The English Novel from Dickens to Lawrence* (New York: Oxford University Press, 1970), 65. References to page numbers refer to this edition.

19. Raymond Williams, *English Novel*, 84.

20. For a Marxist explanation of this process, see Andrew Feenberg, "Culture and Consciousness," in *Lukács, Marx, and the Sources of Critical Theory*, 133-71.

21. In attempting to understand Eliot's work, I have found considerable enlightenment in Alexander Welsh, *George Eliot and Blackmail* (Cambridge: Harvard University Press, 1985). Welsh places Eliot in the revolutionary information culture emerging in the nineteenth century; thus he hopes to discover "why blackmail took hold of the modern imagination" (v). As unpromising as this narrow aim might appear, Welsh yet convincingly represents the processes by which knowledge regarded as information takes on special status and function in modern culture. What use is to be made of information, and by whom, and with what consequences? Throughout the following discussion, I am indebted to Welsh's provocative hypotheses. Welsh notes: "the moment of revelation governs the value of information" (50). Welsh's provocative assertion translates in my own study of crisis-rhetoric to the following hypothesis: given that any moment may be effectively designated a crisis, the designation of a crisis by one interested individual (character or author) implies privileged information. This process we have already seen at work from Richardson onward, most emphatically in the violent turn against turn between Robert Lovelace and Clarissa Harlowe who vie with each other as to which one will designate or, so to speak, authoritatively reveal a crisis.

22. George Eliot, *Felix Holt, the Radical*, 42. References to page numbers refer to this edition.

23. Welsh notes that the word *consciousness* occurs with increasing frequency in Eliot's later novels. He relates her understanding of consciousness to a pathology and a psychopathology of information, to the whole complex notion of privacy/secrecy vis-à-vis publicity, and to Eliot's "fictions of discontinuity" (257). As if invoking White's trope of irony, he suggests that the fiction of discontinuity doubles back upon itself.

24. "The four basic forms of value identified by Marx are the Elementary, Total, Generalized, and Money." Kellner, *Language and Historical Representation*, 234.

25. See "Distribution Effects" in Dällenbach, *The Mirror in the Text*, 60-71.

26. *The Crisis, or the Change from Error and Misery, to Truth and Happiness*, ed. Robert Owen and Robert Dale Owen (London: J. Eanonson, 1833).

27. On this point, I am taking exception to critics of Hayden White's tropology as being necessarily cyclical and, hence, unhistorically dead-ended. Nothing prevents us from seeing the ironical stage as, either sooner or later, converting into an entirely new metaphor or an advanced stage of the original metaphor that initiated the chain. For criticism of White, see James Mellard, 31-32.

28. See, e.g., Bruce Henricksen, "The Construction of the Narrator in *The Nigger of the 'Narcissus'*," *PMLA* 103 (1988): 783-95. Following Henricksen's Bakhtinian analysis, I think that the numerous major characters in *Felix Holt*, each contributing to an informing crisis-consciousness, merge with or are subsumed by an implied author's or narrator's voice, an "I" that first appears in chapter 16 and, as if in unconscious complicity with capitalism, concludes the book with a loaded final word—in effect a troping of materialism—the word *money*. More generally, like *The Nigger of the 'Narcissus,'* *Felix Holt* illustrates how modern individuals are formed out of numerous discursive experiences.

29. An example of how critical scrutiny of a crisis-rhetoric in a novel can enable an interpretation of the entire book can be seen in my essay "The Concept of 'Crisis' in *Middlemarch*," *Nineteenth-Century Fiction* 28 (1974): 450-57.

30. George Eliot, *Middlemarch*, ed. David Carroll (Oxford: Clarendon Press, 1986). References to page numbers refer to this edition.

31. Arthur K. Moore, *Contestable Concepts of Literary Theory* (Baton Rouge: Louisiana State University Press, 1973), 158.

32. Stevenson, *The English Novel*, chap. 14.

33. Norris, *Deconstruction*, 133-34.

34. George Eliot, *Daniel Deronda*, ed. Graham Handley (Oxford: Clarendon Press, 1984). References to page numbers refer to this edition.

35. Barbara Hardy, "Introduction" to George Eliot, *Daniel Deronda* (New York: Penguin, 1967), 27.

36. For a psychoanalytical explanation of Gwendolen's tortured personality, see my essay "Therapist or The Rapist?: George Eliot's *Daniel Deronda* as a Pre-Freudian Example of Psychoanalysis in Literature," *Journal of Evolutionary Psychology* 5 (1984): 55-68.

37. See Mary Ann Caws, *Reading Frames in Modern Fiction* (Princeton: Princeton University Press, 1985), which describes how "certain passages stand out in relief from the flow of the prose and create, in so standing, different expectations and different effects" (xi). Caws thinks such disruptive devices in effect permit other genres to enter a narrative; moreover, modernist narratives peculiarly call attention to themselves as employing such devices. Among the relevant modulations of narrative operators (*agents*

de change) identified by Caws: centering, bracketing, diegetic clues, detachment, estrangement, embedding, larger or smaller contexts, frames of expectation, internal closure, container and contained, detachment, concentration, embedding, figure and field, hinge, grid, highlighting, mind set, silhouette, and surround. In this respect, I think that the crisis-trope effectively embeds or internally frames numerous metaphoric devices, most notably self-reflexive criticism itself.

38. Welsh, *George Eliot and Blackmail*, p. 329.

39. In identifying a major theme in Hayden White's tropology, Kellner notes that the cyclical sequence of tropology from metaphor to irony in fact does not preclude a force that confronts the weight of tradition: human choice. Kellner, *Language and Historical Representation*, 196.

Chapter 3. The Art of Crisis-Consciousness

1. George Levine, *The Realistic Imagination* (Chicago: University of Chicago Press, 1981), 255.

2. David Smith and Phil Evans, *Marx's KAPITAL for Beginners* (New York: Pantheon Books, 1982), 129.

3. Benedetto Croce, *History of Europe in the Nineteenth Century*, trans. Henry Furst (New York: Harcourt, Brace & World, 1963), 36.

4. Honoré de Balzac, *"Père Goriot" and "Eugénie Grandet,"* trans. and intro. E. K. Brown and others (New York: Modern Library, 1950), 239.

5. Emile Zola, *Germinal*, trans. and intro. E. L. Tancock (Baltimore: Penguin, 1969), 85.

6. Gustave Flaubert, *Madame Bovary: Patterns of Provincial Life*, trans. and intro. Francis Steegmuller (New York: Modern Library, 1957), 283.

7. Miller, *Fiction and Repetition*, 4.

8. Peter Brooks, *Reading for the Plot: Design and Intention in Narrative* (New York: Knopf, 1984), 137.

9. Allon White, *The Uses of Obscurity: The Fiction of Early Modernism* (Boston: Routledge & Kegan Paul, 1981), 27.

10. Marshall Brown, "'Errours Endlesse Traine'," 13-15.

11. George Meredith, *The Poems of George Meredith*, ed. Phyllis B. Bartlett, 2 vols. (New Haven: Yale University Press, 1978), II, 786-87 and 1045-47.

12. Taking *consciousness* to mean a "standpoint" for "social subjectivity," Andrew Feenberg works out the relations between Marx's theories of class consciousness and the later revisions of George Lukács (*History and Class Consciousness*). See Feenberg, "Culture and Consciousness," in *Lukács, Marx, and the Sources of Critical Theory*, 133-171.

13. George Meredith, *The Egoist*, Norton Critical Edition, ed. Robert M. Adams (New York: Norton, 1979). References to page numbers refer to this edition.

14. Anthony Farrow, *George Moore* (Boston: Twayne, 1978), 72.

15. George Moore, *Esther Waters* (Boston: Houghton Mifflin, 1963), 189-90.

16. George Gissing, *New Grub Street*, ed. and intro. Irving Howe (Boston: Houghton Mifflin, 1962). References to page numbers refer to this edition.

17. Ivan Turgenev, *Fathers and Sons*, Norton Critical Edition, trans. and ed. Ralph Matlaw (New York: Norton, 1966), 158.

18. Jürgen Habermas, *Legitimation Crisis*, trans. Thomas McCarthy (Boston: Beacon Press, 1973), 1-5. In my chapter 7, Habermas will be used to contextualize my discussion of Robert Coover's *The Public Burning*.

19. Lionel Stevenson, *The English Novel*, 415.

20. Henry James, *Autobiography*, ed. W. F. Dupee (New York: Criterion, 1956), 560.

21. Henry James, *The Portrait of a Lady*, Norton Critical Edition, ed. Robert D. Bamberg (New York: Norton, 1975), 100. References to page numbers refer to this edition.

22. Hugh Kenner, "Neatness Doesn't Count After All," *Discover* 8, no. 4 (April 1986): 88.

23. Henry James, *The Ambassadors*, Norton Critical Edition, ed. Robert Martin (New York: Norton, 1964), 240. References to page numbers refer to this edition.

24. Brown, "'Errours Endlesse Traine'," 9-11.

25. Ibid., 13.

26. Quoted in H. Stuart Hughes, *Consciousness and Society: The Reorientation of European Social Thought, 1890-1930*, rev. ed. (New York: Vintage, 1977), 428-29.

Chapter 4. A Conflicted Trope for a Violent New Age

1. Alan Wilde, *Horizons of Assent: Modernism, Postmodernism, and the Ironic Imagination* (Baltimore: Johns Hopkins University Press, 1981), 16-49.

2. Joseph Frank, *The Widening Gyre: Crisis and Mastery in Modern Literature* (New Brunswick, N. J.: Rutgers University Press, 1963).

3. Karl Barth, *The Epistle to the Romans*, trans. [from the Sixth Edition] Edwyn Hoskyn (London: Oxford University Press, 1933). References to page numbers refer to this edition.

4. John McConnachie, *The Significance of Karl Barth* (London: Hodder and Stoughton, 1931), chap. 2. Critical attention to such extreme opinions and extremes of style as Barth's can be justified in the same way that the French ethnographer Marcel Mauss justifies his close study of certain primitive societies. Mauss characterizes his extreme anthropological examples thus: "the maximum, the excessive, which make it possible to see better the facts than where, not less essential, they remain small and involuted." Cited in J. Hillis Miller, *Fiction and Repetition*, 4. For my argument, I select the strongest possible examples from my own reading experience.

5. D. H. Lawrence, *Twilight in Italy* (New York: Viking, 1958), 43.

6. Eugene Webb, *Philosophers of Consciousness*, 295.

7. D. H. Lawrence, *Lady Chatterley's Lover* (New York: Grove Press, 1957). References to page numbers refer to this edition.

8. Roland Barthes, *The Pleasure of the Text*, trans. Richard Miller (London: Cape, 1976), 14.

9. E. M. Forster, *Aspects of the Novel*. References to page numbers refer to this edition.

10. E. M. Forster, *Howards End*, Abinger Edition (London: Edward Arnold, 1973). References to page numbers refer to this edition.

11. Peter Widdowson, *E. M. Forster's "Howards End": Fiction as History* (London: Sussex University Press, 1977), 62ff.

12. E. M. Forster, *A Passage to India*, Abinger Edition, ed. Oliver Stallybrass (London: Edward Arnold, 1978). References to page numbers refer to this edition.

Chapter 5. A Trope to be Avoided

1. Edmund Husserl, *The Crisis of European Sciences and Transcendental Phenomenology*, trans. and intro. David Carr (Evanston, Ill.: Northwestern University Press, 1970). References to page numbers refer to this edition.

2. Paul Valéry, *The Art of Poetry*, 210-211.

3. General relationships between consciousness and the self are examined in Eugene Webb, *Philosophers of Consciousness*.

4. Paul de Man, *Blindness and Insight*, 16.

5. David Carr, "Translator's Introduction" to Husserl, *The Crisis of European Sciences and Transcendental Phenomenology*, xxxv.

6. Edmund Husserl, "Philosophy and the Crisis of European Humanity," in *The Crisis of European Sciences and Transcendental Phenomenology*, appendix A. References to page numbers refer to this edition.

7. See Alexander Welsh, *George Eliot and Blackmail*, 337.

8. Italo Svevo, *Confessions of Zeno*, trans. [from the Italian] Beryl de Zoete (New York: Random House, 1958), 397.

9. See my essay "The Path of Sympathy: Abstraction and Imagination in Camus' *La Peste*," *Studies in the Novel* 8 (1976): 377-93.

10. Marcel Proust, *Swann's Way*, trans. C. K. Scott Moncrieff (New York: Vintage, 1970), 237. See my essay "Nemerov's Definition and Proust's Example: A Model for the Short Novel," *Studies in the Novel* 11 (1979): 162-77.

11. André Malraux, *Man's Fate*, trans. Haakon M. Chevalier (New York: Vintage, 1968). See my essay "Knowledge of Beings: Concept of 'Crisis' in *La Condition Humaine*," *Journal of Evolutionary Psychology*, VIII (March 1987): 35-40.

12. Thomas Mann, *The Magic Mountain*, trans. H. T. Lowe-Porter (New York: Modern Library, 1952), 439-40. Hans Kellner offers a superb reading of this Bildungsroman as a "curriculum" at the end of which "Hans Castorp is complete, tropologically, ready for death." Kellner, *Language and Historical Representation*, 238-240.

13. Joyce Cary writes: "The power of words, of symbols, is another inevitable consequence of the freedom of the soul. Men are born with very little instinct, and therefore, from childhood, are compelled to form their own ideas of the world. They are alone in mind. Obviously, if they were not, if they were like ants and bees, members of a robot community, they would not be free. Freedom, the power to make instant unique decisions, to respond to change, to crisis, requires the separation of minds, the solitude of the individual, and the need of language for communication." "Author's Preface," *Not Honour More* (New York: New Directions, 1985).

14. Franz Kafka, *The Castle*, Definitive Edition, trans. Willa and Edwin Muir, with an homage by Thomas Mann (New York: Schocken, 1974), 203.

15. Hermann Hesse, *Steppenwolf*, rev. ed. of Basil Creighton's trans., intro. Joseph Mileck (New York: Holt, Rinehart and Winston, 1963), 74.

16. Ralph Freedman, *The Lyrical Novel: Studies in Hermann Hesse, André Gide, and Virginia Woolf* (Princeton: Princeton University Press, 1963), 185-270.

17. See Miller, *Fiction and Repetition*, 227; 241-42 n. 16.

18. Webb, *Philosophers of Consciousness*, 68.

19. Joseph Conrad, *Lord Jim*, Norton Critical Edition, ed. Thomas C. Moser (New York: Norton, 1968). References to page numbers refer to this edition.

20. Robert Penn Warren, "Introduction to *Nostromo*," xviii (see my next note).

21. Joseph Conrad, *Nostromo*, intro. Robert Penn Warren (New York: Modern Library, 1951). References to page numbers refer to this edition.

22. Joseph Conrad, *Victory* (Garden City, New York: Doubleday Anchor, 1957). References to page numbers refer to this edition. See my essay "Beguiled Into Action: Silence and Sound in *Victory*," *Texas Studies in Literature and Language* 16 (1974): 349-62.

23. Alick West, *Crisis and Criticism and Selected Literary Essays*, fwd. Arnold Kettle, intro. Elisabeth West (London: Lawrence and Wishart, 1975), 127.

24. James Joyce, *A Portrait of the Artist as a Young Man* (New York: Penguin, 1977). References to page numbers refer to this edition.

25. Alan Wilde, *Horizons of Assent*, 40.

26. E. M. Forster, *Aspects of the Novel* (New York: Harcourt, Brace, 1927), 179.

27. James Joyce, *Finnegans Wake* (New York: Viking, 1974). References to page numbers refer to this edition.

28. Raymond Williams, *The English Novel from Dickens to Lawrence* (New York: Oxford University Press, 1970), 168.

29. Adaline Glasheen, *Third Census of "Finnegans Wake": An Index of the Characters and Their Roles*, rev. and expanded from the second Census (Berkeley: University of California Press, 1977), 148-49.

30. Michael H. Begnal, "Love That Dares to Speak its Name," *A Conceptual Guide to "Finnegans Wake"*, ed. Michael H. Begnal and Fritz Senn (University Park: Pennsylvania State University Press, 1974), 139-48.

31. Margaret C. Solomon, *Eternal Geomater: The Sexual Universe of "Finnegans Wake"* (Carbondale: Southern Illinois University Press, 1969), viii.

Chapter 6. A Trope to be Exploded

1. For these terms and concepts as part of the unfolding story of modern consciousness, see Eugene Webb, *Philosophers of Consciousness*.

2. Hans Kellner, *Language and Historical Representation*.

3. Howard Felperin, *Beyond Deconstruction*, 27 n. 11.

4. Thomas S. Kuhn, *The Structure of Scientific Revolutions*, 2d ed., enlarged (Chicago: University of Chicago Press, 1970), 108. References to page numbers refer to this edition.

5. William Golding, *Lord of the Flies* (New York: Coward-McCann, 1962). References to page numbers refer to this edition.

6. Eugene Hollahan, "Running in Circles: A Major Motif in *Lord of the Flies*," *Studies in the Novel* 2 (1970): 22-30.

7. Paul Goodman, *The Structure of Literature* (Chicago: University of Chicago Press, 1954), 50.

8. Lawrence Durrell, *Lawrence Durrell and Henry Miller: A Private Correspondence* (New York: Dutton, 1963), 224.

9. Lawrence Durrell, *The Alexandria Quartet* (New York: Dutton, 1957-1960). References to page numbers refer to this edition.

10. Eugene Hollahan, "Who Wrote *Mountolive*? The Same One Who Wrote 'Swann in Love'," *On Miracle Ground: Essays on the Fiction of Lawrence Durrell*, ed. Michael

H. Begnal (Lewisburg: Bucknell University Press, 1990), 113-32. Rptd. from *Studies in the Novel* 20 (1988): 167-85.

11. Durrell, *Private Correspondence*, 327.

12. Hollahan, "Who Wrote *Mountolive?*"

13. With Durrell's death in 1990, critics begin to assess his overall achievement. See, for example, *The Other Lawrence Durrell*, ed. Eugene Hollahan, *Studies in the Literary Imagination* 24 (Spring 1991).

Chapter 7. An Extremist Crisis in Crisis-Consciousness

1. Mark Conroy, *Modernism and Authority: Strategies of Legitimation in Flaubert and Conrad* (Baltimore: Johns Hopkins University Press, 1985), chapter 1.

2. Jürgen Habermas, *Legitimation Crisis*. References to page numbers refer to this previously cited edition.

3. Critics rarely have the courage to admit that a given example pleases by fitting one's developmental or *a priori* assumptions. On this point, I am indebted to Lucien Dällenbach's courageous example in *The Mirror in the Text*, 140. Concerning a text that perfectly illustrates the mise en abyme at a crucial stage of a historical survey of the device, Dällenbach writes: "If this work [*Les Lieux-dits*] is a veritable godsend for my study, this is because it conforms absolutely to a formula not adopted by any previous text." His point is that the example is totally reflexive, hence, so to speak, totally *mise en abyme*. I consider *The Public Burning* to read like one endless crisis-trope and hence to carry my idea to its uttermost development within a single novel. Totally crisis, so to speak.

4. Marshall Brown, "'Errours Endlesse Traine'," 11.

5. Richard Gilman, *Decadence: The Strange Life of an Epithet* (New York: Farrar, Straus, and Giroux, 1979), 90-91.

6. Francois Duchêne, *The Endless Crisis: America in the Seventies* (New York: Simon and Schuster, 1970), 33.

7. Richard M. Nixon, *Six Crises* (Garden City, New York: Doubleday, 1962). References to page numbers refer to this edition.

8. Robert Coover, *The Public Burning* (New York: Viking, 1978). References to page numbers refer to this edition.

9. "Crise du Jour," *National Review*, 8 May 1987, 19-20.

10. Jonathan Green, *Newspeak: A Dictionary of Jargon*. London: Routledge & Kegan Paul.

Chapter 8. Career of a Crisis-Watcher

1. *Philosophical Dimensions of Saul Bellow's Fiction*, ed. Eugene Hollahan, *Studies in the Literary Imagination* 17 (Fall 1984).

2. Judie Newman, *Saul Bellow and History* (New York: St. Martin's Press, 1984), 177.

3. Marshall Brown, "'Errours Endlesse Traine'," 9-25.

4. Eugene Hollahan, "'Crisis' in Bellow's Novels: Some Data and a Conjecture," *Studies in the Novel* 15 (Fall 1983): 249-64.

5. Bellow, *Dangling Man* (New York: Vanguard, 1944). References to page numbers refer to this edition.

6. Bellow, *The Victim* (New York: Viking, 1956). References to page numbers refer to this edition.

7. Bellow, *The Adventures of Augie March* (New York: Viking, 1953). References to page numbers refer to this edition.

8. Bellow, *Seize the Day* (New York: Viking, 1961). References to page numbers refer to this edition.

9. Bellow, *Henderson the Rain King* (New York: Viking, 1959). References to page numbers refer to this edition.

10. Matthew Roudané, "An Interview with Saul Bellow," *Contemporary Literature* 25 (1984): 269.

11. Daniel Fuchs, "Bellow and Freud," *Philosophical Dimensions of Saul Bellow's Fiction*, 59-80.

12. Bellow, *Herzog* (New York: Viking, 1964). References to page numbers refer to this edition.

13. Bellow, *Mr. Sammler's Planet* (New York: Viking, 1970). References to page numbers refer to this edition.

14. Bellow, *Humboldt's Gift* (New York: Viking, 1975). References to page numbers refer to this edition.

15. Newman, *Saul Bellow and History*, 168.

16. Bellow, *The Dean's December* (New York: Harper & Row, 1982). References to page numbers refer to this edition.

17. Bellow, *More Die of Heartbreak* (New York: William Morrow, 1987). References to page numbers refer to this edition.

18. The importance of such an opening gesture is elucidated in Mary Ann Caws, *Reading Frames in Modern Fiction*, 16-19 and 269-70 n. 15, which surveys the literature on the subject of opening gambits and gestures.

19. Daniel Fuchs, *Saul Bellow: Vision and Revision* (Durham: Duke University Press, 1984), 28-49.

20. Newman, *Saul Bellow and History*, 177.

21. Cited in Hans Kellner, *Language and Historical Representation*, 224.

Bibliography

Novels that incorporate *Crisis*

Amis, Kingsley. *Lucky Jim*. New York: Viking, 1953.

Austen, Jane. *Emma*. Norton Critical Edition. New York: Norton, 1972.

———. *Pride and Prejudice*. New York: Holt, Rinehart and Winston, 1960.

Balzac, Honoré de. *Père Goriot*. Translated by E. K. Brown and others. New York: Modern Library, 1950.

Bellow, Saul. *The Adventures of Augie March*. New York: Viking, 1953.

———. *Dangling Man*. New York: Vanguard, 1944.

———. *The Dean's December*. New York: Harper & Row, 1982.

———. *Henderson the Rain King*. New York: Viking, 1959.

———. *Herzog*. New York: Viking, 1964.

———. *Humboldt's Gift*. New York: Viking, 1975.

———. *More Die of Heartbreak*. New York: William Morrow, 1987.

———. *Mr. Sammler's Planet*. New York: Viking, 1970.

———. *Seize the Day*. New York: Viking, 1959.

———. *The Victim*. New York: Viking, 1956.

Camus, Albert. *The Plague*. Translated by Stuart Gilbert. New York: Modern Library, 1948.

Cary, Joyce. *Not Honour More*. New York: New Directions, 1985.

Conrad, Joseph. *Lord Jim*. Norton Critical Edition. New York: Norton, 1968.

———. *Nostromo*. New York: Modern Library, 1951.

———. *Victory*. Garden City, New York: Doubleday Anchor, 1957.

Coover, Robert. *The Public Burning*. New York: Bantam, 1978.

Dickens, Charles. *Bleak House*. New York: Crowell, 1971.

———. *Oliver Twist*. New York: New American Library, 1961.

Durrell, Lawrence. *The Alexandria Quartet*. New York: Dutton, 1957-60.

Eliot, George. *Felix Holt the Radical*. Introduction by George Levine. New York: Norton, 1970.

———. *Middlemarch*. Boston: Houghton Mifflin, 1956.

———. *Daniel Deronda*. New York: Penguin, 1967.

Fielding, Henry. *Joseph Andrews*. Boston: Houghton Mifflin, 1961.

Flaubert, Gustave. *Madame Bovary*. New York: Modern Library, 1957.

Forster, E. M. *Howards End*. New York: Vintage, 1921.

———. *A Passage to India*. New York: Harcourt Brace Jovanovich, 1924.

Fowles, John. *The Ebony Tower*. New York: New American Library, 1974.

Galdós, Benito Perez. *Doña Perfecta*. Translated by Harriet de Onis. New York: Barron, 1960.

Gissing, George. *New Grub Street*. Boston: Houghton Mifflin, 1962.

Golding, William. *Lord of the Flies*. New York: Capricorn, 1959.

Grass, Günter. *Cat and Mouse*. Translated by Ralph Manheim. New York: New American Library, 1963.

Hardy, Thomas. *Jude the Obscure*. New York: Modern Library, 1967.

————. *The Return of the Native*. Norton Critical Edition. New York: Norton, 1969.

Hesse, Hermann. *Steppenwolf*. New York: Holt, Rinehart and Winston, 1963.

James, Henry. *The Portrait of a Lady*. Norton Critical Edition. New York: Norton, 1975.

————. *The Ambassadors*. Boston: Houghton Mifflin, 1960.

Joyce, James. *A Portrait of the Artist as a Young Man*. New York: Penguin, 1964.

————. *Finnegans Wake*. New York: Viking, 1959.

Kafka, Franz. *The Castle*. Translated by Willa and Edwin Muir. New York: Schocken, 1974.

Lawrence, D. H. *Lady Chatterley's Lover*. New York: Grove Press, 1957.

Mackenzie, Henry. *The Man of Feeling*. New York: Norton, 1958.

Malraux, André. *Man's Fate*. Trans. Haakon M. Chevalier. New York: Vintage, 1968.

Mann, Thomas. *The Magic Mountain*. Translated by H. T. Lowe-Porter. New York: Modern Library, 1927.

Meredith, George. *The Egoist*. Norton Critical Edition. New York: Norton, 1979.

Moore, George. *Esther Waters*. Boston: Houghton Mifflin, 1963.

Murdoch, Iris. *Bruno's Dream*. New York: Penguin, 1970.

————. *A Fairly Honourable Defeat*. Greenwich, Conn.: Fawcett Crest, 1973.

Proust, Marcel. *Swann's Way*. Translated by C. K. Scott Moncrieff. New York: Vintage, 1970.

Richardson, Samuel. *Clarissa, or the History of a Young Lady*. Abridged and edited by Philip Stevick. San Francisco: Rinehart, 1971.

Scott, Sir Walter. *The Heart of Midlothian*. New York: Holt, Rinehart and Winston, 1969.

Sterne, Laurence. *The Life and Opinions of Tristram Shandy, Gentleman*. New York: Signet, 1962.

Svevo, Italo. *Confessions of Zeno*. Translated by Beryl de Zoete. New York: Vintage, 1958.

Thackeray, William Makepeace. *Vanity Fair: A Novel Without a Hero*. New York: Modern Library, 1950.

Turgenev, Ivan. *Fathers and Sons*. Translated and edited by Ralph E. Matlaw. Norton Critical Edition. New York: Norton, 1966.

Updike, John. *The Coup*. New York: Knopf, 1978.

Woolf, Virginia. *A Room of One's Own*. New York: Harcourt, Brace and World, n. d. [1929].

Zola, Emile. *Germinal*. Translated by L. W. Tancock. Baltimore: Penguin, 1954.

Critical writings that incorporate *Crisis*

Auerbach, Erich. *Mimesis: The Representation of Reality in Western Literature*. Translated by Willard Trask. Garden City, N. Y.: Doubleday, 1953.

Barthes, Roland. *The Pleasure of the Text*. Translated by Richard Miller. London: Cape, 1976.

Bennett, Tony. *Formalism and Marxism*. New York: Methuen, 1979.

Bloom, Harold. *Kabbalah and Criticism*. New York: Seabury, 1975.

Brooks, Peter. *Reading for the Plot: Design and Intention in Narrative*. New York: Knopf, 1984.

Brown, Marshall. "'Errours Endlesse Traine': On Turning Points and the Dialectical Imagination." *PMLA* 99 (1984): 9-25.

Conroy, Mark. *Modernism and Authority: Strategies of Legitimation in Flaubert and Conrad*. Baltimore: Johns Hopkins University Press, 1985.

Cusac, Marian H. *Narrative Structure in the Novels of Sir Walter Scott*. The Hague: Mouton, 1969.

David, Deirdre. *Fictions of Resolution in Three Victorian Novels: "North and South," "Our Mutual Friend," "Daniel Deronda."* New York: Columbia University Press, 1981.

Delaura, David J. "Newman's *Apologia* as Prophecy," in John Henry Cardinal Newman, *Apologia Pro Vita Sua*. Norton Critical Edition. New York: Norton, 1968.

de Man, Paul. *Blindness and Insight: Essays in the Rhetoric of Contemporary Criticism*. New York: Oxford University Press, 1971.

Forster, E. M. *Aspects of the Novel*. New York: Harcourt, Brace & World, 1927.

Frank, Joseph. *The Widening Gyre: Crisis and Mastery in Modern Literature*. New Brunswick, N.J.: Rutgers University Press, 1963.

Goodman, Paul. *The Structure of Literature*. Chicago: University of Chicago Press, 1954.

Guttmann, Allen. *The Jewish Writer in America: Assimilation and the Crisis of Identity*. New York: Oxford University Press, 1971.

Jameson, Frederic. *The Prison-House of Language: A Critical Account of Structuralism and Russian Formalism*. Princeton: Princeton University Press, 1972.

Kenner, Hugh. "Neatness Doesn't Count After All," *Discover*, vol. 8, no. 4 (April 1986): 86-88; 90.

Longinus. *On the Sublime*, 54-93. In *Criticism: The Major Statements*, second edition, edited by Charles Kaplan. New York: St. Martin's, 1986.

Miller, J. Hillis. *Fiction and Repetition: Seven English Novels*. Cambridge: Harvard University Press, 1982.

Newman, Judie. *Saul Bellow and History*. New York: St. Martin's, 1984.

Norris, Christopher. *Deconstruction: Theory and Practice*. New York: Methuen, 1982.

Scholes, Robert and Robert Kellogg. *The Nature of Narrative*. New York: Oxford University Press, 1966.

Stevick, Philip. "Introduction" to Samuel Richardson, *Clarissa, or the History of a Young Lady*, vii-xxviii. San Francisco: Rinehart, 1971.

Svaglic, Martin J. "The Structure of Newman's *Apologia*." *PMLA* 66: (March 1951): 138-48.

Trilling, Lionel. "Freud and the Crisis of Our Culture" (lecture, 1955), published as "Freud: With and Beyond Culture," in Lionel Trilling, *Beyond Culture: Essays on Literature and Learning*. New York: Viking, 1965.

Valéry, Paul. *The Art of Poetry*. Introduction by T. S. Eliot. New York: Vintage, 1961.

Van Ghent, Dorothy. *The English Novel: Form and Function*. New York: Harper & and Row, 1953.

West, Alick. *"Crisis and Criticism" and Selected Literary Essays*. Foreword by Arnold Kettle. Introduction by Elisabeth West. London: Lawrence and Wishart, 1975.

White, Allon. *The Uses of Obscurity: The Fiction of Early Modernism*. Boston: Routledge & Kegan Paul, 1981.

Wilde, Alan. *Horizons of Assent: Modernism, Postmodernism, and the Ironic Imagination*. Baltimore: Johns Hopkins University Press, 1981.

Williams, Raymond. *The English Novel from Dickens to Lawrence*. New York: Oxford University Press, 1970.

Wimsatt, William K., Jr., and Cleanth Brooks. *Literary Criticism: A Short History*. New York: Alfred A. Knopf, 1957.

Philosophical and related works that incorporate *Crisis*

Altick, Richard D. *Victorian People and Ideas*. New York: Norton, 1973.

Arnold, Matthew. "My Countrymen." In *Culture and Anarchy, with Friendship's Garland and Some Literary Essays*, edited by R. H. Super, V: 3-31. *The Complete Prose Works of Matthew Arnold*. Ann Arbor: University of Michigan Press, 1965.

————. "From Easter to August." In *The Last Word*, edited by R. H. Super, XI: 246-64. *The Complete Prose Works of Matthew Arnold*. Ann Arbor: University of Michigan Press, 1977.

Barth, Karl. *The Epistle to the Romans*. Translated from the Sixth Edition by Edwyn C. Hoskyn, with a new preface by the author. London: Oxford University Press, 1933.

Campbell, Joseph. *The Hero with a Thousand Faces*. Princeton: Princeton University Press, 1968.

Carlyle, Thomas. *Sartor Resartus: The Life and Opinions of Herr Teufelsdröckh*, edited by Charles Frederick Harrold. New York: Odyssey, 1937.

Cassirer, Ernst. *The Philosophy of Symbolic Forms*. 3 vols. New Haven: Yale University Press, 1953.

Cibber, Colley. *An Apology for the Life of Mr. Colley Cibber, Comedian, with an Historical View of the Stage During His Own Time, Written by Himself*. Edited with an Introduction by B. R. S. Fone. Ann Arbor: University of Michigan Press, 1968.

Clausen, Christopher. *The Place of Poetry: Two Centuries of an Art in Crisis*. Lexington: University of Kentucky Press, 1981.

Collier, Peter (ed.). *Crisis: A Contemporary Reader*. New York: Harcourt, Brace & World, 1969.

"Crise du Jour," *National Review*, 8 May 1987, pp. 19-20.

The Crisis, or the Change from Error and Misery, to Truth and Happiness, edited by Robert Owen and Robert Dale Owen. London: J. Eanonson, 1833.

Croce, Benedetto. *History of Europe in the Nineteenth Century*. Translated by Henry Furst. New York: Harcourt, Brace & World, 1963.

Cumberland, Richard. *Memoirs of Richard Cumberland, Written by Himself*. London, 1807.

Davis, Joseph K. (ed). *Man in Crisis: Perspectives on the Individual and His World*. Glenview, Ill.: Scott, Foresman, 1970.

Duchêne, Francois, ed. *The Endless Crisis: America in the Seventies: A Confrontation of the World's Leading Social Scientists on the Problems, Impact, and Global Role of the United States in the Next Decade*. (A Seminar under the Auspices of the International Association for Cultural Freedom). New York: Simon and Schuster, 1970.

Durrell, Lawrence. *Lawrence Durrell and Henry Miller: A Private Correspondence*. New York: Dutton, 1963.

Foucault, Michel. *Power/Knowledge: Selected Interviews and Other Writings, 1972-1977*. Translated by Colin Gordon and others. Edited by Colin Gordon. New York: Pantheon, 1980.

Gurwitsch, Aron. *Studies in Phenomenology*. Evanston, Ill.: Northwestern University Press, 1966.

Habermas, Jürgen. *Legitimation Crisis*. Translated by Thomas McCarthy. Boston: Beacon Press, 1973.

Howe, Irving. *Thomas Hardy*. New York: Macmillan, 1971.

Husserl, Edmund. *The Crisis of European Sciences and Transcendental Phenomenology*. Translated, with introduction, by David Carr. Evanston, Ill.: Northwestern University Press, 1970.

James, Henry. *Autobiography*. Edited by F. W. Dupee. New York: Criterion, 1956.

Kuhn, Thomas S. *The Structure of Scientific Revolutions*, second edition, enlarged. Chicago: University of Chicago Press, 1970.

Lawrence, D. H. *Twilight in Italy*. New York: Viking, 1958.

McConnachie, John. *The Significance of Karl Barth*. London: Hodder and Stoughton, 1931.

Merrell, Floyd. *Pararealities: The Nature of Our Fictions and How We Know Them*. Philadelphia: John Benjamins, 1983.

Mill, John Stuart. *Autobiography and Literary Essays*. Edited by John M. Robson and Jack Stillinger. Toronto: University of Toronto Press, 1981.

Newman, John Henry. *Apologia Pro Vita Sua*. Edited by David J. DeLaura. Norton Critical Edition. New York: Norton, 1968.

Nixon, Richard M. *Six Crises*. Garden City, N.Y.: Doubleday, 1962.

Paine, Thomas. *The American Crisis*. In *The Writings of Thomas Paine*, 4 vols. New York: AMS Press, 1967.

Williams, David. *Mr George Eliot: A Biography of George Henry Lewes*. New York: Franklin Watts, 1983.

Willis, Robert E. *The Ethics of Karl Barth*. Leiden: E. J. Brill, 1971.

Zaner, Richard M. *The Way of Phenomenology: Criticism as a Philosophical Discipline*. New York: Pegasus, 1970.

Other Critical Writings

Barthes, Roland. "To Write: An Intransitive Verb?" In *The Structuralist Controversy: The Languages of Criticism and the Sciences of Man*, edited by Richard Macksey and Eugenio Donato. Baltimore: Johns Hopkins University Press, 1970.

Beardsley, Monroe C. *The Possibility of Criticism*. Detroit: Wayne State University Press, 1970.

Blackmur, R. P. *Form and Value in Modern Poetry*. New York: Doubleday, 1952.

Booth, Wayne. *The Rhetoric of Fiction*. Chicago: University of Chicago Press, 1961.

Caws, Mary Ann. *Reading Frames in Modern Fiction*. Princeton: Princeton University Press, 1985.

Cecil, David. *A Portrait of Jane Austen*. New York: Hill and Wang, 1979.

Contemporary Literary Criticism: Literary and Cultural Studies, second edition. Edited by Robert Con Davis and Ronald Schleifer. New York: Longman, 1989.

Dällenbach, Lucien. *The Mirror in the Text*. Translated by Jeremy Whiteley and Emma Hughes. Chicago: University of Chicago Press, 1989.

Farrow, Anthony. *George Moore*. Boston: Twayne, 1978.

Feenberg, Andrew. *Lukács and the Sources of Critical Theory*. New York: Oxford University Press, 1986.

Felperin, Howard. *Beyond Deconstruction: The Uses and Abuses of Literary Theory*. Oxford: Clarendon Press, 1986.

Haley, Michael Cabot. *The Semeiosis of Poetic Metaphor*. Bloomington: Indiana University Press, 1988.

Fulweiler, Howard W. "Gerard Manley Hopkins and the Evolution of Consciousness." In *Centenary Revaluation of Gerard Manley Hopkins*, edited by Eugene Hollahan. *Studies in the Literary Imagination*, 21, no. 1 (Spring 1988).

Gates, Henry Louis, Jr. *The Signifying Monkey: A Theory of Afro-American Literary Criticism*. New York: Oxford University Press, 1988.

Hollahan, Eugene. "The Concept of 'Crisis' in *Middlemarch*." *Nineteenth-Century Fiction* 28 (March 1974): 450-57.

———. "'Crisis' in Bellow's Novels: Some Data and a Conjecture." *Studies in the Novel*, 15 (Fall 1983): 249-64.

———. "'Of Course the Whole Thing Was Couéism': *The Heart of the Matter* as a Critique of Emile Coué's Psychotherapy." *Studies in the Novel* 21 (Fall 1989): 320-31.

———. "Therapist or The Rapist?: George Eliot's *Daniel Deronda* as a Pre-Freudian Example of Psychoanalysis in Literature." *Journal of Evolutionary Psychology* 5 (March 1984): 55-68.

———. "Who Wrote *Mountolive*? The Same One Who Wrote 'Swann in Love'." In *On Miracle Ground: Essays on the Fiction of Lawrence Durrell*, edited by Michael H. Begnal, 113-32. Lewisburg: Bucknell University Press, 1990. Rptd. from *Studies in the Novel* 20 (Summer 1988): 167-85.

Iser, Wolfgang. *The Act of Reading: A Theory of Aesthetic Response*. Baltimore: Johns Hopkins University Press, 1978.

———. *The Implied Reader: Patterns of Communication in Prose Fiction from Bunyan to Beckett*. Baltimore: Johns Hopkins University Press, 1974.

Kellner, Hans. *Language and Historical Representation: Getting the Story Crooked*. Madison: University of Wisconsin Press, 1989.

Lauber, John. *Sir Walter Scott*. Twayne's English Authors Series. New York: Twayne, 1966.

Lentricchia, Frank. *Criticism and Social Change*. Chicago: University of Chicago Press, 1983.

Mellard, James M. *Doing Tropology*. Urbana: University of Illinois Press, 1987.

Miller, J. Hillis. *The Form of Victorian Fiction*. Notre Dame, Ind.: University of Notre Dame Press, 1968.

Moore, Arthur K. *Contestable Concepts of Literary Theory*. Baton Rouge: Louisiana State University Press, 1973.

Ong, Walter F., "The Writer's Audience is Always a Fiction," *PMLA* 90 (1975): 9-21.

Oppenheimer, Paul. *The Birth of the Modern Mind: Self, Consciousness, and the Invention of the Sonnet*. New York: Oxford University Press, 1989.

Riffaterre, Michael. *Text Production*. Translated by Terese Lyons. New York: Columbia University Press, 1983.

Saussure, Ferdinand de. *Cours de linguistique générale*. Paris: Payot, 1973.

Schwarz, Daniel R. *The Humanistic Heritage: Critical Theories of the English Novel from James to Hillis Miller*. Philadelphia: University of Pennsylvania Press, 1986.

Rimmon-Kenan, Shlomith. *Narrative Fiction: Contemporary Poetics*. New Accents Series. New York: Methuen, 1983.

Van Ghent, Dorothy. *The English Novel: Form and Function*. New York: Harper & Row, 1953.

Webb, Eugene. *Philosophers of Consciousness: Polanyi, Lonergan, Voegelin, Ricoeur, Girard, Kierkegaard*. Seattle: University of Washington Press, 1988.

Welsh, Alexander. *George Eliot and Blackmail*. Cambridge: Harvard University Press, 1985.

White, Hayden. *Tropics of Discourse: Essays in Cultural Criticism*. Baltimore: Johns Hopkins University Press, 1978.

Books Treating of Single Words

Empson, William. *The Structure of Complex Words*. Norfolk, Conn.: New Directions, 1952.

Furbank, P. N. *Reflections on the Word "Image."* London: Secker & Warburg, 1970.

Gass, William. *On Being Blue: A Philosophical Inquiry*. Boston: David R. Godine, 1976.

Gilman, Richard. *Decadence: The Strange Life of an Epithet*. New York: Farrar, Straus, and Giroux, 1979.

Knox, Norman. *The Word "Irony" and Its Context, 1500-1755*. Durham, N.C.: Duke University Press, 1961.

Lewis, C. S. *Studies in Words*. Cambridge: Cambridge University Press, 1960.

Tave, Stuart M. *Some Words of Jane Austen*. Chicago: University of Chicago Press, 1973.

Trilling, Lionel. *Sincerity and Authenticity*. Cambridge: Harvard University Press, 1971.

Tucker, Susie I. *Enthusiasm: A Study in Semantic Change*. Cambridge: Cambridge University Press, 1972.

Williams, Raymond. *Culture and Society: 1780-1950*. New York: Columbia University Press, 1958; 1983.

————. *Keywords: A Vocabulary of Culture and Society*. Revised edition. New York: Oxford University Press, 1983.

Other Works Cited

Altick, Richard D. *The Art of Literary Research*. Revised edition. New York: Norton, 1975.

Roudané, Matthew C. "An Interview with Saul Bellow," *Contemporary Literature* 25 (1984): 265-80.

Stevenson, Lionel. *The English Novel: A Panorama*. Boston: Houghton Mifflin, 1960.

Dictionaries and Related Sources

Dictionary of Philosophy and Psychology. Edited by James M. Baldwin. 3 vols. Gloucester, Mass.: Peter Smith, 1960.

A Handbook to Literature, 5th edition. Edited by William Harmon. New York: Macmillan, 1986.

Partridge, Eric. *Origins: A Short Etymological Dictionary of Modern English*. New York: Macmillan, 1959.

Index